INTERNATIONAL LENDING IN A FRAGILE WORLD ECONOMY

FINANCIAL AND MONETARY POLICY STUDIES

volume 7

INTERNATIONAL LENDING IN
A FRAGILE WORLD ECONOMY

Published by Martinus Nijhoff Publishers on behalf of
the Société Universitaire Européenne de Recherches Financières (SUERF)

For a list of other volumes in this series see final page of the volume.

INTERNATIONAL LENDING IN A FRAGILE WORLD ECONOMY

Edited by

Donald E. Fair in co-operation with Raymond Bertrand

with contributions from:

Jacques R. Artus
Helmut von der Bey
Adrian Blundell-Wignall
Jean-Claude Chouraqui
W. Peter Cooke
Richard Dale
Fritz Diwok
Hermann-Josef Dudler
Frans A. Engering
Rainer E. Gut
Armin Gutowski
Helmut H. Haschek
H. Robert Heller

Manfred Holthus
R. Barry Johnston
Stephan Koren
Alfred Kuehn
David T. Llewellyn
Joël Métais
Jeanne-Marie Parly
Tadeusz M. Rybczynski
Luigi Spaventa
Alexander K. Swoboda
Tom de Vries
David Williams

1983 **MARTINUS NIJHOFF PUBLISHERS**
a member of the KLUWER ACADEMIC PUBLISHERS GROUP
THE HAGUE / BOSTON / LANCASTER

Distributors

for the United States and Canada: Kluwer Boston, Inc., 190 Old Derby Street, Hingham, MA 02043, USA
for all other countries: Kluwer Academic Publishers Group, Distribution Center, P.O. Box 322, 3300 AH Dordrecht, The Netherlands

Library of Congress Cataloging in Publication Data

Main entry under title:

International lending in a fragile world economy.

   (Financial and monetary policy studies ; v. 7)
   Papers from the 10th colloquium arranged by the
Société universitaire européenne de recherches
financières and held in Vienna in April 1982.
   English and French.
   1. Loans, Foreign--Congresses. 2. Debts, External--
Congresses. 3. Underdeveloped areas--Debts, External--
Congresses. 4. Banks and banking, International--
Congresses. 5. International finance--Congresses.
I. Fair, Donald E. II. Bertrand, Raymond, docteur en
droit. III. Artus, Jacques R. IV. Société
universitaire européenne de recherches financières.
V. Series: Financial and monetary policy studies ; 7.
HG3891.5.I58 1983   336.3'435   82-24649
ISBN 90-247-2809-6

ISBN 90-247-2809-6 (this volume)
ISBN 90-247-2605-0 (series)

Copyright

PRINTED IN THE NETHERLANDS

CONTENTS

PREFACE

The Papers collected in this volume are those presented at the tenth Colloquium arranged by the Société Universitaire Européenne de Recherches Financières (SUERF), which took place in Vienna in April 1982.

The Society is supported by a large number of central banks, commercial banks, and other financial and business institutions, as well as by academics and others interested in monetary and financial problems. Since its establishment in 1963 it has developed as a forum for the exchange of information, research results and ideas, valued by academics and practitioners in these fields, including central bank officials and civil servants responsible for formulating and applying monetary and financial policies.

A major activity of SUERF is to organise and conduct Colloquia on subjects of topical interest to members. The titles, places and dates of previous Colloquia for which volumes of the collected Papers were published are noted on page 421. Volumes were not issued for Colloquia held at Tarragona, Spain in October 1970 under the title "Monetary Policy and New Developments in Banking" and at Strasbourg, France in January 1972 under the title "Aspects of European Monetary Union".

In choosing the subject for Vienna, SUERF's Council decided to focus on evolving trends in, and issues resulting from, the growth and pattern of international lending under the impact of rising oil prices, stagflation in the industrialised economies, and a rapidly growing indebtedness of non-oil lesser developed countries and certain Comecon countries. Accordingly, contributions were invited under the general heading "International Lending in a Fragile World Economy".

The Colloquium was attended by about 130 participants representing a wide range of financial activities and academic teaching and research in the financial field.

The Chairman of the Colloquium as a whole was the President of SUERF, Dr. H.E. Scharrer. After opening addresses by Professor Dr. Stephan Koren, Governor of the Oesterreichische Nationalbank, Mr. Rainer E.

Gut, Chairman of the Executive Board, Crédit Suisse and Dr. W.P. Cooke, Head of Banking Supervision, Bank of England (which appear below in Part A, Chapters I to III), the contributed Papers, which had been circulated beforehand, were discussed in four separate Commissions meeting simultaneously. The themes of the Commissions were: "The Growth of International Lending: Determinants and Domestic Implications" chaired by Professor Mario Monti and Mr. Bengt Metelius (Part B, Chapters IV to VIII), "The Role of Banks in International Lending" chaired by Professor J.S.G. Wilson and Mr. P. Martinez Mendez (Part C, Chapters IX to XII), "Aspects of Growing International Indebtedness" chaired by Professor W. Eizenga and Mr. Conrad Reuss (Part D, Chapters XIII to XVI) and "The Stability of the International Financial System" chaired by Professor J.R. Sargent and Mr. Raymond Bertrand (Part E, Chapters XVII to XXI). The Colloquium reassembled for a final plenary session at which a view of the general topic for the Colloquium was presented by Professor A.K. Swoboda and a report on the proceedings of the Commissions was given by Dr. Fritz Diwok (Part F, Chapters XXII and XXIII).

In some cases minor changes have been made to the Papers before publication. The languages of SUERF are English and French. Each Paper is printed in the language in which it was presented.

As on previous occasions the Colloquium was generously sponsored by the local banking community, and special thanks were extended by SUERF to the Creditanstalt-Bankverein and Oesterreichische Länderbank and to Dr. Fritz Diwok, Secretary-General of the Austrian Bankers' Association for the excellent arrangements.

The Colloquium was highly successful both in the quality of the papers and discussions and in the opportunity it provided for contacts between experts from so many different countries. For this success it is a great pleasure to acknowledge and to thank once again Miss M.C. Hinkenkemper, at the time of the Colloquium the Executive Secretary of SUERF, who was unfortunately unable to be present on this last occasion before her retirement, and her assistant and successor as Executive Secretary, Miss Annelies Vugs, for their excellent organisation and invaluable services.

Donald E. Fair
Raymond Bertrand

ABOUT THE EDITORS AND AUTHORS

Editor:

Donald F. Fair, International Economic Consultant, The Northern Trust Company of Chicago, London. Formerly Economic Adviser, The Royal Bank of Scotland Group Ltd.

in co-operation with

Raymond Bertrand, Ancien Directeur des Affaires Financières, OCDE

Jacques R. Artus, Assistant Director of the Research Department, IMF

Helmut von der Bey, Dircktor, Deutsche Bank

Adrian Blundell-Wignall, Deputy Head, Monetary and Fiscal Policy Division, OECD

Jean-Claude Chouraqui, Head of Monetary and Fiscal Policy Division, OECD

W. Peter Cooke, Head of Banking Supervision, Bank of England

Richard Dale, Rockefeller Foundation International Relations Fellow, Guest Scholar at the School of Advanced International Studies of the Johns Hopkins University and at the Brookings Institution, Washington

Fritz Diwok, Secretary General, Austrian Bankers' Association

Hermann-Josef Dudler, Direktor, Deutsche Bundesbank

Frans A. Engering, Director International Financial Relations, Ministry of Finance, The Netherlands

Rainer E. Gut, Chairman, Crédit Suisse

Armin Gutowski, Professor, President HWWA-Institut für Wirtschaftsforschung - Hamburg

Helmut H. Haschek, Chairman of the Board of Executive Directors and General Manager, Oesterreichische Kontrollbank AG, Vienna

H. Robert Heller, Vice President, Economics Department, Bank of America, San Francisco

Manfred Holthus, Head of the Research Group General Development Policy, HWWA-Institut für Wirtschaftsforschung - Hamburg

R. Barry Johnston, Economist, Bank of England

Stephan Koren, Professor, Governor, Oesterreichische Nationalbank, Vienna

Alfred Kuehn, Head of Division, OECD

David T. Llewellyn, Professor of Money and Banking, Head of Economics Department, Loughborough University

Joël Métais, Maître Assistant, Université de Paris-Dauphine

Jeanne-Marie Parly, Professeur, Université de Paris-Dauphine

Tadeusz M. Rybczynski, Economic Adviser, Lazard Brothers & Co. Ltd.

Luigi Spaventa, Professor, University of Rome

Alexander K. Swoboda, The Graduate Institute of International Studies, and International Center for Monetary and Banking Studies, Geneva

Tom de Vries, Alternate Executive Director, IMF

David Williams, Deputy Treasurer, IMF

Part A

OPENING ADDRESSES

Chapter I

INTERNATIONAL LENDING
IN A FRAGILE WORLD ECONOMY

by *Stephan Koren*

I am very pleased indeed that SUERF has decided to hold this year's colloquium in Vienna and that it has chosen a topic of great concern to bankers worldwide. Though a lot of valuable research has been done in this field, problems are increasing.

Let me first outline some of the international developments in the past which were at the roots of the fragile world in which we find ourselves today.

In the post-war period the Bretton Woods system provided a framework within which countries could operate. The system was designed to assist individual countries which were experiencing balance of payments difficulties as a result of their domestic policies being too much out of line as compared with those in other countries. If that happened, the country concerned could turn to the IMF and obtain financial assistance until it got back into line with the help of a programme worked out between itself and the IMF. Thus, a balance of payments problem affected one country and had to be solved by that same country by means of domestic economic and monetary policies.

The keystone of that economic world was the system of fixed exchange rates, which facilitated rational expectation and calculation in the real economy. Together with steady progress in the liberalization of trade and payments the system brought about a tremendous expansion in the international exchange of goods, services and capital as well as a so far unprecedented increase in economic welfare in the western hemisphere.

However, that framework so beneficial for two decades after World War II, over time has undergone dramatic change.

First I should like to draw your attention to the fact that the system of fixed exchange rates began to break apart nearly a decade before the first oil shock. Domestic economic adjustment to the fixed exchange rate regime faced increasing difficulties in the second part of the 1960s; governments and central banks for political and psychological reasons were reluctant to resort to exchange rate adjustments which were economically necessary. Enhanced by the facilities of the Euro-markets, waves of exchange rate speculation ensued. The de facto abandonment of the system of Bretton Woods in 1971 by the Nixon declaration on the end of the convertibility of the dollar into gold therefore was only the last logical step in this chain of developments.

Let us recall that the establishment of floating exchange rates at the very beginning was connected with the sincere hope that they would provide more room for autonomous manoeuvre in monetary policy. And that they would restore the position of policy makers to decide on priorities in domestic economic policy of their own choice. At the same time floating exchange rates were expected also to be able to even out the differences in economic development between countries.

The implicit error of the early 1970s seems to have been the belief that by abandoning the strict rules and regulations of the system of fixed exchange rates the undesirable repercussions on domestic economic policy would vanish and painful domestic adjustment processes could be avoided.

However, the 1970s have taught us that there is no such thing as bypassing necessary economic adjustment – neither in a fixed nor in a floating exchange rate system.

With the arrival of the first oil shock this situation was aggravated – in kind as well as in extent. In kind because now it was not the individual country which was affected, but groups of countries shared a common fate; furthermore, the deterioration for some was not only due to inadequate domestic policies but mainly the result of an exogenous shock beyond the control of individual countries. The extent of such a shock had not been experienced before; you certainly recall that oil prices had more than trebled within a short period of time.

In the aftermath of the first oil shock the non-oil developing countries were doubly affected, by higher oil prices as well as by soaring prices for manufactured goods as a result of inflation in the industrialized countries.

The larger industrialized countries managed to improve their balance of payments rather quickly, mainly by letting the deterioration in the terms of trade affect their domestic growth.

The smaller industrialized countries did not manage to recover as fast and were thus ill-prepared for the second oil shock. They continued to suffer large external deficits.

Just before this new blow the balance of payments surplus of OPEC had disappeared. And there was of course no improvement in the heavy deficit position of the non-oil developing countries.

These groups of countries, after running down their reserves, had to turn to the international capital markets which only then, especially from 1978 onwards, grew at more than US$ 100 billion a year, an increase which had not been experienced before. Resources became available on the supply side, as surplus countries accumulated sufficient funds. At that time, i.e. between the two oil shocks, most funds were provided through the intermediation of the international financial markets with little thought given to country risks and to the question of whether enough real resources are generated in the borrowing countries to enable them to service and redeem their debts.

The second oil shock plunged the oil-importing countries into sizeable deficits, which were matched by a record surplus of OPEC of over US$ 100 billion in 1980. The pattern of adjustment was similar to the one after the first oil shock. In spite of the further rapid erosion of the OPEC surplus and the corresponding swing in the combined OECD current account the distribution of surpluses and deficits within the OECD area became more uneven than after the first oil shock.

Different, also, are the prospects of financing the deficits; the limits may not arise on the supply side of funds, as dwindling surpluses from OPEC countries seem to be replaced by a flow of funds from US banks. The problem is the creditworthiness of the debtors.

The medium and long-term debts of 94 developing countries, which amounted to about US$ 100 billion on the eve of the first oil shock, had quadrupled by 1979. Although these economics and their exports have grown to the same extent during this period and their overall relative burden has thus not deteriorated, the situation of some individual countries has been of great concern. Only recently has this new era started, when lending to sovereign states, which had been considered very safe, proved to have been risky after all.

Most affected are the weaker members of the group of centrally planned economies. Having just returned from a visit to the Soviet Union let me draw your attention to the fact, that the Polish crisis has caused a shock on both sides. The multinational banking system used to assess the CMEA countries as a block risk, not differentiating between countries. The immediate consequence for the CMEA countries was the availability of funds: declining credit ceilings, shorter maturities and higher spreads. The CMEA countries themselves have begun to rethink their policy of tapping the international credit markets. They seem to be aware of the dilemma that they must moderate their demand for Western credit and at the same time promote the productive potential of their economies and their export performance.

But the present situation is even more complicated: the CMEA countries need more assistance and at the same time they face harsher conditions as their creditworthiness declines. This could endanger their liquidity and thus aggravate problems. To be more precise: the attempt to declare Poland's default would have most undesirable economic repercussions for the Western banking system as well as for the Eastern block, not even mentioning the political dimensions.

For the CMEA countries a solution has to be found involving lenders and borrowers. Global problems like this have to be tackled worldwide, with parallel or complementary efforts undertaken in the individual countries. The international financial markets have been very successful in overcoming the problems so far through their vital rôle in recycling funds between surplus and deficit countries, but at the same time they are of growing concern to national monetary authorities.

Nothing would be gained if one lender tried to get an advantage by having a debtor declare default if, as an unavoidable consequence, the whole system is endangered. Therefore, the lenders on their part have to take into account higher risks and the possible need for rescheduling, whereas debtors will have to be more concerned about their own liquidity and their borrowing capacity. But the main focus should be on long-term efforts to enable the badly affected countries to come out of their predicament by their own endeavours.

May I leave it to your imagination, to compare the immediate postwar period up to the mid-1970s with the fragile world we are living in now. Personally I have a strong belief that this present situation needs more cooperation on an international level; but the precondition for this cooperation is to restore confidence between lenders and borrowers. This confidence, which has deteriorated so much in recent years, is in itself indispensable for solving international problems.

If asked to speculate even on the immediate future of economic development I must first remind you of the fragility of forecasting. One might try, however, to reach some conclusions or inferences from observing recent events. Lower balance of payments disequilibria and lower inflation rates in some countries show that they have been successful in coping with the changes which took place in the 1970s. Their success, however, was achieved at the expense of growth in their own domestic economies. Slow growth in the main markets of the world, together with high interest rates and rising protectionism, have aggravated the situation we are finding ourselves in.

Thus, the future will be of our own making. The more we realize the interdependence of the world's economies and the resultant need to harmonize economic policies, the better will be our chances for balanced economic progress.

This includes providing debtor countries with the chance to succeed in their adjustment efforts while preventing, through prudential banking, the international financial structure from being disrupted.

We have learned a great deal in the last few years: we have learned to live with rescheduling, we appreciate the closer contacts established between commercial banks and monetary authorities, we realize how important an institution the IMF is, which does not only give financial support to countries, but also helps them in solving their fundamental problems by advising them on planning adjustment.

I am looking forward to hearing about the findings of this distinguished colloquium and wish all participants success and a happy stay in Vienna.

Chapter II

INTERNATIONAL LENDING
IN A FRAGILE WORLD ECONOMY:
THE POINT OF VIEW OF A COMMERCIAL BANKER

by *Rainer E. Gut*

"A nightmare of debts", "On the brink of chaos", "Facing financial collapse" – these are the headings of recent newspaper and magazine articles dealing with the subject of this meeting. There can therefore be no doubt about its topicality; or, in other words, there may be reasons for concern. As a matter of fact, as a practical banker I have worked in many a bank, but I was never able to bank on a university education. The honour for me to have been invited to address this eminent gathering of the academic world has therefore been all the greater. I would like to extend my sincere thanks for this invitation.

The topic of this Colloquium is "International Lending in a Fragile World Economy". I am sure you will not take it amiss if I view this suggestion of "fragility" with a little scepticism. Even at the outset of my banking career some thirty years ago I heard prominent politicians, businessmen and economists talking about the perils of the time and the threat of collapse. And yet both the world and the economy continued to turn.

At that time it seemed to me that, to executives, the future consisted of dim hopes but definite fears. And today things are not much different. The problems overshadowing the world economy – in particular, the growing international indebtedness since the oil crisis of 1973 – give endless cause for complaint. Yet these worries about the state of the world have not prevented banks from vigorously expanding their international business. Neither is their attitude likely to change in the immediate future. In fact, in a recent survey, all the fifty-two big banks interviewed declared their intention to intensify their international activities in the years to come.

Evidently, there exists a curious conflict between bankers' theoretical and practical approaches. Why is this so? As an explanation, four main factors can, in my view, be cited.

Firstly, the oil price hike created international payments and financing problems on an unprecedented scale. At the time, the banks seriously doubted their capacity to cope with this huge task. However, the governments which were called upon for support not only hesitated, but, moreover, were forced by domestic constraints to cut development aid precisely at a time when it was needed more than ever. The International Monetary Fund as well reacted only gradually to the changed circumstances.

And what were countries – which urgently needed funds to bridge their oil-induced difficulties – to expect of a World Bank which, on average, takes three years from credit application to disbursement? The international banking system had therefore to fill the gap, almost against its will – a further confirmation of the economic law stating that demand always creates its own supply.

Second, the banks had to meet these new financing requirements when political tensions and a monetary system with floating exchange rates considerably heightened the risks. The fear of the consequences of their own courage is understandable and has found expression in a banking climate which might be described as cheerful pessimism.

Third, the oil shock brought about a change in the structure of international financing. Whereas bond issues and export credits guaranteed by supplier countries had previously been the chief instruments of international capital movements, the emphasis has since been shifted to ordinary bank credits. Instead of governments or buyers of foreign bonds, the banks themselves have become the principal risk bearers, a fact that has also contributed to their ambivalent attitude towards international business.

Fourth, the geographical scope of the business has expanded considerably. While up to the end of the 1950s international capital movements took place largely between industrial nations, they now encompass practically the whole world. This widening of the geographical base has naturally boosted the opportunities for international financial operations.

But with the growth in foreign exposure, the appearance of payments difficulties in several countries, and various unexpected political developments, such as in Iran, Poland or Argentina, the banker's always acute sense for risk aversion has been noticeably sharpened of late.

Thus numerous factors and influences, combined with the bad memories of the 1930s, prevent bankers from plunging boldly and confidently into the vast seas of international financing that the oil shocks created. In fact, they were profoundly aware of the existing treacherous depths and eddies. At all events, nothing could be further from the truth than the observation occasionally put forward that Western banks, overwhelmed by the gigantic inflow of petrodollars, have stepped up their international lending in a completely reckless manner unprecedented in financial history. Thereby – so the story goes – they caused countries to go into debt, frequently against their better judgment. The reality is different. Certainly, the economic tasks of banks consist in spanning a bridge between depositors and borrowers. However, the main concern and the chief impulses did not emanate and never have emanated from the deposit side of the balance sheet. Priority clearly belongs to the banks' search for suitable borrowers that seem to assure the payment of interest and principal. The banks generally continued to strictly adhere to this practice even after the oil crisis. Before borrowing petrodollars they looked for credit opportunities that offered an optimum return at a reasonable risk.

In order to achieve this, the traditional methods of lending were supplemented by various new and improved techniques. A notable example is the syndicated loan, which makes it possible to supply borrowers with substantial funds, and yet to limit the commitment – and thus spread the risk – by dividing up the transaction among the members of the syndicate. Another major innovation was the rollover credit running for a number of years with interest rates adjusted periodically; this permits the borrower to acquire the necessary long-term funds, while allowing the banks not only to pass on the interest rate risk, but also to tap the particularly broad money markets for the financing of long-term projects. New avenues were also followed in order to tackle another key problem of international finance, the assessment of country risks. Such assessments have, it is true, long been customary. Today, however, they are incorporated with virtually all international banks in a strict system of country rating. Before this gathering of economists, who are only too conversant with the theoretical and practical aspects of country analyses, I surely do not need to delve any deeper into the problems involved in the timely collection and proper evaluation of all necessary macroeconomic data and political observations.

In any case, in all major international banks country ratings play an important role today. Together with country limits, i.e. the ceiling as determined by the bank's board up to which an individual institution can commit itself vis-à-vis any one borrower, they help to adequately distribute and limit the foreign exposure. Thus the present situation contrasts strikingly with that of the early 1930s. At that time the payment difficulties of Germany and Austria, where international indebtedness was heavily concentrated, led after the payments moratoria of these two countries to a collapse of the international financing mechanism, thus exacerbating the world crisis. Today, however, the international credit pyramid is more solidly based, and the geographical distribution of foreign risks, wider spread.

Now it is sometimes said that this may be well and good, but all that the banks have actually done within the recycling process was to pay the oil bills of the borrowing countries, or, in other words, to indulge in consumer financing on a worldwide scale that left no tangible economic assets behind. Surely, each new international loan or securities issue helps in the last analysis to finance a balance of payments deficit, since the funds provided are ultimately used for the purchase of goods or services abroad and thus inevitably lead to a deterioration of the borrower country's current account.

However, it by no means follows from this that the monies in question necessarily evaporate into thin air. This certainly may have been the case in some instances. On the whole, however, the banks have always insisted, in line with their traditional principles of operation – and the last few years are no exception – that loans granted were used for investment projects which helped the country to cut imports or to raise its export potential, thus providing the amounts of foreign exchange required for servicing the debt. In short, what, broadly speaking, could be labelled "project financing" is at the centre of the international activity of most banks. Precisely for this reason, many a banker is wary of huge accommodations to the tune of billions of dollars – the so-called jumbo loans. For, the purpose of these arrangements is typically the financing of public deficits – a practice which certainly does not make them economically unsound per se. But whether or not this is the case is always difficult to evaluate, especially as governments certainly do not supply private banks with information more willingly than official bodies or international institutions.

The cautious and balanced financing policy of the banks is also reflected in the statistics on international indebtedness. Attention is generally focused only on the quintupling of the developing countries' foreign debt, from $87 billion in 1971 to $524 billion today – which corresponds to an average growth rate of 20 per cent per annum. These enormous figures cause the media to use the colourful phrases quoted earlier.

They would, however, lose a lot of their impressiveness if the foreign indebtedness of the industrial countries were also taken into account; actually, after the oil crisis, these latter temporarily engaged in massive borrowings too, but were more successful in coping with their balance of payments difficulties. Moreover, the figures mentioned represent nominal values, which have relatively little meaning in our inflationary times. If, however, inflation is taken into account, the real – i.e. price-adjusted – increase in the developing countries' indebtedness since 1971 averages merely 10 per cent per year; and in the last few years this rate has even dropped to 5 per cent annually, or practically to the level of the average rate of real economic growth in the developing countries. Overall, therefore, the discrepancy between the rising international indebtedness and the economic performance of the

Third World is by no means so glaring as some people seem to believe.

The same conclusion can be drawn from the figures on debt servicing costs. True, they have increased, in oil-importing developing countries, from 13 per cent of export earnings in 1973 to approximately 21 per cent today. But, in view of recession, depressed commodity prices, high interest rates and rapidly rising amortizations due to shortened maturities, the deterioration is less than one would have feared. This is a further indication that the massive expansion of lending over the last decade has by no means been ineffectual, but, by and large, created substantial economic assets from which borrower countries benefit considerably.

Moreover, amortization which is also included in the figures on debt servicing is basically only a question of refinancing. This should pose no serious issues as long as a climate of confidence can be maintained. An economic burden for borrower countries results naturally from interest payments, the cost of which in the oil-importing developing countries has risen from 5 per cent of export earnings in 1973 to more than 9 per cent in 1981. Overall, they are still confined within the limits regarded as acceptable in theory and in practice. It is therefore understandable that Walter B. Wriston, Chairman of Citibank, New York, once said about the recent development of international credit operations: "It was the greatest transfer of wealth in the shortest time frame and with the least casualties in the history of the world. It was a terrifically difficult thing to do. We did it".

This statement may sound complacent, but it conveys the pride bankers feel with respect to their achievements in the past decade. That their activity has contributed decisively to securing a reasonable degree of prosperity and employment in the world under difficult conditions is undeniable. But this belongs almost to history. Today the crucial questions present themselves differently, namely: Can the international financing system continue to function in the face of markedly increased international indebtedness? Is it able, when handicapped in this way, to cope with the decline in oil surpluses and its consequences?

In point of fact, the observation that the global level of international indebtedness is not excessive does not mean that there are no problems confronting international banking. A statistician might maintain that a man with his head in a deep freezer and his feet in the oven enjoys a pleasant average temperature. But bankers cannot orient their behaviour according to such fallacious averages. For them it is solely the situation of individual debtor countries and of the individual debtors that counts.

From this vantage point, a number of major weaknesses in the financial structure of the world become immediately apparent. First, precisely the system of country ratings had the inevitable result of concentrating the banks' attention on eligible industrial and newly industrialized countries which often had been among their customers for decades, if not for more than a century. As a matter of fact, at least half the growth in the foreign debt of developing countries since 1973 is accounted for by just ten nations – among which, above all, Argentina, Brazil, Mexico, the Philippines, Spain and Korea. This ample flow of funds relieved these countries for a long time of the need to rectify their balances of payments. Moreover, the banks' traditional attitude of considering customer relationships as a long-term proposition had the result that financial accommodation was frequently not denied to friends in spite of worsening circumstances.

In some instances an additional factor may have been the wish not to jeopardize earlier commitments by turning off the credit tap. Thus foreign debts piled up rapidly in some countries, with their servicing requiring an alarmingly growing quota of export earnings. In order to counter this trend, unpopular measures must be taken. But these could cause severe domestic tensions in debtor countries, which in turn may seriously endanger outstanding loans. Accordingly, banks are today particularly concerned with assessing the politically tolerable limits of any programme of economic stabilization.

Difficulties also stem from that group of countries which – either because of economic weakness or political instability – are not rated as creditworthy, and therefore remain entirely or at least largely cut off from international credit flows. As international development aid also dwindled simultaneously, these nations suffered seriously after the oil shocks. The ensuing considerable widening of the gap between economically advancing and stagnating countries created tensions that could seriously affect the long-term outlook of the world economy and politics. These problems, however, cannot be solved by private banks, but solely by the governments of the industrial and oil-exporting countries, from which additional efforts must be expected to increase development aid at least to the long-promised 0.7 per cent of GNP.

Additional complications have been created on the world financing scene by the fact that bankers are not always completely free in choosing the direction of their foreign loans but must occasionally bow to political requirements or wishes. For example, the US banks' large interest in Latin America is probably not entirely coincidental. Similarly, the so-called West German Ostpolitik and the climate of détente undoubtedly constituted a major underlying reason for the substantial loans to Eastern bloc nations, in the arrangement of which particularly German and Austrian banks, but also American, French and British ones participated or, should I say, had to participate. The events in Poland and the behaviour of Rumania have put this type of business in a somewhat questionable light. The famous "umbrella theory" – according to which Moscow would always assume responsibility for the commitments of other COMECON countries – has obviously deserved the scepticism it had always received in some quarters. In fact – and this has generally been our view – going by its logic, it could only justify loans to the Soviet Union, as the "umbrella holder", but not to countries that try to eat their foreign-financed cake under the umbrella's shelter. In addition, the ability of communist governments to impose sacrifices on their own people in order to re-establish economic equilibrium has certainly also been overestimated.

The basic framework of international financing has also been affected by the recent glut in the oil market which gave rise to the question of whether the resulting steep decline in OPEC surpluses, in conjunction with the high international credit demands, might not lead to serious liquidity problems that could weaken the foundation of the entire international credit pyramid. Undoubtedly this development is not entirely unproblematical. Apparently some OPEC countries, such as Nigeria, Mexico and Indonesia, today have to resort to previously accumulated bank balances and credits in order to finance their imports. Notably in the United States this may have contributed in some measure to the resistance shown by interest rates to the downward pressures, emanating from the recession and declining inflation. But these influences should not be overdramatized. The supply of funds to international financial markets is not dependent on a single source; already in the past it had frequently changed its origins; and in future, apart from oil countries, industrialized nations are likely to again play a bigger role in this respect as their current accounts are beginning to show overall surpluses instead of the former deficits. As long as international flows of funds are not impeded, the supply and demand for money on international financial markets will in normal times be brought into balance by the play of interest rates.

Nevertheless, these structural shifts in international finance as well as the increased tension in world politics could evidently not leave the banks unconcerned. As institutions working chiefly with their clients' rather than their own funds, they have to conduct their business in conformity with the obligation to protect their deposits. And in uncertain times one of the banks' traditional methods of averting risks is to grant financing for as short a term as possible in order to withdraw their investments rapidly in case of danger. They are well aware that such a procedure pursued collectively may bring about just that collapse of which all are so afraid. But macroeconomic considerations of this type cannot seriously influence the attitude of institutions which in risky situations do not wish to be the last ones that – as a German saying goes – are bitten by the dogs. This basic policy, together with the distortions during the last few years in the interest rate structure – i.e. short-term rates higher than long-term ones – has pushed up perceptibly the proportion of relatively short-term credits in international financing. As a result, the instability of the international credit structure has certainly increased of late.

In view of these developments the question arises as to what can be done to stabilize the situation and to keep the financial markets open. Not that the banks are particularly pessimistic, nor does the possibility of increased future debt restructurings cause them to panic. Since the end of World War II they have experienced approximately sixty such restructurings, sixteen of which since 1980. Nevertheless, they have not withdrawn from the international scene; on the contrary, as pointed out at the beginning, they even plan to step up their foreign operations. They believe, however, that governments should endeavour to create that institutional framework which international financial markets, just as all free markets, require in order to operate satisfactorily in the long run. Conversely, the authorities apparently have the impression that banks have gone very far in their international business and should therefore be subjected to additional curbs. From different vantage points the views thus seem gradually to converge.

Nevertheless, little love is shown by the banks for initiatives to tighten control over the Euro-markets. They certainly understand the authorities' concern over the complications caused to monetary and credit policies by these markets. But West German, Japanese and Swiss experience has definitely proved that these problems can and must be solved on a national level.

In their view, special supranational interventions therefore do not serve very useful purposes, to say nothing of the difficulties created for such experiments by the insistence of governments on their sovereignty and the diverse structure of banking systems.

If, however, something is really to be done, the most plausible among the measures suggested, would seem to be the Swiss proposal to oblige banks internationally to observe uniform capital ratios. This preference of mine by no means reflects chauvinistic feelings but is based on solid and objective reasons. For one thing, capital adequacy requirements can be applied without major problems to various types of banks; second – and this, after all, is the aim of all bank supervision – they serve to protect depositors and, third, help to channel, if not limit, international operations by harmonizing competitive conditions among banks with respect to refinancing costs.

For the future of international banking, however, interventions of this sort are undoubtedly far less important than other measures of a more fundamental nature. These measures should in my view be oriented chiefly towards three areas. First, the role of governments in international debt restructuring; second, the viability of the international banking system under crisis conditions, and third, the vast field of basic economic policy approaches. Important developments have already taken place in all three fields. But further improvements appear to be both necessary and feasible.

Debt restructuring has for years been handled via the so-called Paris Club which has gained considerable experience in this field. Such restructuring never has been, and never will be, an easy task, since it necessitates communication and compromise not only between the borrower country and the creditor nations, but also between the divergent interests of the many participating banks. In most cases up to now the policy of the so-called "short leash" has been adopted, giving preference to refinancing instead of actual restructuring and limiting financial assistance to the amounts of existing or imminent arrears. Creditors, it is true, are today in a relatively favourable position thanks to the cross default clause, whereby a country not honouring its commitments can be declared in default vis-à-vis all its lenders and thus practically barred from further access to the financial markets. Yet it is quite clear that this clause is a two-edged knife. Resorting to it could, in fact, mean that a problem, which was purely bilateral in character, suddenly assumes international proportions, thus also involving banks that had originally not been affected at all.

In view of this complex situation an atmosphere of mutual trust and low profile is desirable in all such loan renegotiations. In such discussions, as a cynic once put it, bankers act like players on a soccer field who hurriedly gather, for reasons of discretion, around their colleague whose shorts have split.

In contrast, governments frequently show an inclination to use such situations of financial distress for political ends. Admittedly, their participation in such negotiations is important, nor is there any denying that governments have the right to use all possible tools for their ends. But they ought always to take into account the serious reactions that can be triggered by interventions in the delicate fabric of international finance.

Accordingly, the understandable attempt of the US to exploit Polish and Rumanian debt problems for exerting pressure on Moscow and obtaining political concessions recently sent cold shivers down the spine of the markets. With some jitteriness they are at present studying the likely financial effects of the conflict between Argentina and Britain over the Falkland Islands. Notwithstanding the fact that Britain has up to now shown considerable self-restraint in the financial and banking fields too, these recent developments will, even in the best imaginable case, undoubtedly leave behind a serious financial heritage.

In view of this state of affairs and the increased instability of the credit pyramid it is – and with this I come to a second category of institutional aspects – particularly auspicious that the leading Western central banks already agreed years ago – in the so-called Basle concordat – to grant liquidity aid should the international banking system come up against serious liquidity bottlenecks as a result of a confidence crisis caused by extraordinary occurrences.

Of late, however, they have tended to emphasize that this assistance would only be available to support the system, and that it was under no circumstances designed for helping those banks out of their difficulties, which have violated the basic tenets of sound banking.

This viewpoint is understandable. However, in practice differentiating between banks that are deserving of support and those that are not is no easy task. It is thus to be hoped that under crisis conditions the monetary authorities will not become bemired in such casuistic considerations. Rather they ought constantly to remain conscious of the importance of making their financial assistance available speedily, sufficiently, and discreetly if such an emergency is to be mastered.

The IMF, too, owing to the additional funds it has lately received, is in a better position to assist countries that are struggling to maintain their economic equilibrium, and thus to support the entire system. This is all the more the case since for some time now the Fund has shifted its basic policy approach from merely financing balance of payments deficits toward adjustment through measures which help countries to return gradually to a tenable economic equilibrium.

In this context one may also ask whether it would not be advisable to further pursue the idea of setting up an international guarantee system to secure loans to especially poor countries against losses such as political eruptions, bad harvests, or similar catastrophes that are not insurable in the ordinary market. The organization of such a system is unquestionably full of possible pitfalls.

However, in a time when the development of the Third World is one of the major economic goals, but when governments find it difficult to raise the necessary amounts of aid, the elaboration of such a project and the careful examination of its benefits and drawbacks might be well worth the toil and sweat of the experts.

Similarly, the task of international financing would undoubtedly be simplified if the flow of risk capital into the Third World in the form of direct investments by the private sector could be increased. This type of investments, whose return depends on their profitability, would not only facilitate the transfer of the much sought-after technical know-how, but also reduce the strains on the balance of payments – which especially in hard times result from today's prevalence of loan financing. These are of course difficult, emotion-laden questions. Yet the basic attitude towards the problem does appear to be improving. Now that even Cuba has permitted foreign direct investments, it should become possible to discuss this topic in a constructive manner again.

This remark brings me to the third prerequisite for the long-term viability of international banking: international economic policy – for which the industrialized countries bear a special responsibility. At present particular attention must be devoted to two fundamental problems. In the first place, the wave of protectionism, rising dangerously today, must be held in check. Only when the developing countries are guaranteed access to the markets of the industrial world will they be able to earn the export proceeds required to service their debts and to promote employment in industrial countries through their purchases of goods. Secondly, it is indispensable for the industrial nations to persevere with their anti-inflationary policies. For these policies alone can lead the world into a new phase of healthy economic growth, and help to bring down the high interest rates that constitute such a heavy burden today. Gratifyingly, the world seems to be gradually coming closer to this goal.

This, Ladies and Gentlemen, brings me to the end of my remarks. In my view, the free financial markets successfully mastered the difficulties that arose in the wake of the oil crisis. They should be able to continue their task in the future. This, however, can only be the case if the institutional framework of the financial markets remains up to standard in the future, which probably will make certain improvements mandatory. Should these be made, and if world politics throws no spanners in the works, a bright and exciting, though by no means carefree, future can be forecast for international banking. In fact the message that bankers wish to give governments today can best be stated in a paraphrase of the famous words of a French minister of finance to his prime minister: "Faites nous de bonnes politiques et nous vous ferons de bonnes finances".

Chapter III

INTERNATIONAL LENDING
IN A FRAGILE WORLD ECONOMY:
A SUPERVISORY PERSPECTIVE

by *W.P. Cooke*

It has often seemed to me that the relationship of the supervisory authorities to the international banking community has much in common with that of doctors and their patients. Like the single doctor the supervisor at the national level cannot handle every patient or every disease; he may not always know the regulatory diet which his colleague elsewhere has prescribed and he may be a bit out of touch with the latest approach to medication both preventative and curative. Also, like the doctor, the banking supervisor has taken his Hippocratic oath of secrecy and, again like the doctor, he often grumbles that his warnings, usually related to over-indulgence or a lack of care, tend to be ignored until it is too late. In the spirit of this analogy I would like today to take the pulse of the international banking system, to attempt some diagnosis of the problems it faces and possible approaches to treatment.

First, what is the nature of this system? Looking back over the development of international banking during the 1970s, the most striking feature has been the enormous rapidity of the growth of international lending. The annual rate of growth during the 1970s was over 20 per cent. Over the same period the outstanding external indebtedness of developing countries has more than quintupled, according to OECD figures. The indebtedness of some individual countries has grown almost twice as fast as the total. Surges in international borrowing and lending can be seen in association with the oil price rises of 1973-74 and 1979-80. The connection between international bank lending and the growth of world trade cannot be made too precisely, however, since bank lending does not always appear to have grown fastest when the financing needs were greatest.

At the same time as countries' surpluses and deficits – in industrial countries, in OPEC countries, and in developing countries – were growing, the commercial banks came to play a larger part in the recycling process. Their share of the total external debt of developing countries trebled in the 1970s (excluding loans provided under export credit guarantees where the percentage share fell somewhat). The part played by direct investment and concessionary lending, particularly the latter, provided by governments and official agencies correspondingly fell.

There was not simply a quantitative increase in the volume of bank lending, however, but also a series of qualitative changes in the character of the lending. The challenge of meeting new financing requirements and the need to attract new lenders into the market has meant that there has been a constant process of innovation. The techniques of syndication and bond and project finance have grown in complexity and sophistication as the market has grown in size. It can also be maintained that the sheer volume of the new lending has necessarily led to some reduction in the quality of the loans.

There has been a steady stream of new banks entering the market and it is estimated that the number of banks participating in syndicated lending has grown fivefold in the past decade. There are both good and bad aspects to this. The number of new entrants has certainly helped to spread the burden and the risks of international lending to sustain the necessary recycling of funds. On the other hand, a large number of the new entrants have necessarily been smaller and relatively less experienced than the larger and older established banks, and therefore perhaps less well prepared to handle the specialised problems posed by international lending. Such banks also tend to be more reliant on interbank funding and so are more at risk than larger banks if confidence in the system were to waver and previously friendly sources of funds were to be denied to them. Furthermore, it can be argued that the very complexity of modern loan agreements and the number of banks involved, has introduced an element of fragility to the system by increasing the interdependence of those operating in it.

It is not just the rate of growth in banks' international lending, however, which leads people to look closely at the health of the international financial system and prompts the meetings such as the one in which we are currently participating. If that were the only concern, then we might conclude that the patient was a little breathless but basically in sound condition. But rapid growth, as in nature, can bring with it some secondary effects which may make the organism more vulnerable.

What are these effects? Firstly, for the borrowers. The increasing use of bank lending as a means of bolstering, or as a substitute for, more traditional methods of balance of payments financing has had a number of consequences for the borrowers. The greater part of the increase in bank lending has been concentrated in the relatively small number of developing countries which have had access to external financing on a significant scale. Such bank lending has generally borne variable rates of interest rather than the fixed (and often concessionary) rates of official agencies or direct aid. So, because of the worldwide inflation which followed the oil price rises, the interest rates which the borrowers have found themselves paying for bank money have been sustained at an exceptionally high level historically at least in nominal terms, and now in the last two years in real terms also. Also the maturity pattern of this lending, although it appears long by the banks' standards, is nevertheless shorter than that available from some of the official agencies. The combination of these factors has put a severe strain on many developing countries and has increased their financing needs both to meet interest costs and to refinance maturing loans. The accelerating pace of reschedulings in recent years shows how the pressures on these countries have been building up.

New pressures have also emerged for the banks. The majority of the banks involved in international lending come from the industrialised countries. Domestic circumstances in many of these countries are compounding the international problems. The effects of stagflation and high and volatile interest rates have, in many cases, led banks to undertake distress lending to support businesses in their home countries, and this may impair the banks' capacity to sustain losses on their international side. Furthermore, this period of rapid expansion in banks' international business has also put pressure on banks' capital ratios and the last two decades have seen a material worsening in the adequacy of banks' capital in most countries. This is a subject to which I will revert later.

At the same time, the successive waves of banks entering or re-entering the international market coupled with a high level of liquidity in international markets over recent years have kept competitive pressures strong. A proper sense of the relationship between reward and risk has become blurred. Spreads and, as a consequence, profits have been squeezed in international business, making it difficult for banks to earn sufficient return on their capital to maintain its real value in an inflationary environment or to meet losses.

So much for an outline of the system as it is and the strains and pressures inherent in it. Let me now turn to how these strains and pressures can be handled.

I must say at once that I do not come with any of the ready-made universal panaceas of the travelling medicine man. At the same time, I hope that what I have said so far does not make me sound too much like Molière's quack Dr. Purgon in "Le Malade Imaginaire" who was for ever diagnosing serious illnesses so that he could prescribe expensive medicines. As I hope will become clear, I and my banking supervisory colleagues in other countries believe that prevention is better than cure. We prefer to recommend banks to follow a healthy regime, consisting of a well-balanced diet of nourishing loans, avoiding the extremes on the one hand of obesity – lending too much – and on the other of anorexia – losing all appetite for lending, which in macroeconomic terms could produce highly undesirable consequences. However, the preventative regime should not be so limiting as to exclude all risk and stultify all business, so remedies must always be at hand. They may take the form of the placebos of reassuring noises in public, which may indeed suffice to give the system the confidence to sustain its activity, or the use of stronger drugs in the form of imposing some kind of constraints or regulations, although always with a care to the risk that strong drugs can induce excessive dependency and an inability on the part of the patient any longer to look after himself.

The supervisor has two levels of concern for the international financial system, that of the system as a whole and that of the individual bank.

First of all then, how serious is the present condition of the international financial system? There are some who think the condition is acute. This gathering will need no reminding of the views of Professor Kindleberger, for example, who has suggested that Minsky's model of financial fragility can be applied to events during the last decade. According to this thesis, after passing through the classic phases of "euphoria" and "overtrading" as investors were eagerly attracted by new opportunities, the present phase – "distress" – is reached when investors hesitate, worried by signs of weakness in the market, and begin to withdraw. The final phase yet to come – "revulsion" – occurs as the withdrawal turns into a stampede.

I have to say I find this analysis altogether too alarmist. There are of course major and serious issues which need to be considered and it is no part of the supervisor's role to be complacent. "Withdrawal" syndromes and "domino" theories have to be taken seriously, but it does seem to me unlikely that, short of some quite cataclysmic disaster, the world banking system will cease to sustain a major intermediary role. There are dangers, certainly, arising from the possibility that more than one country will run into serious difficulties at the same time, but I draw comfort from the proven resilience and collective good sense of the world's major banks in reacting to the strains of recent years. During this period the market has gained in breadth through the entry of new banks. It has acquired valuable experience of particular problem situations and has greatly improved the important new techniques for handling the risks of international business, notably country risk analysis. It has shown itself capable of coping not only with the pressure waves of the first oil shock, but subsequently with a second oil shock. The experience of individual reschedulings so far has shown that such events can be handled, without raising major doubts about the viability of the system as a whole. Finally, the authorities have also learnt a great deal from the events of the past decade and have enormously improved their methods of co-operation and knowledge of each others' systems. This in turn has led to a greater confidence in the effectiveness of co-operative procedures.

One particular area which seems to me as a supervisor to warrant careful consideration in the period ahead is the relative contribution which should be asked for from the different parties to the recycling process.

The process of intermediating between the deficit countries and the surplus countries will no doubt have to continue on a large scale. All interested parties in this process, the banks themselves, the supervisory authorities, governments and the international agencies can no doubt agree on the desirability of the major objective, which is the smooth recycling of funds through international financial mechanisms. But they may differ in where they put the emphasis of their most immediate concerns. In particular, there are I believe good arguments for saying that the banks have played, and are playing, more than their fair share in the process; and that, on prudential grounds and in the general interests of the soundness of the system, they should not be asked to bear so much of the burden of recycling in the period ahead as they have recently. At the same time, it should not be forgotten that appropriate adjustment of economic policies by borrowing countries to lessen the strains on the system may also have to play an increasingly important role.

Clearly difficult judgements are involved in maintaining the equilibrium of the system. The authorities must, of course, be alive to the macroeconomic consequences of their prudential constraints and the right balance will not be easy to find, or to justify on any wholly objective criteria. On the one hand, the supervisory authorities have the responsibility for restraining banks from overreaching themselves and exceeding the prudent limits of lending, but on the other it is clear that to restrict the recycling capacity of the banking system, in the absence of any viable alternative intermediaries, might precipitate the very crisis which the prudential regime is designed to avoid. In playing their part in coping with this dilemma, the supervisors have to stand up and speak out for *their* first priority which must be to maintain a sound prudential framework for the international banking system. All interested parties will need to recognise that the banks' ability to fulfil their intermediary role should not be impaired by subjecting them to a greater strain than they can bear. It may be better for all concerned that the banks should play a smaller part in future recycling, than that they should be asked to shoulder the whole burden and collapse under the weight.

The supervisor must therefore work to make the system sound. There are three aspects to this work: ensuring that the coverage of the supervisory blanket is complete and effective, working to improve the co-ordination and quality of different national regimes and co-operation in the handling of problem situations.

These all raise difficult and far-reaching questions, but I believe that a great deal has been achieved in coming to grips with these problems in recent years. The first objective – ensuring that there are no gaps in the system through which banks operating internationally can escape supervision entirely – became of increasing importance as large numbers of new banks operating from a wide variety of countries entered the international market.

The second aspect of a sound system is that the practices of different autonomous national authorities operating within their own legal systems and supervisory regimes should not be so wildly disparate that the international market place lacks all homogeneity and stability. There is always the danger that competitive pressures will tend to work to drag down the level of prudent banking to that permitted for the most marginal performer.

Closing supervisory gaps and improving co-operation and co-ordination of supervisory policies and attitudes have been at the heart of the work which has been undertaken in the Bank for International Settlements in Basle under the auspices of the Central Bank Governors of the Group of Ten Countries and Switzerland. I know that many of you will have heard something of the work of the Committee on Banking Regulations and Supervisory Practices at the BIS in a paper given by my Dutch colleague at your meeting in 1980. I do not intend therefore to dwell too long on its activities this morning. There are, however, a few comments I would like to make.

The early work of the Committee relating to supervisory coverage is contained in what has become known as the "Concordat". This document sets out the basis, capable of general application, of allotting the respective responsibilities of host and parent country for the supervision of the solvency and liquidity of banks operating internationally. I should perhaps stress that this agreement relates to supervisory responsibilities not to the lender of last resort role to which I will refer later. The principles promulgated in the Concordat have been generally accepted and endorsed not only by the countries represented on the Committee, but also by a very large number of countries elsewhere. More recently, the Committee has increasingly turned its attention to the second aspect I mentioned, that of improving the co-ordination of different national supervisory practices. One of the most important of these areas of work has been to press ahead to secure agreement on the principle that supervision of banks' international business should be undertaken on a basis which looks at their activity worldwide on a consolidated basis. This was agreed within the Committee, endorsed by the Governors, and the principle has also been accepted by most other supervisory authorities with responsibilities for significant international banking businesses although its full implementation in many countries will take some time. It applies particularly to the monitoring of the solvency and the risk exposure of international banks' worldwide activity and has brought with it reinforcement of the important concept of parental responsibility, both by the bank itself for its branches and affiliates worldwide and also by the supervisors of the parent bank for the supervision of its worldwide business. This consolidation principle of itself, when it is applied in practice, tends to induce co-ordination of national practices impinging as it does on banking business undertaken in different centres. It also makes even more important the achievement of close and effective co-operation between different supervisory authorities.

This co-operation has been manifested in the wide range of the supervisory matters which have been discussed in Basle and in other supervisory groupings which have been set up in recent years. It is also the essential ingredient of the third aspect of the supervisor's work in maintaining the soundness of the system – that of the handling of problem bank situations. The single most important factor in dealing with these situations is a well-based co-operative relationship between the different supervisory authorities concerned, out of which solutions to practical problems can be found. I do not intend to try to outline some kind of blueprint for the authorities' procedures in these cases. The circumstances are always likely to be special. This is also an area where, particularly if it seems that the problem is more than an isolated one, the Governors of the Group of Ten countries and Switzerland will wish to take into account a wider range of considerations than just the supervisory ones. Their views were succinctly expressed in a communique issued in September 1974 after the disturbances and uncertainties surrounding the first oil shock. In this communique they stated that they recognised that it would not be practical to lay down in advance detailed rules and procedures for the provision of temporary liquidity. But they were satisfied that the means were available for that purpose, and would be used if and when necessary. The principle which I think the Americans refer to as "moral hazard" must always be allowed to exert its discipline and would not normally make it appropriate to spell out in advance what, if any, assistance might be forthcoming from the authorities in a particular set of circumstances.

Problem banks and problem situations, however, are essentially those which the supervisor hopes his efforts will render obsolete. This though may be an idle hope in the real world and leads me on to say a few things about the second level of the supervisor's interest – and the essence of his daily work – the health of the individual bank. On the principle that the whole is only as good as its parts, the soundness of individual banks must be a fundamental concern in the interests of the system and I should like to say something about the respective roles and responsibilities of banks and supervisors in the field of international business.

International business involves banks in several important areas of risk, not always present within a domestic operation. There is exchange rate risk; there is that kind of funding risk which can be especially important in the context of international lending where banks tend to be more reliant on interbank borrowing than they are in their domestic markets; in addition, there is the important risk associated with maturity and interest rate mismatch; also, and most importantly in the context of international lending, there is the concept of country risk: that is, the risk that a lender may be unable to secure repayment of his loan because of special factors affecting the country into which he has lent. Such factors may be political or economic or both. I would like to dwell a little on this latter risk because it has come into increasing prominence in the last few years as the realities of the underlying payments flows in the world have sunk home.

The Committee of Supervisors in Basle has given a great deal of thought to the question of country risk and has been doing a lot of work recently on the management of banks' international lending. So much work has been undertaken on this in recent years that any new study is unlikely to be able to make great claims to originality, but the Committee does believe there is a value in trying to establish some kind of consensus on the considerations which banks ought to take into account in establishing their own policies. This way the expertise of the most experienced, both banks and supervisors, can be made more widely available. I am hopeful that it may be possible to conclude this work shortly and arrive at some considered views on the part of the supervisory authorities in the major international countries about the ways in which banks should set about assessing and monitoring the risks in their international lending.

At the heart of the supervisors' approach to this problem is the principle that responsibility for banks' country risk exposure rests primarily with the individual bank's management. The supervisor's role is not to interfere with the bank's commercial judgment or impose arbitrary limits or methods of analysis, but to make sure that all banks who are taking part in international lending undertake the analysis of country risk with adequate resources and in a professional manner. In an adequate system the supervisor will look for the ability to assess the risk attached to different countries, measure the bank's exposure to them and set appropriate limits to control that exposure.

The first step is the assessment of the degree of risk attached to lending propositions. Here the starting point must be an objective appraisal of the economic and financial data available. Banks should be prepared to supplement the many published sources by asking the prospective borrower to be forthcoming with any additional information which is needed. Banks need to be in a position where they can make at least a reasonable assessment of the future cashflow of the borrower and so its ability to meet its obligations. These tests need to be backed up by more subjective judgments which aim to take into account social and political factors. Most importantly, in all such analysis, banks should be careful not to take too short-term a view, but must be alert to the possibility that a favourable short-term outlook can deteriorate in the longer, or even in the medium, term.

This process of appraisal ought to be undertaken by all banks large and small and all bank managements should be alive to the need to take a hard and considered look at the popular loan proposition of the day. Unfortunately, and particularly in the case of syndicated loans, there is sometimes a tendency for country assessment to go by default: the lead managers may be relaxed since they will be selling down participations to other banks, while participating banks may be tempted to place undue reliance on the judgment and experience of the lead managers. As more and more new banks enter the market, both as participants and lead managers, it is important that this analysis continues to be done and done professionally.

Supervisors have a part to play in this process by disseminating best practices throughout the market and offering advice on the setting up of assessment and monitoring systems. The authorities can also help in improving the quality and timeliness of information available on which banks base their judgments. Good judgments are not made in a vacuum. The BIS, the IMF and the World Bank are all important sources of data on international lending and individual supervisory authorities can also do much to improve the consistency, as well as the timeliness of data collected from and disseminated to their banking systems at the national level.

In all of this, there is increasing acceptance of the need for international banks to be able to monitor their own exposure to an individual country on a consolidated worldwide basis. Also, the simple breakdown of borrowers by a bank according to country should be supplemented by a further analysis which recognises that the ultimate risk of the loan may well not rest in the country of the borrower – for example, where it is covered by a guarantee given from another country, as in the case of export credit guarantee arrangements.

Lastly, there should be effective control systems. Once a bank has made its assessment of the creditworthiness of the borrower's country, some appropriate limit should be placed on its exposure to that country. Such limits should be decided at a senior level within the bank and should be reviewed regularly in order to take account of changing circumstances. These limits, which should include commitments, should be based on the degree of risk that was identified in the country assessment and also on the bank's ability to sustain losses. The supervisor has a responsibility to see that the exposure of individual banks is reasonably spread without excessive concentration.

I should now like to turn to another and in my view very important aspect of sustaining a sound international banking system. This is the role of capital and the maintenance of adequate levels of capital.

The importance of capital is that it is the first bulwark both of the individual bank and of the system against a crisis by enabling a bank to meet losses from its own resources. There can be no absolute and precise test of what level of capital is adequate. The only time it can be said with absolute certainty that capital is inadequate is after a bank has failed. Nevertheless, over time some concepts of adequacy of capital have evolved in the market-place. There is no doubt that there are very many international banks who operate within a supervisory regime which does not impose absolute levels of capital, but who nonetheless feel constrained to no small degree by market opinion over the extent to which they can increase their gearing. Ultimately, however, I believe it is the responsibility of supervisory authorities, when they judge it necessary, albeit without an absolute standard, to say to the individual bank enough is enough, particularly in an era where competitive pressures lead aggressive managements to explore all avenues for improving profitability.

Once a limit has been set in this way a bank, and banks generally, have at least one base from which they can judge what has to be achieved in terms of generating profits to be ploughed back into the business if they are to continue to be adequately capitalised as their business grows. This approach also offers supervisors the possibility of exercising some leverage on inadequate levels of spreads. Indeed it can be said that by this means they are helping to save the banks from themselves. In international business, very largely determined by pure market forces, it is difficult for supervisors to influence directly the prevailing level of spreads and the returns on particular parts of the business and thus affect the capacity of banks to sustain adequate levels of profitability, but capital adequacy ratios are one tool with which they can exercise some influence to the general advantage.

Capital adequacy levels very properly differ from one kind of bank to another. They also differ from one supervisory system to another. Some convergence of the capital levels of major international banks would clearly be desirable but it cannot be denied this will be difficult to achieve. What can, I think, be done by supervisors within their own jurisdictions is to hold out against further erosion of their banks' capital ratios. Much could be achieved to prevent further weakening of the units in the international system if this were done. However, if some banking centres are more lax in their approach than others, then business may well tend over time to flow to the less restrictive centres, which could negate what might otherwise be a desirable impact on the general level of spreads.

Of course, a basic source of protection against loss available to banks is to spread their risks. A number of techniques for doing this are available, including diversification of its own portfolio and sharing the risk with other banks through syndication, or securing guarantees of lending from official or other undoubted sources. Syndication brings many benefits, but it also introduces elements of risk. The number of banks involved as creditors for a sovereign borrower can now run into many hundreds, with the result that there is uncertainty about which banks are involved and the total exposure can be obscured. Such banks are tending to become more and more inextricably intertwined under legal provisions, including cross-default clauses involving other unrelated lending, and these may well increase the difficulties of handling situations when countries get into difficulties. A degree of complexity is probably inevitable and certainly understandable as an element of protection for banks, but it may well be in no bank's interest for this process to be taken too far.

Two other methods which are seen as helping to reduce the risk in banks' international loans are being canvassed currently: the various proposals for loan guarantee schemes and for increased co-financing between commercial banks and official agencies. Various kinds of loan guarantee schemes have been proposed, the general intention of which has been to cover commercial banks' lending, especially to lower income developing countries. While the purpose of these schemes has been not so much to protect the banks as to encourage the continued recycling of funds to developing countries, it may be that proposals of this kind should nonetheless be welcomed by supervisors as tending to reduce risks borne by banks. There may, however, be difficulties in practice in persuading appropriate guarantors to come forward.

The second method – co-financing between commercial banks and official agencies – has attractions for both sides: the official agencies are able to supplement the funds at their disposal, while the commercial banks may have access to better information about the borrower and can benefit from the agency's capacity to exercise more effective leverage over the borrower by monitoring the use of the funds and by the imposition of conditions. There are no doubt institutional and political difficulties to be resolved, however, and a certain amount of reluctance and perhaps even suspicion on the part of all of those involved still needs to be overcome. Also I have some doubt whether co-financing, as a concept, should be pursued to the extent of it being used as a device to impel commercial banks into the provision of excessive balance of payments type finance – a role for which, I would argue, commercial banks are not well suited. Nevertheless the agencies involved in developing the present techniques should be encouraged to pursue their efforts. Co-financing could well have a useful role to play, particularly in making some contribution towards shifting the weight of the task of recycling more away from the banks and towards the official agencies. It may also, in some cases, improve the creditworthiness of borrowers and so give them either new access, or help to maintain access, to the world's capital markets.

Even with adequate country risk assessment, and a diversification of risk, however, there is always a likelihood that some countries will come into difficulties and need to reschedule their debt. Indeed, it may reasonably be argued that a substantial rescheduling of developing country debt is going to have to take place in the years ahead. The pace has quickened greatly over the past few years and it certainly looks at present as though this will be one of the major preoccupations of the international banking community through the 1980s. It is going to be very important, therefore, that banks are as well prepared as possible to cope with these contingencies calmly and competently as they arise. Some banks have established special departments or task forces to handle reschedulings, and others might be encouraged to follow their example.

There are several areas where improvements in the banks' practices should be pursued. Firstly, the timely identification of problem countries is important so that the situation can be taken in hand before it becomes too serious. Work is being undertaken to improve the timeliness of the production of statistics, but banks have a responsibility continually to monitor the condition of their borrowers and any arrears of payment that build up.

The second area susceptible to improvement is co-operation between banks in dealing with problems. It is natural that with such a diversity of banks of different sizes and characters and from many countries there should be conflicts of interest and differences of opinion, not least because the situation may be complicated by political as well as economic considerations. Banks must recognise (and in fairness they are generally very well alive to this) that they all share an interest in the orderly resolution of problems. But orderly resolution of problems will not be achieved unless banks organise themselves effectively. Ad hoc arrangements may have worked rather well in practice and those responsible for organising and running these groups, I believe, deserve much credit. But one day this approach may not work so well, and I believe it may be necessary to look carefully at the proposition that international banks should consider the development of mechanisms and fora with some greater degree of formalisation than at present through which common problems can be discussed and difficulties and differences resolved in the general interest.

Finally, and most difficult, once they have mobilised themselves the banks have to decide what action they should take in respect of countries in payments difficulty. They have to decide whether to risk more by continuing to support the borrower or to call it a day and cut their losses. Banks need to, and generally do, take a long-term view both of their own interests and of those of the system as a whole. To cut off support from one borrower in difficulties may of course lead to serious consequences for others and so multiply the banks' problems. The supervisor, from a basically micro-viewpoint, is concerned to minimise the risks taken by individual banks in the international market place. He must be prepared to contemplate the likelihood of loss occurring in international lending, just as it occurs in banks' domestic business. Therefore, if cases occur where it is decided not to continue to provide support, banks should be prepared to, and in a position to, establish provisions or take losses as necessary. This underlines again the crucial importance of the returns on international lending being proportionate to the degree of risk involved so that sufficient profits can be generated to cover such provisions or losses without excessively diminishing the resources of the banks. Supervisors need to consult with each other to ensure that, in their approach to their banks' attitudes to provisions or write-offs, they are acting as far as possible in a reasonably consistent way in respect of similar international indebtedness. It is more likely that banks will be prepared to take timely and prudent action to deal with potential losses if they are confident that by doing so they will not be putting themselves at a competitive disadvantage vis-à-vis other banks.

So, to conclude, what have banks and supervisory authorities as the prospect in the years ahead? There will be a continuing requirement for intermediation on a very substantial scale between surplus and deficit countries and this will call for a careful and continuing appraisal of the role of the commercial banks in this process by all those involved in this field – the banks themselves, their supervisors, governments and international agencies. There will be a need for cool heads, good judgment and a proper balance of the inter-related factors in determining the way the system sustains payments flows and international activity. Boom tends to lead to bust, and a proper restraint, or to put it another way, an absence of excess will be needed by borrowers and lenders alike both in turning the tap on and turning the tap off. It may well be necessary for borrowing countries to temper their ambitions and be prepared to rein in at times; it may also be right for the developed world to look closely at the liberality of its trade policies and the adequacy of the level of concessional flows. Throughout this whole process I believe it will be crucial to maintain prudential standards, even if this may impose a restraining influence on the extent to which banks can take part in the recycling process. The responsibility for the soundness of the banking system is shared. The banks themselves must constantly be sharpening their perception of the risks incurred in their business and differentiating between them. The authorities must be concerned to ensure that individual banks act prudently, whilst also looking at the whole market with a wider perspective. The smooth functioning of the market, and so the survival of all its participants, depends on a general recognition of this interdependence so that the phrase "the banking community" may continue to live up to its meaning.

THE GROWTH OF INTERNATIONAL LENDING:
DETERMINANTS AND DOMESTIC IMPLICATIONS

Chapter IV

EURO-MARKET EXPANSION: MACROECONOMIC CONCERNS, THEORETICAL MODELS AND PRELIMINARY EMPIRICAL ESTIMATES*

by *R.B. Johnston*

1. INTRODUCTION

By the standards of most national financial aggregates the growth of the Euro-market has been quite remarkable. During the last decade the market expanded at a rate of around 25 per cent per annum and by end-1980 the gross foreign currency liabilities of banks in Europe exceeded $1,000 billion. The reasons for this expansion and its macroeconomic implications are subjects of interest and a continuing source of concern among various national authorities. There are, however, important disagreements about the theoretical processes involved and detailed empirical analysis of the issues is almost completely absent. This paper attempts to draw out some of the relationships between macroeconomic concerns about the Euro-market and the model frameworks which are used to explain its growth (section 3), and to examine the reasons for non-US non-bank transactions in Euro-dollars within the framework of a simple theoretical and empirical model (section 4). The preliminary regression analysis of a pooled cross-country and time series sample finds that trade variables, income growth, relative interest rates and national monetary disturbances are the major determinants of non-banks' holding and borrowing of Euro-dollars. The significance of the Euro-dollar market is seen in terms of its role in financing external transactions and as a source and outlet for liquidity in the domestic economy. The analysis begins, in section 2, with a comment on the content of Euro-currency statistics.

---

* The research reported in this paper was undertaken while the author was on secondment to the Bank for International Settlements. The views expressed are the author's alone and do not necessarily reflect those of either the Bank of England or the BIS.

2. EURO-CURRENCY AGGREGATES

The sheer size of Euro-currency aggregates and an inability to provide a general explanation for the rapid expansion of the Euro-market are themselves a source of concern. Frequently, to explain the rapid growth, reliance is placed on the different regulatory arrangements in domestic and Euro-markets, and regulation circumvention, which imply some loss of monetary control.[1] But the reasons for and implications of Euro-market expansion must be more complex when the statistics under investigation are themselves highly complex. Aggregate measures of "the Euro-market" – its gross or net size – are only one-dimensional representations of variables which cover several different categories of depositors and borrowers, from diverse geographical locations, transacting in several currencies.

Breaking down European reporting banks' total foreign currency liabilities, which amounted to just over $1,000 billion at end-1980, shows that only $142 billion were placed directly in the Euro-market by non-bank entities,[2] the remaining $850 billion coming from official monetary institutions ($109 billion) and commercial banks (Table 1). The commercial bank deposits are

Table 1. *Estimated composition of European reporting banks' foreign currency liabilities and assets (end-December 1980)* [a]

	Total	Non-banks	Official monetary institutions	Banks outside [b, c] the reporting area	Interbank trading within the reporting area
Liabilities ($ bn)	1016	142	109	324	441
of which in dollars (per cent)	68.5	73.0	63.0		
Assets ($ bn)	1006	266	10	299	431
of which in dollars (per cent)	68.4	64.5	71.7		

Memorandum: Dollar liabilities to and claims on US resident non-banks ($ bn): *Liabilities:* 19.2; *Assets:* 8.8.

    a. Banks in Austria, Belgium-Luxembourg, Denmark, France, Germany, Ireland, Italy, Netherlands, Sweden, Switzerland, United Kingdom.

    b. On the liabilities side includes trustee funds placed in the Euro-market by Swiss banks.

    c. Includes a proportion of funds switched between domestic currencies and foreign currencies by reporting banks and funds borrowed and lent in the market by reporting banks in their domestic currencies.

broken down further into interbank transactions in foreign currencties between reporting banks ($441 billion),[3] and into deposits placed in the market by banks outside the European reporting area and by banks in the reporting area through switching out of their domestic currency into foreign currencies, and from lending domestic currencies to other banks in the Euro-market. An examination of reporting banks' foreign currency assets also shows that the bulk of claims are on other banks and that only one-quarter are accounted for by claims on non-bank entities (Table 1). The table records that around 70 per cent of transactions are conducted in US dollars – the remainder are largely denominated in Deutsche Mark (about 13 per cent), Swiss francs (6 per cent) and sterling (3 per cent). A memorandum item shows that only some 19 per cent of European banks' dollar liabilities to non-banks are accounted for by US residents, i.e. by non-bank agents transacting in their domestic currency abroad. The overwhelming majority of non-bank Euro-dollar deposits thus represents holdings of foreign currencies by the non-bank transactors involved.

While it is unlikely that the factors explaining each category of transaction in the Euro-market will be independent,[4] strong and unrealistic behavioural and aggregation assumptions would be needed if the aggregate Euro-currency statistics are to be treated as homogeneous for the purpose of economic analysis. The reasons for interbank transactions will be different from non-bank and central bank decisions to place and borrow Euro-currencies; and the motivation when non banks transact in their domestic currency abroad may be quite different from that of non-banks transacting in foreign currencies. The point is simply that fruitful analysis will often require the researcher to define clearly the particular segment (or segments) of "the Euro-market" in which he is interested and, to avoid possible measurement errors, to use disaggregated data for its investigation. Indeed even Euro-currency data disaggregated into bank and non-bank categories requires an aggregation over different Euro-currency centres where the exact definition of "bank" and "non-bank" varies.

Macroeconomic concerns about the unregulated nature of the Euro market are often directed at the volume of transactions undertaken in the market by non-banks, as this is the volume of funds which is roughly excluded from national monetary aggregates and frequently escapes direct monetary controls [see Johnston (1983)]. Approaches to modelling non-bank Euro-market behaviour are therefore emphasised below and disaggregated data on non-bank Euro-currency deposits are used to examine the reasons for non-US non-bank transactions in Euro-dollars. There are other concerns about the influence of the Euro-market on capital movements which

38

are also directed at the volume of interbank transactions and which are not dealt with here. Efficient international markets bring with them benefits, for example, in the form of easier financing of global payments imbalances, and costs, from more closely integrating national money markets, and the implications of efficient markets cannot be disregarded.

3. CONCERNS AND MODEL FRAMEWORKS

The debate over the macroeconomic implications of the Euro-market has highlighted two approaches to analysing the market's growth. One emphasises the role of outside disturbances, the other the market's endogenous growth potential – the Euro-currency multiplier. To crystallise these views market growth might be divided into a systematic or endogenous multiplier component, En, and a non-systematic or exogenous component, Ex, which is due to outside disturbances.

Market growth = En + Ex

The dynamic nature of these processes is illustrated in Figure 1.

Figure 1.

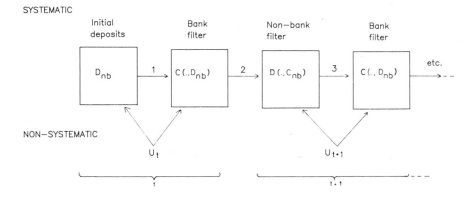

The top half of the diagram shows the systematic multiplier process: an initial stock of non-bank deposits D_{nb}, at time t; this is passed to the banking system [flow (1)] which makes loans to the public. The size of the loans depends on the filter $C(., D_{nb})$, a function of the supply of bank deposits and some other factors. The action of making loans adds to non-bank liquidity [flow (2)] and this additional liquidity is passed through the non-banking sector and its filter D (., C_{nb}), a function of the size of bank loans, C_{nb}, and other factors, and a proportion is then returned to the banking system [flow (3)]. The process can then begin again until some final equilibrium is established which depends on the values of the various filters, i.e. whether they dampen or amplify the deposit and loan flows. The bottom half of the diagram shows the non-systematic part which takes the form of exogenous shocks to the system. These might include a shift in the structure of global payment imbalances, the removal of national capital controls and the changing structure of national monetary regulations and interest rates.

Generally, the causes of Euro-market growth will not divide neatly into systematic and non-systematic processes. The fact that a large volume of capital flows pass through the Euro-market rather than other channels implies that the market has some autonomous role and that the market growth equation should be written in the more general form:

Market growth $= F(En, Ex)$

The intermediate case, where the Euro-market acts mainly as a channel for capital movements but tends to alter their size and thus the ultimate impact of an exogenous disturbance, is arguably the most interesting and important. It would cover, on the one hand, the beneficial effects of the market in the recycling of oil surpluses, and on the other the problems of closer integration of national money markets and the disintermediation of money holdings out of nationally defined monetary aggregates during periods of domestic credit restraint. The *autonomous* influence of the Euro-market on these processes has hardly been analysed at all, however.[5]

The debate over the relative magnitude of the systematic and non-systematic processes is most clearly illustrated by attempts to measure the size of the Euro-currency multiplier.[6] Here there are a broad range of estimates depending on the specific assumptions employed. Examining the model frameworks it is apparent that what is crucial is the extent to which the Euro-market is viewed as segmented from national money markets. The greater the segmentation the more the growth of the market is attributed to an endogenous multiplier process. The different assumptions about the degree of market segmentation and the degree of substitutability between domestic and Euro-market assets and their implications for model frameworks are shown in Table 2.

When the Euro-market is perfectly segmented, the only leakage of funds out of the market is through the reserve holding of Euro-banks, and frac-

Table 2. *Market segmentation and models of the growth of the Euro-currency market*

Degree of market segmentation: borrowers	Degree of market segmentation: depositors			
	Segmented Markets		Integrated Markets	
	Perfect	Partial	Imperfect substitutes	Perfect substitutes
Segmented Markets	Fractional Reserve Multiplier	Leakage Model		
Integrated Markets			Portfolio model (interest elastic supply and demand curves)	Demand determined (Perfect elastic supply curve)
Imperfect substitues				
Perfect substitutes		Supply determined (perfect elastic demand for funds)		

tional reserve multipliers are relevant.[7] Not surprisingly, predictions from this model usually suggest that the systematic multiplier process in the Euro-market is large. Allowing depositors to hold some net additions to liquidity outside the Euro-market – i.e. for domestic and Euro-markets to be only partially segmented – leads to the leakage model.[8] The greater the assumed degree of market integration the larger the leakage and the smaller the multiplier. Mayer (1979), for example, draws an analogy between the Euro-market and an inter-regional banking system with close links with the regional banking systems. His estimate of the size of the leakage is thus large and the multiplier small. Swoboda (1980) compares the Euro-dollar holdings of non-banks with US monetary aggregates and uses the ratio of these stocks as a measure of the average leakage ratio. His estimate of the multiplier is also very small. The assumption is that there is close substitutability between these asset stocks.

The use of a leakage model framework does not resolve, however, the question of how large the systematic multiplier potential of the market actually is nor does it explain the mechanism of market integration. The relevance of Swoboda's comparison between US monetary aggregates and non bank Euro-dollar deposits can be questioned on the grounds that some 80 per cent of non-bank Euro-dollar deposits are held by non-US residents, while US monetary aggregates are predominantly held by US residents. A more valid comparison in determining average asset holding behaviour would be between Euro-dollar deposits and the national money stocks of the non-bank wealth-holders concerned, rather than the US monetary aggregates. Such a comparison would, in fact, yield a much larger leakage and a negligible multiplier.

However, the observation that the largest single group of non-bank transactors in the Euro-market are Europeans would also imply that the Euro-market itself performs a regional borrowing and investment function for non-banks in foreign currencies. Should there exist transaction costs when doing business in one geographical location rather than another – which in all probability is likely – these could cause this regional market to exhibit a degree of segmentation. It is possible to postulate circumstances in which the leakages from a regionally segmented Euro-dollar market would be large or small. For example, if Euro-dollars are predominantly held and borrowed to finance international trade, there could be sizable reflows of dollars to the Euro-market when there is trade between agents in the regional area served by the Euro-currency market. Alternatively, if Euro-dollars are predominantly investments, held as substitutes to domestic currencies, it would be reasonable to expect large leakages out of the Euro-dollar market into national money markets – and vice versa – in the regional area served by the Euro-market. The functional role of Euro-currencies may then be rather important when explaining the size of the multiplier.

At the other extreme to the fractional reserve model are approaches which posit that the Euro-market is perfectly integrated with national money markets. By implication it is meaningless to suggest that the Euro-market has a systematic growth potential independent of national money markets and national regulations which endow comparative cost advantages on one centre over another. That is not to say that the Euro-market has no macroeconomic implications but only that its growth is mainly the result of exogenous forces.

The approaches are based on the near-perfect arbitrage relationship observed between *interbank* interest rates in domestic and Euro-currency markets.[9] One observes that banks will tend to supply funds to the Euro-market whenever Euro-currency interbank rates rise above the effective cost (i.e. the nominal interest rate plus the cost of holding domestic non-interest-bearing reserve requirements) of raising deposits domestically. It is thus argued that the supply of funds to the Euro-market will be nearly perfectly elastic and that the market's growth can be attributed mainly to factors which expand the demand for funds – such as increasing global payments imbalances.[10] These demands are directed towards the Euro-market rather than national money markets because of the efficiency and specialisation of intermediation techniques and the broader geographical base of banks involved in the Euro-market. Another approach argues that the growth of the Euro-market is mainly supply-determined. Banks will tend to fund their business on a global basis so that the *effective* cost of accepting deposits – that is, after allowing for the level of national reserve requirements – will be the same in domestic and Euro-markets. The relative structure of reserve requirements in domestic and Euro-markets will cause the level of *nominal* interest rates to be different in the two markets, however, and this encourages non-banks to hold deposits in one market rather than another.[11] The Euro-market expands when the structure of national regulation causes the differential between Euro and domestic interest rates to widen.[12]

While there are undoubtedly elements of truth in both approaches, the assumption that the Euro-market can be treated as if it were perfectly consolidated with national banking systems is a strong one. It may be true that US banks would consolidate their dollar business at home and abroad, but for other nationalities of banks, Euro-dollar business is foreign currency business and the assumption of perfect consolidation with domestic banking business seems much less likely; and the author has argued elsewhere[13] that it may be inappropriate to aggregate together non-bank and interbank flows when explaining the willingness of banks to intermediate in the Euro-market and the market's overall expansion. The empirical evidence suggests that the volume of deposits placed in the Euro-market by non-banks has had a statistically significant effect on the level of spreads set in the syndicated medium-term Euro-credit market. There is thus some evidence of market segmentation on the side of the banks.

An important intermediate approach to explaining Euro-market growth is the portfolio model framework. Euro and national money markets are closely integrated but Euro and domestic deposits (and loans) are imperfect substitutes. The Euro-market expands when relative interest rates provide incentives to hold deposits there rather than in national money markets, and with the overall growth in investors' portfolios. The models allow for some systematic growth in the market from the interaction between the supply and the demand for Euro-market deposits; but because inflows of new funds into the market are assumed to depress Euro-currency deposit rates, there will be leakages out of the market, which limit the Euro-market's multiplier potential.[14] These models have also some shortcomings, however. First, because of the interbank link between interest rates in domestic and Euro-currency markets, inflows of non-bank Euro-deposits are not generally observed to depress Euro-currency deposit rates. There need be no automatic leakage of funds out of the Euro-market, and portfolio models may therefore underestimate the size of the Euro-currency multiplier. Second, like the leakage model estimates, the portfolio approaches have not allowed for the existence of transaction costs, which may encourage non-banks to undertake business in one geographical location rather than another and which may lead to some degree of Euro-market segmentation. Combined with the use of Euro-currency deposits in the financing of trade transactions it would be possible – as in the leakage model – to postulate circumstances in which the Euro-currency multiplier could be large. Thirdly, the portfolio model does not immediately explain why, in many cases, private Euro-currency deposits have expanded at a faster rate than deposits in national currency markets.

By focussing on the allocation of the stock of wealth, portfolio models emphasise that changes in the equilibrium structure of a wealth-holder's portfolio only occur when the rate of return or the attributes of different assets change, or when the overall size of the portfolio varies because of a rise or fall in the investor's wealth. When the *differential* between the rates of return on domestic and foreign investments widens in favour of foreign securities, investors will adjust their portfolio, reducing their stock of domestic and increasing their stock of foreign assets. But these adjustments are finite, being constrained by the overall size and requirements of the portfolio. Moreover, the existence of international interest rate differentials – say between US domestic and Euro-dollar interest rates – is not necessarily evidence of portfolio disequilibrium or that there is a continuous incentive for wealth-holders to move funds between one money market and another. Thus, for these reasons, if portfolio models are to explain the relatively rapid expansion of Euro-currency deposits, the portfolio adjustment process must be more complex. There may be long lags in adjustment, or Euro-currency deposits may be superior assets in wealth-holders' portfolios.[15]

The state of theoretical and quasi-empirical analysis thus leaves several questions unanswered, and it is necessary to appeal to more rigorous empirical analysis. But up to now, because of the lack of available data, there have been few opportunities to examine directly non-bank behaviour in the Euro-market. Existing empirical work on Euro-currency interest rate determination and aggregate Euro-currency statistics finds evidence of close integration of the Euro-market with national money markets. However, because of the diversity of transactors in the Euro-market noted in section 2, and the importance of interbank arbitrage explanations of Euro-currency interest rates, these estimates cannot claim to explain directly the behaviour of non-banks; and explanations of the reasons for Euro-market expansion using aggregate data will be flawed. Unfortunately researchers continue to interpret equations explaining Euro-currency interest rates in terms of non-bank portfolio behaviour. A recent example is Briault and Howson (1982).[16] The next section thus reports a first attempt to examine disaggregated data on non-US non-bank holdings of Euro-dollars. The period for which a consistent series is available is short, however, and some aggregation is therefore unavoidable in the form of pooling together time series and cross-section data from six countries.

4. A MODEL FRAMEWORK

The empirical estimates are based on the following illustrative framework of the links between domestic and Euro-markets:
– Non-banks outside the United States are assumed to face higher transaction costs when undertaking dollar business in the United States rather than the local Euro-dollar market and thus non-bank transactions in the Euro-dollar market are segmented from the US domestic market. The main alternative to Euro-dollar transactions are transactions in the non-bank's domestic money market.

– Non-bank transactors are divided (artificially) into investors and traders. Investors distribute their stock of wealth, W, between holdings of domestic money, M^d, domestic securities, D_I^d, and Euro-dollar deposits, D_I^e. To keep matters as simple as possible the domestic currency/dollar exchange rate is set to unity.

$$W = M^d + D_I^d + D_I^e \tag{1}$$

Traders import, I_m, and export, X, goods and finance any (temporary) external payments imbalance in dollars by borrowing in the Euro-dollar market, B_T^e, or by borrowing domestic currency, B_T^d, which they sell to the government for dollars.

$$\Delta B_T^e = I_m - X - \Delta B_T^d \tag{2}$$

where Δ is the first difference operator.

– Although the Euro-dollar transactions of non-banks outside the United States are segmented, the Euro-dollar market is linked to the US domestic market through interbank arbitrage flows. The *disaggregated* volume of non-bank Euro-dollar deposits and borrowing have no impact on Euro-dollar interest rates or on the willingness of banks to provide loans. The process of intermediation within the Euro-currency market and Euro-dollar interest rates are thus treated as exogenous. In this respect the framework is only a partial analysis designed to highlight non-bank depositing and borrowing behaviour. [The interbank arbitrage and Euro-bank intermediation processes are examined in Johnston (1979) and (1980).]

As well as equations (1) and (2) other equations could be written to "close" the domestic financial system. In their simplest form they could be specified as follows: the government finances its cumulative deficit, GD, and its holdings of foreign exchange reserves, R, by issuing domestic securities, B_G, and domestic money, M^s:

$$GD + R = B_G + M^s \tag{3}$$

Private investors' holdings of domestic securities equals purchases of government securities and traders' debts:

$$D_I^d = B_G + B_T^d \tag{4}$$

The change in official reserves equals the balance on current account plus private capital inflows, from Euro-dollar borrowing by traders, less private capital outflows from Euro-dollar purchases by investors.

$$\Delta R = X - I_m - \Delta D_i^e + \Delta B_T^e \qquad (5)$$

Combining equations (1)-(5) yields the familiar condition that the change in the total wealth of the private sector – i.e. investors *and* traders – equals the change in the government deficit plus the trade balance:

$$\Delta W - \Delta B_T^e - \Delta B_T^d = \Delta GD + X - I_m$$

The empirical model of the demand for Euro-dollar deposits and loans by non-banks is based largely on equations (1) and (2). It also allows for traders to borrow and to hold Euro-dollar deposits to meet the flow of trade payments;[17] for the possibility that non-banks might systematically redeposit some of their new Euro-dollar borrowings in the Euro-dollar market; and for the influence of domestic monetary disturbances through any excess in the money supplied by the authorities over that demanded by investors. The total demand for Euro-dollar deposits by non-banks is written as:

$$D^e = f(\overset{+}{W}, \overset{+}{r_{E\$}}, \overset{-}{r_d}, \overset{+}{e^*}, \overset{+}{Im_c}, \overset{+}{\Delta B^e}, \overset{+}{M^s - M^d}) \qquad (6)$$

a function of the investor's wealth, the competing return on Euro-dollar and domestic currency assets (Euro-dollar, and domestic currency interest rates, $r_{E\$}$ and r_d respectively, and the expected appreciation of the dollar against the domestic currency, e^*), the volume of imports invoiced in dollars, Im_c, new Euro-dollar borrowing by non-banks, ΔB^e, and the excess supply of money in the domestic economy. The signs over the variables show the expected signs of the partial derivatives of the demand for Euro-dollar deposits by the various variables.

The flow demand for Euro-dollar loans is specified as:

$$\Delta B^e = g(\overset{-}{CB}, \overset{+}{Im_c}, \overset{-}{r_{E\$} + S_p}, \overset{+}{r_d}, \overset{-}{e^*}) \qquad (7)$$

a function of the current balance of payments, CB, the flow of imports invoiced in dollars, and the relative cost of borrowing Euro-dollars and domestic currency (the Euro-dollar rate plus the lending margin in the Euro-market, S_p, the domestic interest rate and the expected appreciation of the dollar). The signs over the variables again show the anticipated signs of the partial derivatives.

In this model the domestic interest rate on traders' debts would be determined simultaneously with non-bank investment and borrowing of Euro-dollars and thus a third equation makes this variable endogenous. This is written:

$$r_d = h(\overset{+}{r_G}, \overset{+}{r_{E\$}}, \overset{+}{e^*}, \overset{-}{CB}, \overset{-}{M^s - M^d}) \tag{8}$$

The domestic interest rate – which in the empirical analysis is taken to be the interest rate on investors' domestic currency in the Euro-market, r_{EC} – is positively related to the yields on competing assets (the yield on government securities, r_G, the Euro-dollar rate and the expected appreciation of the dollar on the foreign exchange markets) and to the demand for finance by traders (inversely related to the balance of payments) and negatively related to any excess in the domestic money stock.

In the complete system of structural equations the yield on government securities, the domestic money stock or the exchange rate would also be jointly determined with the other variables in the model. If the authorities were to set exogenously the interest rate on government securities this would, for example, lead traders to offer a competing interest rate on their domestic borrowing, depending, inter alia, on the external cost of borrowing and investors to allocate their portfolio between securities, traders debts and Euro-dollar deposits. Flows across the foreign exchanges would result, depending on the size of the trade balance and net private sector capital flows [equation (5)]. Under a fixed exchange rate regime and a given government deficit the flows will affect the money stock [equation (3)]; while under a free floating exchange rate regime $\Delta R - 0$, and the exchange rate will move until private capital flows offset the trade balance [equation (5)], insulating the domestic money stock. In the empirical analysis the domestic money stock and the rate on government securities are treated as exogenous variables while the exchange rate was taken to be endogenous to the model. However, it turned out that there was little simultaneous feed-back from changes in the current exchange rate to the other variables in the model and so the equation is not reported in detail. Money demand is derived from a trend estimate of velocity without allowing for interest rate effects. The variable $M^s - M^d$ might then be seen, more appropriately, as measuring domestic "monetary shocks".

The main empirical model thus consists of equations for the demand for Euro-dollar deposits and Euro-dollar loans by non-banks and the interest rate on the domestic currency in the Euro-market. The exogenous variables are the volume of imports invoiced in dollars, the current account balance of payments, the level of private wealth, the Euro-dollar rate, the level of Euro-market lending spreads, the interest rate on domestic government securities and the excess domestic money stock. Lagged values of the non-bank Euro-dollar deposits and loans enter the model as predetermined variables. Expected exchange rate movements are proxied by the lagged value of the rate of change of the spot exchange rates.[18]

5. EMPIRICAL ESTIMATES

The period for which there is a consistent run of data on non-bank holdings and borrowing of Euro-dollars broken down on a country by country basis is relatively short. As from 1977 Q4 there was fairly complete reporting to the BIS by the banks in Austria, Belgium-Luxembourg, Denmark, France, Germany, Ireland, Italy, Netherlands, Sweden, Switzerland, the United Kingdom, Canada and Japan and this data is taken as the start of the sample period, 1977 Q4 – 1980 Q4.[19]

However, this yields only 13 observations on any one country. To overcome the problems of an undersized sample, data on the holdings and borrowings of Euro-dollars by non-banks in six countries were pooled together.[20] The countries are Canada, France, Germany, Italy, Japan and the United Kingdom. The pooled time series and cross-section data provides a sample of 78 observations.

To make the data comparable across countries all variables were expressed in current dollars, rates of change or percentages. The wealth variable was replaced by the rate of change of GNP, as suitable wealth series are not available, and the rate of interest on government securities by countries' official discount rates. To allow for different cross-country responses due to national exchange control regulations dummy variables were also included in the equations and level variables were expressed in natural logarithms. A data annex summarises the notation and the definition of the variables.

The ordinary least squares (OLS) regression results are reported in Table 3.[21] Equation 1(a) is the non-bank demand for Euro-dollar deposits [specified as equation (6)]. Proxies for exchange rate expectations have very little influence and equation 1(b) reports the results after re-estimating the equation without the exchange rate term. A lagged dependent variable has been included to allow for stock adjustments.[22] All variables enter the equation with the correct sign and although some of the t-ratios are slightly low this is not perhaps surprising given the relative diversity of countries in the sample. Overall the fit of this equation is reasonable and nearly all of the explanatory variables are significant at the 90 per cent confidence level. Durbin-Watson statistics are reported, although of course, in present circumstances they do not test serial correlation in the errors. Of interest is the coefficient on the flow of non bank Euro-dollar borrowing, $\Delta \ln B^r$, which suggests a significant redepositing of new borrowed funds in the Euro-market, i.e. an endogenous multiplier process. When simultaneous effects are allowed for using two-stage least square (TSLS, Table 4) the significance of this variable falls sharply, however, thus tending to reject a multiplier process in the simultaneous equation model. The long-run values of the coefficients derived from TSLS are:

Ln Im_c	Ln M^s/M^d	GṄP	$r_{E\$}$	r_{EC}
0.36	2.28	1.56	0.041	-0.032

The coefficient on the volume of imports in dollars, Im_c, is not out of line with the 0.5 predicted by an inventory theoretic approach to the optimal holding of foreign currency balances (Swoboda 1968); the coefficient on the "excess" domestic money stock term, M^s/M^d, suggests that domestic monetary shocks have an important influence on non-bank Euro-dollar holdings and that by implication Euro-dollar deposits are close substitutes to domestic broad money holdings; and the coefficient on the rate of growth of GNP indicates that Euro-dollar deposits are superior assets in wealthholders' portfolios.[23] The coefficients on the Euro-dollar and Euro-currency interest rate terms imply average elasticities of 0.46 and -0.34 respectively.

Equation 2 in Tables 3 and 4 reports the OLS and TSLS results for the flow demand for Euro-dollar loans by non-banks. Although the fit of this equation is rather poor all the coefficients have the correct sign. The growth of Euro-dollar borrowing is positively related to the volume of imports invoiced in dollars and to the cost of borrowing in the domestic currency; and negatively related to the current account balance of payments, the cost of borrowing Euro-dollars (the short-term Euro-dollar interest rate plus the lending spread) and expectations that the dollar will appreciate on the spot exchange market (proxied by the rate of appreciation of the dollar in the previous period). Again, however, the t-ratio on the exchange rate term is low.

Thus, contrary to a priori expectations, exchange rate fluctuations appear to have a small influence on Euro-dollar depositing and borrowing. However, this result may simply reflect a failure to model adequately exchange rate expectations – a not uncommon problem and one made more difficult here by the nature of the sample data.

The results for the Euro-currency interest rate (equation 3, Table 3) follow the specified equation (8). Variables have the right sign but the excess money stock variable is non-significant. As might be expected the official discount rate term has the largest impact but there is evidence that the Euro-dollar rate, the lagged rate of change in the spot exchange rate and the current account balance of payments have an influence. An alternative interpretation of the equation would follow from the interest rate parity relationship between Euro-currencies where r_{DR}, $\dot{e}_{-1}$ and CB are factors influencing the forward discount on the currency vis-à-vis the dollar.

This pooled cross-section and time series regression analysis suggests that non-bank Euro-dollar transactions are related to trade variables, competing interest rates and other arguments in wealth-holders' portfolios. The significance of the Euro-dollar market for non-banks seems to lie in its role as an alternative market for financing external transactions and as a source and outlet for liquidity in the domestic economy. There is evidence that Euro-dollar holdings are superior assets in wealth portfolios and expand at a more rapid pace than the growth of national income; and that Euro-dollar deposits are also close substitutes to domestic broad money holdings. The simultaneous equations do not find evidence for a significant direct redepositing of Euro-dollar borrowing in the Euro-market.

6. SUMMARY AND CONCLUSIONS

An understanding of the factors explaining the growth of the Euro-currency market and its possible macroeconomic implications requires that Euro-data are examined in a disaggregated form. The present paper has concentrated on non-bank transactions in the Euro-market. Some 80 per cent of non-bank Euro-dollar deposits are held by non-US residents and it is plausible that for non-US non-banks the Euro-dollar and the US domestic markets may be segmented to some extent. If so, the size of the redepositing multiplier will largely depend on the links between non-banks' domestic currency market and the Euro-dollar market and the functional role of Euro-dollar deposits and borrowing.

The preliminary empirical work finds evidence of close links between non-

US non-bank transactions in domestic currency and Euro-dollars and that to a large extent the growth of non-bank Euro-dollar deposits reflects wealth-holders' general portfolio allocations. Euro-dollar deposits and borrowing are also related to trade transactions. Here the endogenous expansionary process in the Euro-market is more difficult to disentangle. It is possible that the Euro-market could endogenously expand from its role in financing trade flows: trade between agents served by the Euro-market could lead to an amount of redepositing of funds. However, this amount will also be responsive to relative interest rates in the Euro- and domestic currency markets of the agents concerned; and the functional role of the market in financing trade transactions must generally be regarded as a beneficial one.

Table 3. *OLS Regression Results**

1(a) Ln D^e $= 1.324 + 0.466 \text{ Dum}_{UK1} + 0.562 \text{ Dum}_{UK2} + 0.437 \text{ Dum}_{CA}$
 (2.28) (3.50) (3.82) (3.15)

$+ 0.344 \text{ Dum}_{JP} + 0.111 \text{ Ln Im}_c + 0.704 \text{ Ln } M^s/M^d + 0.487 \text{ G}\dot{N}P$
 (2.72) (1.55) (1.86) (1.94)

$+ 0.011 \text{ } r_{E\$} - 0.0084 \text{ } r_{EC} + 0.151 \text{ } \dot{e} + 0.245 \text{ } \Delta\text{Ln } B^e + 0.704 \text{ Ln } D^e_{-1}$
 (1.58) (2.42) (0.45) (1.68) (8.72)

$\overline{R^2} = 0.987$ $F = 494$ $DW = 2.07$

1(b) Ln D^e $= 1.343 + 0.466 \text{ Dum}_{UK1} + 0.561 \text{ Dum}_{UK2} + 0.440 \text{ Dum}_{CA}$
 (2.34) (3.52) (3.84) (3.20)

$+ 0.348 \text{ Dum}_{JP} + 0.109 \text{ Ln Im}_c + 0.690 \text{ Ln } M^s/M^d + 0.470 \text{ G}\dot{N}P$
 (2.76) (1.52) (1.85) (1.91)

$+ 0.012 \text{ } r_{E\$} - 0.0084 \text{ } r_{EC} + 0.259 \text{ } \Delta\text{Ln } B^e + 0.703 \text{ Ln } D^e_{-1}$
 (1.80) (2.44) (1.83) (8.76)

$\overline{R^2} = 0.987$ $F = 545$ $DW = 2.10$

2    $\Delta\text{Ln } B^e = 0.0089 \text{ Ln Im}_c - 0.000016 \text{ CB} - 0.00673 \text{ } (r_{E\$} + S_p)$
 (1.58) (3.19) (1.54)

$+ 0.0036 \text{ } r_{EC} - 0.371 \text{ } \dot{e}_{-1}$
 (1.58) (1.13)

$\overline{R^2} = 0.232$ $F = 5.70$ $DW = 1.77$

3   r_{EC} $= 1.60 - 2.48 \text{ Dum}_{UK1} - 3.49 \text{ Dum}_{UK2} - 3.89 \text{ Dum}_{CA} - 2.23 \text{ Dum}_{JP}$
 (1.28) (3.94) (4.54) (7.21) (2.43)

$- 1.73 \text{ Dum}_{DE} - 1.70 \text{ Dum}_{FR} + 1.07 \text{ } r_{DR} + 0.101 \text{ } r_{E\$} + 8.78 \text{ } \dot{e}_{-1}$
 (1.73) (2.77) (10.04) (1.44) (1.56)

$- 2.36 \text{ Ln } M^s/M^d - 0.0014 \text{ CB}$
 (0.64) (1.59)

$\overline{R^2} = 0.927$ $F = 88.9$ $DW = 1.72$

---

* t-ratios in parentheses

Table 4. *TSLS Regression Results**

1 $\text{Ln } D^e = 1.340 + 0.362 \text{ Dum}_{UK1} + 0.555 \text{ Dum}_{UK2} + 0.438 \text{ Dum}_{CA}$
   $\qquad (2.16) \quad (3.30) \qquad\qquad (3.49) \qquad\qquad (3.09)$

   $\qquad + 0.344 \text{ Dum}_{JP} + 0.107 \text{ Ln Im}_c + 0.671 \text{ Ln } M^s/M^d + 0.460 \text{ GNP}$
   $\qquad\quad (2.60) \qquad\qquad (1.45) \qquad\quad (1.62) \qquad\qquad\quad (1.69)$

   $\qquad + 0.012 \text{ r}_{E\$} \quad 0.0085 \text{ r}_{EC} + 0.218 \text{ }\Delta\text{Ln } B^r + 0.706 \text{ Ln } D^e_{-1}$
   $\qquad\quad (1.65) \qquad (1.96) \qquad\quad (0.62) \qquad\qquad (8.38)$

   $\qquad \overline{R^2} = 0.987 \qquad F = 522 \qquad DW = 2.07$

2 $\Delta\text{Ln } B^e = 0.0089 \text{ Ln Im}_c - 0.000016 \text{ CB} - 0.0070 \text{ (r}_{E\$} + S_p)$
   $\qquad\qquad\quad (1.58) \qquad\qquad (3.20) \qquad\qquad (1.59)$

   $\qquad + 0.00382 \text{ r}_{EC} - 0.379 \text{ }\dot{e}_{-1}$
   $\qquad\quad (1.66) \qquad\quad (1.16)$

   $\qquad \overline{R^2} = 0.234 \qquad F = 5.8 \qquad DW = 1.76$

* t-ratios in parentheses

DATA ANNEX

Each variable used in the regressions is constructed by pooling together time series and cross-section data from the six countries, Canada, France, Germany, Italy, Japan and the United Kingdom. For each country the time series is 1977 Q4 – 1980 Q4.

The variables are:

D^e: non-bank holdings of dollars in each country with banks in Europe, Canada and Japan (source: BIS);

B^e: non-bank borrowing of dollars in each country from banks in Europe, Canada and Japan (source: BIS);

r_{EC}: each country's three-month Euro-currency interest rate (source: BIS);

$\dot{e}$: $\dfrac{e - e_{-1}}{e_{-1}}$: e is each country's exchange rate against the dollar (number of currency units per dollar, source: BIS);

Im_c: is the dollar value of each country's imports corrected for the estimated amount invoiced in dollars. The estimates of the proportion of dollar invoicing are:

Canada	France	Germany	Italy	Japan	UK
0.90	0.29	0.30	0.43	0.91	0.30

$\dot{\text{GNP}}$: $\dfrac{\text{GNP} - \text{GNP}_{-1}}{\text{GNP}}$: GNP is each country's gross national product at current market prices (national sources).

$r_{E\$}$:   the three-month Euro-dollar rate (source: BIS);

M^s/M^d: is the ratio of each country's broad money stock to a trend estimate of money demand. This trend estimate was obtained by regressing the ratio of the broad money stock to income on a constant and a time trend. The level of income was then multiplied by the constant and trend variable to provide the trend measure of money demand. The period for the regression was 1970 Q1 – 1980 Q4 and the constant and time trend estimated for each country are:

	Constant	Trend
Canada	1.39	0.0094
	(49.7)	(9.02)
France	1.72	0.0061
	(100.9)	(9.49)
Germany	1.57	0.0072
	(183.7)	(22.2)
Italy	3.14	0.016
	(88.0)	(12.1)
Japan	2.91	0.01
	(33.9)	(2.86)
United Kingdom	1.72	− 0.009
	(38.7)	(5.58)

t-ratios in parentheses

(national sources: the money stock definitions are, Canada, total M_2, France, Masse Monétaire, M_2; Germany, Money supply, M_3; Italy, Money and Quasi Money, M_3; Japan, Money and Quasi Money, M_2; United Kingdom, Money Stock, Sterling M_3).

CB: each country's current-account balance of payments in dollars (national sources).

S_p: the average spread on syndicated medium-term Euro-credits charged to major OECD countries (source: Bank of England);

r_{DR}:   the official discount rate in each country (national sources).

The DUMs are country dummy variables taking the value 1 corresponding to that part of the sample drawn from the country identified by the subscript, and 0 otherwise. The subscripts are: CA, Canada; FR, France, DE, Germany; JP, Japan. The dummy variables are used in the case of the United Kingdom: UK1 refers to the period before and UK2 the period after the lifting of UK exchange controls.

Δ: is a first difference operator, $X = X - X_{-1}$ and the subscript -1 denotes that the variable is lagged by one quarter.

Where available, all data are seasonally unadjusted. Ln denotes that the variable is entered in natural logarithms.

NOTES

1. See, for example, Aliber (1980).

2. An additional amount of funds are placed in the market by non-banks through Trustee funds held with Swiss banks. Mayer (1979) estimated that these amounted to $30 billion. These are included in the "Banks outside the reporting area" category in Table 1. As these funds are placed at the risk of non-banks they should, however, be counted as a non-bank source of deposits.

3. This is the amount taken out by the BIS in arriving at its measure of the net size of the Euro-currency market.

4. Ellis (1981) argues that the main determinant of interbank transactions is the volume of deposits placed in the market by non-banks. However, his paper suffers from inappropriate aggregation by treating interbank transactions with banks outside the Euro-market – which often reflect a primary source or final use of funds – in the same way as interbank transactions between banks in the Euro-market.

5. See Johnston (1980) for an analysis of the role of the syndicated medium-term Euro-credit market in facilitating the recycling process; and Johnston (1983) for an analysis of the market's role in short-term capital movements and in the disintermediation of money holdings.

6. For surveys of the approaches involved see Swoboda (1980) and Johnston (1981).

7. The fractional reserve multiplier is

$$m = \frac{1}{r}$$

where r is the fraction of deposits sterilised as holdings of reserves by the banking system.

8. The leakage multiplier is $m = \dfrac{1}{r + b - rb}$

where b is the fixed proportion of additions to non-bank liquidity held outside the Euro-market.

9. For an analysis of the arbitrage links, see Johnston (1979).

10. Heller (1979).

11. See Aliber (1980).

12. For example, during 1979 and 1980 a combination of high US non-interest-bearing reserve requirements and US domestic interest rates gave US investors a large interest rate incentive to hold funds in the Euro-market, and the volume of their Euro-dollar deposits grew by over 300 per cent, from $6 billion to $20 billion.

13. See Johnston (1980 and 1981).

14. See, for example, Freedman (1977) and Hewson and Sakakibara (1976).

15. Knight (1977), in fact, finds evidence of both.

16. Moreover, this paper is flawed by its failure to take into account UK exchange controls, which were enforced up to October 1979. These controls effectively prevented outward arbitrage by UK residents and prior to October 1979 the Euro-sterling/domestic sterling interest rate differential was large and extremely volatile. After 1979 the differential remained close to zero. It is completely inappropriate to interpret the fluctuations in Euro-sterling interest rates as saying anything about UK non-bank portfolio behaviour as this paper does. Prior to the lifting of UK exchange controls there was negligible arbitrage by UK non-banks while, after the removal of the controls, interbank arbitrage dominated the determination of Euro-sterling interest rates.

17. Swoboda (1968) has used Baumol's inventory/theoretic approach to the optimal holding of cash balances to show that when there are transaction costs in moving between domestic and foreign currency traders would hold positive foreign currency balances to meet the flow of trade payments.

18. This is consistent with a view that the rate of change of the spot exchange rate, $\dot{e}_t$, follows a random walk around some constant value, k, measuring the trend in the spot rate:

$$\dot{e}_t = k + \dot{e}_{t-1} + u_t$$

where u_t is a white noise error term.

19. Prior to December 1977 Austria, Denmark and Ireland did not report and although the importance of these countries is relatively small it seemed better to have as consistent a run of data as possible. 1977 Q3 data are, however, used to generate lagged values of the variables when these are needed.

20. Examining countries individually did not provide good estimates because of the colinear nature of the explanatory variable. The pooling together of data from several countries appears to avoid some of the extreme multi-colinearity problems.

21. The OLS equation for the rate of change of the spot exchange rate is:

$$\dot{e} = 0.033 \text{ Dum}_{UK1} - 0.040 \text{ DUM}_{JP} - 0.045 \text{ DUM}_{DE} - 0.0179 \text{ DUM}_{FR}$$
$$\quad\; (2.67) \qquad\qquad (3.04) \qquad\qquad (3.42) \qquad\qquad (1.69)$$

$$+ 0.00385 \text{ } r_{E\$} - 0.00320 \text{ } r_{EC} - 0.00001 \text{ CB} + 0.0359 \text{ Ln D}^e$$
$$\quad\; (2.61) \qquad\quad (2.58) \qquad\quad (4.61) \qquad\quad (1.00)$$

$$\bar{R}^2 = 0.316 \qquad F = 5.5 \qquad DW = 1.91$$

22. Since the series are a combination of time series and cross section data, the lagged dependent variables are constructed by lagging the original country data and then reconcatenating.

23. Johnston (1983) also finds evidence that US non-bank holdings of Euro-dollars are superior assets in their portfolios.

REFERENCES

Aliber, R.Z., "The integration of the offshore and domestic banking system", *Journal of Monetary Economics*, Vol. 6 (1980), 509-26.

Driault, C.B. and Howson, S.K., "A portfolio model of domestic and external financial markets", *Bank of England Discussion Paper*, No. 20 (June 1982).

Ellis, J.G., "Euro-banks and the inter-bank market", *Bank of England Quarterly Bulletin*, Vol. 21, No. 3 (September 1981), 351-64.

Freedman, Charles, "A model of the Euro-dollar market", *Journal of Monetary Economics*, Vol. 3, No. 2 (April 1977), 139-61.

Heller, Robert H., "Why the market is demand-determined", *Euromoney* (February 1979), 41-7.

Hewson, J. and Sakakibara, E., "A general equilibrium approach to the Euro-dollar market", *Journal of Money, Credit and Banking*, Vol. 8, No. 3 (August 1976), 297-323.

Johnston, R.B., "Some aspects of the determination of Euro-currency interest rates", *Bank of England Quarterly Bulletin*, Vol. 19, No. 1 (March 1979), 35-46.

——, "Banks' international lending decisions and the determination of spreads on syndicated medium-term Euro-credits", *Bank of England Discussion Paper*, No. 12 (September 1980).

——, "Theories of the growth of the Euro-currency market: a review of the Euro-currency multiplier", *BIS Economic Paper*, No. 4 (May 1981).

——, *The Economics of the Euro-market: history, theory and policy* (London, Macmillan, 1983).

Mayer, Helmut, "Credit and liquidity creation in the international banking sector", *BIS Economics Paper*, No. 1 (November 1979).

Swoboda, Alexander K., "The Euro-dollar market: an interpretation", *Essays in International Finance*, No. 14 (Princeton, Princeton University Press, February 1968).

——, "Credit creation in the Euro-market: alternative theories and implications for control", *Group of Thirty Occasional Paper*, No. 2 (New York, 1980).

Chapter V

EMERGENCE ET DEVELOPPEMENT
DES MULTINATIONALES BANCAIRES:
ASPECTS THEORIQUES ET EMPIRIQUES

par *Joël Métais*

INTRODUCTION

L'extraordinaire croissance, depuis la fin des années soixante, de l'encours
des créances bancaires internationales – qui a atteint 1542 milliards de dollars au 31-12-1981[1] – a constitué un des domaines de recherche favoris des
spécialistes d'économie financière internationale, au cours de cette période.
Témoin, la floraison d'articles consacrés aux divers aspects des marchés
d'eurodevises sur lesquels se réalisent la majorité des transactions à l'origine
de ces créances.

Les progrès incontestables enregistrés dans la compréhension de ces phénomènes ne sauraient pourtant faire oublier le fait qu'en limitant – au moins
jusqu'à un passé récent – l'analyse aux aspects surtouts quantitatifs de l'intermédiation financière internationale et en privilégiant une approche en termes de théorie monétaire et/ou de mouvements de capitaux internationaux[2] on s'est, sans doute, privé d'une explication plus générale et plus
fondamentale. Pour sa part, cette dernière doit, selon nous, reposer sur des
prémisses aussi simples qu'évidentes pour tout observateur de la scène financière internationale de ces dernières années et qu'on peut résumer ainsi: la
croissance des activités bancaires internationales n'est pas seulement une
simple résultante de la conjonction de divers facteurs d'ordre macro-économique, dont l'influence ne saurait certes être mise en doute: croissance des
échanges internationaux, nouvelle constellation des soldes des paiements internationaux et nécessité corrélative du "recyclage" depuis 1974, etc. Elle
traduit aussi largement des stratégies de croissance et/ou de profit d'un certain nombre de grandes institutions bancaires, pour la plupart originaires
des principaux pays industrialisés. Celles-ci ont trouvé leur expression et leur
aboutissement dans la constitution de ce qu'il convient de qualifier de
banques multinationales (ou de multinationales bancaires). Et ces dernières
dominent aujourd'hui les marchés d'eurodevises par la masse de leurs dépôts et le volume de leurs créances ainsi libellés[3]. Même si on ne peut né-

gliger le rôle – notamment en termes de pressions concurrentielles – qu'y jouent les très nombreuses institutions de taille plus modeste et aux ambitions internationales plus limitées, il est indéniable que l'évolution, à court comme à long terme, de l'intermédiation financière internationale reste largement tributaire des stratégies de ces banques multinationales.

Pourtant, tandis que les firmes multinationales industrielles continuaient à susciter un important courant de recherches théoriques et empiriques, les banques multinationales en demeuraient exclues. Mais des travaux récents et plusieurs articles dans les revues d'analyse économique témoignent de l'intérêt que portent désormais certains chercheurs à cet agent économique qui joue déjà un rôle crucial dans l'allocation internationale des capitaux – notamment entre pays industrialisés et en voie de développement – le rééquilibrage des paiements internationaux ou la transmission des impulsions de politique monétaire, en provenance, surtout des Etats Unis.

Cet article s'inscrit ainsi dans ce courant de recherche qui considère que la compréhension du phénomène de la banque multinationale constitue aujourd'hui un préalable indispensable à l'approfondissement des analyses jusqu'ici consacrées aux marchés d'eurodevises et à l'intermédiation financière internationale. En particulier, si l'on veut en avoir une vision prospective.

Dans une première partie nous définirons la banque multinationale et présenterons ses principales caractéristiques. La seconde partie tentera de formuler une théorie de la multinationalisation bancaire. Celle-ci s'éclairera, dans une troisième partie, à l'aide des résultats des travaux empiriques que nous menons depuis plusieurs années dans ce domaine[4]. Une conclusion dégagera alors les tendances les plus prévisibles de l'activité bancaire internationale au cours des prochaines années.

I. LES BANQUES MULTINATIONALES: DEFINITION ET PRESENTATION GENERALE

Leurs activités et présence internationales sont indissociables de l'histoire des banques. On peut cependant isoler en ce domaine au moins trois grands types d'approche qui, dans le passé, furent relativement séparés.

Dans certains cas, des banques ont établi des filiales dans divers pays étrangers pour s'y livrer à une activité essentiellement locale suivant le modèle sans doute inauguré par les Templiers, et qui connut son expansion la plus remarquable à l'époque des empires coloniaux (anglais et français notamment).

Mais le plus souvent ce sont pourtant les nécessités du financement des échanges commerciaux et des investissements internationaux qui ont conditionné ces activités et implantations bancaires internationales. Ce second modèle a, quant à lui, une histoire qui, bien que plus ancienne encore, ne semble jamais s'être vraiment interrompue depuis les marchands-banquiers italiens du Moyen Age. Un troisième modèle, enfin, est celui fourni par les banques dont la mission essentielle consiste à organiser et animer ce qui devient alors le marché international des capitaux. En ce domaine, les grandes Maisons d'Emission londoniennes apparaissent comme les ancêtres de nos contemporaines Eurobanques consortiales.

Pour sa part, le processus d'internationalisation bancaire, au cours de ces deux dernières décennies, s'est réalisé à partir de, autant qu'il a conduit à la constitution d'institutions géantes qui, le plus souvent, empruntent simultanément leurs caractéristiques aux trois modèles historiques dont nous avons brièvement fait état. Ce n'est pas là le moins original de ses traits, même si ce mouvement s'est initialement engagé pour soutenir le financement des échanges et investissements internationaux. Ce fut notamment le cas pour les banques commerciales américaines qui continuent de dominer la scène financière internationale. Mais bientôt, les deux autres voies ont aussi retenu l'attention comme en attestent l'explosion du nombre de succursales et filiales bancaires sur les places financières off-shore et les acquisitions ou constitutions de banques locales dans plusieurs pays hôtes étrangers.

Cette rapide mise en perspective historique laisse entrevoir, d'emblée, le caractère complexe et multiforme des banques multinationales. Elle ne nous procure pas pour autant une définition opérationnelle et féconde – en termes d'analyse économique – de ces institutions devenues les acteurs prééminents d'un processus d'internationalisation qui englobe aussi un nombre encore bien plus élevé de banques qui ne sauraient – du moins pour l'instant – prétendre à l'appellation de multinationales.

On sait les débats jadis suscités par la définition des firmes multinationales industrielles. Il ne saurait être question de les rappeler ici. Soucieux de nous appuyer sur une définition qui, sans être trop restrictive ni trop extensive, retienne pourtant les traits majeurs des banques multinationales, nous les définirons comme des banques dont les activités internationales conduites, essentiellement, par l'intermédiaire d'implantations dans plusieurs pays étrangers, représentent une part élevée de l'activité et/ou des profits globaux et sont conçues et menées dans une perspective mondiale. Afin de les isoler, en vue surtout de la réalisation des travaux empiriques, au sein de l'ensemble des banques ayant quelque activité internationale significative, il convient de se fixer un seuil critique pour la part de celle-ci dans le total du bilan ou les profits globaux. Nous fondant sur la connaissance que nous avons pu accumuler des activités et stratégies de très nombreuses banques issues de divers pays, nous avons été amenés à situer, de manière très pragmatique, cette valeur critique entre 30% et 40% des grandeurs globales correspondantes. La nature essentiellement qualitative du second critère de la définition en rend, par contre, beaucoup plus délicate l'utilisation à des fins de discrimination entre banques multinationales et banques ayant seulement une importante activité internationale. En l'absence – fréquente – d'informations suffisantes, il semble souhaitable de ne faire jouer à ce critère qu'un rôle subsidiaire; cette démarche a donc été retenue pour établir le tableau 1 ci-après qui ne prétend nullement – en raison du caractère souvent fragmentaire des données – fournir une liste exhaustive des multinationales bancaires. Tout au plus doit-on insister sur leur nombre encore assez restreint, même si un contingent bien plus nombreux de banques qui ne cessent de développer – quantitativement et qualitativement – leurs activités internationales ne devrait pas tarder à venir élargir ce cercle.

Au terme d'une évolution qui, pour la plupart d'entre elles, a connu, en gros trois étapes, les banques multinationales mènent aujourd'hui, au niveau mondial, l'ensemble des activités bancaires de gros, de détail et de service[5]. Au départ, l'expansion internationale privilégia les activités de service et de gros destinées à la clientèle des multinationales industrielles du pays d'origine puis, parfois, de certaines grandes entreprises dans les pays hôtes. Mais dès la fin des années soixantes, les activités de gros sur le marché international des capitaux, à partir des centres financiers offshore prirent le relais. En aspirant une deuxième vague de banques dans l'arène internationale, les perspectives de croissance et de profit alors offertes par les euromarchés allaient conduire à une amplification du processus d'internationalisation qui atteignit jusques et y compris les banques moyennes.

Avec la fin de la décennie soixante dix, marquée par l'érosion de la rentabilité des activités en eurodevises et la montée des risques de l'environnement financier international, les plus grandes banques donnèrent une nouvelle inflexion à leur stratégie internationale en direction des marchés de détail de leurs pays hôtes étrangers. Tandis que les américaines ont jusqu'ici privilégié certains segments spécialisés de ces marchés[6] leurs concurrentes, notamment britanniques et japonaises, ont opté pour la voie de l'acquisition de banques de dépôts, tout particulièrement aux Etats-Unis. Des prises de contrôle spectaculaires, surtout depuis 1978, y ont, en effet, permis à des intérêts étrangers de contrôler 5 des 13 premières banques new-yorkaises et 8 des 15 premières banques californiennes. Ainsi, les banques multinationales

Tableau 1. *Actifs, dépots et profits internationaux des banques dans quelques pays industrialisés. En pourcentage des grandeurs globales correspondantes (e = valeur estimée)*

	1980			1979		
	actifs	profits	dépôts	actifs	profits	dépôts
Etats-Unis[a]						
Bank America Corp.	46	45	48	45	38	50
Citicorp.	62	62	74	66	65	74
Chase Manhattan Corp.	62	49	57	62	47	59
Manufacturers Hanover Corp.	57	50	50	56	49	47
J.P. Morgan and Co.	57	58	58	60	52	56
Chemical N.Y. Corp.	47	38	46	44	34	45
Bankers Trust N.Y. Corp.	51	58	52	53	52	49
Continental Illinois Corp.	37	33	53	38	18	51
First Chicago Corp.	48	–	59	44	4	54
Marine Midlands Banks Inc.	43	38	42	43	27	39
Charter N.Y. Corp.	58	58	44	53	55	40
First National Boston Corp.	49	21	56	48	20	54
Canada						
Royal Bank of Canada	33	44		30	34	
Toronto Dominion Bank[b]	40	45		39	39	
Bank of Montreal	33	31		40	27	
Canadian Imperial Bank of Commerce	33	44		31	28	
Bank of Nova Scotia[b]	57	59		55	45	
Angleterre						
Barclays Bank[c]		34	33		28	31
National Westminster Bank		35e			22e	
Lloyds Bank	51	38		53	30	
Midland Bank		65e			44	
Allemagne						
Deutsche Bank	40e					
Dresdner Bank	33e					
Hollande						
Algemene Bank Nederland	31	44		30	38	
Amro bank	40			38		
France						
BNP[d]			42			35
Crédit Lyonnais[e]		50e		45		51
Paribas[f]		61			39	
Indosuez		75e				

Sources: établi à partir des Rapports Annuels et d'informations de la presse financière internationale.
   a. Pour les banques américaines il s'agit uniquement des dépôts des succursales étrangères.
   b. Pour ces deux banques, seuls sont retenus les actifs en monnaies étrangères.
   c. Barclays Bank International seulement.
   d. Dépôts auprès des succursales, filiales et institutions affiliées étrangères et déposants étrangers en France.
   e. Actifs et engagements en monnaies étrangères. En 1980, il s'agit des profits de la banque seulement.
   f. Seules sont retenues les activités bancaires du groupe.

apparaissent-elles aujourd'hui comme des institutions dont les activités internationales extrêmement variées s'articulent au sein d'un groupe polymorphe qui, le plus souvent, tend à reproduire dans l'espace mondial le modèle de la banque universelle.

Cette diversité des activités s'accompagne – ne serait-ce que pour une meilleure efficacité de fonctionnement, pour satisfaire à des contraintes réglementaires et fiscales et conserver une certaine flexibilité d'adaptation aux évolutions de l'environnement économique et institutionnel – d'une grande variété de points d'appui à l'étranger. Toutefois, des différences sont sensibles entre les banques multinationales quant aux "dosages" respectifs entre bureaux de représentation, succursales, filiales, participations dans des eurobanques consortiales ou des institutions financières locales à l'étranger. Leurs choix, en ce domaine, témoignent incontestablement de stratégies internationales différentes même si souvent ils restent aussi conditionnés par l'héritage historique de chaque institution.[7] Ces stratégies devront d'abord tenir compte des ressources dont dispose la banque pour investir à l'étranger, du niveau et type de risque qu'elle entend y assumer, surtout si elle doit y aborder des activités nouvelles.

Ainsi les grandes banques américaines ont-elles opté pour une approche privilégiant les modes de présence les plus directs – succursales, filiales et bureaux de représentation – , suivant un mode de couverture géographique maximale. Chez leurs concurrents, les sensibilités sont plus diverses mais, en règle générale, le recours aux formules d'association a été plus fréquent tandis que la couverture géographique optimale était plus souvent de règle.[8]

II. LA MULTINATIONALISATION DES BANQUES: ASPECTS THEORIQUES

2.1. *La spécificité de la firme bancaire et l'extension de la théorie de la multinationalisation aux banques: aspects méthodologiques*

Deux séries de raisons expliquent probablement la manifestation tardive de l'intérêt des économistes théoriciens pour la multinationalisation des banques:

La première tient au caractère longtemps insidieux du phénomène lui-même. Il a, de ce fait, moins capté l'attention des observateurs que ne l'a fait l'internationalisation des autres branches industrielles. Cette situation n'a commencé à lentement changer qu'au milieu de la décennie passée, lorsqu'en s'accélérant l'expansion des banques à l'étranger a aussi atteint de nouveaux rivages: après l'Europe, les Etats-Unis, le bassin du Pacifique et le Moyent Orient; maintenant le Canada et l'Amérique du Sud; bientôt l'Afrique.[9]

La seconde est de nature plus directement théorique et comporte au moins deux aspects:

– Pendant longtemps, sinon encore aujoud'hui, on n'a voulu voir dans l'internationalisation bancaire qu'un phénomène dépendant, une résultante, de celle des échanges commerciaux, de la production et des flux financiers. Or, d'une part, il est tout aussi exact que cette internationalisation bancaire a autant favorisé – sinon amplifié – ces phénomènes que ceux-ci ne l'ont provoquée. Et on verra, d'autre part, qu'il est possible de réexaminer à un niveau supérieur d'analyse théorique les liens entre ces deux processus afin de comprendre leurs rapports dialectiques, dans le temps et l'espace.

– Surtout le postulat, communément adopté par les économistes d'une spécificité de la firme bancaire du fait, essentiellement, de son pouvoir de création monétaire et/ou de son caractère hautement réglementé en a certainement retenu beaucoup de franchir le pas pour tenter une analyse du phénomène de la banque multinationale, suivant la voie tracée lors de l'étude des multinationales industrielles. De fait, toute théorie de la banque multinationale ne saurait éluder l'examen préalable de cette question méthodologique[10] fondamentale. A défaut de pouvoir lui consacrer ici les développements assez longs et techniques qu'il appelle, nous ne rapporterons que l'essentiel de la réflexion à mener en ce domaine.

Ainsi, la spécificité des firmes bancaires va-t-elle jusqu'à interdire a priori tout recours aux concepts et outils d'analyse de la théorie de l'entreprise pour étudier leurs comportements et stratégies? Ou bien ce recours reste-t-il possible moyennant cependant certaines hypothèses complémentaires qui intégrent dans l'analyse les particularités des banques issues précisément de leur pouvoir de création monétaire; notamment en ce qui concerne les contraintes qu'imposent à la taille et à la croissance de chaque institution, sa part du marché des dépôts bancaires et la politique monétaire de la banque centrale. Or, il n'y a pas encore à ce jour de réponse claire à ces questions, faute, sans doute, d'une théorie satisfaisante de l'intermédiation financière et de la création monétaire qui lui est associée dans le cas des banques.[11] Et il se peut qu'il faille chercher ici l'origine du défaut premier de la quasi-totalité des modèles microéconomiques de la firme bancaire, impuissants à traduire correctement la réalité du fait de leur incapacité d'intégrer de manière satisfaisante dans un même cadre d'analyse les aspects financiers et réels de la production des banques.[12] Ceci constitue pourtant un handicap majeur lorsqu'on tente d'expliquer des phénomènes aussi importants que la taille et la croissance des entreprises bancaires et la structure de leur branche d'industrie.[13] A plus forte raison leur internationalisation!

Il faut toutefois reconnaitre que les modèles de choix de portefeuille fréquemment utilisés pour représenter le comportement de la firme bancaire peuvent, d'un certain point de vue, rendre compte de ses activités internationales pour autant que l'on se limite à l'analyse de la composition et de la diversification de ses avoirs et engagements internationaux.[14] Mais ces activités internationales peuvent fort bien, compte tenu des hypothèses de ces modèles, être menées seulement à partir d'une base domestique. Dès lors, on ne peut comprendre pourquoi une part importante et croissante de celles-ci est désormais le fait du réseau de succursales et filiales à l'étranger. Or, cette dernière évolution constitue bien le trait original de la banque multinationale qu'il convient, à ce titre, d'expliquer.

Sous réserve des remarques ci-dessus, nous conduirons cette explication en la fondant sur l'hypothèse que la spécificité de la firme bancaire n'est pas de nature à empêcher l'examen de sa multinationalisation à partir d'une extension de l'analyse des multinationales industrielles. Ceci, nous conduit d'emblée à préciser la position des problèmes à l'aide des deux considérations ci-après.

— Ainsi, le problème de la ventilation des actifs internationaux d'une banque suivant qu'ils sont nés d'opérations menées à partir du pays d'origine ou effectuées au sein de points d'appui à l'étranger, ne nous semble pas fondamentalement différent de celui du partage entre exportations et production à l'étranger pour les firmes multinationales industrielles. Aussi, conformément à l'approche retenue dans les analyses récentes de ces firmes, nous faudra-t-il resituer la multinationalisation bancaire dans le cadre plus général de l'ensemble des modalités qui s'offrent à une entreprise de satisfaire une demande sur des marchés étrangers.

— A ce titre, il conviendra aussi bien de s'interroger sur le choix des banques d'être effectivement présentes directement à l'étranger — quoique avec des degrés extrêmement variables d'insertion dans le tissu bancaire local — plutôt que de procéder seulement à des investissements de portefeuille dans des institutions financières étrangères.

2.2. *L'évolution récente des théories de l'entreprise industrielle multinationale*

La décennie soixante-dix a enregistré des progrès aussi nombreux qu'incontestables dans la compréhension du fait multinational, sous la direction de nombreux auteurs comme J.H. Dunning, R. Vernon, C.P. Kindleberger, S. Hymer, ou R. Caves. Dès le début de cette décennie, il était acquis que ce phénomène était passible d'une analyse en termes d'économie industrielle plutôt que de l'approche traditionnelle rattachant l'investissement direct à la théorie des mouvements internationaux de capitaux.[15] Plusieurs explications, essentiellement complémentaires furent alors avancées sans qu'il fût toutefois possible de les rassembler dans un corps théorique unifié, faute de progrès conceptuels suffisants. Intervenus surtout à partir de 1975, sous l'impulsion de J.H. Dunning et, plus récemment, de A.M. Rugman,[16], ceux-ci ont conduit à une percée dans deux directions:

— En premier lieu, ils ont permis une réconciliation et une intégration des théories du commerce international et de la production internationale, dans le cadre plus général d'une théorie de l'engagement international qui combine les notions de *dotations spécifiques de la localisation* qui s'attachent aux pays, et de *dotations spécifiques de la possession*, liées aux entreprises.[17]

— En second lieu, ils ont fait apparaître que les diverses analyses antérieures de la production internationale sont autant de cas particuliers d'une théorie plus générale qui est une extension de celle de la firme et qui s'articule autour de trois notions-clé:

— des avantages spécifiques — notamment sous forme d'actifs immatériels ayant un caractère de biens publics, tels que le savoir-faire, l'information, etc. . . . — possédés de manière monopolistique par une firme.
— l'internalisation du mode d'exploitation de ces avantages par la firme qui aura intérêt à les mettre elle-même en valeur par une production directe à l'étranger plutôt que par le biais d'exportations de biens et services à partir de son pays d'origine ou par l'octroi de licences d'exploitation à des firmes étrangères.
— des variables de localisation caractéristiques des sites d'implantation possible d'unités de production à l'étranger — telles que ressources naturelles, main d'oeuvre qualifiée et/ou bon marché — qui expliquent pourquoi la production a effectivement lieu à l'étranger et dans tel pays particulier, de préférence à tel autre.

Une hiérarchie précise s'établit entre ces trois notions pour expliquer l'internationalisation de la production: en effet, un avantage qui lui soit spécifique doit préexister avant que la firme n'envisage d'en internaliser le mode d'exploitation. En outre, les pays étrangers doivent posséder divers atouts propres pour qu'il soit intéressant d'y établir des unités de production. John

H. Dunning qui a beaucoup contribué à développer cette théorie éclectique de l'internationalisation de la production industrielle[18] montre aussi comment elle *fédère les apports antérieurs de la recherche* en ce domaine: tandis que la théorie de l'organisation industrielle explique surtout la nature des avantages spécifiques possédés par la firme, celle des droits de propriété et de l'intégration verticale permet de déterminer les conditions d'internalisation de ces avantages; celles enfin de la localisation et du commerce international éclairent les facteurs de choix entre les diverses implantations possibles.[19]

Mais plus récemment encore, Alan M. Rugman a cherché à montrer qu'il était possible de dépasser cette théorie éclectique en centrant l'analyse sur le seul concept d'internalisation qui constituerait le nouveau paradigme unificateur de la théorie de l'entreprise multinationale.[20] Au-delà des travaux récents de Casson[21] et des chercheurs de l'université britannique de Reading, cette nouvelle approche trouve en réalité ses antécédents dans la théorie de la firme proposée dès 1937 par Ronald H. Coase.[22] Au coeur de cette analyse, on trouve la notion d'imperfections sur les marchés de biens, de facteurs de production ou de biens intermédiaires, associées à diverses formes d'externalités. Inhérentes à la nature même de ces marchés ou provoquées par l'intervention publique – réglementation – ces imperfections amènent la firme qui y est confrontée à réagir par l'internalisation. Cette dernière consiste à substituer au marché défaillant un marché interne à sa propre organisation qui lui permet notamment de surmonter l'obstacle d'un prix irréaliste, sinon inexistant, pour les biens ou facteurs considérés. Les connaissances technologiques intégrées dans le savoir-faire et l'information en général constituent, à ce titre, des exemples de biens intermédiaires dans la production auxquels le raisonnement ci-dessus est particulièrement bien adapté.

Ce rappel des développements récents de la théorie de la firme multinationale industrielle nous a paru nécessaire dans la mesure où ses principaux acquis vont être reexaminés dans le cadre de l'explication de la multinationalisation bancaire qui va suivre.

2.3. *L'analyse théorique de la multinationalisation bancaire: une première formulation*

Par rapport à de nombreux travaux antérieurs appliqués à montrer pourquoi les multinationales industrielles étaient issues de certaines branches d'activité plutôt que d'autres ou à mettre à jour les facteurs responsables de l'internationalisation d'un nombre plus ou moins élevé d'entreprises au sein d'une branche donnée, cette présentation adoptera une perspective – et de ce fait une démarche – légèrement différente.

– Nous n'avons, en effet, en vue qu'une seule branche: l'industrie bancaire. Au-delà des caractéristiques institutionnelles particulières qu'elle revêt dans chaque pays, on peut pourtant la considérer comme relativement homogène de l'un à l'autre. On admettra ainsi qu'elle est composée de firmes dont l'activité principale consiste à consolider et transformer des risques, d'une part; à servir de courtier et de distributeur sur les marchés de crédit, d'autre part.[23] Les banques offrent en outre divers services financiers spécialisés liés, plus ou moins directement, à leurs octrois de crédit ou à la collecte des dépôts. Nombre de leurs produits ont, pour cette raison, le caractère de produits joints, même si s'est récemment manifestée une tendance à la dissociation des diverses prestations proposées.

– L'attention peut alors se porter plus spécialement sur le fait de savoir, pourquoi, dans chaque pays, seules quelques banques s'internationalisent; d'expliquer la séquence de leur départ pour l'étranger et le choix de leurs pays hôtes. Ainsi cette préoccupation sera-t-elle largement présente dans la suite de l'analyse.

– De même, nous paraît-il important[24] de mettre à jour dans cette analyse les facteurs permettant l'interprétation de trois phénomènes, à nos yeux, essentiels:

– Les différences assez nettes dans le degré d'internationalisation[25] des systèmes bancaires des divers pays. Pour simplifier l'exposé et compte tenu de l'information existante, on se limitera ici aux seuls grands pays industrialisés. Mais l'internationalisation récente d'un nombre croissant de banques issues de pays en voie de développement – Brésil, Corée du Sud, pays du Golfe Persique – mériterait aussi examen.
– L'historique de l'internationalisation de ces divers systèmes bancaires nationaux: est-elle intervenue simultanément dans tous les pays ou y-a-t-il eu des décalages et pourquoi?
– Les spécialisations éventuelles des banques multinationales en fonction de leurs pays d'origine, au regard des grands types d'activités (gros, service, détail) et leurs préférences possibles pour certaines régions du globe.

En raison de la durée de leur expérience de cette phase d'internationalisation – dont le début se situe aux alentours de 1965 – , de leur suprématie encore indéniable sur la scène bancaire internationale[26] – malgré une certaine érosion depuis quatre ou cinq ans – et de la disponibilité des informations statistiques a leur endroit, la démonstration prendra essentiellement comme référence les banques commerciales américaines. Elle procédera en trois étapes, conformément au mode d'articulation de la théorie éclectique de la firme multinationale qu'on vient de rappeler; la mise en évidence des avantages spécifiques propres aux banques multinationales précédera l'exposé des raisons de leur exploitation par la voie de l'internalisation et l'explication de la nécessité d'une présence sur place à l'étranger.

A – *Information, savoir-faire et taille, principaux atouts des banques multinationales*

La relation qui s'instaure entre la banque et ses clients n'a pas la nature de celles qui s'établissent habituellement entre offreurs et demandeurs sur les autres marchés de biens et services.

– Ainsi, si les taux d'intérêt débiteurs sont censés opérer une discrimination entre les emprunteurs, l'information économique et financière détenue par la banque sur son client conditionne pourtant l'étendue de son engagement à son égard.

– Mais la banque doit aussi, en permanence, mobiliser et retenir des fonds obtenus auprès de déposants qui accordent, certes, une grande importance aux intérêts créditeurs qu'elle leur sert mais ne négligent sûrement pas la confiance que leur inspirent sa solidité et sa stabilité.

L'information financière détenue sur les grandes firmes industrielles qui sont leurs clientes de longue date constitue ainsi un des avantages spécifiques possédé de manière monopolistique par leur(s) banque(s) chef(s) de file. Outre un éventuel coût direct d'acquisition et, surtout, d'analyse et de conservation, cette information, généralement accumulée sur une longue période, a plutôt un coût d'opportunité. On peut approximer ce dernier par les pertes consécutives à des concours à des emprunteurs sur lesquels cette information reste encore insuffisante. C'est donc à ce niveau que se situe le premier, sinon le principal élément de l'enchaînement causal qui permet de comprendre pourquoi les banques ont suivi leurs clients à l'étranger lorsque ceux-ci y ont établi des unités de production ou de distribution.

Une relation de clientèle ancienne et étroite avec des entreprises ayant de hautes exigences en matière de services connexes aura ainsi permis à la banque de mettre au point une série de produits financiers nouveaux très élaborés – gestion de trésorerie, couverture du risque de change – et de réunir à cet effet le potentiel humain – souvent hautement qualifié – voire le capital technique – notamment informatique – . Il y a là une autre source d'avantages dont elle cherchera alors à tirer parti avec son client établi à l'étranger, puis avec des entreprises étrangères auxquelles leurs propres banques ne peuvent encore offrir de tels services. Sans anticiper sur les développements ultérieurs, notons déjà que ce sont certainement là les deux principales raisons de l'internationalisation précoce des banques américaines sous l'impulsion de leurs clientes multinationales industrielles, et de leur suprématie encore incontestée en matière de services à ces entreprises.[27]

La taille joue aussi un rôle décisif dans le processus de multinationalisation des banques.[28] De fait, aux Etats-Unis, la quinzaine environ d'entre elles qu'on puisse déjà considérer comme multinationales se classent parmi les vingt premières du pays et sont toujours en tête dans leurs Etats respectifs. En Allemagne, en France, en Grande Bretagne et aux Pays Bas, cette règle ne souffre pas d'exception. Dans le cas des banques, ce facteur confère un avantage spécifique, au même titre que dans le cas des multinationales industrielles, en étant générateur de ressources suffisantes pour affronter les coûts et risques initiaux d'une entreprise à l'étranger. Mais la taille intervient encore (par le biais de divers ratios sur la base des fonds propres) pour déterminer la catégorie d'emprunteurs qu'il sera possible de servir; sans omettre, enfin, la confiance qu'elle inspire aux déposants. Cette dernière constitue, en effet, un véritable bien public intermédiaire dans le processus de production des dépôts. Les déposants – en l'occurence, essentiellement les participants aux grands marchés monétaires notamment ceux d'eurodevises, lorsqu'on se situe dans le cadre international[29] – associent souvent qualité et sérieux de la gestion à la taille de l'institution. Mais ce mécanisme n'est pas seul en cause pour produire la confiance. Un autre, plus subtil, assigne aussi un rôle aux autorités monétaires dans cette production. On admet, en effet, que la banque centrale de son pays d'origine userait toujours de son pouvoir de prêteur en dernier ressort vis à vis d'une grande banque plutôt que de la laisser tomber en faillite. Par ce biais une sorte d'effet externe se trouve associé à la taille de la banque. Il renforce pour cette dernière la valeur de cet actif spécifique.

De même, une banque originaire du pays émetteur de la monnaie international bénéficie d'un autre avantage spécifique lié à la plus grande liberté de manoeuvre et à la sécurité de refinancement que lui confère son accès direct au marché monétaire et à l'escompte de la banque centrale de ce pays. On voit tout le parti qu'on pu effectivement tirer les banques américaines de cette situation. On comprend aussi pourquoi nombre de banques d'autres nationalités ont, à partir des années soixante-dix, cherché à réduire leur handicap en se constituant leur propre base-dollar par le biais du rachat de banques commerciales aux Etats-Unis.

Les banques multinationales possèdent généralement bien d'autres avantages spécifiques qu'on peut regrouper sous le label du know-how. Ceci est flagrant dans le cas de techniques telles que le crédit-bail, l'affacturage, le crédit à la consommation. Désormais, conformément à la théorie du cycle du produit de R. Vernon certaines grandes banques qui en ont une solide expérience implantent des filiales spécialisées dans des pays où une demande pour ces modes de financement n'est pas encore, ou est mal, satisfaite par les institutions financières locales.[30]

Outre ceux que nous venons de présenter[31] et qu'on peut considérer comme détenus préalablement par la banque, il faut encore citer les avantages que celle-ci cherche à acquérir – dans le cadre de son expansion internationale – pour, en quelque sorte, les renforcer du seul fait de leur utilisation dans le cadre de sa propre organisation.[32] Mais ceux qui naissent – ou sont accrus – du fait de l'internationalisation méritent une mention toute particulière. En matière bancaire, le principal réside dans ce qu'on pourrait appeler les effets de réseau.[33] Aux banques dotées d'un réseau dense et global, ceux-ci assurent, entre autres, un accroissement des occasions d'affaires,[34] un refinancement au meilleur coût (en tirant parti des différences de situation sur les divers marchés monétaires du monde), la possibilité de se livrer à des opérations de change faisant intervenir des monnaies exotiques (et génératrices par là-même de fortes commissions). On sait aussi que certains auteurs y ont vu, pour les multinationales industrielles, la possibilité de diversifier leurs sources de profit pour réduire la fluctuation de leurs profits globaux. Cette hypothèse n'est assurément pas à exclure dans le cas des banques!

B – L'internalisation par les banques de leurs avantages spécifiques

La question cruciale en ce domaine a trait, on l'a vu, à l'existence éventuelle d'un marché pour les actifs qui fondent l'avantage spécifique de la firme multinationale. Et dans l'affirmative, celui-ci fonctionne-t-il efficacement: c'est à dire est-il capable de procurer un prix rémunérateur pour le détenteur de l'actif, de promouvoir un niveau satisfaisant des quantités échangées, sans que, par ailleurs, ses mécanismes impliquent un coût opératoire jugé prohibitif par les utilisateurs potentiels? Sinon, ceux-ci y substitueront leur propre ''marché'' ou organisation interne.

Une des originalités de l'activité bancaire réside dans l'absence de brevets pour protéger les techniques financières nouvelles élaborées par les banques innovatrices. Toutefois, la diffusion rapide de ces techniques n'empêche pas certaines banques de témoigner d'un savoir-faire supérieur dans diverses activités, celui-ci n'étant acquis et conservé, il est vrai, qu'au prix d'un flux continuel d'innovations, même mineures.[35] Par ailleurs, la situation de ces banques peut se trouver confortée dans la mesure où la prestation de certains des services issus de ces innovations requiert parfois un potentiel en personnel qualifié et en capital fixe importants.[36] Ceci oppose alors une barrière à l'entrée de concurrents potentiels. Pourtant, le risque d'une érosion rapide de l'avantage spécifique de la banque reste en permanence élevé. L'octroi de licence étant inconcevable – vu l'absence de brevets – l'internalisation de son usage constitue la seule issue pour conserver quelque temps cet avantage.

Que dire de ce point de vue de la confiance inspirée par la banque, qui attire et retient ses déposants? On n'imagine pas que celle-ci puisse la transmettre par un mécanisme de marché quelconque à d'autres institutions puisqu'elle reste, de manière ultime, attachée à son nom.[37]

Surtout, il ne peut exister de marché pour l'échange de l'information financière sur les clients. Ceci serait d'ailleurs en contradiction flagrante avec le rôle et la raison d'être de l'intermédiaire financier qui a, en l'occurence, pour mission de garder la discrétion sur ce type d'information.[38] Dans ce cas aussi l'internalisation du mode d'exploitation de cet avantage spécifique s'impose.

D'un point de vue qui nous rapproche alors du mode d'organisation des processus productifs dans l'industrie – au regard, notamment, du degré d'intégration verticale des activités – il est intéressant de noter que pour toute une série d'activités internationales traditionnelles, la banque conserve le choix entre recourir à ses correspondants et les mener elles-mêmes à l'étranger. Le volume attendu de ces opérations joue un rôle déterminant dans ce choix, eu égard à l'existence éventuelle d'économies d'échelle[39] même si le caractère de produit-joints et les effets externes qui s'attachent à certains services bancaires vont dans le sens d'un renforcement de l'intérêt qu'il y a pour la banque à procéder par internalisation.

C – *Nécessité d'une présence sur place pour exploiter ces avantages spécifiques*

Parmi les facteurs qui incitent les banques à une présence à l'étranger pour tirer le meilleur parti des actifs spécifiques qui fondent leur avantage sur leurs concurrentes, retenons les principaux:

– Le "libre échange" en matière d'actifs financiers n'existe que rarement. Les diverses entraves aux mouvements internationaux de capitaux – qui s'ajoutent, en tout état de cause, aux coûts de transaction associés à la simple nécessité de passer par le marché des changes chaque fois qu'un prêt en monnaie locale doit être accordé à partir de ressources étrangères – ne peuvent être surmontées que par une présence sur place. C'est le lieu de rappeler l'influence qu'ont exercée à cet égard, les diverses mesures de restrictions des mouvements de capitaux américains de 1963 à 1968. En particulier, celles de Mars 1965 (programme VFCR) plafonnant les prêts internationaux des banques à partir des Etats-Unis. Le total de leurs succursales à l'étranger en fin d'année est alors passé de 180 en 1964 (contre 132 en 1959) à 211 cn 1965, 244 en 1966, 295 en 1967 et 373 en 1968.[40]

– En dépit des progrès des télécommunications et autres technologies utilisées par les banques dans les processus de collecte et de transmission de l'information et des fonds – qui sont les éléments de base dc lcur activité d'intermédiation – la distance géographique qui sépare de la clientèle constitue encore une barrière à l'entrée de nombreux marchés bancaires. Cette dernière trouve son fondement dans les coûts de transaction infligés aux clients du fait d'une insuffisante densité du réseau et des trop longs délais de réaction de la banque. Nettement sensibles dans l'activité bancaire de détail au profit de la clientèle particulière, ces coûts le sont moins dans le cas des activités de gros et de service destinées aux entreprises multinationales, par exemple. Quoiqu'il en soit, la meilleure façon de franchir cette barrière à l'entrée réside encore dans l'édification d'un réseau de points d'appui à l'étranger à proximité de la clientèle potentielle.[41]

– Surtout, les banques sont, ces dernières années, devenues extrêmement attentives à l'évolution de leurs charges d'exploitation et donc à toutes les possibilités de les réduire. Avant dc voir comment l'implantation à l'étranger peut y contribuer il convient de formuler quelques remarques qui complètent et renforcent l'ensemble des arguments exposés dans ces trois points, A, B, C.

– En premier lieu, le haut degré de réglementation publique de l'activité des banques – qui selon certains contribue à leur spécificité en tant que firmes – , a un impact particulièrement fort sur leurs coûts opératoires et leur capacité concurrenticllc. Et ce, d'autant plus, que les taux d'intérêt sont plus élevés.[42] S'y ajoute l'effet des diverses formes de fiscalité, notamment celle assise sur les opérations bancaires elles-mêmes (retenue à la source sur les intérêts de certains crédits, par ex.). Ainsi, outre l'impact des dotations en facteurs sur les prix des inputs dans les différents pays,[43, 44] il faut tenir le plus grand compte de l'intervention de la puissance publique pour mettre à jour les *avantages spécifiques des divers pays* au regard des problèmes de localisation des activités des banques multinationales.

– En second lieu, il n'est pas inutile de s'interroger sur les raisons d'un tel intérêt porté par les banques à leurs coûts opératoires.

On a, depuis longtemps, mis en évidence l'influence des structures de mar-

ché oligopolistique sur la multinationalisation des entreprises industrielles.[45] Celles-ci sont ainsi à l'origine des phénomènes de "grappes" ou
d'investissement directs croisés entre pays, au sein d'une même branche
d'industrie.[46] On doit surtout à Raymond Vernon d'avoir montré, à partir
d'une typologie des oligopoles qui en retient trois types – fondés sur l'innovation, parvenus à maturité, senescents – quelle est la nature des barrières
à l'entrée qui, dans chacun de ces trois cas, sous-tendent et confortent cette
structure de marché et quels sont les facteurs d'érosion qui la menacent.[47]

Si le caractère fortement oligopolistique des marchés bancaires des principaux pays industrialisés ne fait aucun doute, il est par contre plus difficile
de caractériser ces oligopoles au regard de la typologie de Vernon. Ainsi, les
innovations financières – non protégées par des brevets – et la diversification des produits, d'une part, la taille et l'expérience accumulée – du moins,
dans les activités de détail[48] – d'autre part, nous semblent-elles constituer
des barrières à l'entrée bien fragiles.[49, 50] Les membres de l'oligopole ne
seront-ils pas alors amenés à rechercher la préservation de leur position à
travers une réduction de leurs coûts de production? Dans ce cas, la (re) localisation d'une partie des activités à l'étranger participe des moyens pour y
parvenir. C'est ici qu'intervient le phénomène des eurodevises. Sur ces marchés, les opérations ont typiquement le caractère d'activités délocalisées par
rapport au centre de production originel d'actifs financiers libellés en une
devise que constitue le pays qui en est l'émetteur. Ceci procède de leur absence de réglementation et de leurs avantages fiscaux liés au statut "offshore" de ces activités sur les principales places financières internationales
à partir desquelles elles sont menées. Il n'est, dès lors, pas surprenant que
les opérations en eurodevises ne soient souvent que de simples substituts des
opérations de crédit domestique. Au niveau des implantations bancaires à
l'étranger, ces phénomènes ont conduit à l'émergence et à la croissance rapide de nouveaux centres financiers internationaux. Le rôle joué à cet égard,
par les Iles Bahamas et Caïmans pour les banques américaines et, plus encore, par Luxembourg pour les banques allemandes puis scandinaves ont
suffisamment fait l'objet d'analyses et commentaires pour qu'il ne soit pas
nécessaire d'insister sur ce point.[51] Et la plus récente illustration, sinon la
plus spectaculaire, de cette importance accordée par les banques multinationales à la nécessité de minimiser des coûts d'intermédiation souvent alourdis
par la seule réglementation publique ou la fiscalité, nous est fournie par les
International Banking Facilities aux Etats-Unis. Mises en place en décembre
1981, celles-ci enregistraient déjà 61,2 milliards de dollars d'actifs au 20 jan-
vier 1982, dont 32,9 pour le compte des banques commerciales américaines![52]

Enfin, le souci des membres des oligopoles bancaires nationaux de défendre leurs parts de marché à la suite de la rupture de l'équilibre antérieur, du fait de l'implantation de l'un deux à l'étranger – ou de l'arrivée de concurrents étrangers – a, semble-t-il provoqué les mêmes phénomènes de grappe que ceux déjà mis en évidence par Knickerbocker. On peut s'en convaincre en étudiant, sur les diverses places financières internationales, la chronologie des implantations de banques originaires d'un pays donné. Londres constitue de ce point de vue un site d'observation privilégié. En outre, la colonie très importante de banques commerciales américaines originaires de régions des États-Unis très diverses – quant aux caractéristiques économiques et à la réglementation sur les implantations des succursales – offre un échantillon idéal pour une première tentative de vérification empirique de cette proposition. A cette fin, le tableau 2 retrace la chronologie de la création à Londres de bureaux de représentation, succursales ou filiales[53] par les banques issues de 11 grands marchés bancaires[54] aux États-Unis. Si l'on excepte le cas des "majors" de New York, établies de longue date dans la City, l'influence des interpendances oligopolistiques entre banques soucieuses de préserver leurs parts de marchés apparaît de manière éclatante. Ainsi, ont-elles sûrement joué un grand rôle dans la décision d'implantation des banques moyennes qui redoutaient, en laissant le champ libre aux seules grandes multinationales bancaires, d'aliéner au profit de ces dernières une large part de leur clientèle industrielle et commerciale établie en Europe. Avec des chocs en retour toujours possibles aux États-Unis.

L'extension de cette étude à la séquence des implantations à Londres, ou dans d'autres grands centres financiers internationaux, des banques des autres pays industrialisés confirmerait vraisemblablement ces premiers résultats. Diverses conclusions en découlent, notamment quant à l'évolution des marchés d'eurodevises au cours de la décennie passée. Ainsi avancerons nous l'idée de l'existence d'un *excédent chronique de la capacité d'intermédiation financière internationale*, conformément aux résultats bien connus de la théorie de l'oligopole industriel. Celui-ci aurait incontestablement exercé une grande influence dans le mouvement d'érosion des marges sur les eurocrédits à moyen terme,[55] certaines banques moyennes nouvelles venues jouant les "outsiders" sur le marché, vis à vis de celles déjà plus solidement établies, pour atteindre un certain volume d'affaires.

En tous cas, ces pressions concurrentielles ont fréquemment été incriminées par certains banquiers inquiets de la détérioration des taux de profits dégagés dans les activités internationales. La troisième section se propose d'apporter quelque information quantitative sur ce point.

Tableau 2. *Séquences d'implantation à Londres des banques issues de 11 Standard Metropolitan Statistical Areas*

SMSA	Noms des banques	Date d'arrivée à Londres	Rang dans la SMSA et volume d'actifs (10^6 \$)			
			A cette date[a]		Au 31 déc. 1980	
New-York City	Chase Manhattan Bank	1887	—	—	2	76.190
	Morgan Guaranty Trust Co.	1897	—	—	4	51.991
	Citibank	1902	—	—	1	114.920
	Bankers Trust and Co.	1922	—	—	6	34.202
	Manufacturers Hanover	1925	—	—	3	55.522
	Chemical Bank	1960	5 (31.12.62)	—	5	41.342
	Fiduciary Trust Co.	1965	—	—	—	—
	Irving Trust Co.	1965	7 (31.12.63)	—	7	18.090
	Bank of New York Co.	1967	10 (31.12.67)	—	8	10.423
	Franklin National Bank	1969	9	3.002	faillie[b]	
	Bank of Tokyo Trust Co.	1971	11 (31.12.74)	1.767	12	3.947
	Republic National Bank	1971	13 (31.12.74)	1.141	10	6.447
	National Bank of North America	1979	10	4.849	11	5.693
Chicago	First National Bank of Chicago	1959	2 (31.12.62)	—	2	28.699
	Continental Illinois Bank and Trust Co.	1962	1	—	1	42.089
	American National Bank and Trust Co.	1969	5 (30.06.73)	1.484	5	2.535
	Northern Trust Co.	1969	4	1.639	4	5.849
	Harris Trust and Savings Bank	1970	3	2.052	3	6.095
	La Salle National Bank	1971	7 (30.06.73)	667	Partie en 1979	
Pittsburgh	Mellon Bank	1968	1	4.365	1	16.157
	Pittsburgh National Bank[c]	—	2	—	2	6.225
	Equibank	1976	3 (30.06.73)	1.238	Partie en 1979	
Philadelphia	First Pennsylvania Bank	1968	1	2.507	2	5.497
	Girard Trust Bank	1968	3	1.750	3	4.386
	Philadelphia National Bank	1969	2	2.328	1	6.210
	Fidelity Bank	1972	4	2.279	4	3.316
Boston	First National Bank of Boston	1922	1 (30.06.73)	5.247	1	15.949
	State Street Bank and Trust	1972	4 (30.06.73)	1.037	4	3.009
	Shawmut Bank of Boston	1978	2	2.891	2	3.456
	New England Merchants National Bank	1981	5	2.890	5	2.890

(Tableau 2, *suite*)

SMSA	Noms des banques	Date d'arrivée à Londres	Rang dans la SMSA et volume d'actifs (10^6 \$)	
			A cette date[a]	Au 31 déc. 1980
Detroit	City National Bank of Detroit	1968	4 1.107 (30.06.73)	Partie en 1979
	National Bank of Detroit	1968	1 3.854	1 10.869
	Detroit Bank and Trust Co.	1969	2 2.156	2 5.668
	Bank of the Commonwealth	1970	5 1.016 (30.06.73)	Partie en 1971
	Manufacturers National Bank of Detroit	1972	3 2.441	3 4.769
Seattle	Rainier National Bank	1968	2 1.318 (31.12.69)	Partie en 1981
	Seattle First National Bank	1973	1 3.969	1 9.588
	Pacific National Bank of Washington	1977	3 —	3 1.882
Dallas – Fort-Worth	Republic National Bank of Dallas	1970	1 2.581	2 11.867
	First National Bank in Dallas	1970	2 2.072	1 13.781
Houston	Texas Commerce Bank	1972	2 2.322 (30.06.73)	1 11.287
	First City National Bank of Houston	1972	1 2.748 (30.06.73)	2 11.275
	Bank of the Southwest	1978	3 3.076	3 4.158
San Francisco	Bank of America	1931	— —	1 111.617
	Crocker National Bank	1964	3 3.392 (31.12.63)	3 19.063
	Wells Fargo and Co.	1969	2 5.935	2 23.638
	Bank of California	1971	4 2.282	4 3.852
Los Angeles	United California Bank	1968	2 4.658	1 32.110
	Security Pacific Bank	1969	2 6.708	2 27.794
	Union Bank	1974	3 4.084	Partie en 1979

Source: Etabli à partir de:
– "Foreign Banks in London. A Survey", *The Banker*, novembre de chaque année.
– "Annual Survey of Bank Performance", *Business Week*, avril de chaque année.
– *Fortune*, mai 1964.

a. Lorsque cette donnée n'était pas disponible, nous l'avons, parfois, remplacée par une autre à une date aussi proche que possible, indiquée entre parenthèses.
b. Franklin National Bank reprise par l'EBIC est devenue European American Bank 9ème banque de New York avec 7.771 millions de dollars d'actifs au 31.12.1980.
c. Pittsburgh National Bank s'est en réalité établie à Paris pour l'ensemble de ses activités européennes. Nous l'avons donc, exceptionnellement, retenue dans ce tableau.

III. LES RESULTATS DES BANQUES MULTINATIONALES: UN PREMIER APERÇU

On peut penser que les banques multinationales obéissent à un objectif de maximisation de leur profit; ou éventuellement de leur croissance. Précisément, ces hypothèses sous-tendent l'exposé de la section II. Qu'en est-il exactement?

Nous n'examinerons ici que la première hypothèse. En outre, les contraintes sur la disponibilité des informations statistiques nécessaires nous obligent à nous limiter aux seules banques américaines. Dans leur cas précis, nous avons pu rassembler des données sur un échantillon de 14 d'entre elles que plusieurs sources américaines s'accordent à classer comme de véritables multinationales bancaires. Leur liste fait l'objet du tableau 3.

Tableau 3. *Groupe des 14 multinationales américaines et bilan au 31.12. 1980 (en millions de $)*

Noms	Origine	Bilan
Citicorp.	New-York	114.920
Bank America Corp.	San Francisco	111.617
Chase Manhattan Corp.	New-York	76.190
Manufacturers Hanover Corp.	New-York	55.522
J.P. Morgan & Co.	New-York	51.991
Continental Illinois Corp.	Chicaco	42.089
Chemical New-York Corp.	New-York	41.342
Bankers Trust New-York Corp.	New-York	34.202
First Chicago Corp.	Chicago	28.699
Security Pacific Corp.	Los Angeles	27.794
Wells Fargo & Co.	San Francisco	23.638
Charter New-York Corp.	New-York	18.090
Marine Midland Banks Inc.	Buffalo (NY)	17.480
First National Boston Corp.	Boston	15.949

Source: Rapports Annuels.

Des informations, extraites de leurs Rapports Annuels, concernant leurs profits et leurs actifs productifs – globaux et ventilés entre secteur domestique et secteur international – nous ont permis de procéder aux divers calculs dont les résultats sont résumés dans les tableaux 4 et 5 suivants.

Dans un premier temps, il est intéressant de comparer les performances de ces 14 banques à celles du reste du système bancaire commercial américain. Cette comparaison porte ici sur les neuf années 1972-1980, qui corres-

Tableau 4. *Evolution des taux de rendement des actifs globaux des 14 banques multinationales et du reste du système bancaire américain (actifs globaux et profits en millions de dollars)*

	1980	1979	1978	1977	1976	1975	1974	1973	1972
14 banques multinationales									
Profits globaux après impôts	3312.1	3012.5	2529	1992.8	1795.6	1747.8	1661.6	1431	1234.1
Actifs globaux moyens	610260	532762	462898	406615	362414	348742	321906	259209	207841
Taux de rendement des actifs (%)	0.543	0.565	0.546	0.490	0.495	0.501	0.516	0.552	0.594
Reste du système bancaire									
Profits globaux après impôts	11114	10096.5	8382	6763	5839.4	5434	5481.4	5129	4288
Actifs globaux moyens ($\times 10^3$)	1157.7	1060.2	955.1	850.4	760.6	703.3	665.1	597.8	530.1
Taux de rendement des actifs (%)	0.960	0.952	0.878	0.795	0.768	0.773	0.824	0.858	0.809
14 banques multinationales									
Profits internationaux	1489	1230	1117	975	889	883	624	489	345

Sources: Federal Reserve Bulletin, Rapports Annuels des banques.

Tableau 5. *Actifs globaux, profits globaux, taux de rendement (évolution 1972-1980)*

	14 banques multinationales		Reste du système bancaire	
	actifs globaux	profits après impôts	actifs globaux	profits après impôts
Taux de croissance moyen annuel	14.4%	13.1%	12.6%	10.2%
Taux de rendement moyen annuel (%)	0.534		0.846	
Ecart type du taux de rendement	0.0333		0.0677	
Coefficient de variation	0.0623		0.0800	

Source: Calculé à partir du tableau 4.

pondent à une période où l'internationalisation des banques américaines, déjà bien avancée, s'est déployée dans l'environnement économique et financier mondial troublé que l'on sait.

Qu'il s'agisse de la progression de leurs actifs ou de leurs profits globaux, les 14 multinationales ont surclassé l'ensemble de leurs concurrentes américaines: leurs actifs globaux ont crû au taux moyen annuel de 14,4%, contre 12,6% pour le reste du système bancaire, les chiffres correspondants pour les profits étant respectivement 13,1% et 10,2%. Or, ces meilleurs résultats sont incontestablement imputables aux activités internationales. On a abondamment fait état de la croissance extrêmement rapide des actifs bancaires internationaux. Mais celle des profits internationaux l'a été tout autant: ceux-ci ont crû au taux moyen annuel de 20% pour les 14 banques de l'échantillon et sont donc largement responsables de leur meilleur score en matière de profits globaux.

En revanche, cela n'a pas empêché ces dernières de réaliser chaque année des taux de rendement de leurs actifs globaux moyens notablement inférieurs à ceux de leurs concurrentes: en moyenne, sur la période, ils s'inscrivent à 0.534 contre 0.846 pour le reste du système bancaire américain. Tout au plus, ces taux de rendement témoignent-ils d'une plus grande stabilité dans le cas des 14 multinationales que dans celui de l'ensemble des autres banques. En effet, en dépit du nombre restreint d'observations, nous avons calculé des écarts types et coefficents de variation (rapport de l'écart type à la moyenne) pour les deux séries de taux de rendement. Pour les 14 banques multinationales ces deux grandeurs prennent respectivement les valeurs 0.0333 et 0.0623; pour les autres banques 0.0677 et 0.0800 respectivement. Ces dernières valeurs traduisent ainsi une plus grande dispersion de ces taux de rendement. Résultat d'autant plus surprenant (a priori) que le reste du système bancaire américain, fort de ses 14 500 banques de toutes tailles et au contact de régions aux caractéristiques économiques fort diverses, pourrait, pense-t-on, diversifier suffisamment ses actifs pour stabiliser le profil de leurs taux de rendement. On voit qu'il n'y parvient pas aussi bien que les 14 multinationales dont les actifs sont sans doute beaucoup plus largement diversifiés, à raison de leurs activités internationales. Ce résultat, certes fragile en raison de la brièveté de la période sous revue, nous semble néanmoins fort intéressant: il est conforme à la thèse selon laquelle les multinationales cherchent à réduire les fluctuations de leurs profits.

Dans un second temps, il nous a paru souhaitable d'examiner plus attentivement les performances individuelles des seules 14 banques multinationales. En effet, si leur stratégie internationale est bien au service d'un objectif de maximisation de profit, les taux de rendement de leurs actifs internationaux devraient être supérieurs à leurs homologues domestiques. En vue de cette comparaison, nous avons dressé le tableau 6. Celui-ci retrace les résultats établis sur la base des taux de rendements des seuls actifs productifs.[56] La période d'observation se termine en 1979 (incluse) et remonte dans la plupart des cas à 1972 (incluse). Soit 8 observations. Malgré cela nous avons encore calculé des moyennes et écarts types de ces taux de rendement, dans les deux types d'activité, respectivement. Contrairement à des opinions souvent exprimées sur la base d'informations relatives à certains segments d'activité ou secteurs géographiques précis, les activités internationales prises dans leur ensemble ne procurent des taux de rendement supérieurs aux activités domestiques que pour 4 banques. Pour 3 autres, taux domestiques et internationaux ne diffèrent pas sensiblement.[57] Pour 7 banques (soit la moitié de l'échantillon!) les taux de rendement internationaux sont très inférieurs aux taux domestiques. Surtout, les écarts-types et coefficients de variation[58] permettent d'éclairer et de préciser de manière intéressante les résultats du paragraphe précédent. En effet, les 7 banques qui enregistrent des taux de rendement des actifs productifs internationaux supérieurs ou équivalents aux taux domestiques connaissent *toutes* des coefficients de variation des premiers inférieurs à ceux des seconds. Inversement les coefficients de variation des taux de rendement des actifs productifs internationaux sont nettement plus élevés que leurs équivalents domestiques pour 6 des 7 banques dont les taux de rendement internationaux sont inférieurs aux taux domestiques.

Ces résultats doivent être considérés avec une certaine réserve ne serait-ce qu'en raison de la fragilité des données à partir desquelles ils sont établis.[59] En tous cas, il est frappant de constater que les banques qui parviennent aux

Tableau 6. *Taux de rendement des actifs productifs internationaux et domestiques (moyennes et écart types sur des périodes terminées en 1979)*

Banques	Nombre d'obser- vations	$\bar{r}_i$	σr_i	$\bar{r}_d$	σr_d	$\bar{r}_i/\bar{r}_d$
Citicorp.	8	0.879	0.118	0.582	0.108	>
Bank America Corp.	8	0.535	0.100	0.727	0.111	<
Chase Manhattan Corp.	8	0.579	0.138	0.494	0.213	>
Manufacturers Hanover Corp.	6	0.678	0.066	0.696	0.083	=
J.P. Morgan and Co.	8	1.006	0.098	1.002	0.163	=
Continental Illinois Corp.	8	0.389	0.156	0.902	0.090	<
Chemical N.Y. Corp.	6	0.500	0.067	0.487	0.069	=
Bankers Trust N.Y. Corp.	8	0.607	0.050	0.344	0.164	>
First Chicago Corp.	9	0.350	0.218	0.849	0.138	<
Security Pacific Corp.	8	0.329	0.126	0.747	0.143	<
Wells Fargo and Co.	7	0.491	0.205	0.684	0.112	<
Charter N.Y. Corp.	8	0.824	0.112	0.404	0.078	>
Marine Midland Banks Inc.	8	0.173	0.061	0.335	0.159	<
First National Boston Corp.	8	0.334	0.101	0.987	0.280	<

$\bar{r}$: taux de rendement moyen annuel des actifs productifs.

σr: écart type des taux de rendements.

i: indice des activités internationales

d: indice des activités domestiques.

Source: Calculé à partir de Rapports Annuels.

meilleures performances internationales sont essentiellement celles dont l'expérience internationale est la plus ancienne.[60] Ainsi doit-on plutôt parler d'un objectif de maximisation du profit à long terme.

Enfin, et surtout, les résultats ci-dessus mériteraient d'être complétés par la prise en compte des risques respectivement encourus par ces banques dans les deux types d'activité. Il est en effet, fort vraisemblable que ce soit le couple taux de rendement/risque qui constitue l'élément déterminant de leur stratégie internationale.

CONCLUSION ET PERSPECTIVES

Les activités bancaires internationales ont suscité ces dernières années de très nombreux travaux de la part des économistes. Mais leur orientation est restée essentiellement macro-économique. Or, le rôle assumé par quelques dizaines de banques multinationales – notamment américaines – dans l'intermédiation financière internationale appelle une analyse théorique et empirique des stratégies et comportements de ces agents. Nous l'avons tentée ici en montrant qu'il était, à cette fin, largement possible de faire appel aux concepts, outils d'analyse et méthodes d'observation de la théorie de la firme multinationale industrielle. Ainsi l'explication articulée autour des trois idées d'actifs spécifiques, d'internalisation et d'avantages associés à la localisation semblent-ils aussi adaptés au cas des banques. Les résultats de quelques travaux empiriques limités aux banques commerciales américaines incitent à une certaine circonspection quant à la rentabilité des activités internationales. Or, celle-ci est cruciale pour la poursuite de leur expansion et de l'acceptation par les banques des risques liés à l'intermédiation financière internationale dans un contexte d'endettement croissant. La détérioration de cette rentabilité sensible pour 6 des plus grandes banques de l'échantillon sous revue, entre 1972 et 1979, fait redouter un désengagement relatif de ces banques. Mais il est vrai que l'influence des interdépendances oligopolistiques dans leur engagement a jusqu'ici été si fort qu'il est bien difficile de savoir des deux facteurs lequel l'emportera. Si l'on admet que les problèmes se posent en des termes peu différents pour les multinationales bancaires des autres pays on perçoit mieux à quel niveau se déterminera, dans le proche avenir, le "sort" de l'intermédiation financière internationale.

NOTES

1. D'après les évaluations trimestrielles de la Banque des Règlements Internationaux.

2. Nous pensons, en particulier, aux diverses analyses suscitées par la croissance du marché des eurodevises fondées sur le modèle de multiplicateur de crédit, ou par l'amplification des mouvements internationaux de capitaux, faisant appel à la théorie des portefeuilles.

3. A défaut de statistiques plus générales, on peut se faire une idée de cette concentration des activités en eurodevises en ne considérant que le cas des banques commerciales américaines. Les dépôts de leurs succursales étrangères correspondent pour beaucoup à des dépôts en eurodevises. Or, au 31 décembre 1976 leur volume global, après élimination des opérations intragroupe, s'élevait à 155, 3 milliards de dollars, tandis que les 10 banques américaines qui détenaient le plus de dépôts à l'étranger en retenaient à elles seules — et ce sur la base de montants consolidés au niveau de chaque groupe — 127 milliards de dollars, soit 82%! Des calculs identiques appliqués aux grandeurs au 31 décembre 1980 conduisent aux résultats suivants: chiffres globaux: 284 milliards de dollars. Encours auprès des 10 premières banques par leurs dépôts à l'étranger: 218 milliards de dollars, soit 77% (calculs effectués à partir des statistiques du *Federal Reserve Bulletin* et des Rapports annuels des banques concernées).

4. Les premiers résultats étaient contenus dans: Joël Métais, *La multinationalisation des banques commerciales,* Thèse d'Etat de Sciences Economiques. Université de Paris Dauphine, juin 1978.

5. Pour de plus amples développements sur ce point, cf.: Herbert G. Grubel, "A Theory of

Multinational Banking'', *Banca Nazionale del Lavoro Quarterly Review*, décembre 1977, pp. 349-363.

6. Essentiellement le secteur du crédit à la consommation. Par exemple, en Grande Bretagne, Allemagne Fédérale, France et aussi à Hong Kong ou au Japon, Citibank est incontestablement le leader dans ce secteur. Mais les ambitions de Bank of America, Chase Manhattan Bank, Chemical Bank ou Security Pacific National Bank sont aussi, en ce domaine, indéniables.

7. Ce poids du passé est particulièrement flagrant dans le cas des deux clearing banks londoniennes Barclays Bank et Lloyds Bank – au niveau des réseaux et activités légués par Barclays DCO et Lloyds and BOLSA – et des deux anciennes banques coloniales anglaises Standard and Chartered Bank et Hong Kong and Shanghai Bank.

8. Dans le cas d'une couverture géographique maximale, la banque s'implante dans tous les pays où elle est susceptible de réaliser un volume d'affaires suffisant, sachant aussi que l'étendue du réseau peut être génératrice d'effets externes favorables en termes de relations de clientèle. Dans celui d'une couverture géographique optimale, elle ne retient que les principaux centres financiers internationaux, à partir desquels elle espère mener le maximum d'affaires ou minimiser la perte de celles qu'une insuffisante présence internationale pourrait lui infliger.

9. Ce n'est bien sûr pas tant d'un début de présence que de la priorité accordée au renforcement de cette présence auxquels nous faisons allusion dans cette séquence.

10. Encore que cette omission soit notable chez les auteurs des quelques articles théoriques sur les banques multinationales portés à notre connaissance comme par exemple: Robert Z. Aliber, "Towards a Theory of International Banking", *Economic Review,* Federal Reserve Bank of San Francisco, Spring 1976, pp. 5-8; Herbert G. Grubel, "A Theory of Multinational Banking", *op. cit.*; Jean M. Gray et H. Peter Gray, "The Multinational Bank: a Financial MNC?", *Journal of Banking and Finance*, février 1981, pp. 33-63.

11. Cf. par exemple: George J. Benston et Clifford W. Smith, Jr., "A Transactions Cost Approach to the Theory of Financial Intermediation", *The Journal of Finance*, mai 1976, pp. 215-231.

12. Les aspects financiers ont de loin fait l'objet du plus grand nombre d'articles. Ils ont été le plus souvent analysés à l'aide de modèles de choix de portefeuilles.

13. Les modèles microéconomiques de la firme bancaire ont donné lieu à un article de synthèse critique par: Ernst Baltensperger, "Alternative Approaches to the Theory of the Banking Firm", *Journal of Monetary Economics*, février 1980, pp. 1-37. Celui-ci met particulièrement bien en relief leurs faiblesses auxquelles il est ici fait référence.

14. Parmi ces modèles, citons celui formulé par R.B. Johnston, "Banks International Lending Decisions and the Determination of Spreads on Syndicated Medium-term Euro-credits", *Discussion Paper n° 12,* Bank of England, London, Sept. 1980.

15. S. Hymer puis R. Caves furent parmi les principaux artisans de cette nouvelle orientation: Stephen H. Hymer, *The International Operations of National Firms: A Study of Direct Foreign Investment*, M.I.T. Monographs in Economics, 14, Cambridge, Mass., 1976 (cet ouvrage reprend en fait sa thèse de Ph.D. soutenue dès 1960 et dans laquelle Hymer s'est posé en pionnier de cette nouvelle approche); Richard E. Caves, "International Corporation: The Industrial Economics of Foreign Investment", *Economica*, N.S. London, 1971, pp. 1-27.

16. Cf. sur ce point: John H. Dunning, "Trade, Location of Economic Activity and the MNE: A Search for an Eclectic Approach" in Bertil Ohlin et alii, eds., *The International Allocation of Economic Activity*, Holmes and Meier Publishers, Inc., New-York, 1977; John H. Dunning, "Explaining Changing Patterns of International Production: in Defence of the Eclectic Theory", *Oxford Bulletin of Economics and Statistics*, November 1979, pp. 269-295; Alan M. Rugman, "Internalization as a General Theory of Foreign Direct Investment: A Re-

Appraisal of the Literature'', *Weltwirtschaftliches Archiv*, Bd. CXIV (1980), pp. 365-379.

17. Cf. John H. Dunning (1977), *op. cit.*, p. 395.

18. Notamment dans les deux articles déjà cités.

19. Cf. en particulier John H. Dunning (1979), *op. cit.*, p. 275.

20. Cf. Alan M. Rugman, *op. cit.*

21. Mark Casson, *Alternatives to the Multinational Enterprise,* London, 1979.

22. Ronald H. Coase, "The Nature of the Firm", *Economica*, 1937, pp. 386-403, repris dans George J. Stigler et Kenneth E. Boulding, eds., *Readings in Price Theory*, Homewood, 1953, pp. 331-351.

23. Cf. Ernst Baltensperger, *op. cit.*, p. 1.

24. Compte tenu des préoccupations en matière de crédits et mouvements de capitaux internationaux et de stabilité du système financier international qui constituent le cadre général de ce colloque.

25. Envisagé ici du seul point de vue du pays d'origine. On peut le mesurer par la part des actifs internationaux dans les actifs globaux pour autant que les banques du pays soient astreintes à communiquer aux autorités des informations sur une base consolidée. Ou par divers autres critères tels que le nombre de banques disposant de points d'appui à l'étranger, le nombre et la répartition géographique de ces derniers.

26. Ainsi, leur part dans le total des créances bancaires internationales se situe aux alentours de 30% et n'est égalée par celle d'aucun autre groupe national de banques. Par ailleurs, le tableau 1 a déjà permis de montrer que les Etats-Unis sont, de loin, le pays d'origine du plus fort contingent de banques multinationales.

27. Par exemple, en 1980, Bankers Trust traitait avec plus de 400 multinationales; Continental Illinois avec 275 dès 1978.

28. L'influence de ce facteur sur la multinationalisation des firmes à l'intérieur d'une même branche d'industrie avait été soulignée dès 1972 par Thomas Horst, "Firm and Industry Determinants to Invest Abroad: an Empirical Study", *Review of Economics and Statistics*, août 1972. Celui-ci écrivait notamment: "Tout ceci suggère qu'en ce qui concerne les facteurs intra industrie, une théorie du comportement d'investissement direct peut être structurellement identique à une théorie en termes d'organisation industrielle des parts de marché domestique" (p. 261). Nous reviendrons sur ce point.

29. Essentiellement des grandes entreprises (dont les multinationales) et des institutions financières, privées et publiques (dont les banques). Tous ces agents sont très sensibles au risque de leur placements, en fonction des institutions auxquelles ils les confient.

30. Parmi les exemples récents, relevons la fondation au Japon par Bank of America d'une filiale avec la société de crédit Nippon Shinpan pour y développer le marché de l'affacturage au profit des petites et moyennes entreprises (*Financial Times*, 7 avril 1981). Celle par Citibank de la première société de crédit-bail jamais créée en Corée du Sud. Son partenaire dans l'opération, Korea-First-Bank, souhaite acquérir par là la connaissance de cette technologie financière (*Financial Times*, 24 mars 1981).

31. Rappelons que nous n'avons nullement cherché à en dresser une liste complète mais seulement à donner quelques exemples.

32. L'exemple qui vient ici plus directement à l'esprit est celui de l'acquisition de banques californiennes par des banques étrangères, en particulier les clearing banks britanniques. Ces dernières très orientées vers l'activité de détail sont fort intéressées – entre autres – par l'avance des banques californiennes dans le domaine des guichets électroniques.

33. Ils ont, en effet, au sens de la théorie économique, la nature d'effets externes liés au seul nombre des points d'appui à l'étranger et à leur dispersion sur la planète.

34. Ne serait-ce que dans le domaine de l'obtention de mandats pour la syndication d'euro-crédits. Mais c'est sans doute à l'endroit de la clientèle des sociétés multinationales que cet atout acquiert toute sa valeur. Ainsi les grandes banques américaines semblent-elles avoir renforcé, grâce à leur réseau mondial, leur avantage initial lié à l'étendue et la qualité de la gamme des services à ces entreprises. En effet, une étude menée, en l'été 1980, par Greenwich Research Associates, révélait que six banques américaines dominaient le marché des services pour les six cents multinationales que compte environ l'Europe. Parmi les raisons de leur succès, on signale l'étendue de leur réseau et la qualité de leurs cadres (*Financial Times*, 16 février 1981).

35. La floraison des formules proposées aux emprunteurs et aux prêteurs dans le domaine des euro-obligations et des eurocrédits à moyen-terme illustre parfaitement cette proposition.

36. Par exemple la gestion de trésorerie internationale qui exige des systèmes informatiques complexes.

37. On peut s'en convaincre à travers l'exemple des mésaventures des eurobanques consortiales sur les marchés monétaires internationaux en l'été 1974. Filiales *communes de plusieurs banques*, parfois importantes, elles n'inspirèrent pas pour autant toujours confiance en raison du sentiment de dilution de la responsabilité des actionnaires que provoquait cette formule. Pour la rétablir il fallut l'intervention de la Banque d'Angleterre auprès des banques mères pour leur faire préciser l'étendue de leurs engagements.

38. En effet, si l'emprunteur était disposé à révéler l'intégralité des informations sur sa véritable situation il serait sans doute mieux servi en recourant directement à un processus de finance directe par le biais d'un marché financier.

39. Celles-ci doivent en l'occurence être appréciées au niveau du point d'appui étranger plutôt qu'à celui de l'ensemble de la banque.

40. Sans qu'on puisse, bien sûr, imputer cette évolution à la seule mesure de 1965. Le rôle de la politique monétaire restrictive de 1965 exerçait déjà son influence. Cette dernière sera pourtant plus nette à partir de 1969.

41. Cette explication est le complément indispensable de celles des points A et B pour réinterpréter en termes théoriques le lien si souvent souligné entre multinationalisation industrielle et multinationalisation bancaire. En l'occurence, au niveau de ses manifestations spatiales.

42. Par exemple, en accroissant le coût d'opportunité de la constitution de réserves obligatoires non rémunérées ou de l'assurance obligatoire des dépôts.

43. Nous utilisons à dessein la terminologie de la théorie pure du commerce international, en effet, pertinente pour expliquer la localisation des activités des firmes multinationales.

44. Parmi les inputs à prix avantageux dont une banque multinationale cherchera à tirer parti en s'établissant à l'étranger, viennent souvent en tête les dépôts dans des pays à forte capacité d'épargne.

45. Cf. Richard Caves, *op. cit.*; Stephen Hymer, *op. cit*, etc.

46. Ceux-ci ont fait l'objet d'une étude très attentive de la part de Frederick T. Knickerbocker, *Oligopolistic Reaction and Multinational Enterprise*, Boston, 1973.

47. Cf. notamment, Raymond Vernon, *Storm over the Multinationals: The Real Issues*, London, 1977. Pour leur part Alan M. Rugman, *op. cit.*, et Ian H. Giddy ont montré comment l'argumentation de Vernon pouvait s'intégrer dans la théorie de la firme multinationale centrée sur le concept d'internalisation. A ce titre, elle trouve donc sa place dans l'ensemble des développements de cette section. Cf. Ian H. Giddy, ''The Demise of the Product Cycle Model in International Business Theory'', *Columbia Journal of World Business*, Spring 1978, pp. 90-97.

48. Dans le cas des activités de gros, la taille joue plus nettement son rôle de barrière à l'entrée. Pas tant du fait de l'influence des économies d'échelle que de celui du montant des ressources globales et des fonds propres nécessaires pour pouvoir servir des grandes entreprises, des gouvernements ou d'autres grandes institutions financières.

49. Nous avons consacré une analyse détaillée à ces questions dans le cas des banques commerciales américaines. Cf. Joël Métais, *Thèse, op. cit.*, Ch. 5, "Multinationalisation des banques américaines et interdépendances oligopolistiques". L'argumentation nous semble susceptible d'extension aux oligopoles bancaires des autres pays.

50. La réglementation publique de l'activité bancaire apparaît, par contre, à beaucoup d'économistes comme le meilleur garant du maintien des positions acquises par les membres de l'oligopole. Cette thèse mérite pourtant réexamen dès lors que cette réglementation se révèle de plus en plus inadaptée aux conditions nouvelles d'exercice de l'activité financière qui ont souvent pour effet de permettre une redistribution des rôles entre intermédiaires financiers. L'exemple présent de la situation américaine illustre parfaitement cette proposition.

51. En septembre 1981 on dénombrait ainsi 30 filiales de banques allemandes à Luxembourg et 14 filiales de banques scandinaves.

52. Source: Salomon Brothers, cité dans "International Capital Markets", *Financial Times*, 15 mars 1982.

53. Les participations, en particulier dans des eurobanques consortiales, ne sont donc pas prises en compte.

54. Ceux-ci, par souci de rigueur, ont été définis sur la base du découpage statistique opéré par le Système de la Réserve Fédérale. Les Standard Metropolitan Statistical Areas (SMSA) qu'il délimite lui servent de référence pour ses divers travaux de recherche économique sur le système bancaire américain. Rappelons surtout que compte tenu du cadre institutionnel dans lequel s'exerce l'activité bancaire outre-Atlantique il est largement pertinent de considérer ces marchés bancaires régionaux comme effectivement séparés les uns des autres. En particulier, au moment de la grande vague d'internationalisation retracée dans ce tableau.

55. Précisément, ces marges doivent rémunérer les services d'intermédiation des banques. Elles évoluent donc au gré de la plus ou moins grande volonté, ou capacité, de celles-ci d'offrir ces services. Cette offre doit être dissociée de celle des fonds à prêter. Confrontée à la demande d'emprunts, cette dernière détermine le coût du refinancement bancaire représenté, en l'occurence, par le LIBOR.

56. Afin d'éviter, dans le cas des banques qui ne donnent pas de précisions à ce sujet les difficultés liées à l'imputation des immobilisations et autres actifs entre les deux secteurs d'activité.

57. Encore doit-on noter que pour Chase Manhattan Corp., J.P. Morgan and Co., Bankers Trust N.Y. Corp. et Charter N.Y. Corp. les taux de rendement internationaux sont légèrement sur-évalués et les taux domestiques corrélativement sous-évalués. En effet, nous ne disposions pour ces banques que d'encours d'actifs productifs à l'étranger auxquels on a dû rapporter les profits internationaux.

58. A interpréter, rappelons le, avec une extrême prudence compte tenu du faible nombre d'observations.

59. Celle-ci tient notamment à la difficulté qu'il y a à séparer correctement grandeurs liées aux activités domestiques et internationales respectivement. Cf. aussi note *supra*.

60. Nous l'avons vérifié sur la base de l'ancienneté de leur présence à Londres souvent antérieure à la seconde guerre mondiale.

Chapter VI

THE EURO-CURRENCY MARKETS: THEIR CREDIT EFFECTS AND THE DYNAMICS OF MONETARY POLICY

by *David T. Llewellyn*

One of the major analytical and empirical disputes with respect to the Euro-currency markets is the extent to which they are passive in response to money and credit conditions determined in national markets, or alternatively are largely autonomous. The latter view holds that Euro-currency markets have an internal dynamism and an effect on world monetary and credit conditions independently of developments in national markets. An important implication of the latter view is that financial intermediation and credit flows through the markets may respond to national monetary policy in a way that substantially weakens monetary policy autonomy. Regrettably, the important distinction between international capital movements in general, and the specific role of the Euro-markets, is not always made in the analysis. Some analysts would extend the argument by imposing various forms of controls or reserve requirements etc. to limit the role of the Euro-currency markets.

It is these and related issues that are the concern of this paper. The emphasis is upon the *credit* rather than *monetary* aspects of the market and, in the context of a particular analytical framework, concludes that the independence of the markets is in practice very limited. In this respect their power to undermine monetary policy is circumscribed though there is such a potential if monetary policy is conducted in a particular way. Focusing upon *credit* raises the issue of what form the credit generation takes: (1) pure financial intermediation where there is a new savings counterpart to the deposit being loaned, (2) credit creation where there is a net rise in lending but no new savings counterpart, (3) multiple credit creation through a mechanism whereby the Euro-lending market itself, through its effect on income, creates a higher demand for the lending institutions' liabilities, or (4) credit diversion where an existing savings deposit is switched from a domestic to a Euro-currency market and lending business is also diverted. While these distinctions can be made conceptually, they are not measurable and there may therefore be some doubt about their usefulness. It cannot be said that lending by non-bank financial intermediaries has no impact upon aggregate demand because there is necessarily a *savings* counterpart (the deposit) to the loan. NBFIs, to the extent that they activate idle balances and cause wealth holders to switch away from banks, have the capacity to increase the volume of credit at given levels of the money supply and savings.

The two central issues addressed in the paper are: (1) the extent to which financial intermediation through the Euro-markets adds to the total volume of world credit, and (2) the extent to which the impact of domestic monetary policy can be weakened through offsetting Euro-market intermediation. These might be termed the *static* and *dynamic* credit effects. The discussion is conducted in the analytical framework of non-bank financial intermediation and in the context of profit maximising liability management by financial intermediaries.

Interest arbitrage between national and Euro segments of a money market is a major factor determining the degree of credit autonomy of the Euro-currency market. In general, the higher the degree of financial integration between national and Euro-currency markets, the less scope the Euro-markets have to undermine domestic monetary policy. But it also depends critically upon the profit maximising and liability management strategies of banks. One of the objectives of the paper is to integrate liability management and profit maximising strategies into the analysis of the determination of the credit effects of the Euro-markets and their potential to frustrate domestic monetary policy.

LIABILITY MANAGEMENT

The development of active liability management and profit maximisation behaviour by banks and other financial institutions has important implications for the conduct and operation of monetary policy. As it also has specific implications for the two credit effects of the Euro-markets, a brief review is made of the principal features of liability management.

In essence, liability management involves financial institutions acting aggressively to determine the level and structure of their liabilities, as opposed to simply manipulating assets on the basis of exogeneously determined liabilities. Profit maximising institutions engage simultaneously in asset and liability management in order to maximise overall risk-adjusted rates of return. At its most basic level, a bank short of reserves but with profitable lending opportunities will seek to increase its own reserves by bidding for deposits in the open market. Any excess demand for credit at current interest rates induces banks to bid for reserves and deposits.[1] The resultant rise in deposit and loan rates continues until the initial excess demand has been eliminated. Banks individually are essentially bidding to increase their share of a given total of high powered money, though in aggregate they may also induce a rise in total. Arbitrage tends to equalise the cost of funds in all markets in which banks compete for funds. It is argued below that the more aggressive is liability management, and the greater is the profit-maximising strategy of banks, the smaller is the potential for Euro-currency market intermediation to thwart the effect of monetary policy.

In any dynamic analysis of the money supply or credit process the role of profit-maximising banks must be incorporated as their portfolio decisions are important in three ways: (i) banks are able directly to induce a rise in the money supply through their asset management; (ii) they are unlikely to passively accept changes in their reserves if this conflicts with their profit strategies; and (iii) through liability management they may collectively induce a rise in both the money supply and the monetary base.

Liability management brings severely into question both the multiplier analysis and the notion of an exogeneously determined monetary base. By aggressively competing for deposits not only individual banks but the banking system can, under some circumstances, induce changes in both the money supply (bank deposits) and the monetary base though the outcome depends crucially upon the response of the central bank whose liabilities make up the monetary base (see Llewellyn, 1982).

How banks respond to a loss of reserves depends upon their excess reserves position and risk/return calculations on the profitability of competing to restore their reserves. One possibility is that banks respond by reducing their earning assets (asset management). But in general, the response depends largely upon the interest rate sensitivity of the demand for bank credit and the interest rate sensitivity of the demand for bank deposits. The lower is the former and higher is the latter, the more profitable it becomes to bid aggressively for deposits to restore the initial reserves position and the greater is the potential rise in interest rates. The net effect upon interest rates and the money supply depends upon whether the central bank reacts by eliminating the excess demand for reserves by increasing the monetary base, or whether it allows interest rates to rise to the extent necessary to eliminate the excess demand for bank reserves by reducing customers' demand for bank credit and hence the banks' demand for reserves. This is the key issue in the debate on monetary base control. If the central bank operates exclusively on the monetary base, interest rates become the equilibrating mechanism.

In the final analysis the ultimate constraint on the banks is the profitability implications of rising interest rates. The central bank can with determination refuse to create reserves by adopting a floating exchange rate, and by allowing market interest rates to find their own level on the basis of a given supply of high powered money. While banks can force the central bank into "dilemma situations", the central bank cannot be forced to create reserves (high powered money). However, if it chooses not to supply reserves it is constrained to accepting the interest rate and exchange rate consequences; that is the nature of the dilemma.

If banks have profitable lending potential and through liability management in the way described can force the central bank to create reserves, the supply of reserves becomes endogenous and determined by aggressive bidding for funds by the banks. In this way the supply of reserves is likely to be a function of the demand for bank advances.

Traditional multiplier analysis tends to implicitly assume that the banking system adjusts passively to changes in the monetary base to the full extent of the multiplier potential. No consideration is given to whether the demand for credit exists to support the full potential of the multiplier or of the profitability of the banks extending their balance sheets. Neither does it incorporate the potential for the banking system itself to induce changes in reserves through aggressive bidding in a profit-maximising strategy. If it is profitable for banks to extend their balance sheet because there is profitable lending business, the banking system is likely to attempt to induce a rise in reserves. In this sense, causality runs from a change in the demand for bank credit or money to changes in the monetary base. Banks, like all economic agents, have profit strategies and this is an integral part of the money supply process though is neglected in simplified multiplier analysis.

The standard multiplier analysis frequently applied to domestic banking systems is not a fruitful approach to the analysis of credit creation in the Euro-currency market as there is no clearly defined reserve base in the Euro-markets, the reserve ratio is not constant, and the leakages are high (redeposit ratio low) as interest rates adjust quickly. Indeed, as already implied, portfolio balance theories of banking behaviour question the usefulness of the traditional multiplier concept even when applied to domestic banking systems and the determination of the money supply within a purely national economy. The substantial growth experienced in the Euro-dollar market, for instance, is associated not with a high internal multiplier but with a similar rapid growth in monetary and financial aggregates in the United States. Thus, in line with standard portfolio balance theory, all markets share in the distribution of any increase in the total supply of dollar assets and through a learning process and a strong competitive position, the Euro-dollar market has tended to increase its share of the total. This is similar reasoning to that applied to the growth of non-bank financial intermediaries within domestic financial systems. Thus as the leakages are high and, because interest rates adjust quickly a continuous flow of funds from the United States is unlikely, the concept of an internal multiplier is of limited value and, in any case, is likely to be low. The centrepiece of the analysis should be the elasticity of the supply and demand curves for Euro-currency funds, rather than the concept of a multiplier.

MONEY v. CREDIT

The focus of the paper is upon the *credit* potential of the Euro-markets rather than their monetary or liquidity implications. The appropriate target of monetary policy has been debated at great length. But there is the issue of whether some part of Euro-market liabilities should be included in any targeted monetary aggregate. Some analysts contend that a proportion of Euro-currency liabilities should be viewed as equivalent to domestic liquidity and that their exclusion from targets may mean that income velocity measures in terms of purely domestic monetary aggregates can increase faster than would otherwise be the case. In a comprehensive survey of this issue McClam (1980) quotes Governor Wallich of the Federal Reserve Board:

"... if monetary authorities focus exclusively on the growth of domestic aggregates, ignoring the effects of the more rapid growth of liabilities to non-banks that is occurring in the Euro-currency market, they may facilitate more expansionary and more inflationary conditions than they intend, or may be aware of. Indeed, there is a risk that, over time, as the Euro-currency market expands relative to domestic markets, control over the aggregate volume of money may increasingly slip from the hands of central banks."

The measurement is complex and the issue has been well surveyed by McClam (1980), Mayer (1976) and Johnston (forthcoming) amongst others. The issues are essentially: (i) whether any inter-bank Euro-currency liabilities should be included in a monetary aggregate target, (ii) whether domestic residents foreign currency bank assets (held at domestic and overseas banks) should be included, and (iii) whether Euro-currency assets (in the country's currency) of residents and non-residents should be included. This is only a part of a more general issue which also considers whether, for instance, liabilities of some non-bank financial intermediaries should also be included in a targeted "monetary aggregate". The UK monetary authorities have recently extended the coverage of published aggregates by new concepts of

Private Sector Liquidity 1 and 2.[2] But any aggregate must to some extent be arbitrary and financial innovation frequently distorts the interpretation of particular aggregates. There is also a school of thought which suggests that *credit* rather than *monetary* aggregates are more significant. In this respect it is not so much whether Euro-currency assets should be included in monetary aggregates, but whether Euro-market intermediation adds to the volume of credit. McClam's analysis focuses upon credit. "The analysis leans towards those views which place emphasis on the demand for credit as distinct from the demand for money. Basically, it sides with the Gurley/Shaw 'new view' of financial markets, which stresses the need for a *financial* policy designed to influence credit creation over financial markets as a whole instead of a *monetary* policy focussing on the control of specific banking sector monetary liabilities." This is also the view adopted in this paper.

It is not likely that Euro-currency liabilities are quantitatively very significant with respect to the measure of "true" monetary aggregates for three main reasons: (i) in Group of Ten countries foreign currency deposits by residents with banks are included in domestic monetary aggregates,[3] (ii) deposits by non-bank residents with banks abroad, while excluded, are generally not large and (iii) bank deposits in the Euro-market (the bulk of Euro-market deposits) should not be included as the ultimate liability is against non-banks and these are already included in domestic monetary aggregates (see McClam, 1980 for a detailed analysis). In a similar study, Johnston (forthcoming) estimates that the total size of relevant Euro-balances currently excluded probably amounts to no more than 4 per cent of measured aggregates.

In reviewing the empirical evidence with respect to Wallich's hypothesis, McClam notes that "there is nothing in the behaviour of the income velocity of total credit that would seem to reflect an unrecorded influence on domestic spending coming from the stock of dollar claims held by non-banks in the Euro-currency market . . . It would not appear, therefore, that the Euro-dollar market has contributed in any direct way to the increases in M_1 velocity that have occurred since 1972".

STATIC AND DYNAMIC CREDIT EFFECTS

The focus of attention is therefore upon the two *credit* effects noted earlier. The *static* effect considers the extent to which the credit flows through the Euro-markets add to the total volume of credit; it focuses upon portfolio equilibrium with respect to the global allocation of wealth and credit as between competing markets and media. The *dynamic* effect relates to the ability of the Euro-markets to undermine domestic monetary policy measures. While related, the two effects raise different analytical and policy issues. The *static* effect may be positive while the *dynamic* effect is neutral. Thus, there may be competitive factors which enable the Euro-markets to provide credit that would not otherwise be given by domestic institutions. These competitive factors produce a stock equilibrium which may imply a higher volume of outstanding credit. But the competitive advantage is not constantly changing. Unless these competitive factors are determined in part by monetary policy measures, the markets do not pose a significant threat to monetary policy.

Banks operating in the Euro-currency markets (accepting deposits and making loans) tend to have a competitive advantage relative to those operating in corresponding domestic markets. The market and control factors giving rise to this are well established.[4] They give rise to a situation where the market's deposit rate can be higher, lending rate lower and lending margin narrower than in domestic banking systems. This secures funds and borrowing customers. The issue in the *static* effect is whether this lending adds to or substitutes for lending that would otherwise have been undertaken by domestic banks.

The basic contention here is that the most suitable analytical framework for considering these issues is that of non-bank financial intermediation. This suggests that Euro-banks stand with respect to domestic money and credit markets in the same currency in the same way as do NBFIs within a country stand with respect to banks. The analysis is very similar in both cases and raises similar issues with respect to credit creation. The parallels are close at two levels. Firstly, the Euro-market is a market in domestic bank deposits in that Euro-market transactions involve changes in the ownership but not the total of bank deposits in the country whose currency is being used. When a transfer is made from, say a bank deposit in the US to the Euro-dollar market the funds are not lost to the US banking system. This is similar to NBFIs within a country who are borrowing and lending bank deposits.[5] Secondly, this means that the Euro-market has the capacity to increase the volume of credit relative to money in the country concerned in a way similar to the potential of NBFIs. Whether this capacity is in practice used, and whether it is applied at times of restrictive policy, is the issue discussed here. The key issue in both cases is the degree of interest rate integration between institutions.

Thus, the methodology to be applied in analysing the Euro-currency market is that of non-bank financial intermediation. A Euro-bank can make new loans only to the extent that it receives a deposit, and when it makes a loan it loses reserves automatically. Thus, a transfer of deposits from a bank in New York to a Euro-bank may induce: (i) an increase in the total volume of world credit as the lending capacity of the Euro-bank is increased while that of the New York bank is not decreased; this also implies increased velocity of circulation of money; (ii) a multiple increase in credit to the extent that, until interest rate differentials adjust, a proportion of funds loaned by the Euro-bank might be subsequently redeposited in the Euro-currency market; or (iii) merely a change in the location of credit rather than the total in that borrowing from a Euro-bank may be an alternative to borrowing from a US bank. Each of these possibilities has a direct parallel in the process of financial intermediation by NBFIs in domestic economies. With respect to (i), it means that there is a *potential* net credit effect in that, being outside the immediate control of domestic monetary authorities, Euro-banks raise the credit capacity of a given volume of domestic bank reserves.

It is useful, therefore, to consider the analytical framework of non-bank financial intermediation, and its implications for credit creation, as it yields relevant insights into the operation of the Euro-currency markets. A transfer of funds from a bank to an NBFI (and the subsequent on-lending) adds to the total volume of credit, rather than substitutes for credit that would otherwise have been provided by the banks, when one or more of the following conditions are satisfied: (1) NBFIs, because of their "efficiency", are able to offer credit at lower interest rates than are banks and credit demand is interest sensitive; (2) banks are either unable or unwilling to compete in the credit market for NBFIs, and hence NBFI lending does not directly displace bank lending though indirectly it may cause bank credit to be repaid; (3) banks ration credit and cause an excess demand for credit at current interest rates which can be absorbed by NBFIs; (4) the profit-maximising level of bank credit is constrained by an officially imposed limitation on bank reserves and banks are not aggressive liability managers; (5) the banking system is not fully competitive with the result that profits are excessive and derive from an uncompetitively wide differential between deposit and lending interest rates and/or, (6) NBFIs are able to increase the *demand* for credit. These six conditions will be applied in the subsequent analysis of credit effects and are referred to as the "basic conditions". If both banks and NBFIs are fully competitive, in that their interest-rate structures are such as to eliminate excess demand for credit, NBFIs may increase credit only to the extent that, at their lower interest rates, the demand for credit is raised. Without this, any expansion of NBFI credit must be at the expense of credit that would otherwise have been given elsewhere.

Precisely similar arguments apply to the credit effects of the Euro-currency markets, bearing in mind that these markets may be taken to be fully competitive with no excess demand at prevailing interest rates, and that domestic banks do compete in the same credit markets as Euro-banks.

In effect, and abstracting from the complications of borrowers and lenders through the Euro-currency market frequently being in different countries, the Euro-dollar market may add to the total volume of credit in much the same way as, within a national monetary system, non-bank financial intermediaries add to the total volume of domestic credit. The abstraction is important as such flows may also imply switches between *currencies* and hence, under some circumstances, credit capacity of banks in different countries may be affected by the effect on bank reserves of central bank intervention in foreign exchange markets. The abstraction is made because this issue relates more generally to international capital movements rather than specifically to Euro-market intermediation. The broader issue is discussed in Llewellyn (1980).

On the other hand, the Euro-dollar market may be an alternative channel for credit that would otherwise have occurred in a different way. Thus, because of their competitive strength, Euro-banks may cause borrowers to switch their demand from banks in the United States which, because there is no excess demand for credit, are unable to find alternative borrowers. Also, in a situation where US banks have no excess reserves, Euro-market borrowers might otherwise have attempted to borrow from banks in the United States and, in order to prevent interest rates rising, the Federal Reserve might in these circumstances have increased the reserves and the lending capacity of the US banking system. In both cases, the existence of Euro-dollar market lending does not add to the volume of credit that would have existed without the Euro-market.

If there is a net credit effect deriving from the competitive position of the Euro-market this could be eliminated in one of three ways: (i) by imposing similar controls on Euro-banks as exist on domestic banks, (ii) by easing controls etc. on domestic banks and/or (iii) paying interest on reserves.

The universal application of control mechanisms (such as compulsory reserve requirements in line with those in domestic markets) would undoubtedly impair the competitive position of the Euro-markets. But in themselves they would not alter the aggregate demand for world credit; existing borrowers would still seek funding. If such demand were switched to the US banking system the initial excess demand for bank credit would induce a rise in US interest rates. The Federal Reserve would then have two broad options: (i) it could ease the pressure on interest rates by supplying bank reserves to enable the banks to meet the increased credit demands; or (ii) it could refuse to increase the lending capacity of domestic banks by failing to increase the supply of bank reserves. In the first case, Euro-market controls would have an effect upon the aggregate volume of world credit only to the extent that credit demand was sensitive to the previous small difference in interest rates between the Euro- and domestic segments of the dollar bank credit market.

In the second case the total volume of US bank credit is constrained by the availability of reserves. While alternative intermediation channels might emerge, the rise in domestic interest rates needed to eliminate the excess demand for bank credit might be substantial and politically unacceptable. Again the effect of the controls is seen to be dependent upon the interest rate sensitivity of the demand for credit. But this issue transcends the distinction between the "static" and "dynamic" credit effects and therefore amalgamates two concepts which analytically should be kept separate.

EURO-STERLING

There are circumstances, therefore, when financial flows through a Euro-currency market may represent a net addition to the total volume of credit relative to the volume of money. Intermediation via the Euro-sterling market may, under some circumstances, also have purely *monetary* effects.

A Paris bank may bid for sterling funds that would otherwise have been maintained as either interest bearing deposits by UK residents at banks in the UK or invested in public sector debt. A transfer of an existing sterling deposit from a bank in the UK to one in Paris does not imply any loss of funds to the UK banks. Only the ownership of the deposit changes from, say, a UK resident to a foreign bank. At this point sterling M_3 is reduced (as the non-resident holding is excluded from the definition) but eligible liabilities are unaltered. If, however, the Paris bank on-lends to a UK resident the overall net effect upon sterling M_3 is zero as the Paris bank has induced a transfer of bank deposits between domestic residents. In the process credit availability to UK residents has been increased with a given stock of money.

Alternatively, if a Paris bank successfully competes for funds previously invested in public sector debt not only is the lending capacity of the Euro-sterling market increased, but that of the UK banking sector too. This is because the induced net switch from public sector debt by UK residents may imply a higher volume of government financing through the monetary sector. Initially there is no net effect upon sterling M_3 as, while initially it rises through the effect of UK residents switching from public sector debt to bank deposits, this is cancelled when the deposit is transferred to a non-resident bank. If the Paris bank subsequently lends to a UK resident sterling M_3 rises. If the debt is purchased by the Bank of England (because of its interest rate policy) bank reserves also rise. In this case intermediation by the Euro-sterling market raises the lending capacity not only of Euro-banks but domestic banks too.

DYNAMIC CREDIT EFFECT

If any of the six "basic conditions" exist, credit generated within the Euro-currency market adds to the total volume of credit. In effect, even if the elasticity of supply of the monetary base is zero the total volume of credit need not be constrained by the supply of bank reserves in the domestic market. But if the supply of reserves is demand determined any move to impair the competitive position of Euro-market banks will not constrain the total volume of credit as the demand for credit is switched to the domestic market and, with excess demand for credit with the previous level of reserves, the central bank increases reserves to prevent interest rates rising.

The *dynamic* credit effect relates to whether, from an initial competitive equilibrium between the domestic and Euro-markets, the effect of restrictive monetary policy is offset by increased Euro-market intermediation. The distinction between the *static* and *dynamic* credit effects is one between stock equilibrium and the distribution of credit due to portfolio preferences, and changes in the relative competitive positions of the two markets due to monetary policy. The dynamic effect of the Euro-currency markets is positive if, following a restrictive monetary policy, the reduction in domestic credit induces a rise in Euro-market credit. It is the contention here that this follows only in circumstances where monetary policy itself causes one of the "basic conditions" to arise and which enhances the competitive position of the Euro-market.

The same argument applies to *disintermediation* by NBFIs (e.g. building societies in the UK) within domestic financial systems. Recent developments in the UK are interesting as banks are now (unlike in the past) competing vigorously for mortgage lending. "Basic condition" 2 is being eroded in the UK and the building societies' share of mortgage lending declined sharply between December 1980 and March 1982 from around 95 per cent to about 80 per cent. This *reintermediation* has had an important "cosmetic" problem for the monetary authorities in that it raises the money supply relative to the total volume of bank and NBFI credit. However, it has implied a willingness by the Bank of England to supply the requisite volume of bank reserves to prevent what would otherwise have been a sharp rise in UK money market interest rates following from bank bidding for deposits and reserves. This is directly analogous to the dilemma postulated above for the Federal Reserve in circumstances where Euro-market credit demand was switched to the domestic banking system. A monetary policy problem arises if the target of policy is a *monetary* rather than a *credit* aggregate.

The *domestic* and *Euro* segments of money markets are, in the absence of exchange control and distortions such as the now largely inoperative Regulation Q in the United States, highly integrated. If there is a high degree of substitutability between the *Euro* and *domestic* segments of money markets, and if a competitive equilibrium exists between them, monetary policy directed at domestic markets will usually affect not only domestic monetary and credit conditions but also the availability of credit in external markets. The relationship between the *Euro-* and *domestic* money market is strictly analogous to that between member and non-member banks of the US Federal Reserve System.[6] Because of the power of arbitrage, and the highly integrated system, the behaviour of non-members' balance sheets reflects almost identically that of member banks. Thus, while US monetary policy measures may have their immediate impact upon member banks, this is generalised throughout the US banking system as, within a highly integrated national financial system, significant interest rate differentials between different components cannot be sustained. Similarly, credit conditions are also generalised through any integrated system.

The same applies to the Euro-currency markets. It follows, therefore, that the Euro-markets reflect the monetary policy stance of governments throughout the world. They are a reflection of monetary and credit conditions determined by policy and, as such, cannot be regarded as a significant independent factor in world inflation, etc.

But before this conclusion can be universally accepted, consideration must be given to the form and instruments of monetary policy adopted. The key issue is the extent to which monetary policy measures influence the "basic conditions" noted earlier as giving rise to a net credit effect deriving from Euro-market intermediation. These conditions are affected differently by different policy measures. Consideration is given to three alternatives: (1) direct control over domestic bank lending, (2) a rise in reserve requirements on domestic banks and (3) a reduction in the monetary base (bank reserves) through market operations by the central bank. The *dynamic* effect is found to be critically determined by which of these measures is adopted to reduce the volume of credit and is positive in the first two cases but, providing domestic banks are profit maximising and engage in liability management, is neutral in the third. A more formal analysis is given in the Appendix.

(1) *Direct Control*

The monetary authorities may impose a credit limit on domestic banks at current asset levels in a situation where the demand for credit rises (shift in the demand curve). In this situation banks may respond in one of two ways: (i) by maintaining the current level of interest rates and causing an excess demand for credit to arise, or (ii) by maximising profits in the constrained situation by charging a higher lending rate to eliminate the excess demand. In this latter case there is no incentive to offer a higher deposit rate as the banks need no more deposits or reserves as the volume of credit is constrained to the current level. In both cases there is scope for increased Euromarket intervention which at least partially offsets the effect of the domestic controls.

The excess demand case corresponds to condition 3 of the "basic conditions". In the absence of exchange control, Euro-market banks compete for deposits in order to meet the excess demand that exists in the domestic market. While Euro-market interest rates rise to attract deposits (and implies a corresponding rise in the lending rate) borrowers are assumed to be prepared to pay it as they are prevented from doing so in the domestic market by the policy of the banks in maintaining an excess demand situation. The net effect is some rise in credit and an increased share for the Euro-market. Some of the initial excess demand is not met as interest rates rise.

In this case the domestic monetary policy measure is offset by Euromarket intermediation as the policy itself causes one of the "basic conditions" to arise. The Euro-markets exploit an imperfection in the domestic market where banks seek to sustain excess demand by not clearing the market through interest rate adjustments.

In the "profit maximising" case the result is the same because "basic condition" 5 is met. Banks maintain a constant deposit rate but raise the lending rate to clear the excess demand that exists at the initial level of interest rates when there is an imposed ceiling on domestic bank credit. The implied "excess profits" can now be competed away by Euro-market banks and this is done by simultaneously offering a higher deposit rate and lower lending rate than domestic banks, while still maintaining their own lending margin. The analysis is described formally in the Appendix.

(2) *Reserve Requirements*

A restrictive monetary pol'cy designed to reduce credit availability may take the form of the imposition of higher reserve requirements on domestic banks. This directly reduces the competitive position of domestic banks relative to Euro-market banks. Other things being equal it causes the domestic deposit rate to be lowered and the lending rate to be raised. Euro-market banks respond as the change in relative interest rates induces a once-for-all portfolio adjustment as domestic depositors and borrowers switch to the Euro-currency market. This raises the lending capacity of Euro-market banks while still maintaining the same margin. But the adjustment is finite, and ultimately determined by the elasticity of demand for credit, being greater the lower is the elasticity. The full effects are described in the Appendix.

In both these cases (lending controls and higher reserve requirements) monetary policy induces a greater volume of financial intermediation to be undertaken by the Euro-market. The restrictive monetary policy is (only) partly offset because they create one of the "basic conditions" of net credit expansion to materialise. However, as in both cases the offset is only partial it means that the targeted credit effect can be achieved with a correspondingly larger policy adjustment. But, following the analysis below, it also means that the same *net* credit effect could also be achieved through operating directly on the monetary base and that this could be done with more precision, less distortion and greater equity as between domestic and Euro-market banks.

(3) *Monetary Base Control*

A policy induced reduction in the monetary base reduces the lending capacity of domestic banks though, in itself, does not alter the capacity of the Euro-market. In order to avoid reducing earning assets banks individually bid for deposits and reserves by offering a higher deposit rate. This may be successful to an individual bank to the extent that it is able to increase its share of the smaller total of reserves. It may be collectively successful if, in order to prevent the rise in interest rates and/or the exchange rate, the central bank reverses its policy with respect to the monetary base. It may have overestimated the elasticity of demand for bank credit and underestimated the interest rate and exchange rate consequences. It is assumed here that there is no such reversal.

The banks' demand for reserves is a derived demand on the basis of the ultimate demand for bank credit. Interest rates rise as banks bid for deposits and reserves. This has the effect of the banks paying a higher interest rate for the same volume of deposits and reserves. The process continues until it is no longer profitable to bid, which will be when lending rates have risen to the point where the demand for credit equals the supply capacity given by the lower level of reserves. Arbitrage by banks, borrowers and depositors will equalise interest rates in the two markets. If there is any tendency for domestic deposit rates to rise relative to Euro-market rates banks switch the source of funding to the Euro-market and depositors switch to the domestic market. Conversely, borrowers would switch to the Euro-market. External funding does not induce a rise in the total volume of reserves available to domestic banks unless it is conducted in foreign currency markets and the central bank intervenes to prevent the exchange rate moving. Borrowing in the Euro-market of the domestic currency is no different from funding domestically in that it involves only changes in the ownership of given balances at the central bank.

Arbitrage keeps interest rates in close alignment and the effect of the contractionary monetary policy is generalised to the Euro-market sector. Providing all interest rate adjustments are instantaneous, there is no scope for increased financial intermediation by the Euro-market. It does not pose a threat to monetary policy conducted through this mechanism. The net result is that credit is reduced in both sectors (see Appendix) and the rise in interest rates is determined by the elasticity of demand for credit.

Adjusting the supply of bank reserves is fundamentally different from altering reserve requirements as: (i) in the former case banks bid for more deposits while in the latter case they bid for less; (ii) the lending margin in the domestic market widens in absolute and relative terms with reserve requirements but not with a fall in reserves, and hence (iii) the Euro-market gains a competitive advantage with reserve requirements but not with a fall in reserves. There is a resultant intermediation effect in the case of reserve requirements that does not exist with a fall in reserves designed to achieve the same effect. It means, however, that in order to induce a lower volume of credit, the required reduction in reserves is less than the arithmetical equivalent change in reserve requirements.

Monetary policy is not weakened by the Euro-markets if policy is conducted in terms of adjusting the volume of bank reserves. None of the "basic conditions" for a net credit effect are altered with a change in the monetary base. This conclusion holds providing: (i) banks respond by aggressive liability management in a profit maximising strategy, (ii) they bid in all available markets, (iii) there is no exchange control impeding arbitrage and (iv) adjustments occur at the same speed in all markets. In these circumstances there are no changes in relative interest rates and no excess demand, even temporarily, emerges.

A qualification needs to be added to the extent of any effect deriving from the "tax" effect at different interest rate levels. If interest is paid on all deposits, the "effective tax" implied by reserve requirements on domestic banks is nec :ssarily greater the higher are market interest rates. The effect of the tax, which rises with interest rates, is to reduce profits of domestic banks. Dependent upon the level of the reserve requirement there is always some level of market rates (assuming a constant differential between domestic banks' deposit and lending rates) that causes losses to be made. In themselves, high interest rates need induce no extra disintermediation effects (on the pattern of deposit and credit flows) through the Euro-market, or change the *relative* competitiveness of the two markets. This is because high interest rates (with reserve requirements placed only upon domestic banks) do not in themselves imply any different interest rate *differentials* as between the two markets than is the case with low interest rates.

But to the extent that the greater tax and lower profits induce banks to widen the differential between loan and deposit rates there is a change in the competitive structure of the two markets which would induce stock-adjustments on both sides of the banks' balance-sheet. However, to the extent that domestic banks receive interest-free deposits, the endowment effect on domestic bank profits rises as interest rates rise increasingly above the cost of services not charged to customers. This could induce the opposite effect on margins.

If reaction speeds are different and slower in the domestic market (perhaps because of regulations, reluctance to raise lending rates, oligopolistic market structures and any institutional contraints) there may be a net offset through the Euro-market even when policy relates to a change in the monetary base. This is because the competitive structures of the two markets are different. This would imply an excess demand for domestic bank credit which would be exploited by Euro-market banks: it implies a degree of credit rationing by controlled banks. This disintermediation with monetary base control arises only as a result of short-run disequilibrium conditions where interest rates do not adjust instantaneously to excess demand conditions. Alternatively, they may arise if domestic banks are not invariably profit-maximisers in the short run, and hence do not bid for funds to satisfy an initial excess demand for credit. Both imply a degree of imperfection in the domestic banking sector.

EURO-STERLING AND THE CORSET

Prior to the abolition of UK exchange control in October 1979, the Euro-sterling interest rate was frequently significantly above the UK domestic inter-bank rate (figure 2). This occurred when the forward discount widened sharply (figure 1) as, through the invariable interest parity condition of the Euro-currency markets, this was reflected in Euro-market interest rates. Exchange control prevented outward arbitrage from the UK and hence the widening forward discount did not have to be reflected in domestic interest rates. This also implied that when the forward discount was wide there would frequently be a substantial covered interest differential against domestic sterling assets (figure 1) though not against Euro-sterling (e.g. 1974, 1976, 1977). Since 1979, following the abolition of exchange control, the domestic covered differential has remained at close to zero notwithstanding sharp fluctuations in the forward exchange rate (figure 1). The interest rate implications of the abolition of exchange control are discussed further in Nellis (1982) and Llewellyn (1980). For much of the 1970s, the monetary authorities sought to constrain the banks' expansion by the *Corset* mechanism. This imposed a "tax" (in the form of interest free deposits at the Bank of England) if banks' interest bearing liabilities rose beyond a specified amount. It was effectively a constraint imposed on banks' liability management.

This, therefore, created two of the "basic conditions" for effective Euro-market intermediation: (i) a wider interest rate differential due to a higher reserve requirement and (ii) a constraint on liability management. But in this respect it was of little significance prior to the abolition of exchange control as banks in the Euro-sterling market could not have access to London money market funds. But after October 1979 this was made possible. A bank in the UK with zero excess reserves, and against its *Corset* limit, could not meet increased credit demand at the same interest rate as in the Euro-sterling market because of the "tax". A Paris bank would find it profitable to bid for sterling funds (as it was unconstrained by the *Corset*) and lend within the UK. This would have no net effect upon the UK money supply (and hence perhaps was of little concern to the authorities) but would raise the volume of credit. The Euro-sterling market did expand rapidly during the period between the abolition of exchange control (October 1979) and the ending of the *Corset* (June 1980).

This was an unsustainable position as, while cosmetically acceptable in terms of the £M$_3$ target, it was grossly distorting the interpretation of money supply data. Credit was diverted outside the controlled sector which

Figure 1. *Sterling forward discount and covered interest rate differential: UK inter-bank and Euro-dollar rates (%)*

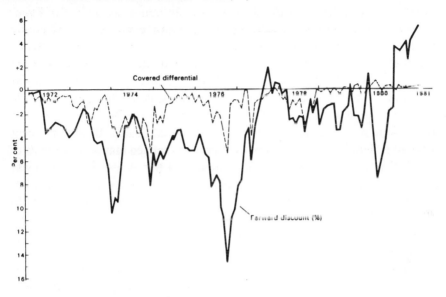

Figure 2. *Euro-sterling and UK inter-bank rates (%)*

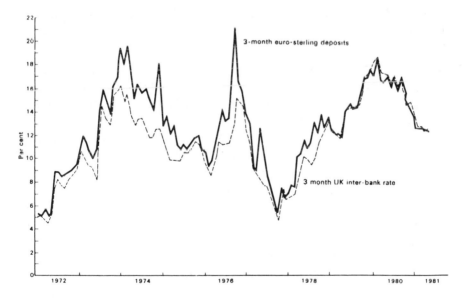

Source: Nellis (1982)

was also inequitable for UK banks who were being taxed relative to Paris banks. There was a sharp reintermediation effect after the suspension of the *Corset* which similarly distorted money supply figures as credit flows previously outside domestic banks (and hence not captured in £M$_3$) were brought within the domestic system.

Since the abolition of exchange control the domestic and Euro-sterling markets have been highly integrated and interest rates have been almost identical (figure 2). This is because, unlike most countries, there is no reserve requirement "tax" imposed upon UK banks. Up to August 1981, UK banks were required to maintain reserve assets equivalent to 12½ per cent of eligible liabilities. But as all but 1½ per cent carried market interest rates this was not an effective "tax". In August 1981 the reserve assets ratio was abandoned and replaced by a "cash" ratio (balances at the Bank of England). Although no interest rate is paid, as it is set at ½ per cent of eligible liabilities (plus operational bankers' balances) again the "tax" effect is negligible. The implication is that UK banks are not at a competitive disadvantage vis à vis the Euro-sterling market and hence domestic deposit rates are not lower or lending rates higher than in the Euro-sterling market. This clearly contrasts with interest rates in the US relative to the Euro-dollar market (figure 3). This also means that the Euro-sterling market is unlikely to have significant credit effect unless monetary policy is conducted through direct control or non-market mechanisms.

CONCLUSION

The paper has considered static and dynamic credit effects of the Euro-currency market in the analytical context of profit maximising liability management behaviour of financial institutions. A series of "basic conditions" for net static credit effects were established in the analytical framework of non-bank financial intermediation. The static effects are shown to be determined by the profit maximising strategy of both domestic and Euro-banks, and the competitive structure of the domestic market.

The *dynamic* effects relate to whether, from an initial competitive equilibrium between the domestic and Euro-markets, the effect of restrictive monetary policy is offset by increased Euro-market intermediation. The conclusion is that there is a positive *dynamic* effect only in circumstances where the monetary policy itself causes any of the static conditions to arise. This depends upon the form monetary policy takes and in particular the extent to which it relies on non-market and control mechanisms and influences

Figure 3. *Euro-dollar and US money market rates*

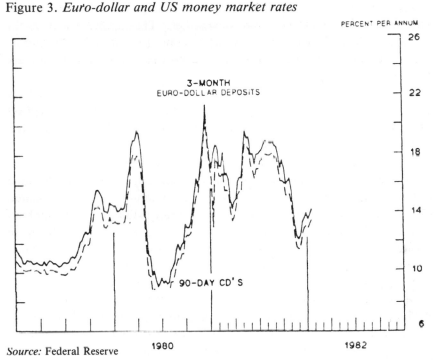

PERCENT PER ANNUM

Source: Federal Reserve

the competitive position of the domestic sector vis à vis the Euro-sector. If policy is conducted in terms of interest rates and banks are not constrained in their liability management, and maximise profits in both the long and short run, the Euro-markets pose no threat to the conduct of monetary policy. This implies instantaneous interest rate adjustments in both markets.

Thus, as with the *static* effect, any net positive *dynamic* effect is due to imperfections in the domestic banking sector and which constrain banks in their liability management.

APPENDIX
MONETARY POLICY AND EURO-MARKET INTERMEDIATION

Three techniques of monetary policy, and the response of the Euro-currency market, are represented in terms of a simple analytical framework. For simplicity it is assumed that initially the domestic and Euro-market of the same currency are in equilibrium with: (i) identical supply and demand schedules, (ii) the same lending margin and interest rates and (iii) the same volume of deposits and lending. It is further assumed that there is no exchange control to prevent arbitrage between the two markets. The supply of deposits in each sector of the market (domestic and Euro) is determined by the considerations in portfolio balance theory. With a given constellation of interest rates, a total portfolio of wealth is allocated across a range of alternative assets. Both of the two banking sectors are competing for shares of portfolio and in two ways: (i) each is competing with the other for the distribution of the total portfolio allocated to bank assets and (ii) both are competing with non-bank forms of holding wealth. The elasticity of the schedules is determined by the interest rate sensitivity of wealth holders between bank and non-bank assets, while the position of each supply of deposit schedule is determined by: (i) the level of interest rates on non-bank assets (assumed to be constant) and (ii) the level of the deposit rate in the competing banking sector. The supply of deposits (S_D) to both banking markets is therefore taken to be a rising function of the own interest rate (while interest rate differentials remain constant),[7] and shifts in each function are determined by any changes in the interest rate differential between the two banking markets. If the deposit interest rate in one sector rises relative to the other sector, the former will gain a larger volume of deposits at each interest rate, i.e. the supply curve shifts. While, at each interest rate, it gains no extra funds by competing with non-bank assets, its share of the bank sector rises because of the change in the interest rate *differential* at each level of interest rates. The supply of loans (S_L) is also a rising function of the level of interest rates with a constant margin above the supply curve of deposits determined by the costs of intermediation including any reserve requirements.

The total demand for loans (initially divided equally between the two markets) is a function of the rate of interest and the distribution between the two markets is determined by changes in the loan rate differential.

1. *Direct Controls*

In figure A1 the two markets are initially in equilibrium with S_{D0} being the supply curve of deposits in the domestic market, S_{L0} the supply curve of loans in the domestic markets and S_{DA} and S_{LA} being the respective supply curves in the Euro-market. Demand is initially represented by D_0 and D_A. Equilibrium is determined at deposit rates i_1 and loan rates i_0 with the total volume of credit equal to (OA + OB). From this position a ceiling of OA is placed on the total lending of domestic banks but demand shifts (in the domestic market alone for simplicity) from D_0 to D_1. At initial interest rates there is excess demand for credit of EF. Two responses are considered:

Figure A1. *Analysis of lending controls*

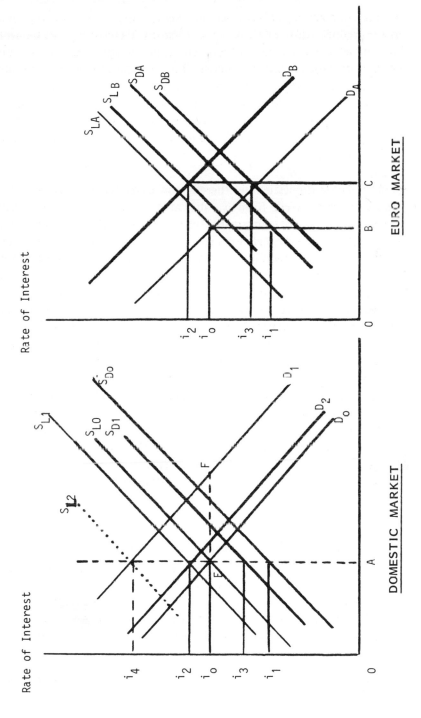

(a) domestic banks initially maintain excess demand by not raising interest rates; (b) domestic banks seek to maximise profits by charging a higher lending rate while keeping deposit rates constant. In either case, as noted in the main text, there is scope for increased intermediation and credit extension by the Euro-market and the effect of the measure is partly offset. This is because the relative competitive positions of the markets change by virtue of the monetary policy measure. In terms of the "basic conditions" noted above, in the first case condition 3 applies and in the second condition 5.

(a) *Excess Demand*

At constant domestic rates there is now excess demand EF with the domestic volume of credit fixed by policy at OA (figure A1). Banks in the Euro (uncontrolled) sector perceive profitable lending business meeting this excess demand (albeit at higher interest rates) by bidding for deposits. Similarly, the demand for credit is switched to the Euro-market. As the Euro-banks bid for funds, the Euro-deposit rate can be higher than the corresponding domestic rate and this induces equal and opposite shifts in the supply curves of deposits from S_{D0} to S_{D1} and S_{DA} to S_{DB}.[8] The supply curve of loans shifts correspondingly to S_{L1} and S_{LB}. Similarly, the demand curves shift from D_1 to D_2 and D_A to D_B in view of excess demand as borrowers are assumed to know that credit is available in the Euro-market.

In competitive equilibrium the final result is constrained to the requirement of similar interest rates in the two markets. The new equilibrium is given at interest rates i_3 and i_2 and results from the net shifts in supply and demand: fall in demand in the domestic market, rise in the Euro segment and a fall in supply in the domestic but rise in the Euro-market. There is nothing to indicate that margins or interest rates should be different as between the two markets. With the level of domestic lending fixed at OA the net result is: (i) a rise in interest rates, (ii) a rise in the volume of credit in the Euro-market (BC), and (iii) an increased share of lending by the Euro-markets. The rise BC must be less than EF (initial excess demand) if there is any elasticity to the demand for credit as interest rates must necessarily rise as demand in total has risen (D_0 to D_1). The offset due to Euro-market intermediation is determined by the elasticity of demand for credit.

In this case the Euro-markets have exploited an imperfection in the domestic market where banks seek to sustain excess demand by not clearing the market through interest rate adjustments.

(b) *Profit Maximising*

Initial equilibrium is again at OA and OB with deposit rates at i_1 and loan rates at i_0 in both markets. A lending limit of OA is placed on domestic banks while demand shifts from D_0 to D_1. In this case (figure A1) faced with an imposed limit of OA, domestic banks maintain a constant deposit rate (i_1) as they need no more deposits than OA but, with an initial excess demand at prevailing interest rates, banks are able to charge i_4, i.e. S_{L0} shifts to S_{L2} but S_{D0} remains the same. This is a disequilibrium position as domestic banks have excess profits (i_4 $i_0 \times$ OA). These would be competed away by the Euro-market.

The unconstrained Euro-market is in a position to compete by offering a higher deposit rate and lower lending rate than domestic banks in the now controlled environment. The new equilibrium is constrained to there being a net rise in interest rates (due to higher demand) but final equality of interest rates as between the two markets. There need be no net change in lending margins. The net (equal and opposite) shifts are S_{D0} to S_{D1} and S_{DA} to S_{DB} (due to aggressive liability management and bidding for deposits by the Euro-market inducing an initial interest rate move in its favour) and D_1 to D_2 and D_A to D_B due to the initial offer of lower lending rates.

The net result must necessarily be the same as in the previous case. In this case, Euro-banks are frustrating monetary policy because they are exploiting and competing away excess profits of domestic banks ("basic condition" 5).

2. *Reserve Requirements*

From an initial competitive equilibrium, reserve requirements are increased on domestic banks. In figure A2 the initial equilibrium implied deposit interest rates of i_0 and lending rates of i_1 in both markets. The total volume of credit is (OA + OB). The rise in reserve requirements must widen the differential between deposit and lending rates in the domestic market and relative to the Euro-market. The competitive position of the Euro-market is thereby enhanced as it can offer a combination of a higher deposit rate and lower lending rate relative to domestic banks. The effect of the reserve requirement is to shift S_{L0} to S_{L1} in the domestic banking sector. The lending rate rises to i_2 and, because of the effect on the demand for credit, the deposit rate is reduced to i_3 as a smaller volume of deposits is required to fund lending. Euro-banks compete for deposits to fund increased lending and this enhanced competitive position raises the deposit rate and lowers the lending rate relative to the domestic market. The change in interest rate dif-

112

Figure A2. *Analysis of reserve requirements*

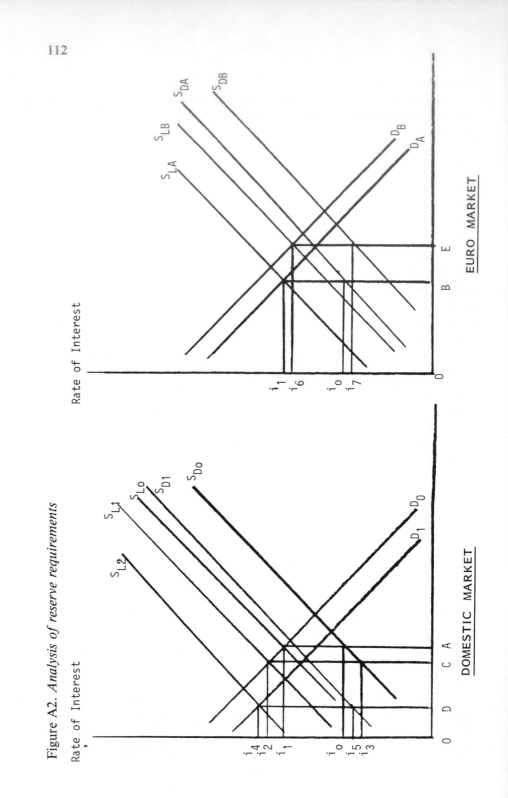

Rate of Interest

DOMESTIC MARKET

Rate of Interest

EURO MARKET

ferentials induces a shift in the demand for credit: D_0 to D_1 and D_A to D_B. The supply curves of deposits shift from S_{D0} to S_{D1} and S_{DA} to S_{DB} which produces corresponding shifts in the supply curves of credit from S_{L1} to S_{L2} and S_{LA} to S_{LB}.

The new equilibrium is constrained in figure A2 to produce a pattern of interest rates where the Euro-lending rate is below the domestic lending rate and the Euro-deposit rate is equal to or higher than the domestic rate. The net effect of the increase in reserve requirement is: (a) a higher lending interest rate in the domestic market (i_4) but a lower lending rate (i_6 in the Euro-market (the effect of the change in the relative competitiveness is distributed between the two markets), (b) the deposit rate falls in both markets (to i_3 and i_7); as the effect on the reserve requirement is likely to both raise the lending rate and lower the deposit rate in the domestic market and, as the lending margin remains constant in the Euro-market, the Euro-deposit rate must be lower in line with the lower lending rate; (c) the volume of domestic credit falls by AD but is partly offset by a rise (BE) in the Euro-market as demand and deposits have been switched to this market, and (d) there is a net fall in the total volume of credit. The reduction in aggregate credit derives from the net effect of the rise in the domestic lending rate and fall in the Euro-lending rate given that the Euro-market's lending capacity is constrained by the requirement that the deposit rate cannot fall below the domestic rate. The net effect depends upon the elasticity of demand for credit. The effect of reserve requirements is to induce both shifts and movements along supply and demand curves; this limits the offsetting effect of intermediation through the Euro-market.

3. Reduced Monetary Base

The monetary base is reduced by a sale of debt by the central bank which constrains domestic banks' lending capacity to OA_1. At initial interest rates, there is now an excess demand for credit CD. Banks bid for reserves (individually attempting to secure a higher share of the smaller total) in an attempt to avoid reducing earning assets. As noted earlier, the rise in the lending rate to i_2 continues until the excess demand position has been eliminated; the extent of the rise is determined by the elasticity of demand for credit. As the fall in reserves does not alter the lending margin both the supply curve of deposits and loans shift from S_{D0} to S_{D1} and S_{L0} to S_{L1}. S_D shifts as banks *offer* a higher rate for deposits.[9] The higher deposit rate in the domestic market induces a similar movement in the Euro-market. Also, domestic banks will be simultaneously bidding for deposits in both markets

114

Figure A3. *Analysis of monetary base*

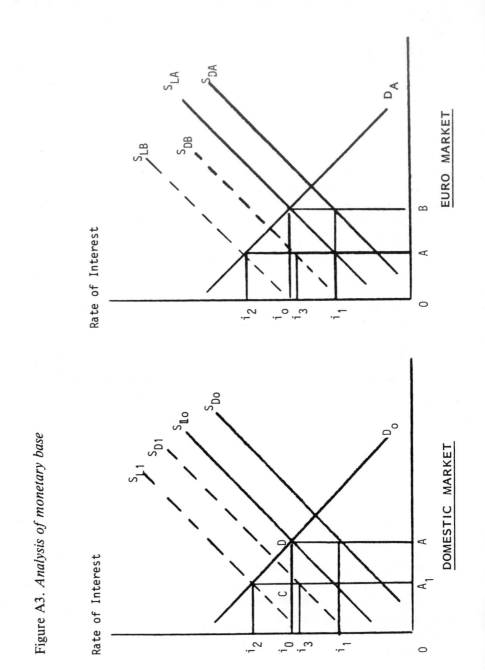

DOMESTIC MARKET

EURO MARKET

and bank arbitrage will keep deposit rates in the two markets in close alignment. Competitive pressure and potential shifts in the demand for loans keeps the lending margins equal and constant and hence the two lending rates are maintained in close alignment. Providing there is perfect and instantaneous bank arbitrage between the two markets, the Euro-market supply curves shift from S_{LA} to S_{LB} and S_{DA} to S_{DB}. There is a fall in Euro-market credit (AB) in line with domestic credit not directly because of the lower level of reserves cut because of the rise in Euro-market interest rates induced by arbitrage and domestic banks bidding for reserves.

Providing liability management is not impeded or constrained, that the fall in reserves does not alter the preferences of depositors and borrowers as between the two markets, and that banks are profit maximisers in both the short and long run (so that there are no differences in reaction speeds) then the Euro-market poses no threat to monetary policy executed via interest rate adjustments induced by changes in the monetary base.

NOTES

1. Throughout the analysis it is assumed that a successful bidding for deposits also secures reserves. This is the case whether the focus is upon an individual bank or banks collectively though the dynamic processes are different in the two cases.

2. The former adds to $£M_3$: private sector holdings of treasury bills, other bills, finance house deposits, and certificates of tax deposits. PSL_2 adds further: building society deposits, deposits at trustee savings banks and national savings bank and holdings of national savings securities. In both series adjustments are made for the institutions' holdings of bank deposits.

3. The official monetary target in the UK relates to the concept "sterling M_3" which excludes foreign currency bank deposits which are, however, included in M_3. In fact, in the two years after the abolition of exchange control foreign currency bank deposits rose by 139% with M_3 rising by 44% compared with 36% for $£M_3$.

4. For a review see Llewellyn (1981).

5. This is not always the case, however. See Llewellyn (1979).

6. This analogy with member and non-member banks has not been valid since the US Bank Control Act, 1980, as reserve requirements are now imposed upon both member and non-member banks and also thrift institutions.

7. It is therefore assumed that the elasticity of substitution between non-bank assets and each of the two banking markets is identical.

8. In all the figures final equilibrium schedules are given which result from net shifts which may be less than initial shifts. The figures therefore describe comparative static positions rather than dynamic processes.

9. A technically more accurate (though also more cumbersome) representation would treat separately the banks' demand for deposits and depositors' *supply* of deposits.

REFERENCES

Johnston, R.B., *The Euro Markets: History, Theory and Policy*, Macmillans (forthcoming).

Mayer, H., "The BIS Concepts of the Euro Currency Market", *Euromoney*, May 1976.

McClam, W.D., "US Monetary Aggregates, Income Velocity and the Euro Dollar Market", *BIS Economic Paper*, No. 2, April 1980.

Llewellyn, D.T., "Do Building Societies Take Deposits from Banks", *Lloyds Bank Review*, January 1979.

Llewellyn, D.T., *International Financial Integration*, Macmillans, 1980.

Llewellyn, D.T., "The Money Supply Process: A Generalised Approach", in Llewellyn, D.T. (ed.), *The Framework of UK Monetary Policy*, Heinemann, 1982.

Nellis, J., "The International Context of Monetary Policy", in Llewellyn, D.T. (ed.), *The Framework of UK Monetary Policy,* Heinemann, 1982.

Wallich, H., Statement before Sub-committee on Domestic Monetary Policy and the Sub-Committee on International Trade, Investment and Monetary Policy of the Committee on Banking, Finance and Urban Affairs, US House of Representatives, July 1979.

Chapter VII

EURO-MARKET GROWTH, RISKS IN INTERNATIONAL BANK LENDING AND DOMESTIC MONETARY MANAGEMENT

by *Hermann-Josef Dudler*

INTRODUCTION

1. The rapid growth of international bank lending and the spectacular expansion of the Euro-currency market have fascinated financial analysts and academics, international traders and commercial bankers as well as central bank and government officials for many years. Outside observers, market participants and representatives of public sector institutions naturally view these world-wide financial trends from differing micro- and macro-economic angles. Judgements and opinions on the Euro-system therefore tend to differ quite substantially depending on individual commentators' doctrinal convictions, their national or business interests, and their specific public responsibilities. The present paper addresses concerns and issues debated among major central banks since the late 1970s, after commercial banks' foreign claims and the gross and net volumes of the Euro-currency market had dramatically expanded at annual average rates of 20 to 30 per cent for about a decade (Annex 1). The author thus views the evolution of the international banking system from a monetary policy perspective.

2. The paper is broadly devoted to a range of topics covered in expert meetings held under the auspices of the Bank for International Settlements (BIS) in Basle in recent years. It does, however, neither purport to give a detailed and complete account of these discussions (whose confidentiality must be respected), nor does it subscribe without reservation to all of the arguments and propositions presented on the following pages (which are partly still controversial). Nevertheless, the author takes a personal stance in the sense that he singles out for closer examination those aspects of the functioning of international currency markets which, in his view, still give rise to well-founded public concern. This includes a certain range of policy questions which might become highly relevant only in future years, should the internationalisation of banking operations continue to progress at a rapid pace. The functioning of the Euro-currency market – as defined in a

wider geographical sense – provides the focus of the following discussion, but bank foreign lending in local currency is sometimes included, especially where reference is made to country or "name" risks. Since the requirements and concerns of financial control and domestic monetary management are a central theme or "leitmotiv" of this paper, it cannot venture to offer an adequate basis for assessing the Euro-markets' overall performance. The world-wide welfare benefits derived from the unique services provided by the international banking system, which are not explicitly considered here, are – needless to say – fully recognised by the author.

3. Part A of the paper briefly discusses the analytical and quantitative framework within which the monetary policy implications of the Euro-currency system might be most appropriately addressed. In Part B an attempt is made to identify four broad areas of policy concern originating from the explosive expansion of the Euro-currency system in the more recent past. Part C describes possible and actual policy responses to the challenges emanating from the existence and fast growth of the Euro-currency market, including measures both at the national and international level.

A. DETERMINANTS AND LIMITS OF EURO-MARKET GROWTH

4. The monetary significance and the relevance of macroeconomic concerns associated with the expansion of the Euro-currency market have been the subject of a long-standing controversial academic debate which dates back to the late 1960s. Various schools of thought have come to fundamentally different conclusions concerning the controllability and monetary nature of the growing stock of liquid Euro-currency liabilities. This "theological" dispute, in some respects, still influences the way monetary officials look at the policy implications of the Euro-market and explains certain differences of view among them. Nevertheless, on a number of principal matters official attitudes have begun to converge. Few central bankers and treasury representatives would deny today that the spectacular expansion of international banking deserves the joint attention of major central banks. Current developments and trends in the Euro-market are thus regularly and commonly reviewed by monetary officials notably at the BIS in Basle, whose staff has made continuous efforts to improve the analytical and statistical tools for monitoring the Euro-currency market. In this context a broad conceptual framework appears to be emerging within which central bankers from the larger industrial countries are able commonly to identify the politically essential characteristics of the Euro-system. Before specific

policy issues are taken up an attempt is made in the following to outline what in the author's opinion could be regarded as an evolving consensus approach to a forward looking and policy-oriented Euro-market analysis.

I. *The Euro-Multiplier Controversy*

5. Against the background of the fast expansion of the Euro-currency market in the 1970s, many monetary economists, notably those with monetarist leanings, tended to explain or analyse the growth of the system using a "money-multiplier" framework. In its simplest form, a comparison was drawn between the expansion of dollar-denominated demand and time deposits of foreign banks held at domestic US banks on the one hand, and the gross and net size of the Euro-dollar market on the other. This suggested that Euro-banks were, over time, willing or able to incur rapidly rising dollar liabilities in the Euro-market while feeling less and less constrained to hold liquid dollar reserve balances in the United States. In the same vein, efforts were made to measure the growth potential of the Euro-currency market on the basis of rigorously formulated multiplier models (Annex 2). These were conceptualised with varying degrees of complexity. They may broadly be categorised as follows:

(a) *Deposit multipliers.* Comparing Euro-banks to a fractional reserve banking system (where balances held by Euro-banks in home currency markets represent their "cash reserves", and "leakages" occur whenever Euro-loan proceeds are not redeposited with Euro-banks by their nonbank clients), various authors have constructed flow or stock deposit multipliers for the Euro-market. These show the growth or volume of Euro-currency liabilities to be dependent on Euro-banks' holdings or receipts of "primary" deposits held with national banking systems.

(b) *Three-stage reserve multipliers.* A more complex family of multipliers has been based on the assumption that domestic banks maintain reserve balances with their central bank on a voluntary or compulsory basis against deposits held by domestic nonbanks as well as by the Euro-banking system. Deposit growth in the Euro-market is thus seen to depend indirectly on the supply of base money made available to domestic banks (at least as long as Euro-banks voluntarily keep "primary" deposit balances with the national banking system). This methodological procedure allows construction of multiplier terms which explicitly capture the deposit-creating power of Euro-banks through the base money savings which they can achieve. Such savings occur, because deposits held with domestic banks carry higher reserve ratios than those created by Euro-banks, whose activity gives rise to only a fractional absorption of national base money, namely to the extent that Euro-banks voluntarily hold deposits with home banking systems.

(c) *Consolidated base multipliers.* It was soon found, however, that relationships between Euro-banks and national banking systems are apparently unstable or difficult to capture through simple, mechanistically operating "ratios". Attempts were therefore made to relate domestic and Euro-deposits as a whole for each currency denomination in one step to their respective national monetary base. The resulting uniform multiplier term was intended to provide an indirect measure of the amplifying influence which the Euro-market may exert on the deposit generating power of the consolidated national and international banking system as a whole.

6. The proponents of multiplier models invariably encountered difficulties in defining or estimating the relevant "leakages" and "reserve ratios". As a result, these authors often tended to overestimate the money-creating capacity of the Euro-banking system, its contribution to the growth of the world money stock, and the specific role of the Euro-market as an independent source of world inflation and exchange market disturbances. Moreover, academic experts committed to a portfolio approach to monetary analysis in the Yale tradition questioned the validity of the fractional reserve banking analogy, on which the Euro-multiplier concept was built, from a point of view of principle. They stressed the dependence of Euro-market activity on banks' risk attitudes and profit maximisation behaviour, underlined the influence exerted on nonbanks' demands for Euro-deposits and Euro-loans by changes in Euro-deposit and Euro-lending rates, while they saw the latter closely linked to corresponding short-term interest rates in national money markets. These authors therefore concluded that central banks might well be able to contain the growth of Euro-aggregates by appropriately controlling domestic money market conditions. Still others felt Euro-deposits were mainly held for investment purposes and could not effectively serve as a means of payments and medium of exchange. This contention was based on the observation that Euro-deposits first had to be converted into a chequeable deposit with a nationally located commercial bank directly participating in a multilateral clearing system of the home country of the Euro-currency concerned. The "moneyness" of Euro-deposits and the macro-economic relevance of Euro-banking was thus called into question on purely technical grounds.

7. Gauged from a present-day monetary policy perspective, these past opposing views on the macroeconomic implications of international banking appear to have gone to unnecessary extremes in many respects. Euro-multiplier models have appropriately drawn attention to the Euro-system's capacity for supplying monetary assets which are not normally included in national money stock measures and monetary targets. They have illustrated also its specific function of economising on national reserve money injections on a global scale. But fractional reserve approaches overemphasise the role of "primary" deposits and thus the supply side of the Euro-market; they more or less overlook the market's potential for interbank deposit redistribution and switching between currency denominations and disregard its ability to "tap" simultaneously different national money and deposit markets. In short, they tend to underrate the Euro-banking system's scope for aggressive liability management. Simple portfolio approaches, on the other hand, tend to neglect specific preferences of international depositors and lenders which turn to the Euro-banking system and attach little weight to the particular competitive advantages it enjoys. They accordingly fail more or less to offer an adequate explanation of the disproportionately fast expansion of Euro-aggregates in relation to domestic money and credit aggregates notably during the 1970s. Turning finally to the technical aspects of the past debate, it would no longer seem to be justified to doubt the monetary importance of Euro-banking operations merely on *a priori* grounds today. While differences in emphasis persist, many central bankers would probably share some or most of the following views with respect to the "moneyness" of short-term Euro-aggregates:

– Short-maturity Euro-currency liabilities are at least in part close substitutes to domestic time deposits, and Euro-currency loans easily replace domestic overdrafts. Central banks which pursue broadly defined money supply targets (e.g. those of the United States, Japan, Germany, France, the United Kingdom) or impose domestic lending ceilings (e.g. in Italy, the Netherlands, Belgium) must therefore keep an eye on Euro-aggregates denominated in their respective currencies and/or on short-term Euro-currency transactions of their domestic nonbanks.
– Even if Euro-currency deposits are not counted as monetary liabilities, their growth can be relevant from the viewpoint of domestic reserve targeting, since they may be held as substitutes for reserve-carrying time deposits held with the domestic banking system.
– The sharp acceleration of inflation and the upward shift in nominal and real interest rates since the mid-1970s have induced firms and households

to economise on their holdings of cash and non-interest bearing demand deposits in order to limit the erosion of the real value of their liquid assets. Traditional distinctions between money and quasi-money have therefore been blurred both at the national and Euro-currency level.

— Innovations in the field of payments technology, notably the electronic transfer of funds, are increasingly enabling sophisticated cash managers of multinational companies to convert "overnight" Euro-deposits quickly and without significant cost into checking accounts at commercial banks located in an issuing country of a Euro-currency. In other words: certain Euro-deposits can now virtually be held as transactions balances.

II. *Euro-System Specific Portfolio Analysis*

8. The apparent shortcomings of simplified approaches to Euro-market analysis have given rise to systematic attempts to describe and explain the behaviour of the Euro-system on the basis of more complex disaggregated portfolio models which take the specific features of Euro-banking into account. Empirical work done in this field in recent years has included single equation approaches for estimating global nonbank demands for Euro-deposits, simultaneous testing of asset demand functions for certain types of Euro-loans and Euro-deposits, closer analysis of the pivotal role which the large interbank portion of the Euro-market plays for the smooth functioning of the whole system, and explanations of the observed links between Euro-currency interest rates and key domestic money market rates. The earlier more simplistic quantitative conceptions of the Euro-market may thus be regarded as "reduced" special cases of a fully-fledged portfolio model of the Euro-currency system.

9. Given the complexity of the Euro-currency market, an empirically testable complete structural model of its functioning is, of course, not within reach. Nevertheless, the newly evolving approach could have a certain appeal to central bankers, since it helps them to formulate their concerns and policy prescriptions in a consistent and analytically acceptable framework. Most officials would probably agree today that the money- and credit-creating power of the Euro-market cannot be properly assessed, if the market is regarded as a segmented, independently operating closed banking system. Arbitrage transactions by banks and large multinational companies establish strong links between key Euro-rates and corresponding domestic money market rates and they maintain interest parity through instantaneous forward cover adjustments between the various Euro-currency interest rates. Euro-banking can therefore hardly be regarded as an isolated autono-

mous source of monetary expansion, disequilibrating capital flows, or exchange rate pressures.

10. On the other hand, the Euro-banking system undeniably enjoys comparative advantages and preferences, which favour its activities. These may grow over time as national regulatory arrangements change, the opportunities offered by the system are more widely recognised, and economic or political events favour a shift of nonbank loan and deposit demands to the Euro-currency market. These special features of Euro-banking, which in part directly concern the monetary authorities, should be appropriately allowed for in policy-oriented efforts to model the activities of the Euromarket. The distinguishing characteristics of the market to be considered in this context may be classified tentatively as follows:

(a) *Self-Generated Competitive Advantages*

Many attractions of Euro-banking business originate from well-known market properties which reduce Euro banks' transaction costs and make particular groups of international clients turn to the Euro-market. One may mention here explicitly

- the efficiency of wholesale banking and the specialisation of Euro-banks in international lending, trade financing and currency portfolio management;
- cross-country risk pooling through the Euro-interbank market or syndicated loan arrangements in which the largest banks operating on a worldwide scale take a stake;
- favourable geographical location;
  anonymity and freedom of the Euro-market system from political interference with loan arrangements and deposit management;
- financial innovations offered by the Euro-market, such as roll-over credits, international CDs, "zero-bonds" and "floating-rate" lending arrangements.

(b) *Windfall Privileges*

Other competitive inequalities strengthening the position of Euro-banks result largely from their ability to evade national control and legislative arrangements and, in part, give them significant pecuniary advantages over national banking systems. Domestic financial burdens and constraints which Euro-banking escapes notably exclude:

- compulsory reserve requirements,

−interest rate ceilings on domestic or foreign deposits,
−direct credit controls,
−legally binding prudential rules,
−income and other national taxes.

(c) *Clientele Demands and Preferences*

Given the comparative advantages which Euro-banks can bring to bear in their favour, business opportunities for international banking may improve disproportionately over time and even grow dramatically in the aftermath of particular events. The comparatively fast growth of world trade and the increasing internationalisation of nonbanks' financial portfolio management could give the Euro-banking system superior long-run market chances. Temporary increases in international payments imbalances, oil-recycling requirements, needs for "unconditional" large-scale financing of development projects and national budget deficits as well as rising demands for the discreet handling of liquid official reserve portfolios, on the other hand, enable Euro-banks at times to expand their loan and deposit business at an exceptionally fast pace.[1]

11. Taken together, the special characteristics of the Euro-market described in the foregoing offer a variety of explanations, why Euro-banking has been so successful since the early 1970s. This international financial trend had many favourable implications and benefitted the world economy as a whole. But it also produced macroeconomic repercussions which have given rise to concern among central bank and treasury officials, in particular in countries which act as an issuer or a host for an important segment of the Euro-currency market.

B. MONETARY POLICY CONCERNS

12. The attitudes and concerns of policy makers presented in the following are not in all cases fully shared among major central banks. Some of them derive from specific conditions created by particular national policy arrangements. Other arguments have typically attracted attention in certain circumstances, but may become less important in a changing worldwide economic environment.

I. *World Inflation, Balance of Payments Disequilibria, and International Reserve Creation*

13. A variety of policy considerations has been inspired by the apparent macroeconomic repercussions associated with the activities of the Euro-banking system. These are felt to complicate the pursuit of national stabilisation goals and, by the same token, make life of central bankers more difficult. Concerns of this sort have their origin in the Euro-market's potential role as an amplifier of worldwide monetary disturbances from which national monetary policies may be unable to insulate themselves.

14. The sheer *size of the Euro-currency market*, which reached a net volume of about $900 billion towards the end of 1981 and grew at an average annual rate of about 25 per cent since the early 1970s, has seriously disconcerted many central bankers, since Euro-banks' claims and short-term liabilities vis-à-vis nonbanks are not normally included in national credit and money supply measures and objectives. In an age of monetary "targetry", extra-territorial growth of money and credit aggregates – for which no individual central bank feels responsible – may entail a significant degree of collective "slippage" at the world level. This could inadvertently facilitate the monetary accommodation of world inflation, even if national central banks appear to be in full control of their domestic monetary situation.

15. The capacity of the Euro-market for smoothly satisfying the large-scale financing needs of sovereign borrowers at attractive and "soft" terms may in some cases have served to erode national budgetary and balance of payments discipline. By *delaying the external adjustment process*, the activity of Euro-banks may thus have contributed in an indirect manner to exchange crises and international financial disruptions which threatened to "spill over" also to countries which pursued tight domestic monetary and fiscal policies. During the first recycling period (1974-1976), when new syndicated Euro-loans to official borrowers amounted to an annual average of about $20 billion, several larger countries tolerated excessive current account and budget deficits and later had to arrange official "conditional" assistance from the IMF and the EEC under crisis conditions. In the subsequent three years (1977-1979), during which syndicated Euro-lending to sovereign debtors climbed to an annual average of more than $45 billion, "overrecycling" phenomena seem to have been even more in evidence.

16. Another global financial concern associated with Euro-banking has its roots in the *uncontrolled growth of official exchange reserves* over the past decade. In this area the Euro-market has played a dual intermediary function. On the one hand, it facilitates the build-up of officially held "bor-

rowed reserves" due to Euro-banks' generous lending to sovereign borrowers. In recent years loans to public institutions amounted to about 75 per cent of Euro-banks' total syndicated lending. On the other hand, Euro-banks offer official reserve holders inconspicuous and profitable investment outlets. At the end of 1981, official currency reserves to the tune of $100 billion were held in the Euro-market (of which more than $70 billion in Euro-dollars and close to $20 billion in Euro-deutschemarks). Euro-market investments thus accounted for about one quarter of total world currency reserves. The unconstrained use and "reshuffling" of these reserves, which can be most easily arranged in the Euro-market, is felt by some to constitute a potential source of global monetary disturbance.

II. *Destabilising Capital Flows and Exchange Rate Disturbances*

17. The Euro-currency market acts as a powerful international intermediary today which efficiently links all important domestic financial centres. By offering financial arbitrage opportunities at an increasing scale to commercial banks, traders, international investors and large corporations across national borders, it has undoubtedly served as a vehicle or accelerator of international financial integration over the past 10 to 15 years. In performing this "catalyst" role, the Euro-market promotes the rapid transmission of internationally relevant economic and political information. At the same time it offers unique facilities for short-term borrowing in various currencies and diversification of liquid international currency portfolios. This enables internationally oriented asset holders to quickly and extensively "reshuffle" the composition of their currency holdings in response to relevant news.

18. The indicated properties of the Euro-market will rarely act as an autonomous source of global monetary turmoil. Exchange rate pressures are normally initiated through uncoordinated domestic policy actions, unanticipated swings in current account balances, changes in inflation differentials and other economic and political surprises. Nevertheless, by reinforcing the international impact of such events, the Euro-currency market is likely to increase the speed and size of short-term international capital movements and exchange rate adjustments and, in this way, it may effectively reduce the autonomy of domestic monetary management in relatively small and open economies.

19. It is tempting to relate the Euro-market's potential for propagating information and promoting the "reshuffling" of currency portfolios to the wide fluctuations of "real" exchange rates since the general transition to a floating rate regime in 1973. Exchange rate movements have apparently

been dominated by financial portfolio adjustments over extended periods of time. "Real" exchange rates thus have tended to deviate quite substantially from their long-run "equilibrium" adjustment path or their "warranted" trend deemed appropriate by policy-makers in the light of economic fundamentals. Between 1978 and early 1982 the Japanese yen and the D-mark depreciated by 22 per cent and 11 per cent respectively in real terms, while the US dollar and sterling experienced real appreciations of 22 per cent and 32 per cent. Using the "purchasing power parity" theorem as a rough and ready yardstick, which "explains" the long-run behaviour of the DM/Swiss franc rate reasonably well, these two smaller reserve currencies apparently appreciated excessively against the US dollar after the mid-1970s, and they lost considerable ground during the past few years (Annex 3). Faced with such disturbances central banks outside the United States often had to accept heavy exchange rate shocks, which threatened to jeopardise the achievement of their domestic stabilisation goals, or they drastically changed their domestic monetary stance in order to mitigate excessive exchange rate fluctuations.

III. *Erosion of Domestic Monetary Targeting*

20. The expatriation of domestic credit and monetary aggregates into the Euro-system, which may cause collective monetary targeting errors at the world level (see para. 14 above), is a matter of immediate concern for those countries issuing an important Euro-currency or performing a host function for a large sector of the Euro-market. Their position is complicated if the use of particular monetary instruments (such as minimum reserve requirements, interest rate regulations, or credit ceilings) provides incentives to Euro banks to set "privileged" lending or deposit rates in the Euro-sector of the individual currency concerned. This will tend to attract domestic borrowers or deposit holders into the Euro-market. Similarly, familiar rigidities in "cartelised" domestic interest rate adjustments may temporarily cause significant nonbank sector "circular flows" between the home and the Euro-market, since Euro-banks normally bring their "libor"-based short-term lending and deposit rates quickly into line with key interest rates in national money markets.[2]

21. Deposit and credit disintermediation flows can induce offsetting international arbitrage transactions in the interbank market. "Circular flows" may thus be perfectly symmetrical and therefore leave no lasting impact on the exchange rate. Nevertheless, they are likely to complicate the implementation of quantitative monetary objectives in several respects:

(a) If a significant portion of the domestic demand for money and credit is met in the Euro-market, *familiar macroeconomic relationships* between policy goal variables (e.g. incomes and prices) and conventional monetary aggregates may be *destabilised*, and movements in the latter could give misleading signals to monetary policy makers.

(b) Central banks may no longer be able to exercise appropriate control over their *operating variables* in the domestic money market. *"Reserve multipliers"* could become unstable, if Euro-bank activities lead to unforeseeable reductions in banks' demand for cash assets (see para. 5, section (b) above). If, on the other hand, short-term interest rates are systematically manipulated by the central bank, the authorities may have difficulties in setting them at correct levels. The *interest-rate elasticities* of money and credit demands are likely to change, as long as extra-territorial money aggregates grow rapidly and are priced at "privileged" interest rates. As a consequence familiar interest rate relationships may no longer serve as a guide for efficiently controlling monetary aggregates.

(c) Changes in *policy instruments*, such as compulsory reserve ratios or credit ceilings, may *reinforce "circular flow"* phenomena. Central banks might accordingly not be able to use their familiar most powerful quantitative weapons in an efficient way.

IV. *Macro-Prudential Risks and Lender of Last Resort Obligations*

22. Official supervisory authorities and internationally operating banks themselves have long been recognising that international banking is prone to large specific risks. During the period from around the mid-1970s up to the present a wide measure of agreement seems to have been achieved that some or all of the following potential sources of fragility of the international banking network deserve close attention:

- country or transfer risks (the case of Turkey or Poland),
- excessive foreign exchange exposure (or "Herstatt symptoms"),
- maturity mismatching (which may cause unexpected interest losses),
- earnings or capital inadequacy (due to competition pressure on "spreads"),
- lack of Euro-market-specific lender of last resort facilities.

23. While it may be left to national supervisory authorities to ensure the soundness or solvency of individual banking institutions, monetary policy makers feel called upon also to look into these matters, because any mate-

rialising of international banking risks could entail far-reaching macroeconomic and monetary implications. It has been noted that individual Euro-banks may tend to overlook the actual size of country or transformation risks born by the international banking system as a whole. Such risks may be widely distributed among banks due to the complex linkages established through the Euro-interbank network with individual institutions regarding their interbank claims always as highly liquid or sound. Similarly, banks may be overly complacent about their funding risks, since the Euro-interbank and national money markets have up till now always been satisfying all liquidity needs with individual institutions of a normal standing hardly encountering any serious difficulty.

C. POLICY RESPONSES

24. The articulate expression of various kinds of monetary policy unrest arising from the rapid expansion of the Euro-currency market – which reflects an improving understanding of its functioning (cf. paras. 8-11 above) – has inspired a rather sophisticated line of thinking about the ways in which policy should respond. In principle, the authorities seem to be ready to pair the various identified sources and areas of concern with specific policy measures and solutions. In practice, the scope for differentiated policy action appears to be quite limited, however, and it has been observed that any type of intervention dampening the growth of Euro-banking might serve simultaneously to reduce the "catalyst" role of the Euro-market in the transmission of international currency disturbances, decelerate the expatriation of domestic credit and money stock components, and limit the concentration of risks associated with international banking activities. The following sections discuss indiscriminately specific as well as multi-purpose types of policy measures which the monetary authorities of major industrial countries have either seriously considered or actually taken in recent years to tackle the macroeconomic problems created by the explosive growth of Euro-banking.

I. *Possible Routes of Collective Action*

Co-ordinated Domestic Monetary Management
25. Conventional "Euro-multiplier" analyses as well as the international interest rate linkages emphasised in portfolio-theoretic conceptions of Euro-currency market behaviour have been cited to support the view that an "ex-

cessive'' growth of Euro-banking could, perhaps, be prevented, if monetary policies in the larger industrial countries were consistently tight. Historic events such as the phasing out of capital export controls in the United States in 1974, the expansionary monetary policy pursued by the Federal Reserve System in subsequent years and the sharp widening of the US balance of payments deficit in 1977/78, indeed, appeared to provide some empirical evidence that policy-induced ''supply pressures'' might have contributed to the fast growth of the Euro-dollar sector during those years. Temporary squeezes on ''spreads'' also seemed to prove that market growth might have been promoted by supply-side factors. The suggestion has therefore been made that major central banks should collectively pursue comparatively restrictive policies to contain the growth of the Euro-currency system in a subtle and market-oriented way.

26. Both the relevance and the feasibility of such a policy approach have been seriously questioned. The basic reasoning on which it builds takes little account of the special advantages and ''privileges'' which favour the growth of Euro-banking. In this context it is interesting to recall that Euro-aggregates grew more than twice as fast as the corresponding domestic monetary aggregates during 1974-1979: Euro-bank lending and broadly defined monetary liabilities in the Euro-currency market rose, on average, by almost 30 per cent annually while comparable domestic aggregates in industrialised countries expanded only at rates of between 10-15 per cent. Moreover, a co-ordination of national monetary policy objectives is notoriously difficult, and it would be hard to decide which contribution individual countries should make to restraining the activity of Euro-banks from the demand and supply side.

Ceilings on International Bank Lending

27. Going to the opposite extreme, jointly adopted administrative measures – such as capital import controls and quantitative ceilings on Euro-lending – have also been proposed to limit the room for manoeuvre of the international banking system. Central banks from larger countries, notably those acting as an issuer or host of a Euro-currency, have, however, come to the conclusion that such steps could hardly be efficiently implemented and, above all, that they would be inconsistent with market economy and free competition principles.

Abolition or Reduction of Windfall Privileges

28. Such principal objections have not been raised against various proposals aiming at an internationally co-ordinated removal of unjustifiable in-

equalities of competitive conditions which seem to have nourished the growth of Euro-banking. Steps of this kind would at the same time abolish obstacles to the efficient use of particular instruments of monetary policy, remove distorting competitive advantages which large private and sovereign borrowers with easy access to the "wholesale" Euro-credit market enjoy, and improve prudential standards in international banking. But there is a fundamental difficulty standing in the way of rapid progress in this field. It arises from the fact that national *instruments of monetary management* and their current use, *banking legislation* notably with respect to minimum capital and liquidity requirements as well as *tax regulations* would have to be harmonised in a large group of countries. This is not only necessary in order to eradicate as far as possible all existing artificial incentives to Euro-banking business; it would also serve to avoid the unintentional creation of new competitive distortions that might be associated with "harmonisation" efforts (e.g. the introduction of a reserve requirement on Euro-deposits) which took no account of differences in regulations governing domestic banking activities. Historically rooted differences in domestic financial structures and institutional arrangements, opposing economic policy principles and preferences, and diverging national interests – which do not necessarily coincide in issuing, host and mere user countries of Euro-currencies – make it a rather complex task to achieve international agreement on uniform harmonisation procedures, even if such efforts were confined to the most relevant areas of concern.

29. A revealing illustration of these difficulties was provided by the outcome of extensive discussions that major central banks held in 1979/80 over a proposal by the United States authorities for compulsory minimum *reserve requirements on Euro-currency deposits* on a global consolidated basis. Hardly anybody doubted that growth of the Euro-dollar and Euro-deutschemark sectors of the international currency market has been aided by the existence of domestic compulsory reserve systems in the United States and Germany on the one hand, and the lack of such requirements in the Euro-market on the other. Due to these inequalities (which work out differently in both cases due to the divergent treatment of borrowing from banks abroad), deposit rates for three-month Euro-dollars have tended to exceed comparable domestic rates by up to 100 basis points in recent years (Annex 4), while three-month Euro-deutschemark deposits have been quoted around 50 basis points below corresponding German interbank funds (Annex 5). The Euro-dollar market has therefore been highly attractive to US nonbank depositors, while internationally operating banks were able to offer favourable lending rates to German borrowers in the Euro-currency mar-

ket. The resulting expatriation of domestic money and credit aggregates has, at times, complicated the task of domestic monetary management in the countries concerned. Given the worldwide financial services that both countries provide to the international community by issuing and guarding important reserve and investment currencies, the United States and Germany saw some justification for asking their trading partners to agree to the introduction of a uniform Euro-reserve requirement in order to preserve the effectiveness of their monetary policies. Other countries, where compulsory reserves are unknown, have been opposed to such proposals on grounds of principle. They expected new inequalities to arise, if reserve requirements had only been imposed at the Euro-market level while local-currency bank liabilities were left free from such requirements in their home markets. Needless to say, the predictable legal and administrative complications, the danger of evasion of Euro-business to "exotic" centres and the expected reporting burdens on banks were also cited in support of some countries' doubts concerning the efficacy and feasibility of a Euro-reserve requirement.

II. *National Policy Reactions*

30. Given the limited scope for worldwide concerted action on Euro-market problems, a number of countries have taken defensive steps at the national level to shield their domestic monetary policies as far as possible from undesired international influences. Economies not fully integrated in international financial markets have in many cases resorted to familiar administrative measures by introducing capital controls or managing a dual exchange rate system. Larger open economies, notably those issuing or sheltering a Euro-currency, have found new solutions to reconcile in some degree the pursuit of quantitative domestic monetary objectives with external concerns. The following sections report on some recent developments in this field.

Explicit Allowance for Exchange Rate Constraints

31. Virtually all countries outside the United States, which adopted formal monetary targeting practices since the mid-1970s, saw their new policy approaches sooner or later eroded or falling under severe strain, because "unwarranted" real exchange rate movements threatened to jeopardise the achievement of domestic stabilisation objectives. Excessive currency appreciations weakened countries' price competitiveness, dampened investment propensities in export-oriented industries and reinforced recessionary devel-

opments. Excessive exchange rate depreciations stimulated domestic inflation and tended to undermine confidence in the longer-run stability of the
currencies that had come under pressure. In a number of cases the monetary
authorities first attempted to firmly pursue their domestic monetary objectives, but later sought to stabilise the exchange rate by adjusting their domestic interest rates even if this entailed an obvious loss of credibility of their
quantitative monetary objectives. The most conspicuous examples were
cases of severe monetary "overshooting" associated with excessive currency
appreciation (Germany 1977/78, Switzerland 1978, United Kingdom 1980).

32. Learning from these experiences, central banks now seem to be prepared to solve such conflict situations in a systematic and forward-looking
manner. They explicitly associate their domestic monetary targets with
longer-run exchange rate considerations while attempting to preserve public
confidence in the soundness of their overall stabilisation course. Since 1979,
the German central bank specifies external and internal conditions under
which the authorities are prepared to deliberately deviate from the mid-point
path of their annual target ranges for the growth of the central bank money
stock. In Switzerland, the authorities warned the public in 1981 in advance
that an "undershooting" of their monetary target might be desirable in
order to stop the downward movement of the Swiss franc and prevent a further acceleration of domestic inflation. Similarly, the British monetary
authorities have made it known that the behaviour of the exchange rate is
a consideration which will be given due weight in implementing monetary
policy.

Monitoring of Composite Domestic and Euro-Currency Aggregates

33. In order to avoid inadvertent mis-specification of monetary target variables or mis-reading of movements in domestic monetary indicators, major
central banks have begun to monitor composite monetary aggregates, in
which conventional domestic credit and money stock measures are combined with Euro-currency components which are likely to owe their existence to artificially induced expatriation or "circular flow" phenomena.
Not surprisingly the United States and — with a lesser degree of urgency —
Germany have taken the lead in systematically devising such wider monetary constructs. Already during the year 1978 short-term Euro-dollar liabilities held by US nonbanks are estimated to have risen at a rate equivalent to
about 1 per cent of the traditional basic US money supply (M1). This clearly
constituted a "threshold" level at which the monetary authorities could no
longer assume that domestically defined monetary aggregates continuously
provided a reliable guide for target-oriented monetary policies. In Germany,

the volatile replacement of domestic short-term bank borrowing by the private sector through short-term Euro-currency loans has in recent years more or less eroded the significance of short-term domestic credit expansion as a supplementary monetary indicator (Annex 6). Moreover, since early 1981 growth of Euro-currency deposits in the hands of German nonbanks also approached a "sensitivity threshold". Such extra-territorial money holdings temporarily expanded at an annual rate of about 1 per cent in relation to the domestic money stock.

34. The authorities in the two countries most seriously affected by Euromarket disintermediation are now continuously looking at indicators which are supplemented by the relevant Euro-currency components:

— Overnight Euro-dollars issued by Caribbean branches of US banks to US residents are included in the revised broader US money stock M2, while term Euro-dollars are additionally incorporated in the Federal Reserve's new liquid assets measure "L".
— For internal monitoring purposes, the Bundesbank adds a fictitious domestic minimum reserve equivalent, which is imposed on German nonbanks' Euro-currency holdings outside the Federal Republic, to the central bank money stock and watches a combined indicator of short-term bank borrowing by the private sector at home and in the Euro-market.

35. It would be rash to conclude that such statistical adjustments constituted a satisfactory policy solution. Data on Euro-aggregates become partly available only with considerable delay and their behaviour can hardly be predicted with confidence. Moreover, in order to allow for the growth in Euro-aggregates, bank reserve or interest rate pressures will have to be kept disproportionately high in the domestic money market to take account of base money savings and "privileged" underpricing of loans on the part of the Euro-banking system. This puts a discriminatory burden on domestic credit institutions and smaller nonbanks with little or no access to Euromarket facilities. The ensuing competitive and allocational distortions could clearly become significant if expatriated Euro-aggregates continued to grow at disproportionately high rates.

Repatriation of "Privileged" International Banking

36. A defensive national step specifically designed to attract Eurobanking business away from "exotic" centres back into the local financial market was taken by the United States in December 1981. Banks in New York City were allowed to establish so-called International Banking Facili-

tics (IBFs) which are permitted to conduct deposit and lending business with non-residents under "privileged" conditions. This includes freedom from domestic minimum reserve requirements, interest rate limitations and state and local taxes. From a national monetary policy point of view the measure could have the advantage that international banking business that would otherwise have been conducted elsewhere – outside or inside the United States – will now be geographicaly concentrated in the home market and thus become more transparent. On the other hand, given the conspicuous inequalities between interest rates offered to non-residents and resident US nonbanks, large US corporations might feel encouraged to discover mays and means of placing funds at preferential terms with IBFs.

37. In a global perspective, the measure taken by the United States might in the long run turn out to be counter-productive. Since it tends to perpetuate and possibly enlarge Euro-market-type inequalities, other larger countries might be tempted to "retaliate" and follow the US example. This could provide additional artificial incentives to international banking on a global scale and permit borrowers and depositors to utilise the new facilities "cross-wise": domestic US banking business might begin to emigrate at an even faster pace into other financial centres with highly attractive new IBFs, while the United States might increasingly attract regular domestic banking business from other industrial countries.

CONCLUDING REMARKS

38. The spectacular expansion of Euro-banking since the beginning of the last decade reflected growing international trade and increasing world financial integration. International banking was also favoured by specific demands for international financial services associated with two oil price shocks, large-scale international budget financing and unusual world payments imbalances. Moreover, growth of the Euro-currency system was facilitated by inequalities in national monetary arrangements, prudential rules and tax legislation. This accorded substantial pecuniary "privileges" to Euro-banks and their clientele. The beneficial influence of the smoothly functioning international banking system on the world economy must clearly be recognised. However, with the growing importance of international bank lending and the disproportionate widening of Euro-currency markets the potential weaknesses of the system and its global implications for monetary stability and inflation control have become more apparent. It would, undoubtedly, be counter-productive to subject the system to undue adminis-

trative and regulatory constraints. But in the longer run the market may well need some degree of internationally coordinated guidance or monitoring with a view to containing its global monetary repercussions and dormant macro-prudential risks. If international banking and currency markets continue to expand with unrestrained speed, it will become self-evident at some stage that "Euro-money does neither supervise nor manage itself".

NOTES

1. At times, the increasing willingness or ability of particular national banking systems to diversify their portfolios by moving into the Euro-banking business seems to have favoured the growth of the Euro-currency market from the supply side, as "newcomers" offered innovative or more competitive international banking services.

2. In the case of Germany, this factor played a more important role than changes in reserve requirements (or the existence of reserve requirements on domestic bank liabilities) in recent years in explaining fluctuations in the German corporate sector's borrowing in the Euro-deutschemark market (see Annexes 5 and 6).

ANNEX 1

Table 1. *Alternative measures of the Euro-market and of international bank lending (BIS-concepts) (in $ billions)*

End of year or quarter	Euro-currency market		International bank lending	
	Gross	Net[1]	Gross[2]	Net[3]
1969	57	44	—	—
1970	75	57	—	—
1971	98	71	—	—
1972	132	92	196	—
1973[4]	192	132	290	(180)
1974	222	177	361	220
1975	259	205	442	260
1976	311	247	548	330
1977[5]	396	300	690	430
1978[5]	511	377	893	535
1979	666	475	1,111	665
1980 March	676	493	1,117	680
June	728	537	1,206	745
September	742	551	1,248	775
December	801	575	1,322	810
1981 March	809	590	1,349	820
June	792	588	1,347	825
September	821	623	1,423	875
December	892	662	1,542	940

1. Adjusted for interbank transactions.
2. Foreign assets in domestic and foreign currencies of banks in European BIS reporting area, Canada, Japan and the United States including certain offshore branches of US banks.
3. Adjusted for double-counting due to interbank transactions within the reporting area.
4. New series.
5. Break in series.

Source: BIS.

Table 2. Alternative measures of international bank lending and gross size of extended Euro-currency market (Bank of England estimates)

Gross measures of international banking[1]; in $ billions: amounts outstanding

	Lending by banks in the BIS reporting area to non-residents in:		Lending by banks in offshore centres to non-residents[2]	Total lending to non-residents (1+2+3)	Lending by banks in the BIS reporting area in foreign currencies to residents[3]	Gross size of the Euro-currency banking market (1+3+5)	Swiss trustee accounts	Total international bank lending (4+5+7) or (2+6+7)
	Foreign currency	Domestic currency						
	1	2	3	4	5	6	7	8
End-December 1977	422	177	168	767	151	741	30	948
End-December 1979	701	282	263	1,246	242	1,205	53	1,540
End-September 1981	886	369	387	1,642	360	1,633	88	2,089

1. There are minor breaks in some of the series. The figures for different dates are affected by changes in the dollar value of non-dollar currencies.
2. Comprising *branches of US banks* in the Bahamas, the Cayman Islands, Panama, Lebanon, Hong Kong and Singapore (for all of which figures are reported to the BIS) together with estimates for non-reporting banks in these centres and all banks in Bahrain and the Netherlands Antilles. The business is assumed to be all in foreign currency.
3. Excluding lending by banks in the United States, which is believed to be negligible.

Source: Bank of England.

ANNEX 2. DERIVATION OF EURO-MONEY MULTIPLIERS*

I. *Simple Money Multiplier: The Basic Model*

$(1)\quad B = C + R$

$(2)\quad M = C + D$

$(3)\quad R = r \cdot D$

$(4)\quad C = c \cdot M$

B:	Monetary base
C:	Currency in circulation
R:	Bank reserves
M:	Domestic money stock
D:	Domestic (demand and time) deposits
r:	Reserve ratio
c:	Currency ratio

Substitution of (4) and (3) into (1) gives:

$(5)\quad B = c \cdot M + r \cdot D$

Utilizing (2) equation (5) can be written as:

$(5')\quad B = (c + r(1 - c)) \cdot M$

or

$(6)\quad M = \dfrac{1}{c + r(1 - c)} \cdot B$

where the *money multiplier* is given by

$(7)\quad \dfrac{M}{B} = \dfrac{1}{c + r(1 - c)}$

or, rearranging (7):

$(7')\quad \dfrac{M}{B} = \dfrac{1}{1 - (1 - r)(1 - c)}$

---

* I am indebted to Dr. Friedmann from the Bundesbank's research staff for preparing this Annex.

II. *Primary or Initial Deposit Multiplier: The Flow Approach*

$$(8) \quad D = D_{NB} + ER$$

$$(9) \quad M^* = D_{NB} + ED$$

$$(10) \quad ER = r_E \cdot ED$$

$$(11) \quad D_{NB} = q \cdot M^*$$

Substitution of (11) and (10) under consideration of (9) into (8) gives:

$$(12) \quad D = qM^* + r_E (1 - q) M^*$$

or

$$(12') \quad D = (q + r_E (1 - q)) M^*$$

or

$$(13) \quad M^* = \frac{1}{q + r_E (1 - q)} D$$

or

$$(13') \quad M^* = \frac{1}{1 - (1 - r_E) (1 - q)} D$$

Where the *total-deposit multiplier* is given by:

$$(14) \quad \frac{M^*}{D} = \frac{1}{q + r_E (1 - q)} = \frac{1}{1 - (1 - r_E) (1 - q)}$$

D:	Deposits with the domestic banking system
D_{NB}:	Deposits of non-banks with the domestic banking system
ER:	Reserves of Euro-banks in the form of deposits with the domestic banking system
M^*:	Nonbanks' deposits with domestic banks and Euro-banks
ED:	Euro-deposits of nonbanks
r_E:	Reserve ratio for Euro-deposits
q:	"Leakage" coefficient

The formal structure of (14) is obviously identical with the Simple Money Multiplier relations (7) and (7') respectively. The *Primary or Initial (Euro-) Deposit Multiplier* can be obtained from (14), if equations (9) and (8) are interpreted as first differences with a zero national component, so that substituting

$$\Delta M^* = \Delta ED \quad \text{and} \quad \Delta D = \Delta ER \quad \text{into (14) gives}$$

$$(15) \quad \frac{\Delta ED}{\Delta ER} = \frac{1}{q + r_E (1 - q)} = \frac{1}{1 - (1 - r_E) (1 - q)}$$

This interpretation of the Primary or Initial (Euro-) Deposit Multiplier within the familiar simple money multiplier framework clearly indicates that this particular model is based on a *partial* equilibrium assumption (flow approach), whereas the regular multiplier approach can be seen as a full equilibrium approach (stock approach). (In the line of this argument: see M. Willms, "Money Creation in the Euro-Currency Market", *Weltwirtschaftliches Archiv*, Vol. 112 (1976), p. 209).

III. *Bank-Reserve Multiplier in a Two-Stage Banking System: The Stock Approach*

The relationship between Euro-banks' reserves in the form of deposits with the domestic banking system and the volume of Euro-deposits of nonbanks

$$(10) \quad ER = r_E \cdot ED$$

can be transformed into the multiplier relation

$$(16) \quad ED = 1/r_E \cdot ER$$

where

$$(17) \quad \frac{ED}{ER} = \frac{1}{r_E}$$

is the *Two-Stage Bank Reserve Multiplier* for Euro-deposits.

Note: Leakages can be seen as reductions of ER within the context of this simple two stage stock model.

IV. *Bank-Reserve Multiplier in a Three-Stage Banking System*

$$(18) \quad R = RD + RE$$

$$(8) \quad D = D_{NB} + ER$$

$$(9) \quad M^* = D_{NB} + ED$$

$$(10) \quad ER = r_E \cdot ED$$

R: Total reserves of the domestic banking system

RD: Bank reserves against deposits of residents with the domestic banking system

RE: Bank reserves against deposits of Euro-banks with the domestic banking system

(19) $RD = r_1 \cdot D_{NB}$

(20) $RE = r_2 \cdot ER$

(11) $D_{NB} = q \cdot M^*$

r_1: Reserve ratio on deposits of residents with the domestic banking system

r_2: Reserve ratio on deposits of Euro-banks with domestic banks

Substitution of equation (10) into (20) gives:

(20′) $RE = r_2 \cdot r_E \cdot ED.$

By means of (20′) and (19) equation (18) can be transformed into:

(21) $R = r_1 \cdot D_{NB} + r_2 \cdot r_E \cdot ED;$

utilizing (11) and (9) equation (21) can be rewritten:

(22) $R = (r_1 \cdot q + r_2 \cdot r_E (1 - q)) M^*$

or

(23) $M^* = \dfrac{1}{r_1 \cdot q + r_2 \cdot r_E (1 - q)} R$

where

(24) $\dfrac{M^*}{R} = \dfrac{1}{r_1 \cdot q + r_2 \cdot r_E (1 - q)}$

is the *Three-Stage Bank-Reserve-Multiplier* of nonbanks' total (domestic as well as Euro-) deposits.

V. *Base-Money Multiplier*

(1′) $B = C + RD + RE$

(8) $D = D_{NB} + ER$

(9′) $ME = C + D_{NB} + ED$

(19) $RD = r_1 \cdot D_{NB}$

ME: Domestic money stock, extended by Euro-deposits of nonbank residents

(20)　$RE = r_2 \cdot ER$

(10)　$ER = r_E \cdot ED$

(11')　$D_{NB} = q \cdot ME$

(4')　$C = c \cdot ME$

Substitution of (4'), (19), (10) and (20) into (1') gives:

(21')　$B = c \cdot ME + r_1 \cdot D_{NB} + r_2 \cdot r_E \cdot ED$

which can be rewritten with respect to (11'), (9') and (4') as follows

(22')　$B = (c + r_1 q + r_2 r_E (1 - c - q)) \cdot ME$

or

(23')　$ME = \dfrac{1}{c + r_1 q + r_2 r_E (1 - c - q)} \cdot B$

where

(24')　$\dfrac{ME}{B} = \dfrac{1}{c + r_1 q + r_2 r_E (1 - c - q)}$

is the *Base-Money Multiplier* of nonbanks' total deposits.

ANNEX 3. LONGER-TERM COMPARATIVE TRENDS IN THE MONEY STOCK, INFLATION RATES AND EXCHANGE RATES

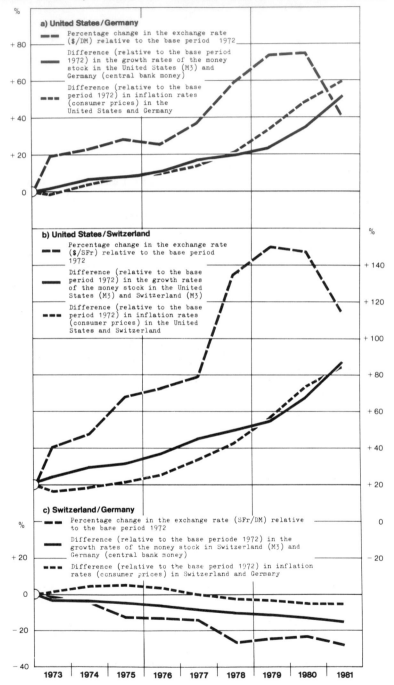

ANNEX 4. INTEREST RATE DIFFERENTIAL BETWEEN THE US MARKET AND THE EURO-DOLLAR MARKET

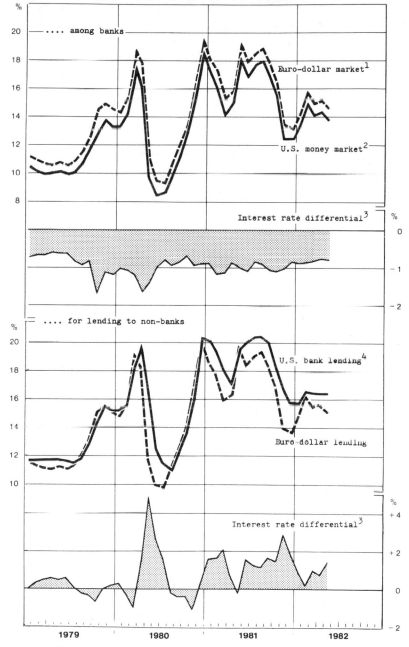

1 Rates for three-month funds.   2 Certificates of Deposit.
3 U.S. market above Euro-dollar market.   4 Prime Rate.

ANNEX 5. INTEREST RATE DIFFERENTIAL BETWEEN THE DOMESTIC MARKET AND THE EURO-DM MARKET

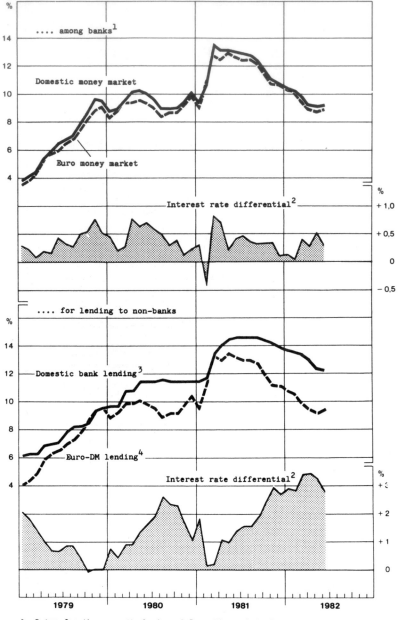

1 Rates for three-month funds. 2 Domestic market above
Euro-market. 3 Rates for credit in current account of
DM 1 million and over but less than DM 5 million.
4 With maturity of three months.

ANNEX 6. SHORT-TERM LENDING TO PRIVATE DOMESTIC NONBANKS (SEASONALLY ADJUSTED)

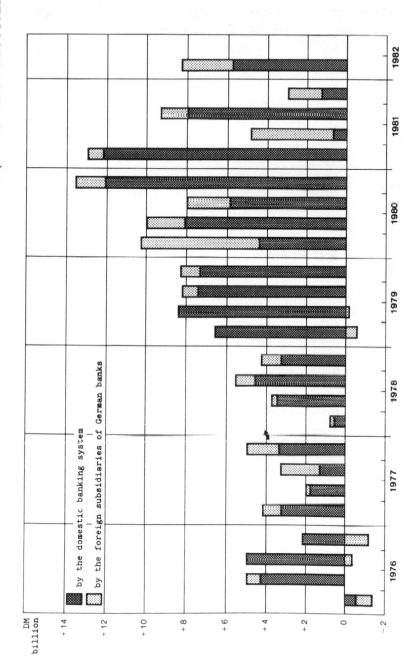

Chapter VIII

INTERNATIONAL CAPITAL FLOWS, EXCHANGE RATES AND DOMESTIC MONETARY POLICY*

by *Adrian Blundell-Wignall* and *Jean-Claude Chouraqui*

A. INTRODUCTION

Under the Bretton Woods system exchange rates were essentially fixed and were adjusted only periodically to correct fundamental balance of payments disequilibrium. Central banks were required to buy or sell domestic currency on the exchange market at the pre-determined rate. Net capital flows were thought mainly to depend on interest rate differentials and, in the relatively stable decades of the 1950s and 1960s, were not accorded much importance in the analysis of economists or in the priorities of policy-makers. This situation changed during the 1970s, however, after a period of large US payments deficits and the withdrawal of the convertibility of the dollar into gold. The international monetary system came under hitherto unknown pressures and the final attempts to maintain fixed parities failed largely because national authorities found that it had become increasingly difficult to reconcile external and internal objectives.

The purpose of this paper is to assess the relationship between domestic monetary policy and capital flows in a situation where exchange rates may be permitted to float. In section B a brief summary of events throughout the 1970s is presented. In section C, the ways in which economists have attempted to analyse the relationships between capital flows, money and exchange rates are discussed. In section D the main conflicts in policy objectives that arise are set out. Finally, in section E, possible implications for current policy making are summarized.

* The present paper reflects the opinions of the authors and does not purport to represent those of the institution (OECD) to which they belong. It has benefited from comments by Val Koromzay. The authors are responsible for any remaining errors and omissions.

B. CAPITAL FLOWS, INTEREST RATES AND EXCHANGE RATES: HISTORICAL OVERVIEW

Chart 1 shows the growth of the broad money, net capital flows and the balance for official settlements for the major seven OECD countries, expressed as a percentage of the lagged money supply over the period 1973 to 1981.[1] With the exception of Japan, where flows have generally fluctuated within a narrow range close to zero, most countries have experienced periods of substantial capital movements. The United States was characterized by substantial outflows until the late 1970s, during which time there had been a sustained interest rate differential against the dollar. Intervention by foreign central banks to support the rapidly deteriorating external value of the dollar during 1978 was followed with similar action by US authorities after the dollar support package of November. Subsequently, both exchange rates and yield differentials have tended to move to a much greater extent, while official intervention has been close to zero.

Its close financial ties with the United States meant that Canada was a substantial importer of US capital through most of the 1970s. Pre-emptive changes in monetary policy rather than intervention have been used to maintain a relative stable exchange rate vis-à-vis the US dollar. Other major OECD economies are not so closely linked with the United States, and policy has frequently varied over time with respect to domestic and external objectives. Net capital inflow declined to be slightly negative in Germany in the years immediately following the switch to floating, but subsequently has tended to fluctuate around zero. Intervention to support the exchange rate has largely reflected movements in current account balances. In the United Kingdom, capital inflows rose very sharply in 1977, following the tightening of domestic monetary policy in response to the exchange rate pressures of 1976. A similar pattern emerged in Italy following periods of severe pressures on the external value of the lira in 1976 and after 1980. Large capital inflows in France have been mainly associated with the emergence of current account deficits, partly as the result of the two oil price shocks (1974, 1980). Intervention has been relatively small in relation to the domestic money supply for much of the period, suggesting that other instruments (interest rates and foreign borrowing) have been used to maintain the relative stability of the franc.

Zero intervention implies that the exchange rate is permitted to find its own level and current and capital accounts offset each other. In this case monetary growth is normally determined by domestic factors. Non-zero intervention allows external factors to influence monetary conditions in an

Chart 1. *Monetary expansion, net capital flows and balance for official settlements*

_____ *Broad money growth*
_ _ _ *Net capital flows*
_ . _*Balance for official settlements*

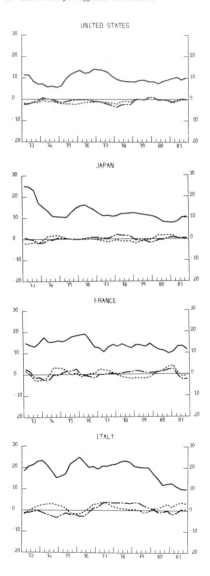

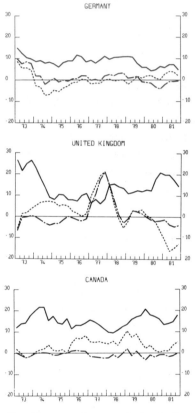

Note: Figures are the sums of quarterly flows over the same quarter one year earlier, expressed as a percentage of the broad money supply at the beginning of the period. The money supply concepts used are: United States, M1; Japan, M2 (+ CD since 1979); Germany, M3; France, M2; United Kingdom, sterling M3; Italy, M2; Canada, M2.
Source: OECD.

ex ante sense, but whether or not this is reflected in observed outcomes will depend on private portfolio behaviour and the (possibly offsetting) actions of the authorities. Most of the countries considered have attempted to meet domestic monetary targets, but at the same time have not wanted interest and exchange rates to move too sharply. Their joint attempts to reconcile possibly conflicting goals with respect to these variables have led to outcomes which are frequently difficult to interpret. For example, during 1977/78 interest rate differentials moved in favour of the dollar; yet it is precisely this period which is associated with a weak external value of the dollar (Chart 2). Similarly, there are no readily observable consistent patterns between current accounts and exchange rates (Chart 3). Any analysis of the interrelationships between capital flows, domestic monetary policy and exchange rates requires detailed empirical analyses with causal relationships in mind. While this is far too ambitious for the present paper, an attempt will be made briefly to spell out how economists have attempted to come to grips with these problems, and to isolate some of the main policy implications.

C. THE ANALYSIS OF CAPITAL FLOWS

1. *Accounting Relationships Between Money and Capital Flows*

Capital inflow is defined to be the net purchase of foreign exchange by the central bank, less the current account of the balance of payments.[2] Such capital inflow may represent net borrowing by the government or the private sector. An ex-ante rise in capital inflow, given the current account, will increase the demand for domestic currency on the exchange markets. If the authorities choose to intervene to fix the exchange rate, the supply of domestic currency will rise by the same amount. If institutional arrangements (e.g. as in the United Kingdom) are such that an inflow to purchase newly-issued government debt substitutes for bank lending to the government, its effects on the monetary base and the broad money supply will be *automatically* "sterilized". The composition of assets held by banks would change towards higher reserves and smaller holdings of government debt with no net impact on monetary aggregates. Otherwise, in the absence of active sterilization policies, the monetary base and the broad money supply will rise by an equivalent amount in the first instance. Subsequent portfolio substitutions within the private sector and/or policy actions by the authorities may alter the final outcome.

152

Chart 2. *Interest rate differentials and exchange rates*

———— *Interest rate differential (left scale)*
— — *Spot exchange rate (right scale)*

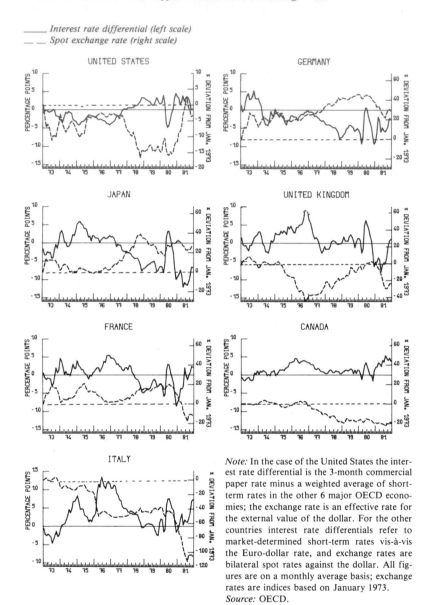

Note: In the case of the United States the interest rate differential is the 3-month commercial paper rate minus a weighted average of short-term rates in the other 6 major OECD economies; the exchange rate is an effective rate for the external value of the dollar. For the other countries interest rate differentials refer to market-determined short-term rates vis-à-vis the Euro-dollar rate, and exchange rates are bilateral spot rates against the dollar. All figures are on a monthly average basis; exchange rates are indices based on January 1973.
Source: OECD.

Chart 3. *Effective exchange rates and current account balances*

– – – – – *Effective exchange rate (left scale)*

Current balance (right scale)

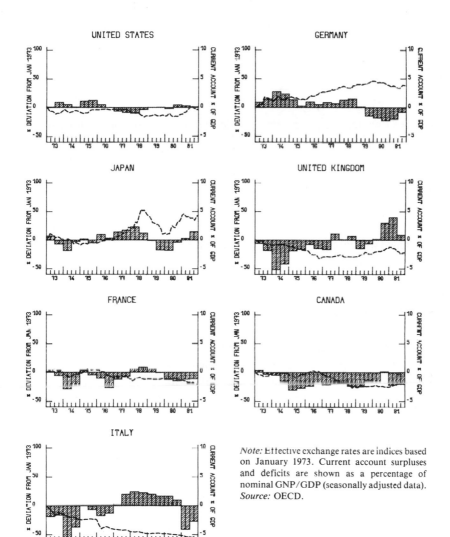

Note: Effective exchange rates are indices based on January 1973. Current account surpluses and deficits are shown as a percentage of nominal GNP/GDP (seasonally adjusted data). *Source:* OECD.

The authorities may also choose not to intervene on the exchange market. In this case an ex ante rise in net capital inflow will cause the actual exchange rate to appreciate to the extent necessary to ensure that the current account and the capital account offset each other. The current account may deteriorate, or the exchange rate may appreciate to a level sufficiently high as to reverse capital inflow through expected depreciation. Between these extremes the authorities may choose partly to intervene and partly to permit the rate to move.

2. *Determinants of Capital Flows and Exchange Rates*

There are two main approaches to the explanation of short-run capital flows:

— the monetary approach, and
— the portfolio balance model.

The monetary approach to short-run capital flows applies to the case of fixed or heavily managed exchange rates, and a relatively small open economy is typically assumed.[3] It is generally agreed that the private sector's demand for money is related to money income and interest rates. The current supply of money, which is influenced by domestic monetary policy actions, may diverge from this demand.[4] If the authorities fix the exchange rate the supply of money may be adjusted to demand by external payments imbalances. This may occur through the current account, to the extent that money affects domestic real demand, but in the short run such adjustments are likely to occur through capital flows. Thus, for example, domestic credit policies that are appreciably more expansionary than those prevailing externally will lead to capital outflows and falling international reserves, possibly putting pressure on the exchange rate. Eventually a change in policy would become necessary. Domestic credit would have to be tightened, or the commitment to fix the exchange rate relaxed.

At an empirical level, the monetary approach has found support in a wide range of countries considered individually.[5] However, when all countries are taken together, the approach may not lead to a predictable relationship between domestic credit expansion and the balance of payments, given the demand for money. For example, if all countries simultaneously expand domestic credit it will not be possible for all to adjust to monetary equilibrium through payments outflows. Other variables, e.g. inflation, would have to adjust. The relationship between domestic credit and the balance of payments comes to depend on the nature of foreign monetary policies and may not, in this sense, lead to stable predictions.

The portfolio balance approach to capital flows is to some extent more general.[6] It is internationally consistent, in the sense that portfolio demands may be defined so that world flows always sum to zero, and many of the results of the monetary approach may be derived from it as a special case. Wealth holders are assumed to diversify their portfolios, holding assets in different currencies depending on expected relative yields, given some allowance for exchange rate risk. That is, the proportion of wealth held in each asset will depend on interest rate differentials, expected exchange rate movements and risk premia on different currencies. Exchange rate expectations are thought mainly to be related to:

– perceived disequilibrium in the level of the real exchange rate, including movements in the relationship between domestic and foreign price levels and the influence of unexpected developments in the current account of the balance of payments, and
– expected inflation differentials.

Movements in the overall holdings of international reserves may also influence expectations about the timing of exchange rate movements.

Under freely floating exchange rate balance of payments flows will not normally be able to influence the money supply. Both of the above approaches to capital flows then provide an explanation of the exchange rate. Under the monetary approach, given that the supply of money cannot adjust through overall payments imbalances, the exchange rate shifts to clear the money market through the price level.[7] In the portfolio balance model the spot exchange rate adjusts in relation to the expected exchange rate (hence affecting the expected rate of depreciation) to ensure that asset demands and supplies are equated. Intervention may be used to reduce the extent to which the exchange rate would otherwise adjust. In the monetary model this is because the authorities permit the money supply to adjust towards demand through payments imbalances in the short run. In the portfolio balance model, this occurs because official intervention affects the net supply of foreign currency assets to domestic residents.

The main insight of the monetary approach is that policies affecting domestic credit which are inconsistent with the private sector's demand for money may lead to offsetting payments flows and/or pressure on the exchange rate. Some examples of the rapidity with which such mechanisms have operated are given below. The portfolio approach, on the other hand, stresses the importance of monetary policies in a wide range of countries. It also emphasizes the role of more complex factors related to expectations and risk, which are likely to complicate, if not dominate, the external pressures that tend to emerge. Depending on particular circumstances, both approaches may have relevance for understanding the types of pressures and conflicts in policy objectives that have developed in practice.

D. MAIN CONFLICTS IN POLICY OBJECTIVES

Most major economies from the middle of the 1970s began to formulate their policies in terms of an objective for the rate of growth of some measure of the money supply or credit.[8] If these objectives are not internationally consistent, i.e. excessively inflationary or deflationary vis-à-vis each other, capital flows are likely to be generated under either of the above approaches. In these circumstances any commitment to fix the exchange rate will require sterilization of unwanted capital flows in order to achieve the monetary target.[9] But in the long run "sterilization" is not a feasible strategy, because it tends to recreate the conditions that led to the capital flows in the first instance.[10] Consequently, the continued achievement of monetary targets may require the exchange rate to be permitted to move.

A problem arises, however, because authorities in most of the major economies have, at times, also attempted to avoid large (possibly destabilising) exchange rate movements. Where depreciation has been involved, efforts to control inflation may be endangered. Appreciation, on the other hand, threatens output and employment in industries producing for export and/or import competing sectors. Of the economies considered, the United States has generally paid least attention to the exchange rate, because of its small share of trade in GNP and the special position of the dollar as a reserve currency.[11] In the period immediately following November 1978, however, "excessive" depreciation did lead to considerable intervention by the Federal Reserve. At the other extreme, Canada has almost always attempted to adjust interest rates to maintain the relative stability of its currency against the dollar, whatever the consequences for domestic monetary conditions.

In the other major economies there has been more scope for conflicts in policy objectives to emerge. All are exposed to international developments so that, to varying degrees, the exchange rate is given consideration. But at the same time each is sufficiently large that domestic objectives may also be given priority. France and Italy are both within the EMS and are committed to parities, the general path of which tends to be dominated by the Deutschemark. Both have attempted to reconcile this with domestic monetary objectives by operating on domestic credit expansion, but periodic realignments within the EMS have been necessary. Germany has traditionally placed more emphasis on domestic monetary control and has been prepared to allow the exchange rate to move. Nevertheless, as recent experience has shown, if the rate is thought to move to levels which bear no relation to "underlying realities" and threaten to undermine objectives such as inflation or growth, the Bundesbank is prepared to adjust its domestic policy. During the latter part of the 1970s and early 1980s the United Kingdom and Japan have been more prepared to see the exchange rate move. More recently, however, exchange rate considerations have again been given more priority in the United Kingdom.

As this picture suggests, policy objectives have varied between countries, and over time within individual economies. Part of the reason for this is that authorities operate in a situation where there is considerable uncertainty about the causes of various pressures, leading them to persist with a particular intermediate target for some time. Where the target is not appropriate, pressures will simply be forced into other areas, and eventually there may be departures from, or the complete abandonment of, the initial objective. Examples of these problems are discussed below for the cases of monetary and exchange rate intermediate targets, respectively.

1. *Independent Domestic Monetary Policy*

If authorities attempt to achieve domestic objectives which are globally inconsistent, either in an expansionary or a contractionary sense, pressures tend to be forced upon the external sector. For example, if domestic interest rates are held at low levels compared to foreign rates, given exchange rate expectations, capital outflows will tend to develop. Where this tendency is reinforced by deteriorating exchange rate expectations – which is likely to be the case if expansionary policies have led to relatively high inflation and a deterioration of the current account – very heavy pressure can be put upon the level of international reserves. The problem may not only be the reallocation of assets stressed by the portfolio balance model, but the large scope for financing capital outflows by borrowing on favourable terms from domestic banks. Conversely, if domestic policies are relatively tight, capital inflows may induce monetary expansion which is excessive. In either case the exchange rate is likely to come under pressure.

Numerous examples of domestic monetary policy generating external pressures exist. In 1972 and 1975/76 in the United Kingdom, and in France and Italy in 1975/76, expansionary domestic policies put severe downward pressure on the exchange rate. Relatively tight policies in Germany resulted in upward pressure on the Deutschemark from 1973 to 1977. Eventually, in all cases, domestic monetary policy was forced to re-adjust. For example, in 1976/77 a sharp squeeze on domestic credit was implemented in Italy and the United Kingdom on the recommendation of the IMF. Intervention to reduce upward pressure on the Deutschemark in 1978 led to a substantial overshooting of the Bundesbank's target for central bank money.

2. *Exchange Rate Targets*

The portfolio balance model suggests that exchange rates may move for reasons other than those emphasized by the monetary approach. For example, current account "news" may have an immediate effect on rates as a consequence of, say, vagaries in movements of the price of oil.[12] Currency preferences may shift, causing movements of the risk premia attached to each. Interest rate differentials may change because of large unexpected changes in budget deficits in different countries. Even exchange rate pressures resulting from movements in foreign interest rates may not readily be explicable within the framework of the monetary approach. For example, the latter would tend to predict an appreciation of exchange rates against the dollar as a consequence of a rise in interest rates in the United States, since the demand for money in that country would tend to fall. Recent experience, however, suggests that reverse pressures have tended to emerge.[13]

The achievement of a stable exchange rate in the face of random disturbances at home and from abroad may require substantial changes in domestic monetary policy. This may be inconsistent with other domestic goals. An important example in this respect is Canada. To avoid unwanted exchange rate movements the authorities in this country have been forced to adjust domestic interest rates in line with movements of those prevailing in the United States. During most of the early 1980s the Bank of Canada has undershot its target for M1, in part because US interest rates have remained at very high levels. In France and Italy authorities have attempted to reconcile the commitment to stabilize the exchange rate with domestic monetary objectives through a comprehensive set of administrative controls. This leads to financial market distortions and, in any case, periodic changes in domestic policies have not been avoided.

E. POSSIBLE IMPLICATIONS FOR POLICY MAKING

The main policy issue arising from the above discussion concerns the conflict between domestic objectives and unwanted capital flows and/or exchange rate pressures. These instabilities tend to arise because:

(i) domestic money policies are too "independent", i.e. in the sense of being excessively restrictive or expansionary in respect to other major economies over a long term horizon, or

(ii) shorter-term exogenous shocks to the real exchange rate through real wage resistance, current account "news", movements in currency preferences and the like, may lead to unwanted developments which can be reinforced through "band-wagon" speculative cycles.

1. *The Longer-Term Stance of Monetary Policies*

In recent years there has been a rather "shaky" consensus that intermediate domestic monetary policy objectives should be couched in terms of targets for money supply or credit aggregates. Such targets can prove useful for ultimate domestic policy goals. The main advantages include:

(i) Stabilizing influences on nominal GNP in the face of exogenous disturbances to spending (e.g. budget deficits). In particular, interest rates tend to act as automatic stabilizers.

(ii) The reduction of the level and variance of inflation over a long time horizon. This may also enable long-term interest rates to be reduced through lower inflationary expectations.

(iii) By making monetary policy more predictable, targets for the money supply may provide depending on the institutional setting – a more appropriate environment for wage negotiations, investment decisions, etc., thus avoiding the possibility of destabilizing expectations frequently associated with monetary "fine tuning".

However, the foregoing discussion of capital flows and exchange rate pressures suggests that an "independent" approach to monetary targetry may possibly be untenable in the medium term. In these circumstances there may be some advantages in moving towards the establishment of internationally consistent medium-term financial strategies. The view that steps in this direction are an essential ingredient of any long-term reform of the international monetary system has recently been advocated by a number of authors.[14] Moreover, the potential usefulness of such an approach has been underlined by the mixed success of optimum currency areas in bringing about similar results via less direct channels. It has been argued, for example, that the joint EMS float has not been sufficiently successful in bringing domestic policies and economic performance of participating countries into line with each other.

It should be noted that coordinated monetary targeting implies that the countries concerned have a joint objective function. In the broadest terms this might involve, for example, a forecast for the growth of real income and a targeted rate of inflation in each. When weighted together in a common currency, area money and money income growth should be consistent. If they are not, pressures which could have been avoided would normally tend to emerge. It should be borne in mind that even with a coordinated approach to policy, disturbances could still arise for reasons such as:

— money demand instability;
— real wage resistance; and
— monetary policy in non-participating countries.

However, a coordinated approach to setting intermediate monetary targets, might eradicate some rather obvious sources of pressure between countries.

2. *Short-Term Shocks*

Where short-term random disturbances are responsible for exchange rate pressures, it is sometimes argued that domestic monetary policy could be used to "counter-shock" the markets. Any assessment of whether such policies are desirable will depend on the nature of any resulting expectations effects. If external pressures were essentially of a transitory nature, the cure could prove more disadvantageous than the disease. An excessively rapid domestic credit squeeze to counteract a weak exchange rate resulting from temporary pressures, for example, may needlessly lead to a sharp downturn in real activity. In practice, authorities are not always able to distinguish "temporary" shocks from more fundamental developments which could justify a change in intermediate targets. Moreover, "band-wagon" effects may amplify otherwise "innocent" disturbances. However, the adoption of particularly severe short-run policies would not normally be consistent with a coordinated approach to policy.

F. DIRECT CONTROLS ON NATIONAL AND INTERNATIONAL BANK LENDING

It is sometimes argued that conflicts between exchange rate targets and monetary growth can be reduced by quantitative controls on bank lending. This, however, tends to lead to market distortions which undermine the reasons for targeting a particular monetary aggregate in the first place. For example, credit may be disintermediated through bank acceptances, so that the targeted aggregate may become less closely related to private expenditure and money income.

Similarly, quantitative controls on Euro-market operations are sometimes proposed in order to reduce external pressures. For example, it is argued that such operations increase the speed and size of short-term capital movements and exchange rate pressures, which it would be wise to avoid. However, it seems more likely that the development of the Euro-currency market has itself been largely a response to the existence of various domestic administrative controls. To the extent that this is the case, it is arguable that the Euro-markets have a useful role to play in reducing inefficiency in domestic financial markets. Similarly, exchange rate speculation through the Euro-market is a symptom rather than a cause of exchange rate disturbances which mainly originate from inconsistent policy objectives between countries. Again, this may reflect perfectly efficient behaviour on the part of agents in international financial markets.

NOTES

1. The balance for official settlements, BOS, is a measure of exchange market intervention by the authorities.

2. Changes in the net external assets of commercial banks may be treated as though they were domestic credit expansion.

3. The monetary approach is usually attributed to Mundell (1978) and Johnson (1977). See also Whitman (1975) and Swoboda (1977) for useful summaries of these views. The small open economy assumption does not invalidate the insights of this approach for larger economies. The smaller and more open the economy, however, the more important will be the balance of payments channel for adjustment to domestic monetary disequilibrium. Moreover, the more valid will be the assumption of parametric prices and interest rates in the rest of the world.

4. The empirical relevance of monetary disequilibrium is sometimes disputed by economists, depending on their preferred views on the size of various elasticities of substitution. The possible existence of this phenomenon is not in dispute. Consider a model with a goods market, a money market, and a bond market. If the bond market is assumed to clear by interest rate adjustments, then monetary disequilibrium will be a counterpart of goods market disequilibrium.

5. Studies include Kouri and Porter (1974), Argy and Kouri (1974), Courchene and Singh (1976), Bean (1976), Guitian (1976), Zecher (1976) and Genberg (1976), all of whom used essentially reduced form approaches to estimation. Tests of this approach using full system techniques include Jonson (1976), Knight and Wymer (1976), Sassanpour and Sheen (1976), and Atkinson, Blundell-Wignall and Chouraqui (1983).

6. The portfolio approach is generally attributed to Branson (1968). Empirical evidence over the fixed rate period may be found in Branson and Hill (1971). Subsequent developments over the period of floating exchange rates include Branson (1977) (1979), Branson, Halttunen and Masson (1977) and Branson and Halttunen (1979). This approach has been built into the OECD International Linkage Model, with complete global consistency properties. See Frenkel, Gylfason and Helliwell (1980) for a synthesis of the monetary and portfolio balance approaches.

7. Examples of the monetary model include Frenkel (1976), Bilson (1978) (1979). Dornbusch (1976) provides an interesting variant with different speeds of adjustment in goods and asset markets. His model demonstrates the possibility of exchange rate "overshooting".

8. See "Monetary Targets and Inflation Control", *OECD Monetary Studies Series* (1979).

9. "Sterilization" refers to the attempt to offset the effects of payments imbalances on domestic monetary conditions by domestic credit policies.

10. See Emminger (1979) and Mundell (1978) for a discussion of the difficulties with such a policy from a practical and theoretical point of view, respectively.

11. This implies that foreign central banks frequently intervene to stabilise the dollar.

12. See Dornbusch (1980), for example.

13. In sum, at a theoretical level, portfolio balance and monetary models can lead to similar empirical predictions under fixed or heavily managed exchange rates when changes in domestic monetary policy are considered. However, important differences emerge in the way external shocks can be integrated through expectations effects in these models. In this respect the portfolio balance/"news" models seem to be both more general and intuitively appealing.

14. See McKinnon (1982), Polak (1981) and Reuber (1981).

REFERENCES

Argy, V. and P.J.K. Kouri (1974), "Sterilization Policies and the Volatility in International Reserves", in Aliber, R.Z. (ed.), *National Monetary Policies and the International Monetary System*.

Atkinson, P., A. Blundell-Wignall, & J.C. Chouraqui (1983), "Budget Financing and Monetary Targets With Special Reference to the Seven Major OECD Economies", *Economie et Sociétés*, forthcoming.

Bean, D.L. (1976), "International Reserve Flows and Money Market Equilibrium: The Japanese Case", in Frenkel, J.A. and H.G. Johnson (eds.), *The Monetary Approach to the Balance of Payments*.

Bilson, J. (1978), "The Monetary Approach to the Exchange Rate: Some Empirical Evidence", *IMF Staff Papers*.

Bilson, J. (1979), "Recent Developments in Monetary Models of Exchange Rate Determination", *IMF Staff Papers*.

Branson, W.H. (1977), "Asset Markets and Relative Prices in Exchange Rate Determination", *Sozialwissenschaftliche Annalen des Instituts für Höhere Studien*.

Branson, W.H. (1979), "Exchange Rate Dynamics and Monetary Policy", in A. Lindbeck (ed.), *Inflation and Employment in Open Economies*, North-Holland.

Branson, W.H. and H. Halttunen (1979), "Asset Market Determination of Exchange Rates: Initial Empirical and Policy Results", in J.P. Martin and A.D. Smith (eds.), *Trade and Payments Adjustment Under Flexible Exchange Rates,* Macmillan.

Branson, W.H. and R.H. Hill (1971), "Capital Movements in the OECD Area: An Econometric Analysis", *OECD Economic Outlook, Occasional Studies.*

Branson, W.H., H. Halttunen and P. Masson (1977), "Exchange Rates in the Short-run: The Dollar-Deutschemark Rate", *European Economic Review.*

Courchene, T.J. and K. Singh (1976), "The Monetary Approach to the Balance of Payments: An Empirical Analysis for Fourteen Industrial Countries", in J.M. Parkin and G. Zis (eds.), *Inflation in the World Economy.*

Dornbusch, R. (1976), "Expectations and Exchange Rate Dynamics", *Journal of Political Economy.*

Emminger, O. (1979), "The Exchange Rate as an Instrument of Policy", *Lloyds Bank Review.*

Frenkel, J.A. (1976), "A Monetary Approach to the Exchange Rate: Doctrinal Aspects and Empirical Evidence", *Scandinavian Journal of Economics.*

Frenkel, J.A., T. Gylfason and J.F. Helliwell (1980), "A Synthesis of Monetary and Keynesian Approaches to Short-run Balance of Payments Theory", *Economic Journal.*

Genberg, A.H. (1976), "Aspects of the Monetary Approach to Balance of Payments Theory: An Empirical Study of Sweden", in Frenkel and Johnson, *op. cit.*

Guitian, M. (1976), "The Balance of Payments as a Monetary Phenomenon: Empirical Evidence, Spain 1955-71", in Frenkel and Johnson, *op. cit.*

Johnson, H.G. (1977), "The Monetary Approach to Balance of Payments Theory and Policy: Explanation and Policy Implications", *Economica.*

Jonson, P.D. (1976), "Money and Economic Activity in the Open Economy: The United Kingdom 1880-1970", *Journal of Political Economy.*

Kouri, P.J.K. and M.G. Porter (1976), "International Capital Flows and Portfolio Equilibrium", *Journal of Political Economy.*

Knight, M.D. and C.R. Wymer (1975), "A Monetary Model of An Open Economy with Particular Reference to the United Kingdom", in M.J. Artis and A.R. Nobay (eds.), *Proceedings of the AUTE Conference,* Cambridge University Press.

McKinnon, R. (1982), "Stabilising the World's Money", *Financial Times,* 3rd June, 1982.

Mundell, R. (1978), *International Economics,* Macmillan.

OECD (1979), *Monetary Targets and Inflation Control,* Monetary Studies Series.

Polak, J.J. (1981), "Coordination of National Economic Policies", *Occasional Paper No. 7, Group of Thirty.*

Reuber, G.L. (1981), "Steps to Improve International Economic Policy Co-ordination", *Canadian Public Policy,* VII: 4, Autumn.

Sassanpour, C. and J.R. Sheen (1976), "A Comparative Study of Money and Economic Activity in France and Germany; 1959-73", in H.G. Johnson, M. Mussa and C.R. Wymer (eds.), *Proceedings of the AUTE Conference.*

Swoboda, A.K. (1977), "Monetary Approaches to Worldwide Inflation", in Krause, L.B. and W.S. Salant (eds.), *Worldwide Inflation: Theory and Recent Experience.*

Whitman, M.v.N. (1975), "Global Monetarism and the Monetary Approach to the Balance of Payments", *Brookings Papers on Economic Activity.*

Zecher, J.R. (1976), "Monetary Equilibrium and International Reserve Flows in Australia", in Frenkel and Johnson (eds.), *op. cit.*

Part C

THE ROLE OF BANKS IN INTERNATIONAL LENDING

Chapter IX

WESTERN GOVERNMENTS AND WESTERN BANKS: HOW TO RECONCILE THEIR OBJECTIVES IN INTERNATIONAL LENDING

by *F.A. Engering*

I. COMMERCIAL BANKS AND INTERNATIONAL LENDING

a. *Introduction*

Western governments and Western banks each have their own objectives in international lending. The question that is being dealt with in this paper is how, from the point of view of a Western government, these objectives can best be reconciled.

In section I we will look at the objectives of commercial banks in international lending, and we will review the developments of international lending since the first oil crisis. In section II we will look at the objectives of governments with respect to international capital flows. In section III we will review the means that are at the disposal of governments to influence international capital flows. In section IV, we will try to make some concluding remarks and try to determine, given the objectives of Western governments, which sort of instruments are the most appropriate to use for the government.

Finally we try to reach a conclusion about the role of the government in international lending in the next decade under different current account scenarios in the world.

b. *Behaviour and Objectives of Commercial Banks in International Lending*

The objectives of commercial banks in international lending do not differ much from their objectives in domestic lending or in other aspects of regular banking activities. The banks try to make a profit in order to maintain or strengthen their relative position and in order to safeguard their continued existence. That does not mean, however, that activities cannot be reconciled with the objectives of the government. It only means that they will try to invest their deposits as safely and as profitably as possible. According to a study by Salomon Brothers (*United States Multinational Banking: Current and Prospective Strategies,* June 1976), the profit of the thirteen largest US multinational banks from their international operations increased from US$ 117 million in 1970 to US$ 836 million in 1975. Profits from domestic operations did not increase at all during this period, and by now 50 per cent of profits of these banks are generated by their international operations. But the overall risk of lending increased. On the one hand banks tried to compensate for this by increasing the interest and other charges. On the other hand banks tried to limit the risks of international lending by spreading these risks over different areas, over different sectors, over different kinds of projects, etc. It is questionable, however, whether commercial banks indeed do reach sufficient spread of risks in their portfolios. Quite often banks will lend because they expect to be able to continue providing other services to the borrower that are important to their profits, like the financing of trade. Trade, however, is to a large extent geographically determined. Therefore it is not surprising that most lending to developing countries in Latin America and the Caribbean is done by commercial banks in the United States. In contrast, Eastern European countries borrowed mostly from Western European banks, and especially from banks in West Germany. Table 1 shows the geographical distribution of international debts to US and non-US commercial banks.

Table 1. *Geographical distribution of debts to commercial banks, December 31, 1976 (in billions of US dollars)*

	All banks	US banks	non-US banks
Non-oil LDCs	76.8 (59%)	52.0 (75%)	24.8 (40%)
of which Brazil	21.2 (16%)	13.9 (20%)	7.3 (12%)
Mexico	17.9 (14%)	13.0 (19%)	4.9 (8%)
OPEC	24.8 (19%)	13.0 (19%)	11.8 (19%)
Eastern Europe	29.2 (22%)	4.3 (6%)	24.9 (40%)
Total	130.8 (100%)	69.3 (100%	61.5 (100%)

Source: A. Angelini, M. Eng, F. Lees, *International Lending, Risk and the Euromarkets*, 1979.

c. *The Pattern and Development of International Lending by Commercial Banks Since 1973*

The total volume of published international bank lending has increased considerably since 1973. Whereas this lending amounted to around US$ 21 bil-

Table 2. *Published medium and long term loans (in millions of US dollars)*

	1973	1974	1975	1976	1977	1978	1979	1980	1981
OECD	12,354 (59.3%)	18,291 (64.1%)	6,224 (30.2%)	9,903 (35.5%)	13,041 (38.6%)	30,368 (46.1%)	29,082 (35.8%)	41,191 (51.6%)	39,794 (46.0%)
Eastern Europe	590 (2.8%)	830 (2.9%)	1,946 (9.5%)	1,725 (6.2%)	1,409 (4.2%)	3,071 (4.7%)	3,719 (4.7%)	2,666 (3.3%)	1,509 (1.71%)
OPEC	2,100 (10.1%)	644 (2.4%)	2,468 (12.0%)	2,472 (8.9%)	4,266 (12.6%)	9,719 (14.8%)	8,763 (11.1%)	6,686 (8.4%)	5,566 (6.51%)
Developing countries	5,267 (25.2%)	7,520 (26.3%)	3,776 (42.6%)	11,895 (42.6%)	13,622 (40.3%)	21,844 (33.2%)	36,021 (44.5%)	28,206 (35.3%)	39,131 (45.4%)
of which Brazil and Mexico	2,000 (9.6%)	3,083 (10.8%)	4,286 (20.8%)	5,283 (18.9%)	5,211 (15.4%)	10,602 (16.1%)	16,936 (20.4%)	11,259 (14.1%)	17,074 (19.8%)
Other (including international institutions)	543 (2.6%)	1,205 (4.2%)	1,168 (5.7%)	1,924 (6.9%)	1,443 (4.3%)	805 (1.2%)	1,517 (1.9%)	1,155 (1.4%)	273 (0.3%)
Total	20,864 (100 %)	28,541 (100 %)	20,583 (100 %)	27,920 (100 %)	33,781 (100 %)	65,807 (100 %)	79,107 (100 %)	79,904 (100 %)	86,273 (100 %)

Source: Financial Statistics, OECD.

lion in 1973, it exceeded US$ 86 billion in 1981 (excluding take-over financing in the US which amounted to US$ 48 billion). The annual volume of lending has increased continuously except for 1975 when a decline of around US$ 8 billion occurred. Quite considerable increases occurred in 1974, 1976 and 1978. In the latter year the lending volume nearly doubled.

There are various factors that influence the volume of international lending to individual countries as well as to groups of countries. These factors include the size of their balance of payments deficit or surplus, the demand for credit by the private sector, the availability and conditions of credit, the reserve position and the total debt of the country concerned, as well as political developments.

Lending to *OECD countries* has shown a clear relationship with the development of their aggregate balance of payments as well as with credit conditions. The oil price increases of both 1973-74 and 1979-80 caused the balance of payments position of OECD countries as a whole to change from one of surplus to one of deficit. At the same time there was a strong increase of commercial bank lending to OECD countries. This lending decreased again, however, as soon as the balance of payments position of these countries improved. The latter was especially the case in 1975.

Table 3. *OECD: current account balances and international bank lending, 1973-1981 (in billions of US dollars)*

	1973	1974	1975	1976	1977	1978	1979	1980	1981
Current account balance	10	− 27	0	− 18	− 24	10	− 33	− 73	− 35
International bank lending[a]	12.4	18.3	6.2	9.9	13.0	30.4	29.1	41.2	39.8

a. Published medium and long term credits only.

Source: OECD.

In 1978 and 1979 there was a "borrowers' market" and "aggressive selling" led to considerably lower spreads. Both government and private borrowers, in the OECD area as well as elsewhere, benefitted from this. They borrowed even more than required to cover their immediate needs in order to be in a favourable position when credit would become scarcer once again.

Also in lending to *non-oil developing countries* the impact of the balance of payments position and of the conditions in international capital markets can be seen. Apart from these factors also the debt position and the policy of adjustment of the country concerned are important in determining the willingness of banks to lend to these countries. In addition also the reserve position of these countries turns out to be a factor in determining the demand for credit.

Of course we have been talking here about those non-oil LDCs that have access to international capital markets. Commercial banks do in general not lend to the poorest countries because the credit risks involved are too large. These countries depend primarily on official development assistance.

Table 4. *Non-oil developing countries: current account balances and international bank lending, 1973-1981 (in billions of US dollars)*

	1973	1974	1975	1976	1977	1978	1979	1980	1981
Current account balance	− 6	− 23.5	− 30	− 17	− 12	− 23	− 38	− 60	− 68
International bank lending[a]	5.3	7.5	8.8	11.9	13.6	21.8	36.0	28.2	39.1

a. Published medium and long term credits only.

Source: OECD.

Commercial bank lending to non-oil developing countries increased continuously from about US$ 5 billion in 1973 to about US$ 36 billion in 1979. In 1973 about one quarter of all international bank loans went to non-oil developing countries. In 1979 their share had increased to over 45 per cent (see Tables 2 and 4).

In 1978 and 1979 many developing countries used the relatively favorable market conditions to strengthen their reserve position. The reserves thus accumulated were a great help to many of them in 1980, when their aggregate balance of payments deficit increased by about US$ 22 billion, while conditions in international capital markets were hardening at the same time. Borrowing by developing countries decreased by about US$ 8 billion in 1980. Of this decrease, Mexico and Brazil accounted for nearly US$ 6 billion, because of an increasing preoccupation on the part of commercial banks with the debt positions of these countries. Especially in 1978 and 1979 lending to these countries increased extremely rapidly. The willingness of banks to lend to these two improved again in 1981, because of the structural adjustment policies in these countries and because of the higher spreads that could be achieved. Also lending to other developing countries increased again in 1981.

The demand for capital by *OPEC countries* shows, as expected, a strong relationship with their current account position. International lending to these countries decreased sharply in 1974, but in the years 1975 through 1977 it reestablished itself at a level of around 10 per cent of total international lending by commercial banks (see Table 2). In 1978, a year in which these countries experienced a very low balance of payments surplus, international lending to them increased strongly both in relative and in absolute terms. In 1980 and 1981 the demand for international capital by OPEC countries decreased. Now that their surplus is declining, their demand for international capital is on the rise again.

Table 5. *OPEC countries: current account balances and international bank lending, 1973-1981 (in billions of US dollars)*

	1973	1974	1975	1976	1977	1978	1979	1980	1981
Current account balance	7.5	59.5	27	36	29	4	62	110	60
International bank lending	2.1	0.6	2.5	2.5	4.3	9.7	8.8	6.7	5.6

Source: OECD.

International commercial bank lending to *Eastern European countries* is determined, apart from by their balance of payments position, also by their international debt position and, recently, by payments difficulties (Poland and Romania). International commercial bank lending to Eastern Europe increased considerably in 1975, decreased over the next two years, and rose again in 1978 and 1979. Over the past two years there was a strong decline again, especially in 1981, which illustrates the reluctance of the banks since the payments difficulties in Poland.

d. *The Distribution of International Commercial Bank Lending*

In general one can be satisfied about the way in which international commercial banks have contributed to the recycling of petro-dollars. Table 2 shows that international lending by commercial banks has generally been directed towards the areas with a large or increasing balance of payments deficit. The figures do certainly not bear out the contention that developing countries were crowded out as soon as the demand for capital in OECD countries increased. The figures for 1976 and 1978 for example show that both groups of countries could acquire a large volume of international capital at the same time.

In 1980 there was a case in which international lending to non-oil LDCs decreased, whereas lending to OECD countries increased strongly. The decrease, however, was mainly caused by Mexico and Brazil. In these countries debt had increased rapidly during 1978 and 1979, making commercial bankers more careful when the balance of payments deficits increased strongly in 1980. The generally accepted policy of structural adjustment in these countries and larger spreads, however, caused banks to expand their lending to these countries again in 1981.

The decrease in 1980 of published international lending to developing countries other than Brazil and Mexico is probably caused in part by lower demand for credit because of the accumulation of reserves in prior years. The unfavourable development of interest rates and the existence of unpublished "club deals", may also have been of influence. According to some bankers, club deals accounted for about 15 per cent of total international lending in 1980. If this were true these deals would amount to about $ 20 billion out of a total of $ 135 billion bank loans and bond issues together in 1980. Partially because of international lending by banks the reserve position of developing countries has not strongly deteriorated and these countries themselves were able to maintain an average rate of real growth of around 6 per cent per annum during the period 1974-1980.

It can be concluded that commercial banks contributed greatly to a successful recycling of petro-dollars in the period 1973-1981, and that there has been no crowding out of developing countries.

II. THE OBJECTIVES OF GOVERNMENTS WITH RESPECT TO INTERNATIONAL CAPITAL FLOWS

In section I the international capital flows have been looked at from the perspective of commercial banks. In this section we will look at international capital flows from the perspective of governments.

A first objective of governments in the area of international capital flows is to maintain and promote an efficient international capital market. Otherwise also the governments' own objectives in international lending will be frustrated. The improvement of the international capital market will therefore be the topic of the first sub-section. In the second sub-section we will discuss the various other objectives of governments. In doing so we will deal separately with capital flows to the OECD countries, to the non-oil developing countries, and to (and from) the OPEC countries.

a. *Improvement of the International Capital Market*

The market for international bank loans functions rather well. It reasonably well satisfies the criterion that there have to be many "buyers" and many "sellers", as well as the criterion that the market has to be transparent. There are many governments and many private corporations that want to borrow and many commercial banks that want to lend.

Sometimes banks are being restricted in their international lending activities, as in Japan and Germany, but the market as a whole is not affected very much by these restrictions that, moreover, are generally temporary.

The transparency of the international capital market has increased quite considerably over the past few years. This is at least in part a consequence of the statistical activities of OECD, BIS and IMF. Most individual loans are published.

In general the banks are quite well informed about the debt position of their borrowers. There are however also some factors that impede a full transparency. The product is not homogeneous, because there is a variety of kinds of loans (various maturities, various currencies, etc.). In the last few years the market partners themselves have affected the transparency by concluding so-called "club deals" or "one-to-one deals", that are not published. Such deals certainly diminish the knowledge of market partners of the situation of supply and demand as well as their understanding of the price formation process. Often it is the high price (the spreads and the fees) that borrowers have to pay for new loans that leads to the conclusion of such secret deals. The efforts of governments ought to be directed towards diminishing this market imperfection.

b. *Social Economic Objectives of Governments*

In this sub-section we will try to assess the role of commercial banks in the realization of the objectives of the government of an industrialized country. In doing so we will first look at capital flows to OECD countries. After that we will deal with flows to non-oil developing countries and to (and from) OPEC countries.

(i) *OECD Countries*

In the national economic policy of the Netherlands five main objectives can be distinguished. These are: full employment, price stability, balance of payments equilibrium, economic growth, and an equitable distribution of income. The first three objectives can be considered to be cyclical objectives, whereas the last two objectives are structural ones. It does not seem unreasonable to assume that these objectives are shared by all industrialized countries although there can be a difference in emphasis from country to country.

In assessing the role of international lending it is important to keep in mind that the character and function of international lending with respect to the financing of balance of payments deficits of OECD countries as well as of other groups of countries have changed because of the oil crisis of 1973-1974.

Prior to the first round of oil-price increases in 1973-1974 current account deficits could generally be regarded as a sign of cyclical overheating. Domestically this implied inflationary tendencies and a tight labour market. International commercial bank lending, which was of relatively minor importance if compared to the period after 1974, hardly had a role in financing these current account deficits. The main role was played by the IMF.

IMF credits are of course intended to finance balance of payments deficits, but the objective of this is not to postpone the required cyclical adjustment. The conditionality attached to these credits made them into a means for reaching this adjustment.

Although prior to 1974 the international commercial bank lending in most cases was directed to finance projects and investments, this lending still implied a way of financing the current account. As such it could enlarge the business cycle in capital importing countries. In other words, this lending generally turned out to be *pro-cyclical*. On the other hand these capital movements probably helped reaching the structural objective of economic growth: international commercial lending generally was directed towards investment projects that contributed to the strengthening or necessary changing of the economic structure of the deficit countries.

Since 1974 the character and size of the balance of payments problems of OECD countries have changed dramatically. The oil-price increases had an unfavourable impact on the traditional cyclical objectives: the inflationary effect of the oil crisis caused a considerable increase in unemployment in nearly all OECD countries in 1975; the average rate of inflation in the OECD area increased strongly because of the high energy intensity of production and consumption; all countries with exception of the Netherlands and Germany, experienced a worsening of their current account.

It is remarkable that in 1974 many governments used an expansionary monetary and budgetary policy in a situation of a deficit on the current account. Towards the end of 1974 monetary policies were loosened in many OECD countries, especially in the United States and, to a lesser extent, in Germany.

Table 6. *OECD countries*

	1973	1974	1975	1976	1977	1978	1979	1980
Real growth in GDP (% increase)	6.1	0.9	−0.4	4.9	3.7	3.8	3.4	1.3
Unemployment rate* (%)	3.2	3.5	5.1	5.2	5.3	5.1	5.1	5.8
Consumer prices (% increase)	7.8	13.4	11.3	8.6	8.9	8.0	9.8	12.9
Balance on current account ($ bln)	10	−2.7	0	−1.8	−2.4	10	−33	−73

Source: OECD, *Economic Outlook.*

* in the 15 largest OECD countries.

In a number of European countries it was decided in 1974 that the reduction of unemployment ought to get a higher priority.

After that also the United States and other countries started to give priority to fighting the recession. It is important to note that preventing the deterioration of the balance of payments position was in many countries not considered to be a side-condition for policy of demand stimulation.

One of the causes of this was undoubtedly the relatively easy way in which current account deficits could be financed. International commercial lending became increasingly important in financing balance of payments deficits. At the same time the role of the IMF in financing these deficits was strongly reduced in relative importance. As was already noted these IMF credits were anti-cyclical in character because of the conditions attached to them. Unlike the times before the first oil crisis, in 1974, the role of international lending in financing balance of payments deficits was thought to be *anti-cyclical* as well, but in the opposite direction. It enabled countries to take measures against increasing unemployment that was thought to be of cyclical character.

By now one can wonder whether the cyclical response to the oil crisis of 1973-1974 and the supporting role of international lending has been a good thing. It is a fact that unemployment continued to increase after 1974 and that economic growth was only partially restored. The question arises whether international lending has not been counter-productive as far as the structural objective of economic growth is concerned, by allowing the necessary structural adjustment to the increased energy prices to be postponed. In this connection one has to think of the effects that allowing an increase in real income which exceeds the increases in productivity had on the profitability of private enterprise.

While commercial bank lending before the oil crisis mostly strengthened the economic growth but destabilized the business cycle, after 1974 international bank lending hampered the structural adjustment but prevented a sharp decline in expenditures in the short run.

Policies in the OECD area after the second oil crisis of 1979-1980 differ considerably from those of the first oil crisis. Now a restrictive monetary and budgetary policy prevails. One no longer tries to avoid the impact of worsening terms of trade on real wages. At the same time there is attention to strengthening the economic structure in the medium term. It is clear that under these circumstances a certain amount of commercial credit to finance balance of payments deficits is both necessary and justified. It permits a process of structural adjustment that otherwise would be endangered by the external position of the country. Of course this is not to say that all the international lending to OECD countries satisfies this criterion.

From the above it can be understood that international bank lending, unlike IMF credits, is generally adaptive and supportive of the policies of borrowing countries. In practice these credits therefore have sometimes an anti-cyclical and sometimes a pro-cyclical character, they sometimes lead to an improvement and at other times lead to a deterioration of the economic structure. It would of course not be fair to hold in the first place the commercial banks responsible for these positive or negative effects. The first responsibility rather lies with the policy-makers in the borrowing countries.

(ii) *Non-Oil Producing Developing Countries (NODCs)*

In our view capital flows to NODCs have to serve two purposes: increasing the economic independence of these countries, and alleviating their extreme poverty.

Conceivably international commercial lending could play a role in reaching both objectives. Probably, however, the alleviation of poverty will generally require official multilateral or bilateral development assistance. With respect to increasing the economic independence, a structural objective, commercial banks could play a more important role, however. By increasing economic independence we mean in this connection the promotion of a process of economic growth that implies a re-allocation of the factors of production towards the external sectors of the economy. Increasing economic dependence will finally have to manifest itself in a declining current-account deficit, and thus in a decrease of dependence on foreign capital.

It is important to note that after the first oil crisis the oil bill of the NODCs increased by US$ 16 billion, or about 2½ per cent of their GNP. Nevertheless, in retrospect these countries were able despite all these and other international problems to reach an average real economic growth of around 6 per cent per annum in the period 1974-1980.

Table 7 shows that, partially because of the ample availability of credits by international commercial banks, these countries could finance the substantial deficit that unavoidably accompanied this level of real growth.

Of course this picture is somewhat oversimplified. As has already been shown in section I, international commercial lending has in fact restricted itself to the so-called newly industrialized countries and to a very small group of other developing countries. Apparently the market does not meet the need for capital of all countries. In addition it has to be realized that maintenance of economic growth does not automatically imply an increase in economic independence. International credit can also be used for consumption purposes. This of course leads to the maintenance of effective demand, but at the same time it leads to a postponement of the process of structural adjustment, resulting in ongoing unsustainable deficits on current account.

Some countries that did not succeed in improving their external position despite due credits are now confronted with enormous debts (Philippines, Brazil). This indicates that commercial bank loans have not always been used in a sufficiently productive way. Nevertheless there are also examples of more favourable developments like Peru and Sri Lanka. The total picture for NODCs is thus mixed.

(iii) OPEC Countries

International commercial lending is of essential importance to the objectives of the economic policy of OPEC countries. From the point of view of the industrialized countries the following objectives of OPEC countries are of importance:

- to initiate a process of economic expansion and diversification with the help of oil revenues, without causing a cyclical overheating that may lead to social and political instability;
- in connection with the previous objective, to create investment opportunities for the surplus oil revenues.

Realization of the second objective is related to international commercial lending. Here there is a two-way relationship. Because OPEC countries have balance of payments surpluses there are deficits elsewhere in the world. Because there are balance of payments deficits and thus demand for credit, banks are able to offer OPEC countries investment opportunities in the

Table 7. *Balance of payments of non-oil developing countries (in billions of US dollars)*

	1973	1974	1975	1976	1977	1978	1979	1980
Exports, fob	67½	98	92	115	134½	154½	185	207½
Imports, fob	75	121½	130½	140	159	191½	232	267
Trade balance	-7½	-23½	-38½	-25	-24½	-37	-47	-59½
Services and private transfers, net	-4½	-8	-9	-9½	-9	-1½	-14	-16
Official transfers, net (ODA)	6	8	10	9	9½	2½	14	15½
Current balance	-6	-23½	-37½	-25½	-24	-36	-47	-60
Capital balance	13½	25	34½	35	36½	51½	54	59½
Direct investment	3	3½	3¼	3¼	4	4½	5½	6
Aid (ODA)	4	5¼	7¼	7	6¾	8½	9½	10½
Other official flows (OOF)	2½	3¼	4½	4½	4¼	5	5½	6
Portfolio and banking flows		5	6	8	8½	15	16	20
Official export credits	4	1¼	2	3¼	4¾	5½	6½	7
Other capital, including errors and omissions*	6¾		11½	9	8½	13	11	10
Net transactions of monetary authorities	7½	1½	-3	9½	12½	15½	7	-½
Other official financing	0	1¼	1¾	2	-½	-½	1	1
Changes in international reserves	7½	2¾	-1	11½	12	15	8	½

Memorandum items

Percentage changes in trade:

			1975	1976	1977	1978	1979	1980
Volume: Exports			-10	26	5½	7	8	3
Imports			-3	5½	5½	7½	7	4¼
Price**: Exports			5	-½	13	7	11½	9
Imports:			11	1	8	12	13	10½

* Including Euro-borrowing ** Average values in $ terms.

Source: OECD.

form of interest-bearing deposits. In addition it has to be noted that international commercial lending means that the credit risks are not born by OPEC countries. An interesting question for policy makers is to what extent commercial banks are willing to go in assuming this credit risk. The closer the risk limits to which banks will go are approached, the more their willingness to accept OPEC deposits will decrease. In these circumstances the following things are possible:

- recycling stops; for many reasons this should be deemed both unlikely and undesirable;
- the risks are transferred from the commercial banks to the governments of industrialized countries;
- OPEC countries are urged to invest directly or through multilateral institutions in deficit countries.

The problem mentioned does not however look very acute at this moment because of the rapidly decreasing surpluses of OPEC countries that are caused by the present international energy situation.

III. THE INFLUENCE OF GOVERNMENTS AND CENTRAL BANKS ON INTERNATIONAL CAPITAL FLOWS

In this section we will deal with the instruments at the disposal of Western governments with which they can influence the amounts and allocation of international financial flows to reach their own international economic and financial objectives.

There can be made a distinction between market disturbing and market oriented instruments.

a. *Market Disturbing Instruments*

Influencing international capital flows is not the objective of the means mentioned in this context, like the nationalization of commercial banks, foreign exchange restrictions, investment guidelines, and prudential controls. Nevertheless these means, that are used primarily for internal political and economic motives or in order to maintain the position of commercial banking, can have implications for international capital flows.

(i) *Nationalization of Commercial Banks*

Nationalization has a large amount of ramifications, and it usually takes place because of domestic political motives. The impression exists that it does not matter much for international capital flows whether or not the banks in a country have been nationalized. Although it is very well possible that the lending by a nationalized bank is more politically determined than lending by a private commercial bank. Profitability and the assessment of risk are then no longer the only criteria and the operation of the market mechanism is therefore affected.

(ii) *Foreign Exchange Restrictions and Investment Guidelines*

Foreign exchange restrictions generally serve as a tool of domestic economic policy: the introduction or the abolition of these restrictions can influence international lending. Japanese and German commercial banks for example have in the past during short periods of time been subject to formal and informal restrictions in this area. Investment guidelines are generally advocated by those who think that domestic savings should also be used domestically. These guidelines mostly imply restrictions for international lending.

(iii) *Prudential Controls*

Also prudential controls by monetary authorities that are primarily meant to maintain a healthy commercial banking sector, can influence international lending to certain countries or groups of countries; in this connection one can especially think of different solvency and liquidity guidelines that can be issued, and the informal evaluation that can be done with respect to credits to different countries. It is important that the supervising authorities are very flexible in their guidelines. As soon as a country for example with the help of the IMF and possibly after restructuring of its debts has clearly started with a good adjustment policy, it is undesirable to maintain the former strict prudential controls any longer. In general in exercising the control the supervising authorities should avoid taking over the responsibilities of the commercial banks. Therefore it is preferable that the supervising authorities make sure that the banks have an adequate machinery to assess risks rather than that the supervising authorities apply rigid country limits. In this way the market mechanism is least affected.

b. *Market-oriented Instruments*

There are various ways in which governments can influence international capital flows without violating the rules of the market game. In considering these ways it will have to be kept in mind that actions that influence international capital flows can be taken for quite different purposes. The purpose can be financial, e.g. balance of payments support, but it can also be humanitarian, e.g. disaster relief aid, economic, e.g. export credits, or strategic, e.g. the OECD aid to Turkey.

In this section we will distinguish means of influencing international capital flows without disturbing the market mechanism. This can be done on the basis of whether or not the government enters the market itself as an independent market agent. First we will deal with two ways the government can use to influence the behavior of the existing market agents. Secondly, we will deal with those ways that imply that the government enters into the market itself.

(i) *Guarantees*

If the government does not want to supply the capital itself, the most effective way of influencing international capital flows is to provide guarantees for such flows. From the viewpoint of the supplier of capital a 100 per cent guarantee transforms the loan almost into a bond issue of the donor government. In fact, except for accounting purposes the differences are minor. However, mostly only partial guarantees are given. In this way, the government can steer the market flows without losing the benefit of its independent judgement: if the risk is really bad, even a 95 per cent guarantee may not provoke a response from the market.

(ii) *Interest Subsidies*

Another way in which the government can influence capital flows without entering the market itself is by providing interest subsidies. Whereas guarantees are intended to lure lenders into lending, interest subsidies are intended to lure borrowers into borrowing.

As with most other means to influence international capital flows, one can distinguish two reasons for giving interest subsidies. The first is to improve the economy of a recipient country that needs capital but cannot generate sufficient earnings to pay the going rate for it. This explains the various forms of interest subsidies that have at one time or another been given through the Bretton Woods institutions.

The second reason is to improve the economy of the donor country. All subsidized export credits fall into this category. The difference from the first category of interest subsidies is clear if one considers that the availability of subsidized export credits is generally most strongly limited for countries that, from an "ability to pay" point of view, would need them most.

(iii) *Direct Bilateral Supply of Capital*

If the government wants to influence capital flows by entering into the market itself, the most simple way is the direct transfer of capital by the government to a government or institution in another country.

Direct transfers of capital take place under a variety of terms, from grants to loans on near-market conditions. Two aspects of these transfers are interesting to us in the present context: the degree of concessionality and the degree of conditionality.

The degree of concessionality will be determined by the budgetary position of the donor country and by the donor country's estimate of the recipient country's ability to carry debt.

The degree of conditionality will be determined by the intentions of the donor, and by his ability to attach conditions to the intended capital transfer. The latter ability clearly depends on the size and concessionality of the transfer – clearly, one can attach more conditions to a large grant than to a small loan on hard terms.

The conditions that can be attached to a capital transfer, be it a loan or a grant, are basically of two kinds. First, there are the conditions as to the domestic policies of the recipient country. In the case of project loans these conditions are normally limited to various aspects of the execution of the project itself. In the case of balance of payments loans, the conditions are generally of a macroeconomic character. This is only logical since here the financial situation of the country as a whole can be considered as "the project".

A second type of condition relates to procurement. There are very few official transfers of capital that do not specify the way in which the goods and services to be financed by them have to be procured. In the extreme case one can point here to official export credits. Here the main, if not the sole purpose is to foster the procurement of goods and services by the donor country. But also in other forms of capital transfer this aspect is rarely forgotten. Even disaster-relief aid quite often has to be spent in the donor country. In fact, it is not wholly correct to consider the bilateral ODA figures as an indication of capital flows. Quite often aid flows really are flows of goods and services, which are translated into money terms only for purposes of comparison and addition.

(iv) *Multilateral Supply of Capital: The International Financial Institutions*

If a government wants to influence international capital flows by entering the market, it does not need to do so by itself. The government can channel its funds through international institutions. I am especially thinking here of the multilateral development banks. The IMF is a chapter apart, to which other participants in this conference have already quite ably contributed.

Given the prevalent "gearing ratios" the multilateral development banks actually operate like government guarantees. (The development funds operate more by the way of direct capital transfers.) However, the multilateral character of these operations makes them differ in some important respects from guarantees and direct transfers by individual governments. First, procurement is not tied to a particular country but has to be from member countries, and the widespread membership of most MDBs means that their loans are practically untied. Secondly, bilateral political considerations do not, or at least should not, play a role. And thirdly, because of this, and because of the relatively large volume of capital these institutions can provide, they are in a much better position than an individual donor government to convince a country's policy makers of the desirability of certain actions.

Of course, the multilateral approach also has some disadvantages. Desirable measures can be blocked by disagreement, and even if countries do agree, procedures are often cumbersome – one only has to think of the legal steps that have to be taken to implement the capital increase of the World Bank, decided upon in January 1980. The lack of a direct relation between an individual country's contribution and its procurement can give certain governments great difficulty in defending their contribution at home. But in general, MDBs have been remarkably successful in generating flows of capital that could not have existed without them. Since the need for most of these flows has increased dramatically in the last few years, it is all the more alarming that just now a move towards a dramatic curtailment of the activities of these institutions seems to be under way.

(v) *Other Market Means*

If one thinks long enough, an almost interminable list of ways to influence capital flows without violating the rules of the market can be thought of. Mixed credits, co-financing with different types of cross default clauses, or with different ways of distributing the maturities between the governmental and the non-governmental institutions, various approaches to debt rescheduling or to the supply of funds by, for example, the IMF, all these measures and instruments do have an impact on international capital flows. But we have limited ourselves here to what are, in our view, the main categories.

In the next section we will see what determines our choice of the various means at our disposal.

IV. CONCLUDING REMARKS

We have discussed the international lending of banks and dwelt upon the special role of banks in the recycling of OPEC surpluses in the 1970s. Further, we have assessed the functioning of the banking sector in international lending in light of the economic and financial objectives of Western governments. Finally we have seen what sort of instruments Western governments have at their disposal to influence the amount and allocation of international lending. We could draw the conclusion that the way in which banks operate in international lending does not force governments to take stringent and market disturbing control measures. Instead of that governments should use market oriented instruments bilaterally or through the multilateral institutions when their objectives are not realized by the market alone.

The degree to which Western governments have to play a role in international lending during the next decade depends strongly on developments in balance of payments disequilibria in the world. We could distinguish two scenarios:

a. As a consequence of the energy prices OPEC surpluses remain on a very high level and recycling of these surpluses has to take place. The situation that emerges then is characterized by an accumulation of risks with the international banking sector, and, related to that, unsustainable debt positions of deficit countries. Without a substantially closer involvement of Western governments, the international banks will not be able to play the same important role in the recycling process as before. First, governments should stimulate, through an adequate conditionality especially by the multilateral institutions, structural adjustment in deficit countries to reduce balance of payments disequilibria. But during the adjustment process the financing of the current deficits has to be continued. Western governments should, bilaterally or through the multilateral institutions, take part in the recycling themselves. In a situation in which Western industrialized countries face their own deficits and adjustment problems this will be a very difficult mission, financially as well as politically, even apart from the fact that the role of governments could only be complementary to that of the banks. Because of that governments should enable the banks to continue their activities in the recycling process, by providing adequate forms of guarantees and co-financing.

b. The OPEC surpluses will disappear while the remaining deficits of the NODCs are mirrored in savings surpluses in the OECD countries. Also in this situation the necessity of structural adjustment of deficit countries has to be stressed to reduce current account deficits to sustainable levels as soon as possible. In the meantime financing of probably somewhat lower deficits has to be carried on. On the one hand the financial restraints and disequilibria in Western countries are somewhat smaller, on the other hand Western banks will reorientate themselves to the financing of the resuming economic growth in Western economies. It is clear that as far as international lending of the banking sector will continue, it will be reallocated from current account financing toward project lending. In this scenario the role of governments in the financing of current account deficits will become relatively more important. As far as the deficits are reversible and temporary, the IMF is able to provide the financing. In situations where countries' current deficits have a more structural character real savings have to be transmitted from surplus countries.

In both scenarios it seems that Western governments have to be prepared, given their international economic and financial objectives, to increasingly participate with market oriented instruments in the process of an optimal international allocation of capital flows.

Chapter X

OPPORTUNITIES AND CONSTRAINTS IN INTERNATIONAL LENDING

by *David Williams**

I can, perhaps, best indicate the nature of my remarks to this colloquium by attempting to give some answers to three questions that bear on the topic of opportunities and constraints in international lending: What has determined the growth in international banking? What have been the consequences of the growth in international banking for the functioning of the international economy? What is the role of the official institutions, in particular the International Monetary Fund, in the area of international banking?

I. GROWTH OF INTERNATIONAL BANKING

The growth of international banking, or in its narrower, but better known phenomenon of the Euro-dollar markets, has been extraordinary over the last 25 years. From virtually nothing at the time of the sterling crisis of 1957, Euro-currency deposits, measured on a gross basis, now amount to approximately US$ 2 trillion – a compound annual rate of growth of over 20 per cent.[1]

While the year-by-year fluctuations in the rate of growth of international lending have been marked, there has at no time – even during the worrisome days of 1974 when a number of commercial banks became over-extended in their international operations[2] – been a sustained contraction in activity in the Euro-dollar, or given its expansion into other currencies, in the Euro-currency markets – in particular the Euro-sterling, Euro-Deutsche mark, and Euro-Swiss franc markets. Indeed, the expansion of international lending into currencies other than the US dollar has been a very important steadying element in the growth of international banking when conditions in

---

* The remarks presented in this paper are personal, and should not be interpreted in any way as representing official views of the International Monetary Fund.

some markets – in particular the markets for dollars – were pointing to a slow down in growth. Since about 1970, when the dollar component of the market amounted to approximately 65 per cent of the total, the share of the US dollar has declined to less than one half; the share of the Deutsche Mark, the next largest component, has grown from about 5 per cent in 1970 to 20 per cent at the present time.

The proliferation of currencies used in foreign lending is a measure, not only of the extraordinary relaxation of controls on international capital movements and the interconvertibility of currencies that have taken place over the last 20 years, but in particular of the rapid internationalization of domestic financial institutions which, in part, have been associated with the long post-war boom in the world economy. In any event, the internationalization of the banking system has importantly contributed to the more even distribution of savings in the world economy and that has benefitted both large and small economies, developed and developing.

In addition to the growth of the overall size of the market and the increasing diversification of currencies used in the operations of the market, there has also occurred a phenomenal growth in the number of financial institutions that participate in international lending. At the end of last year some 600 banks, from about 85 countries, were operating in countries outside the legal domicile of their headquarters. These banks controlled about 450 subsidiaries, owned a network of about 5,000 foreign branches and had well over 1,000 direct affiliations. The physical presence of foreign banking establishments is not new and was, for example, a marked feature of the development of overseas banking by the British banks in the last half of the nineteenth century. That expansion, however, occurred in the then newly developing territories such as Australia, Africa (in particular South Africa) and Asia (in particular the Indian sub-continent). As regards the present expansion, it is striking that much of the expansion is in countries with well established banking systems and money market centers such as the more highly developed countries in Europe and North America and South and East Asia.

The physical expansion of international banking is to some extent a matter of the banks following, if not sometimes leading, the growth of overseas trade and international investment by domestic corporations; for example, the great wave of US bank expansion in Europe was in the 1960s which in part coincided with the great wave of US overseas direct investment in Europe. However, the configuration of the main centers of international banking, especially centers such as London, Switzerland, Luxembourg, Bahrain, Singapore, Hong Kong, the Cayman Islands, Bahamas, Panama and, the newest but far from the least, the International Banking Facilities

(IBFs) in New York, reflect not only the influence of domestic regulatory and tax considerations but, perhaps more importantly, the absence of *domestic* controls and regulations, including the application of domestic interest rate ceilings, reserve requirements, and exchange controls on the *foreign* operations of banks as well as highly efficient international communications systems. In other words, the rapid expansion of international banking can be related to a considerable extent to the privileged position of banks as regards their nondomestic activities compared with their domestic operations. The banks have responded, beyond imagination, to the stimulus of non-regulated banking, which has provided not only a high rate of profitability as compared with domestic banking but also a wide scope to experiment with new financial and credit instruments, new interest rate mechanisms and new ways of meeting customer needs and of tapping financial resources. International banking has been an undoubted major economic success story of the last quarter of a century, but with its success have come problems for the working of the monetary system – both domestic and international – that are still to be tackled.

The rapid growth of international lending has not, of course, taken place in a vacuum. Over the entire post-war period, the scale of the world economy has grown at impressive nominal annual rates. Since the mid-1950s, world trade in goods, services and private transfers has grown at a compound rate of almost 10 per cent expressed in US dollar terms. Over much of the post-war period up to 1973, the period of the long boom, very impressive rates of growth in volume terms were also recorded. The numbers of financial transactions, for which no reliable data exist, have grown at substantially higher rates. In short, despite the slower real growth rates of the 1970s, the world economy has been buoyant by the standards of the past over most of the post-war period, and recessions, with very few exceptions, have been short-lived and comparatively shallow.

II. RESERVE CREATION BY THE BANKS

The international banking system has reflected the rapid growth in the world economy, and indeed can take credit for a major role in facilitating the growth in international trade and payments that has contributed so much to the unprecedented international prosperity of the post-war years. International banking has also been an integral part of the development process in the third world as well as elsewhere over much of the period. However, these aspects of the role and function of international banking would not, of themselves, single out the international banking system for special consideration. The international banking system performed a similar role in the last third of the nineteenth century and the early years of this century. No doubt an efficient international financial infrastructure is a necessary condition for furthering international economic development. Over the last decade or so, the international banks have also been performing a major function that was not a major function in earlier years – namely, the provision of balance of payments finance on a continuing basis and on a large scale to official borrowers. Formerly, the preponderant role of the international banks was to provide finance for trade and development. Issues bearing directly on the balance of payments positions of countries were dealt with mainly, though not exclusively, on an intergovernmental basis and balance of payments adjustments involved essentially domestic deflation or, in the event countries had an effective choice, given their exchange rate arrangements, of letting the exchange rate float ("going off the gold standard") with an accompanying deflation of domestic demand. The possibility of financing a balance of payments deficit from the banking system over a prolonged period of time was not an option that was practically available to countries prior to the 1960s.[3]

Over the last decade, the working of the international monetary system has been transformed, in part because the commercial banks have become the main providers of balance of payments financing and the suppliers of international reserves to official entities. This unique extension of the role of the international banks has brought with it unique responsibilities and duties in the conduct of the activities of the banks. In a very real sense, the heart of the international monetary system is now a network of international banks which operate without their activities being subject to regulation by central institutional authorities that are directly charged with the responsibility of helping to keep the system on an even keel. The question is, therefore, whether self regulation by the banks is a sufficient form of control and a stabilizing influence in the international monetary system taken in the context of the peculiar constraints and regulations on domestic banking activities in various countries and which may also have to serve to regulate the foreign operations of the banks.

During the decade of the 1970s, official holdings of foreign exchange reserves quadrupled, which is an unparalleled rate of accumulation. During this period almost one-half of net current account deficits and the reserve accumulation of the non-oil developing countries were financed by net borrowing from banks and from the international bond market; over the last few years those proportions have risen and reliance on market financing has increased generally. The same phenomenon of large-scale market financing of balance of payments deficits may be observed for the smaller industrial countries. The tables in the Annex present some data that bear on this issue. It can also be seen that, following the sharp increases in the price of oil in 1973/74, the major oil-exporting countries have been the major sources of funds for this financing. It is also noteworthy that the outflow of short-term banking funds from the industrial countries has tended to accelerate on the occasions that outflows have diminished from the major oil-exporting countries. The constancy of the flow of resources to the non-oil developing countries has thus been maintained, in terms of their current account deficits, to a remarkable extent. The complementarity of the sources of funds underscores the demand-determined nature of the international operations of commercial banks. The same mechanism has also applied, but in a much less systematic way and on a smaller scale, to the smaller industrial countries in Europe. The larger industrial countries have financed their deficits to a considerable extent by the creation of liabilities – the counterparts of the currency diversification in the Euro-currency market and the source of the multi-currency reserve standard, which is a distinguishing feature of the present phase in the evolution of the international monetary system.

The international operations of the commercial banks must, therefore, be looked at not only from the point of view of their impact on the growth of world trade and income – their traditional commercial financing functions – but also from the point of view of the development of the international monetary system as a whole and, in particular, from the stability of that system. To some extent, the result of the two main functions of the international banking system are indistinguishable. Countries that borrow finance for trade and development can, and do, use those resources as holdings of international liquidity – or reserves. Indeed, it is difficult to construct a comprehensive series of uses for the resources provided by the international banks over the last 25 years. A great deal of data exist as regards the maturity distribution of international bank claims and also the country distribution of debt. A significant question, however, is how the proceeds of the debt have actually been used and whether they have generated, or are in the process of generating, sufficient foreign exchange earnings to effect the transfer of the repayment of interest and principal and, at the same time, generate reasonable domestic economic growth in the debtor countries. This question arises in particular for that part of the debt incurred as balance of payments financing, because this "transfer problem" is, in view of the extraordinarily large volume of outstanding international indebtedness, an integral part of what is now usually referred to as the balance of payments adjustment process.

The change in the system of reserve creation has also profound implications for the evolution of the financial system. The disintegration of the par-value system in the late 1960s and the move to generalized floating of exchange rates in the early 1970s was, of course, a major change in the functioning of the monetary system that had profound implications for the role of reserves in the system. The system of reserve creation that was in effect during the 1950s and early 1960s, and which depended on the supply of newly mined gold (and use of the IMF) and on the US incurring balance of payments deficits while surplus countries accepted US dollars, has been transformed into a system in which the commercial banks are the main source that generate liquidity in response to demands for it. This has profoundly affected the initiative of the IMF to substitute over the long run the system of reserve creation based on gold and US balance of payments deficits with a system based on SDR creation.[4] Furthermore, and as pointed out in the Fund's Annual Report, changes in official reserves represent, on the one hand, the results of portfolio choices of countries whether to place the proceeds of their borrowings or their net current receipts in commercial banks or in official monetary agencies and, on the other hand, most countries can acquire the reserves they demand either through exchange market intervention at exchange rates consistent with external surpluses or through borrowing in international capital markets.

III. LIMITS TO INTERNATIONAL BANKING

In view of the pervasive nature of international banking in the world economy and its fundamental role as purveyor and creator of international credit, the issue naturally arises regarding the limits to the growth of international banking, and of the ability to control the system in the interests of monetary stability. Domestic banking systems are subject to the ultimate control of central banks which, despite the awkwardness of having the residual obligation to finance net official deficits of the government, can impose a sufficient degree of restraint on the domestic activities of the banking system to achieve the broad aims of the authorities, at least over the short-term. While no similar institutional arrangements exist on the international level, and it is for consideration whether that state of affairs is in the general good, the growth of international banking is subject, over the short run, to severe constraints from developments in the international economy itself. The banks' responses to these developments will help determine the course of the international economy in the 1980s.

I do not need to dwell at this point on the current disturbing developments in the world economy. The world economy is in a period of exceptionally sluggish rates of growth, particularly as measured by post-war standards. Rates of growth of output of 1 to 2 per cent, and lower, have been widespread over the last three years, and the immediate prospect is for little improvement. These low rates of growth of output and trade, and accompanying high rates of unemployed resources in the labor and product markets, make it more difficult to effect policies of structural adjustment but act as a considerable incentive for countries to borrow as a means of helping to maintain domestic demand and thereby delay the adjustment to adverse circumstances.

Secondly, the widespread reliance on policies of monetary restraint to curb the endemic inflationary pressures of the last decade has resulted in extraordinary volatile interest rates and, recently, in very high real levels of interest rates. Volatile interest rate structures have been associated and indeed have helped induce very high short-run variability of exchange rates between some of the leading industrial countries – the group of countries in the EMS being a particularly noteworthy exception. With these developments a shift to shorter maturities in lending operations by the banks has become noticeable, and many new forms of borrowing have been introduced in the market as a means of reducing the high effective cost of borrowing.[5] The high variability of exchange rates and, more particularly high interest rate levels, have importantly increased the risks as well as the costs of international banking.

Thirdly, the massive payments imbalances of the past few years will diminish to a considerable extent, but the aggregate deficit of the non-oil developing countries, which was approximately US$ 63 billion in 1980, and about $ 75 billion in 1981 is expected to fall only slightly in 1982. Massive financing will again be needed of which, on recent past experience, about one half can be expected to be derived from the international banks. Without such assistance these countries would need to contract their imports on a major scale and severely curb their already inadequate rates of growth.

However, further large-scale deficits partly financed by borrowing will add to an already burdensome load of debt. Total indebtedness of the non-oil developing countries amounts to approximately $420 billion in 1980, which represents a compound annual rate of growth of almost 21 per cent since 1971. The ratio of debt service payments to exports of the non-oil developing countries is now at approximately 23 per cent, in contrast to a ratio of approximately 17 per cent in 1978. High interest rates compound the burden of large absolute amounts of debt and worsen the current account problems to service such debts – 1 percentage point change in interest rates in the Euro-dollar market is equivalent to $ 2 billion in debt service to the poor countries. Furthermore, these conditions are spawning increasing demands for debt reschedulings on a scale that makes countries and institutions increasingly vulnerable. Finally, and perhaps not unexpectedly, the general quality of debt, both official and corporate, in both the industrial countries and the developing countries, is deteriorating under the pressure of low growth, high inflation and high real interest rates.

In short, the international banking system is facing an increasingly difficult economic environment in which it operates. In the light of that deterioration and the fact that the former high rates of profitability on international lending have fallen quite sharply recently, there is a risk, particularly from the smaller institutions, that the flow of bank credit will start to dry up. The creditworthiness of some countries, and corporations, has fallen dramatically. The banking system itself is having to adapt to a new environment of considerable instability of interest rates and exchange rates, declining adequacy of capital to loans ratios and increasing demands for debt rescheduling with consequential declines of creditworthiness. Furthermore, the declining surpluses of the major oil-exporting countries, and compensating declines in the deficits of the industrial countries, remove the virtual assurance of new international resources flowing to the banks (indeed there may be a net absorption of resources by the major oil-exporting countries) that could be used to help meet the large deficits of the non-oil developing countries.

There are then, from a number of viewpoints, grounds for the banks to become increasingly cautious in extending new loans. In some cases this would clearly be prudent because exposure has reached levels that are high in relation to the banks' own resources. As noted above, the weakening capital base of the banks will also result in further potential restraints on lending. The Bank for International Settlements has also noted that "certain measures now being taken by the banking regulatory authorities, notably the spread of banking supervision on the basis of worldwide consolidated accounts, may somewhat limit the scope for further growth of international bank lending".

However, there is no reason for a generalized indiscriminate slow-down in international lending by the banks. Indeed, in the present darkening economic circumstances, it is clearly in the general interest to assure an adequate flow of funds through the international banking system and in particular to the non-oil developing countries. At the same time, there is need for further balance of payments adjustment in the endemic deficit countries. Clearly, the financing and adjustment mechanisms need to be fully reconciled with one another. However, the present institutional arrangements do not assure, or even provide for such reconciliation of these two functions. The next phase in the evolution of the international monetary system may well be concerned with this dichotomy between the reserve-creating institutions and the reserve-controlling institutions. In the meantime, the banks themselves can undertake to a greater extent than hitherto a series of steps that would help reduce the risks of international lending and help maintain some of the financial discipline associated with balance of payments adjustment.

IV. ROLE OF THE BANKS IN ADJUSTMENT

The orderly evolution of international banking would seem to call for market participants themselves to adopt formal measures of self control that would help the banks as a group to avoid becoming overcommitted in any one country, and any individual bank from becoming unduly exposed. A greater collaborative effort by the leading international commercial banks would be an important stabilizing element in international banking. This effort could take a number of different forms: first, it would be useful if the international banks implemented a system to provide for a continuous exchange of information with each other in critically important areas bearing on their operations – e.g., the extent of the reporting bank's involvement in each individual country, and information on the term structure and the amounts of credit outstanding in individual countries both in aggregate and by key sectors. Secondly, a further improvement would be the development of a comprehensive approach for the management of external financial risks, including the establishment of a country risk assessment or ratings bureau. Thirdly, the major commercial banks could arrange publicly outstanding swap lines of credit with each other. A financial pooling arrangement through the creation of swap credit lines could provide an automatic short-term source of liquidity for the banks and could also encourage the development of banks providing stand-by facilities to their overseas branches and to smaller international banks. A further development could be the creation of an international deposit insurance, or credit guarantee fund, which would increase the confidence of depositors and reduce the risks of international lending. These are all measures that the banks themselves could initiate and put into operation.

V. THE ROLE OF OFFICIAL INSTITUTIONS

The large-scale operations of the international banks and their pervasive influence over the working of the world economy have raised the issue of official regulation over these operations, particularly in the event of a faltering in the working of the international banking system which could affect the international financial system as a whole. The major responsibility for virtually all the prudential aspects of international banking continues to fall on the individual international commercial banks themselves. However, since December 1974, a great deal of work has been done under the aegis of the Committee on Banking Regulation and Supervisory Practices and the BIS as regards the surveillance of banking practices, the clarification of the relationships between local central banks, head offices and branches and affiliates of the international banks, and the systematic monitoring of international banking developments – including a strengthening of prudential control over the international banks by the supervision of banks' international business on a consolidated basis and by a better assessment of country risks.

The formal arrangements for supervision and surveillance of international banking are comprehensive and the rules for supervision and surveillance are reasonably fully articulated. Cooperation – if not already operational – is increasing though it is essentially untried as a method of self-control over the operations of the banks. The exchange of information between the major central banks, the inspection by central banks of the commercial banks operating in the international field as well as the degree of central bank control over the international operations of the banks is at present at a level that, at least, would provide the central banks with an early warning system if not the ability to avoid a crisis from developing with the inevitable need for more direct official intervention. However, the growing scale of foreign operations of the commercial banks, both in terms of borrowing from abroad as well as lending to foreign entities, could result in circumstances in which the local central bank could not adequately cushion all strains that might adversely affect the local commercial banks. As a consequence, the central bank may itself experience a severe drain on its international reserves and perhaps an unjustified downward pressure on its exchange rate as a result of the foreign-related operations of the commercial banks.[6] This in turn raises the question of what role, if any, is there for the international financial institutions, such as the International Monetary Fund?

Individual official institutions in need of liquidity will probably turn if not before then in the last resort to the international official institutions for assistance. In this respect the International Monetary Fund can be regarded as a backstop – or a residual source of liquidity for an individual country in need of balance of payments financing. However, a Fund member has access at any time to the various facilities of the Fund provided it meets the policies attached to the use of those facilities, and the member is encouraged to use those resources earlier rather than later in its external financial difficulties. The conditional resources of the Fund can be made available only on the basis of an agreed stabilization program with the member. The policies relating to the implementation of a stabilization program are not intended, nor are they designed, to meet an emergency situation in a member's balance of payments and reserve position. The Fund is not legally precluded, however, from developing a policy on the emergency use of its resources if it should determine that there was a need for such a policy.

However, the Fund's particular relationship with its members raises difficult issues for the Fund in widening its relationship beyond the official circle. For example, the possibility of closer cooperation between the Fund and private commercial banks has been discussed on many occasions, and I have referred above to the increasing need to relate in some systematic fashion the processes of reserve creation with policies to ensure balance of payments adjustment over reasonable periods of time and without members resorting to policies destructive of the growth of trade and payments. The Fund and the commercial banks are in an essentially complementary relationship, particularly as the Fund makes available short-term conditional resources to its members. In this way, the Fund helps to provide a stable environment for the orderly market financing of member's long-term trade and development needs. However, the Fund's legal and practical responsibilities are solely to its membership, and the membership regards its relations with the Fund as sensitive and confidential. This relationship in practice would generally preclude a close ongoing link between the Fund and the operations of the commercial banks. For example, major difficulties would arise for the Fund if it published its reports and evaluations of members' economic policies and prospects; there is also a limit to the amount of information that the Fund, at its initiative, could publish or otherwise make available that bears on the economic and financial performance of a member. It also follows that the Fund cannot reasonably advise banks on their lending activities with individual countries.

There are, of course, some positive ways in which the Fund can and does help its members in relation to their activities with the commercial banks. For example, there has been concern that excessive lending by commercial banks can lead to debt service problems for borrowing countries, which in turn could threaten the stability of the international banking system. In response to this concern, the Fund can play a useful role in helping to resolve crises that might arise in the servicing of bank debt, especially as they bear on the balance of payments position of members. The Fund has also, at the request of its members, advised on members' relations with the commercial banks, including assisting in the compilation of adequate information as regards their external financial situation. Furthermore, banks have been lending to some countries on a net basis only in the context of the country having concluded a stabilization agreement with the Fund. In this latter respect, the commercial banks lend conditional resources in support of the balance of payments adjustment effort of the borrower.

The Fund itself also closely monitors developments in international banking, which includes ongoing discussions with the commercial banks, central banks, and international agencies bodies such as the BIS and OECD. Obviously, the present overall scale of operations by the international banks is of an order that attracts official concern, particularly in view of the lack of central control in the international banking system. The present decentralized system of prudential control over the international banking system, which rests essentially with the commercial banks themselves and secondarily with individual central banks, needs further improvement in order to safeguard the stability of the banking system and of the international monetary system. The process of improving prudential control in its many aspects no doubt needs to be maintained, and the Fund will, within the limits of its primary responsibility of meeting its members' financing needs, play a role in this area.

VI. CONCLUSIONS

The responsibilities of the International Monetary Fund in the international monetary system are directly with its membership. The broad range of the Fund's responsibilities, for example in its surveillance of members' exchange rate policies, the impact of its reserve creating activities (including the creation and allocation of SDRs), and its policies on use by members of its conditional facilities, have effects of varying degrees on the financial markets and the institutions that compose those markets. Under present arrangements, the Fund's role vis-à-vis the private banks is, however, inherently limited and largely indirect, because its impact is felt through its influence – and persuasiveness – with its members. It would be of doubtful benefit if the Fund in its day-to-day activities with its members would compromise that relationship in any way because of closer direct working associations with market institutions. Nevertheless, there is an inherent weakness in the present international monetary system which arises from an absence of central control over the balance of payments lending operations of the commercial banks, and which result in the creation of international reserves, and the overwhelming need to link that availability of balance of payments financing with policies of balance of payments adjustment, which the banks cannot themselves provide. This is the major challenge in the working of the monetary system – to make reserve creation serve the purposes of balance of payments adjustment. That is a challenge not only for the commercial banking system but also those official international institutions that are charged with safeguarding the stability of the international monetary system.

NOTES

1. This is not the place to delve into the origins of the Euro-dollar market. I have dated the growth of the market from 1957 because, as part of the stabilization measures introduced by the UK Government in September 1957, the authorities imposed a ban on the use of sterling credits in the financing of third country trade. The British overseas and merchant banks quickly shifted the basis of financing this highly profitable third country trade from sterling to dollars, for which there was a pool to tap partly as a result of Eastern European deposits of US dollars in London, rather than in US based banks, but perhaps more importantly, because the US market was a ready source of funds that could be borrowed, especially in the light of the effects of domestic interest rate ceilings because of Regulation Q. The Euro-dollar market is a classic case of financial markets developing a particular form mainly because of the imposition of official controls – in this case controls in the UK and, of a different sort, in the United States.

2. This is not the place to trace the growing difficulties of a number of banks in the period 1973/74, starting with the collapse of the National Bank of San Diego in the US. Those developments, however, were symptomatic more of the speculative proclivities of the banks themselves rather than because of major difficulties in any large-scale country borrower of foreign funds.

3. Developments during the late 1920s leading up to the international financial crisis of 1931 were not essentially a matter of unsustained financing of balance of payments deficits but rather a progressive involvement of the banks in financing projects that would not permit early realization of the banks' commitments, thereby laying the basis for a pervasive liquidity crisis in the international banking system.

4. It is interesting to note the conclusion of the IMF Executive Board that "The first decision to allocate SDRs was predicated on the assumption that the earlier process of reserve creation had substantially come to an end"; *Reform of the International Monetary System*, Report by the Executive Board of the IMF to the Board of Governors, Washington, 1972, p. 6. It was not fully perceived at that time that a new system of reserve creation was already operative based on market responses by the commercial bank.

5. Floating rate note issues are now almost the standard form of borrowing, but in addition potential buyers of medium-term bonds have been tempted with bonds convertible into equities, with issues incorporating a currency swap element, zero coupon and deep discount issues and, shades of the 1920s, commodity-backed financings – of which one such issue was linked to the price of gold and another to the price of oil.

6. This is not to say, of course, that coordinated central bank action would not be sufficient to halt or prevent a crisis from developing. An important example of coordinated central bank action at a time of incipient crisis was the announcement made in September 1974 by the governors of the central banks of the Group of Ten and Switzerland. The significance of this action was that the major central banks created a precedent to commit liquidity to the international banking system if needed and thus acted as a major stabilizing element.

ANNEX.

Table 1. *Changes in net positions of countries vis-à-vis commercial banks (negative figures indicate increase in net borrowing) (in billions of US dollars)*

	1974	1975	1976	1977	1978	1979	1980	Jan.-Sept. 1981
Industrial countries	n.a.	29	8	2	25	− 3	8	26
Oil-exporting countries	30	6	3	2	− 8	31	38	7
Non-oil developing countries	n.a.	− 28	− 11	− 1	− 10	− 26	− 45	− 25
Others	n.a.	− 6	—	− 3	− 7	− 1	—	− 8

Source: International Monetary Fund

Table 2. *International bank and bond finance*
(in billions of US dollars)

	Average 1971-72	1973	1974	1975	1976	1977	1978	1979	1980	Jan.-Sept. 1981
International bank lending (net)	25	33	50	40	70	68	90	130	165	112
Industrial countries	16	16	22	10	31	39	40	71	100	80
Oil-exporting countries		3	3	8	9	9	14	7	6	1
Non-oil developing countries	8	10	15	15	21	14	25	41	52	27
Others	1	4	10	7	9	6	11	11	7	4
International bond issues (net)	n.a.	8	10	20	30	31	30	30	28	30
Less double counting due to bank purchases of bonds	n.a.	−1	−2	−2	−4	−5	−8	−9	−10	−8
Total	n.a.	40	59	58	96	94	112	51	183	134

Source: International Monetary Fund

Table 3. *Disposition and financing of current account balances, 1970-81 (in billions of US dollars)*

	Current account balance[1] (1)	Capital account (inflow +) Total[2] (2)	Commercial banks[3] (3)	Change in liabilities to foreign official agencies[4] Total (4)	Use of Fund credit (5)	Changes in reserves[5] Total (6)	Reserve positions in the Fund (7)
I. Industrial countries							
1970	12.3	− 4.5	—	4.1	− 0.3	11.9	0.7
1971	16.3	− 10.8	—	26.3	− 1.9	31.8	− 0.8
1972	16.9	− 6.6	—	11.0	− 0.5	21.3	—
1973	19.6	− 17.5	—	5.7	—	7.8	0.2
1974	− 12.4	− 4.7	—	19.7	1.8	2.6	1.7
1975	16.0	− 20.8	− 29.0	7.0	2.0	2.2	1.4
1976	− 1.6	− 3.1	− 8.0	15.1	2.8	10.4	4.7
1977	− 4.9	3.2	− 2.0	39.9	1.2	38.2	1.1
1978	31.4	− 19.4	− 25.0	29.6	− 2.5	41.6	− 2.4
1979	− 8.4	− 2.7	3.0	5.8	− 3.2	− 5.3	− 2.3
1980	− 43.8	48.1	− 8.0	21.3	− 0.9	25.6	3.5
1981			− 35.0				2.1
II. Major oil-exporting countries							
1970	− 0.5	1.2	—	0.1	—	0.8	—
1971	1.0	4.1	—	0.1	—	3.2	—
1972	1.7	1.0	—	− 0.3	—	2.4	0.1
1973	4.1	− 0.8	—	—	—	3.3	0.1
1974	53.9	− 22.5	− 30.0	0.1	—	31.5	1.9
1975	31.8	− 18.8	− 6.0	− 0.2	—	12.8	2.8
1976	33.3	− 22.2	− 3.0	—	—	11.1	1.2
1977	26.4	− 11.0	− 2.0	—	—	15.4	0.2
1978	− 3.6	− 8.9	8.0	—	—	− 12.5	− 0.8
1979	36.9	− 16.4	− 31.0	—	—	20.5	− 1.8
1980	70.9	− 82.1	− 38.0	—	—	23.6	1.2
1981			− 9.0				1.5
III. Non-oil developing countries							
1970	− 10.5	12.5	—	− 0.4	− 0.5	1.6	0.2
1971	− 13.2	14.8	—	0.1	0.1	1.7	0.1
1972	− 8.1	15.9	—	0.2	0.3	8.0	—
1973	− 9.8	19.2	—	0.2	0.1	9.6	0.2
1974	− 33.3	33.0	—	1.6	1.5	1.3	− 0.3
1975	− 43.3	43.3	28.0	2.3	2.0	− 2.3	− 0.2

(Table 3, continued)

| | Current account balance[1] (1) | Capital account (inflow +) | | Change in liabilities to foreign official agencies[4] | | Changes in reserves[5] | |
		Total[2] (2)	Commer-cial banks[3] (3)	Total (4)	Use of Fund credit (5)	Total (6)	Reserve positions in the Fund (7)
1976	− 30.3	38.5	11.0	4.1	3.0	12.3	− 0.1
1977	− 25.9	37.3	1.0	0.2	− 0.1	11.6	—
1978	− 33.0	51.0	10.0	0.2	− 0.1	18.2	0.5
1979	− 49.3	58.7	26.0	0.2	0.2	9.6	0.2
1980	− 63.6	66.5	45.0	0.9	1.1	3.8	1.2
1981			33.0				− 0.3

1. Excluding official transfers.

2. This balance is computed as the difference between the balance financed by changes in reserve assets and the sum of the current account balance and the change in liabilities to foreign official agencies; it includes net errors and omissions, as well as reported capital movements, government transfers, SDR allocations, valuation adjustments, and gold monetization (see also footnote 4).

3. Based on BIS data.

4. The concept of "liabilities to foreign agencies" used in this table encompasses use of Fund credit and short term balance of payments financing transactions in which the liabilities of the borrowing country are presumably treated as reserve assets by the creditor country.

5. The changes in reserve assets indicated here are calculated as the changes in US dollar equivalents of period-end stocks of total reserves with gold valued at SDR 35 per ounce. It may be noted that official agencies of some countries hold external financial claims that are not classified as reserves. Changes in such claims are included in column (2), "Capital account". The dividing line between capital movements and reserve asset changes remains particularly uncertain for some oil exporting countries.

Chapter XI

THE ROLE OF BANKS IN INTERNATIONAL CAPITAL MARKETS

by *T.M. Rybczynski*

In the last decade or so, and especially since the first oil shock, the nature, scope and role of banks both as regards their domestic and international activities have altered very significantly. This paper endeavours to examine the changes which have taken place and their implication with respect to one fairly narrow area, viz. that covering their involvement in international capital markets. To see the development in this area in the wider framework of the changes and issues arising in international financing, we first provide a brief description of international capital markets and their main characteristics. This is followed by a brief examination of the size and growth of the total financial market and its principal components and of the role this market has played in the international financing of the world economy and the main groups of countries. We then discuss the nature of banks' involvement in international capital markets, its impact on international financing and conclude by posing the main issues arising from banks' participation in international capital market activity.

Known in everyday parlance as Euro-bond markets, the international capital markets form a part of world capital markets which include also traditional foreign bond markets and domestic capital markets. The dividing line between these three sectors of world capital markets and above all between international markets and traditional foreign bond markets, has become increasingly blurred especially in the last year or so. There are three basic features which distinguish international capital markets from the other two sectors (and are also used as a basis for statistical and other purposes). They are, first, that these markets issue and trade in securities issued on behalf of borrowers outside the countries of the markets where they are originally sold; secondly, that such securities are originally made available simultaneously on the markets of at least two countries but are denominated in a currency which need not be the currency of either; finally, that such securities are brought to the market by financial syndicates comprising participants in several countries.

In contrast, traditional foreign bond markets are concerned with securities, which although also issued on behalf of non-residents of the country on whose market they are sold, are denominated in the currency of a country where they are originally marketed. Domestic capital markets issue securities on behalf of residents of a country where they are introduced and are denominated in the currency of that country.

In addition to these three basic features, international capital markets – which comprise primary and secondary markets, that is those concerned with original marketing and subsequent trading – have three other important characteristics. First, they are unregulated markets, that is to say that in principle they are not subject to the rules and regulations of the regulatory bodies supervising the activities of domestic capital markets including the foreign bonds sector, such as the Securities and Exchange Commission in the US, The Stock Exchange in the UK, The Capital Markets Sub-Committee in Germany. Secondly, these markets so far are concerned only with bonds and convertibles and warrants and do not include – as domestic capital markets and also foreign sectors of domestic markets do – ordinary shares and other securities such as preference shares, etc. Thirdly, at least until now these markets although broad, that is to say covering about 5,000 different securities, appear not to have sufficient depth, i.e. the quantities that can be traded at any particular time are relatively limited, or in other words, their secondary markets with some exceptions are insufficiently active.

Although unregulated in principle, in the sense that membership of the selling syndicate and the way they and trading firms operate is not subject to any rules, the original flotations of securities denominated in currencies other than the US and Canadian dollar and various "currency cocktails" such as the European Unit of Account (ECA) are indirectly controlled by national authorities whose currencies are used. The authorities, as in the case of Switzerland, either forbid such issues completely, or, as in the case of Germany, Japan, the UK and other countries, regulate them through the requirement that syndicates introducing them are led by a domestic bank (or banks) and therefore indirectly fall within the scope of the regulatory power of the authorities.

Although such regulations aim at insulating domestic capital markets from international capital markets, their effectiveness is increasingly limited, blurring the distinction between external bonds issued in domestic markets and international bonds. This is especially true for countries with no exchange control, such as Germany and the UK, whose residents are free to purchase them outside their own frontiers and indeed gain certain tax advantages inasmuch as international issues, as a rule bearer bonds, are easily transferable and all of them pay interest rates gross of tax. This blurring of the dividing line between the international markets and external bond markets denominated in currencies other than the US and Canadian dollar raises important policy issues, to which I will return later on.

Looking at the evolution of the international capital markets in the last seven years or so, four main developments stand out. First, the absolute size of gross issues (i.e. the involvement of primary markets) has been growing. The expansion in the value of gross and net issues has been accompanied by a rise in the relative importance of the Euro-bond market in relation to traditional foreign issues in domestic markets – the section of the world capital markets directly comparable with international capital markets. (These two sections of world capital markets cover the international flows of capital obtained in capital markets.) The rise in the share of international capital markets is indicative of the greater attraction these markets have in relation to traditional external bond markets and probably of a less restrictive attitude, especially in the last five years, of the national authorities, which impose restriction on such issues denominated in their currencies, mainly because of balance of payments pressures. This development has a bearing on the evolution of international monetary arrangements, and the role of financial markets as a whole (that is to say including money and credit markets).

Table 1. *Gross issues of Euro-bonds and foreign bonds*
(in billions of dollars and percentages)

	1976		1977		1978		1979		1980	
	$	%	$	%	$	%	$	%	$	%
Euro-bonds	15.4	44.9	19.5	54.0	16.0	74.4	17.8	47.1	22.1	57.7
Foreign bonds	18.9	55.1	16.6	46.0	21.5	25.6	20.0	52.9	16.1	42.3
Total	34.3	100.0	36.1	100.0	37.5	100.0	37.8	100.0	38.3	100.0

Source: World Bank.

Secondly, since the mid-1970s there has been a marked decline in the relative importance of the US dollar-denominated obligations floated on primary international capital markets and a marked rise in the relative importance of DM-denominated securities accompanied by a small increase in 1980 and, according to preliminary estimates, also in 1981 of sterling, Dutch guilder and yen-denominated obligations. There is little doubt that a rise in the relative importance of the DM and other currency denominated securities floated on primary international capital markets is indicative of a change in preferences on the part of investors, reflecting in turn changes in the international monetary arrangements to which national authorities outside the US and Canada – which do not restrict issues in their currencies outside their frontiers – have had to respond. This trend in turn has been influenced by and influences international financing and the place and functions of banks.

Table 2. *Currency denomination of Euro-bonds issued (in billions of dollars and percentages)*

	1976		1977		1978		1979		1980	
	$	%	$	%	$	%	$	%	$	%
US$	10.0	65.1	12.3	63.3	7.7	48.2	10.6	59.7	13.7	60.6
DM	2.8	18.4	5.2	26.8	6.5	41.0	4.7	26.2	4.3	18.9
Dutch guilder	0.5	3.0	0.4	1.9	0.4	2.4	0.4	1.9	0.7	3.3
French franc	0.1	0.4	—	—	0.1	0.7	0.3	2.1	1.0	4.5
Sterling	—	—	0.2	1.1	0.3	1.8	0.3	1.6	1.1	4.9
Yen	—	—	0.1	0.6	0.1	0.5	0.1	0.6	0.3	1.4
Composite units*	0.1	0.7	neg.	0.2	0.2	1.5	0.4	2.3	neg.	0.5
Other**	1.9	12.4	1.9	6.1	0.7	3.9	1.0	5.6	0.9	5.9
Total	15.4	100.0	19.5	100.0	16.0	100.0	17.8	100.0	22.1	100.0

* neg. means less than $0.05 billion.
** Including Canadian $, Kuwait dinar, Saudi Arabian riyal, Austrian schilling, Norwegian kroner, and others.

Source: World Bank.

Thirdly, in the last five years or so there has been a marked shift from straight Euro-bonds in favour of convertibles and floating rate notes. The two important factors contributing to this change have been an increasing involvement of the corporate sector in industrial countries and a greater volatility of interest rates. The former reflects the tendency on the part of the corporate sector to regard international markets as an alternative to domestic markets, the latter is indicative of borrowers' and lenders' preferences for reducing the risk of changes in the interest rate.

Inasmuch as banks, especially international banks, are also buyers, holders of and traders in securities originally issued in international capital markets, their attitudes affect and are affected by this development.

Finally, the examination of fund-raisers in Euro-bond markets brings out that the bulk of fund raising has been done by borrowers in industrial coun-

Table 3. *Euro-bond borrowing by instrument*
(in billions of dollars and percentages)

	1977		1978		1979		1980	
	$	%	$	%	$	%	$	%
Straight	15.7	94.4	11.1	69.6	11.1	62.5	14.2	64.1
Convertible and warrants	1.2	6.0	1.3	8.2	1.6	9.1	2.6	11.7
Special placement	0.8	3.7	0.8	5.3	0.8	4.7	0.9	4.5
Floating rate notes	1.8	9.4	2.6	16.3	4.2	23.6	4.2	19.1
Others and unknown	neg.	0.2	0.1	0.2	—	—	0.1	0.5
Total	19.5	100.0	15.9	100.0	17.8	100.0	22.1	100.0

Source: World Bank.

tries, including official and semi-official borrowers, and to a much smaller extent by international organisations. The share of fund raising by developing countries has been very small and has tended to comprise in the main a few countries such as Mexico and Brazil, falling into either an oil-exporting group or a newly industrialised countries group. In other words, international capital markets have so far mainly helped, at least in the first instance, the flow of medium-term capital among industrial countries rather than between developed and developing countries. This development is important in the context of the world financial flow and the way it is affected by the behaviour of banks.

Looked upon in the context of global international financing provided by financial markets – taken here to comprise international (i.e. Euro-) and domestic credit and money markets and international (i.e. Euro-) capital markets as well as traditional foreign bond markets, whose relative importance has been increasing while that of official and officially-sponsored financing in various forms has been declining – the contribution of international capital markets to total market financing which started growing in the 1960s is still modest. In the last two years (1980 and 1981) it accounted for about 10 per cent of funds so raised, having been around 16 per cent in the four years ending in 1978.

While any comparison with domestic financial flows is subject to important qualifications and reservations and must be treated with extreme caution, such tentative estimates as can be made tend to indicate that capital markets in the major industrial economies contribute on the average about one-third of financial flows – the figure not significantly out of line with 30 per cent or so contributed to international flows by *both* international capital markets and foreign bond markets.

Table 4. *Gross Euro-bond issues by groups of countries*
(in billions of dollars and percentages) [1]

	1976		1977		1978		1979		1980	
	$	%	$	%	$	%	$	%	$	%
International organisations	3.1	20.1	2.4	12.3	2.7	16.9	2.8	15.7	3.1	14.0
Industrial	11.0	71.4	13.2	67.7	9.8	61.3	12.7	71.3	17.4	78.7
Developing oil-exporters	0.2	1.3	0.5	2.5	1.1	6.9	0.3	1.7	0.1	neg.
Developing non-oil exporters	0.9	5.8	2.2	11.3	2.1	13.1	1.6	9.0	1.3	5.9
Centrally-planned economies	0.1	neg.	0.2	0.5	neg.	neg.	neg.	neg.	neg.	neg.
Others	0.1	neg.	1.0	5.2	0.2	1.3	0.3	1.7	0.1	neg.
Total	15.4	100.0	19.5	100.0	16.0	100.0	17.8	100.0	22.1	100.0

1. neg. means less than 0.5% or $0.5 billion.
Note: Totals may not add up due to rounding.

Source: World Bank.

Table 5. *International flows through bank lending and international and*
foreign bond markets (net) and world deficits on current account
(in billions of dollars)

	1971 -1973	1974	1975	1976	1977	1978	1979	1980
International bond issues (net)	3	4	9	14	16	16	15	15
Foreign bond issues (net)	5	6	11	16	15	14	15	13
International bank lending (net)	27	50	40	70	68	90	130	165
Less double counting due to bank purchases of bonds	neg.	− 1	− 2	− 4	− 5	− 8	− 9	− 10
Total[1]	33	59	58	96	94	112	151	183
Sum of deficits on current account	18	76	78	73	76	85	93	153

1. Net of double counting due to bank purchases of bonds.

Source: World Bank and author's estimates.

The international movements of funds through credit and capital markets are nowadays often related to the sum of current account deficits of all world economies. Such totals increased sharply in 1974 following the first oil shock (see Table 5), did not alter significantly in the following four years, but rose sharply again in 1980 in the wake of the second oil shock. The total of international finance raised through credit and international and foreign bond markets, however, since 1976 has quite comfortably exceeded the sum of deficit – which of course is also financed by official and private non-debt creating flows.

A closer examination of the total of the world's current account deficits, however, conceals rather than reveals two different developments bearing on their financing and the role of international capital markets, foreign bond markets and credit markets.

The first development is that there is fairly close connection between the current account deficit and the movements of funds through financial markets (i.e. credit markets and international and foreign bond markets) for planned economies, also for non-oil developing countries.

The reason why private financing obtained to a large extent in international credit and only to a negligible extent in international capital markets approximates the deficit on current account for the planned economies is simple. This is that their external transactions are strictly controlled, and that apart from holding a small amount of funds abroad to finance their current transactions, these countries do not own nor buy assets overseas, be it on account of their enterprises or on behalf of their residents. In other words, the current account deficit of this group of countries is directly re-

Table 6. *Planned economies: current account deficit and finance abroad (in billions of dollars)*

	Current account deficit	Increase in debt to banks overseas	Bond issues in the West
1974	− 5	nil	nil
1975	− 11	nil	nil
1976	− 13	nil	0.1
1977	− 9	+ 4	+ 0.3
1978	− 6	+ 5	neg.
1979	− 3	+ 2	0.1
1980	− 5	nil	nil

Source: World Bank.

lated to their ability to obtain necessary finance either by way of suppliers' credit or their ability to raise funds needed in the credit markets in the market economies and in international and foreign bond capital markets – all transactions being controlled by their authorities.

Broadly speaking similar factors are also relevant to the involvement in international financing of non-oil exporting developing countries. It is now recognised that this group consists of four sub-groups with different characteristics, which in turn determine the nature and the degree of their participation in international financing including the Euro-bond market. These four sub groups comprise net oil exporters, major exporters of manufactured goods, low income countries and other non-oil developing countries. It is only the first two sub-groups, net oil-exporters and major exporters of manufactured goods, which have been able to use Euro-bond and foreign bond markets to a very small degree, but even then mainly as part of deficit financing under direct control of the authorities. Furthermore, the recourse to Euro-markets and foreign bond markets has been limited to a very small number of countries, such as Brazil and Mexico, the remainder participating only to a very small extent or not at all.

Table 7. *Non-oil developing countries: current account and private finance (in billions of dollars)*

	1974	1975	1976	1977	1978	1979	1980
Main exporters of manufactures							
Current account deficit	− 19	− 20	− 12	− 8	− 10	− 22	− 32
Borrowing from credit markets	n.a.	n.a.	11	6	13	18	24
Borrowing from capital markets	1	1	1	1	2	2	1
Net oil-exporters							
Current account deficit	− 5	− 10	− 8	− 7	− 8	− 8	− 11
Borrowing from credit markets	n.a.	n.a.	7	3	6	11	14
Borrowing from capital markets	n.a.	n.a.	6	2	5	10	14

n.a. = not available.

Source: World Bank.

As far as low-income and other non-oil developing countries are concerned, for practical purposes they have not been involved in fund-raising in international and foreign bond markets. Indeed, their use of private finance has been and continues to be very small, the bulk of their external financing coming in one way or another from official sources in industrial countries. This pattern of financing indicates that private markets perceive that the risks involved in lending to them are too high.

The involvement of oil-exporting countries in international financing, including Euro- and foreign bond markets and credit markets has been different from that of the non-oil developing countries and planned economies on the one hand and industrial countries – discussed later on – on the other. Unlike non-oil developing countries and planned econonomies this group of countries has had and continues to have a current account surplus and its most important and major members do not impose any restrictions on movements of capital (and on current transactions). In the context of international markets these countries have been net providers of liquid funds advanced by way of placing bank deposits in industrial countries. They have also been lenders by way of purchasing securities in the primary and secondary Euro-bond, foreign bond and domestic capital markets and also – but to a very small extent – denominated in their currencies. Finally, they have increasingly become directly involved in international financial flows and intermediation by setting up and expanding their banks and financial institutions engaged in banking, investment banking and other financial transactions.

Table 8. *Oil-exporting countries: current account position, net bank borrowing and disposition of cash surplus*
(in billions of dollars)

	Current account	Bank borrowing (net)	Cash surplus	Placed in bank deposit	Other uses
1971-73 (average)	n.a.	n.a.	n.a.	n.a.	n.a.
1974	+ 68	3	58	30	28
1975	+ 35	8	39	11	28
1976	+ 40	9	42	13	29
1977	+ 31	11	40	13	27
1978	+ 3	18	20	5	15
1979	+ 68	7	69	40	29
1980	+112	6	120	42	82

Source: World Bank.

In contrast to both non-oil developing countries and planned economies on the one hand and oil-exporting countries on the other, whose involvement in international financing and international credit and capital markets, though for different reasons, has broadly speaking tended to reflect their current account position, the industrial countries' participation has been markedly different in character. Their borrowing has far exceeded their net current account deficit since 1974 (and also before 1973, when they had a net surplus), and indeed the sum of their deficits, indicating that the current account deficit has played a limited role in the financial flows to and from international markets and that there have been and continue to be other factors of even greater importance.

These factors include, first, the function of intermediation relating to the re-channelling of oil exporters' surpluses to non-oil developing countries and to planned economies; secondly, the intermediary function among industrial countries themselves; and finally – and this is subject to a debate – the function of money creation by international credit markets referred to nowadays as "privatisation" of world liquidity.

The role of Euro-bond markets in re-channelling funds from surplus countries – OPEC between 1974 and 1977 and in 1979-1981 and industrial countries before 1974 and in 1978, when the pre-1974 pattern of world payments re-asserted itself – has been rather modest as has been that of foreign bond markets. This is so because the number of countries capable of raising funds in this way is limited and comprises, as mentioned before, a small number of developing oil-exporting countries and major exporters of manufactures. Their Euro-bond issues cover flotation either by governments (i.e. sovereign risk) or government-owned enterprises in basic industries, above all oil, and of securities issued by privately-owned enterprises but carrying a government guarantee (i.e. again sovereign risk).

The Euro-bond market plays a much more important role in the flow of funds among industrial countries. While direct government issues and government guaranteed issues for balance of payments reasons, particularly for smaller industrial countries, have played quite an important role, corporate issues, especially by multinational companies based in countries with no exchange controls and motivated by the cost and other relevant factors, have been quite prominent and growing. For such operations the Euro-bond market has been and continues to be an alternative source of funds.

Euro-bond issues are also a part of the "privatisation" of world liquidity, inasmuch as they are used to raise funds by international banks, enabling them in turn to accelerate the growth of their assets. I will return to this aspect later on.

It is interesting to note here that within the broad framework of international financial markets the relative importance of Euro-bond markets, notwithstanding marked year-to-year fluctuations associated with changes and expectations of change in interest rates, has displayed a secular increase, indicating their growing integration into the world credit and capital markets.

Table 9. *Industrial countries: current account position* [1] *and borrowings from international credit and bond markets* [1]
(*in billions of dollars*)

	Sum of current account deficits	Sum of current account surpluses	Net current account position	Borrowing from international financial market (net)			
				Banks	Foreign bonds	Euro-bonds	Total
1971-73 av.	5.1	15.0	+ 9.9	16	3	2	21
1974	38.1	18.8	− 19.3	22	3	2	27
1975	21.9	28.2	+ 6.3	10	7	7	24
1976	31.3	18.9	− 12.4	31	11	10	51
1977	40.3	21.7	− 18.6	39	9	11	60
1978	31.7	48.0	+ 16.3	40	10	8	58
1979	33.3	16.4	− 16.9	71	11	9	91
1980	63.0	10.6	− 42.4	100	7	14	121

1. Inclusive of official transfers.

Source: IMF.

Against this background the role played by banks in international capital markets can be seen best by examining the functions they perform in this area and the way they have changed in the recent years and compare their position with that of other firms.

Before describing the nature of banks' involvement in the international capital markets it is worth emphasising that this market is in principle an unregulated market (i.e. there are no restrictions on entry or regulation of operations), and that firms in primary markets comprise banks, taken here to denote deposit-taking banks and investment banks (i.e. financial institutions engaged in the selling of securities). While deposit banks in the US and Japan are not allowed to engage *domestically* in underwriting activities (Glass-Steagall Act of 1932 and post-World War II legislation based on American approach in Japan), banks in other industrial countries generally, though there are some exceptions, have been free to do so and in fact have been heavily engaged in this activity, except until recently in the UK, where large deposit-taking banks of their own volition refrained from doing so, leaving this area to merchant banks and specialised underwriting firms (i.e. issuing houses not undertaking banking). However, through the acquisition of merchant banks, big deposit banks in the UK have in effect entered domestic underwriting business.

Both large and not-so-large deposit banks and investment banks in all industrial countries have also been managing funds in fiduciary capacity on behalf of private individuals, pension funds and various savings-collecting bodies – the sector of business which has been growing very rapidly – and consequently have been acting in fiduciary capacity as buyers of securities issued in primary markets and as buyers and sellers of securities in secondary markets.

Reflecting these different legal approaches to underwriting, the primary international capital market has come to comprise large deposit banks from the European countries, merchant banks from the UK and private banks and issuing houses from Europe, and specially established merchant banking subsidiaries of American deposit banks (permitted to do so overseas), large Japanese deposit banks (permitted to do underwriting overseas), Japanese security houses (i.e. underwriters), as well as the US investment banks. The large European deposit banks' as well as other European and Japanese banks' and merchant and private banks' operations in the primary international capital market are undertaken either directly or through special subsidiaries.

In primary markets deposit banks' involvement comprises, first, underwriting – that is to say arranging to sell newly-issued securities or buying them outright for sale to others – the function they undertake in common with other participants; secondly, they themselves are issuers of securities the proceeds of which are used to expand the basis of their banking business. In the secondary markets some of the deposit-taking banks also act as market-makers in some securities, that is to say they are traders. Virtually all deposit banks as well as investment banks also act as buyers and sellers of existing securities either for their own account or on behalf of their clients, whose funds they manage in fiduciary capacity.

It should be emphasised here that the secondary international capital market is dominated by institutional and a relatively small number of large private investors whose affairs are managed by fund-managing institutions. This contrasts strongly with domestic secondary capital markets, including the foreign bond sector, where private small investors are still quite important. Also, secondary international capital markets – as I mentioned at the beginning – at present do not possess the same depth as domestic capital markets. According to existing estimates, of the total of some 5,000 Euro-securities, about one-third of Euro-bonds has no effective secondary market, about one-third has a fairly limited market and only for the remaining one-third are trading conditions reasonably satisfactory.

In what way have the functions performed by banks in the international capital markets, and outlined above, affected and influenced the evolution of international financing in the last ten years or so and what are the implications of this development?

Broadly speaking, the participation of large deposit banks, of not-so-large deposit banks, as well as of investment banks in primary markets by way of acting as underwriters and as original issuers of securities and their involvement in secondary markets as buyers and sellers of "old" securities and also as market-makers, has affected the evolution of international financing in two principal ways. First, it has led to growing integration of world financing by effectively improving the flow of funds between different national markets and consequently reducing the obstacles separating various domestic financial markets, including capital markets. Secondly, it has led to a reduction in segmentation between various sections of financial markets both domestically and internationally, resulting again in an increase in integration of financial markets on a worldwide scale.

The contribution of international capital markets and of banks involved in them to the integration of world capital markets and world financial markets has consisted in the opening and widening of access to the pool of world saving, by raising the awareness of the prospective investors to financing possibilities, and by offering to savers financial instruments of appeal to them. By bringing world investors and world savers together the international capital market and international credit particularly have helped to reduce the gap between risk-adjusted rate of return on investment in various countries and the rate of return to savers allowing for their risk and liquidity preference.

The basic mechanism through which this has been achieved consists in a further strengthening of the already close relationship, first, between the Euro-bond markets and foreign bond markets and secondly between the foreign bond markets and domestic markets. Banks' involvement in these areas has extended to the function of pricing commercial risk – which they have been performing and which all domestic capital and credit markets engage in – to pricing and marketing of foreign exchange risk, political risk and sovereign risk.

The undertaking of the pricing and marketing of risk attaching to international financing has added an additional source of funds available to new or "old" borrowers and provided an additional avenue to savers, thus breaking down the barriers between various domestic capital (and credit) markets.

For developing countries with a high rate of growth and/or beginning to realise their growth potential, international capital markets have provided the machinery for pricing and marketing the risks attaching to international financing they need to continue to expand and previously not easily accessible to them or not accessible at all. Their borrowings in the international capital markets have been limited so far to fund-raising operations by their governments or government-sponsored institutions whose risk – as one would expect at this stage of development – can now be priced and marketed.

For developed countries, whose borrowers in addition to government comprise non financial and financial corporations, the international capital market has opened a new source of finance whose transactions and intermediation costs are often lower, since such operations bring in line the rates of return on various investments in different countries and rates of return to savers in different countries – allowing for risk and liquidity preference – and by doing so help improve the efficiency of capital markets.

Accompanying the inter country or geographical integration of capital (and financial) markets, of which the international capital market has been an integral part, there has been also a reduction in segmentation within capital markets and as between capital and credit markets. There are two aspects here. The first relates to the ability of bank and non-bank intermediaries as a whole to increase their ability to engage in maturity transformation and risk diversification. The second has to do with the increasing overlap and substitutability of financial liabilities they incur and financial assets they acquire and in turn held by bank and non-bank financial intermediaries and savers.

As regards the latter, Euro-bond markets have developed a variety of financial instruments which have enhanced the range of options available to savers (i.e. investors) and borrowers, the effect of which has been to reduce the segmentation among various sectors of capital market and between capital markets and credit markets. Straight bonds with maturities between five and fifteen years supplement foreign bond and domestic markets which are involved principally with debt of between ten and twenty-five years. Convertibles with or without warrants are complementary to similar instruments issued in domestic markets. Floating rate notes provide a bridge between fixed coupon and other instruments and together with relatively short bonds provide an alternative to roll-over medium-term banking credits.

One important consequence of the involvement of banks in international capital markets has been to increase the ability of banks operating in this area to enhance their ability to carry out maturity transformation and risk diversification – the two basic functions performed by banks and non-bank financial intermediaries. By raising funds by floating rate notes in various currencies, banks can fund their medium-term and longer-term lending, while spreading the risk among a larger number of borrowers, thus imparting a new flexibility. By raising debt, including convertibles, in various currencies they can widen their capital base while simultaneously extending the scope of their operations, thus enhancing their risk diversification.

A reduction of geographical separation and market segmentation of capital markets and their integration with credit markets has reduced the transaction and intermediation costs to providers of funds and users of funds and has reduced the disparity between rates of return earned by users of funds and those received by providers of funds.

In the longer perspective an increasing participation of banks in international capital markets represents a further advance in the growth of world financial integration and intermediation associated with the real growth of world economy and its members. Indeed – and this cannot be emphasised too strongly – international capital (and credit) markets emerged in the 1960s, well before the first oil shock, and there is no doubt that they would have expanded – though perhaps not as rapidly – even if oil prices had not been increased in 1973 and 1979.

World financial integration involves, first, a shift in international financing towards market finance (i.e. towards international and domestic credit and capital markets) and away from non-market finance (i.e. government transfers and direct investment); secondly, from indirect finance (obtained through banks) to direct finance obtained by fund-users from fund-providers through capital markets.

Looked upon in this framework changes in external financing of two sub-groups of developing countries, i.e. net oil-exporters and major exporters of manufactures, involving a shift away from official financing towards mainly indirect market financing (i.e. through banks), and a first modest shift towards financing through international capital markets reflects a secular trend associated with real growth of world economy and its members and accompanying it changes in the mix and pattern of financing. This also holds true as regards changes in external financing of industrial countries. In their case the important element, apart from the balance of payments financing operations undertaken by governments – especially of the smaller countries but now rapidly diminishing in importance particularly for major countries – has been the growth in foreign financing by the corporate sector involving increasingly direct raising of funds from savers through capital markets, and above all international capital markets.

Finally, a few comments on the principal issues which the expansion of international capital (and credit) markets has brought to the fore in the macroeconomic and microeconomic areas. In the macroeconomic area two main problems have come to the top of the agenda. The first concerns the extent to which (if any) banks' involvement in the international capital market contributes to the "privatisation" of world liquidity creation. The second relates to the way and the degree to which the international capital markets impair the pursuit of independent exchange rate and interest rate and therefore economic policies by individual countries and justifies the imposition of restrictions on issues on Euro-bond markets by countries which do so.

The problem of the contribution of the international capital market to "privatisation" of world liquidity is a part of a wider question of the role played in this process by Euro-credit markets. If it is accepted that Euro credit markets do have a certain power to create world liquidity then, by funding themselves in Euro-bond markets, banks also raise their lending and liquidity-creating power. This raises the important issue of world liquidity creation, which is outside the scope of this paper.

As regards the second issue, the regulation of Euro-bond issues by countries other than the US and Canada is justified on the grounds that they prevent or contain the internationalisation of their currencies – the development which would make domestic management more difficult. However, the experience of the recent years tends to indicate that controls of capital movement (outwards and inwards) at least for the major countries are becoming increasingly ineffective. For this reason regulation of Euro-bond issues by countries which exercise such powers at present must be considered by reference to the desirability and practicability of having capital controls as such.

In the microeconomic area the main issues are those of competition and prudential regulation. More specifically, the questions that need posing and answering are how to preserve competitive pressures leading to a reduction in transaction and intermediation cost, while preserving adequate stability and maintaining the confidence of fund-providers.

No doubt both sets of problems will be high on the economic and political agenda in the future, and I hope that the issues will be tackled with vigour, resolution as well as prudence and wisdom based on full understanding of the problems involved.

Chapter XII

THE INTERRELATIONSHIPS BETWEEN EXPORT FINANCING AND COMMERCIAL BANKING ACTIVITY

by *Helmut H. Haschek*

OUTLINE

For the future well-being of the world economy further growth of international trade is a precondition. The recent and current situation is marked by increasing deficits between surplus and deficit regions on current account which in all probability will continue to grow in the future. In order that world trade will continue to develop favourably the bridging of these gaps will be the major task of the international financial community, a task which will be, however, much more difficult than hitherto.

In the 1970s the commercial banks assumed a predominant role in bridging these gaps. But they were forced to assume risks far beyond their traditional involvement in foreign trade consisting in providing services to accommodate the real flow of goods and services and to bridge payment deferred on short term. In fact, the abundance of funds at their disposal forced them to become merchant banks involved in medium- and long-term financing of sovereign risks. The flow of financial resources has been separated from the flow of goods and services. Therefore the advantages of export risk insurance could not be made use of, increasing the commercial banks' vulnerability in view of the magnitude of the volume which had to be transacted.

To deal with the future, a much closer cooperation between the lending operations of the commercial banks, the international institutions such as the IMF, the IBRD and the regional development banks and in addition the export financing agencies is called for as a *deliberate* strategy and not be left more or less to coincidence.

It could well be imagined that the export financing agencies arise, with a new type of borrower in the international markets, to a much greater degree than hitherto, to perform the transformation task which has become too risky for the commercial banks which are already burdened with sometimes excessive country risks. In the future even more so as there is the threat that economic policy will be used as an integrated tool in foreign policy which cannot be influenced by the private banking sector (see the Iran case and the RMCA issue at present).

The existing and the growing imbalances among the trading regions of the world tend to increase the nationalization of credit risks in international trade. This means the essence of the art of banking, the diversification of risks, becomes more and more fragile.

Therefore new forms of risk-sharing have to be found. The closer co-operation between the commercial banks and the export financing agencies on an international scale may provide part of the answer. It could be insti-tuted without delay. It would be preferable to the creation of new large in-ternational lending agencies and mutual insurance funds which tend to result in the creation of new international bureaucracies removed from the actual scene where the needs occur and the solutions to their satisfaction have to be found.

I

It has become fashionable over the past few years to comment on the further development of the world economy in terms of more or less pronounced pes-simism. While in the aftermath of the first publication of the Club of Rome the intensity of pessimism was correlated to the extent of the exponential growth factor which was inserted into the various equations which simulat-ed the future, recently a new element in international politics has overshad-owed the future perspectives with a more imminent danger: the outbreak of *economic warfare* originating from different sources – be it the growing protectionism as a tool of economic self-defence, or the use of economic sanctions as an integral part of foreign policy in the struggle over the bal-ance of power within the community of nations.

Economic warfare was barely visible at the roots of the destruction of the monetary order at the beginning of the 1970s, it was apparent in the forma-tion of the oil cartel, it came to the surface during the Iran crisis and it is in the forefront at the brink of a new cold war between East and West and latent in the North-South confrontation at present.

II

One thing remains certain: there is and there will be for some time a basic disequilibrium between surplus and deficit regions in the world and the basic challenge offered will be to continue to find ways and means to transform financial assets into real transfers of goods and services though the volume of financial surpluses changes from time to time as a result of economic development and the consumption pattern of energy.

Without wanting to minimize the problems for the future development of the world economy and the challenges the present generation and the coming ones are confronted with it is both useful and necessary to point out the very positive developments which have taken place in the past quarter of the century.[1]

Oil conservation in the industrialized countries in particular and rising imports of the OPEC countries are the forces which can offset the imbalances created. But even optimistic forecasts project that in the next five years the non-oil LDCs might accumulate an additional deficit of some $ 200 billion over the existing debt burden of some $ 100 billion of current bank debt and the COMECON countries including China may accumulate another $ 35 billion over the accumulated bank debt of $ 55 billion.

In all probability the private banking system will be unable to provide such enormous amounts in recycling surpluses because in a number of cases banks have arrived at their lending limits. It is certain that a substantial increase in official lending is required. Whether this will be forthcoming in the volumes required remains to be seen. New strategies seem necessary to be developed.

These new strategies will require intensified international cooperation on the basis of *existing instruments* and *institutions* which seems easier to be accomplished than drafting a new monetary world order. Pragmatic approaches are required beyond ideological and bureaucratic limitations.

In the following, the attempt is made to demonstrate that a substantial contribution to meet successfully this challenge needs the establishment of a much closer cooperation than hitherto between the commercial banking community, the International Monetary Fund together with international and regional development banks, and the export financing and insurance institutions in the industrialized world, and the creation of integrated export financing and insurance agencies in less developed countries, to achieve both increased flows of goods and services to the regions where demand accrues and the foreign exchange earnings to pay for these imports on the one hand and diversified, self-liquidating financial assets on the other to assist in the reinvestment of accumulated foreign exchange surpluses.

III

The world economy has changed radically since 1970. There has been the disestablishment of the monetary order. There is the energy problem, which created basic disequilibration between the trading regions of the world.

The energy problem helped to create the first recession in the post-war period. It helped to create the present painful situation in which one hopes for a recession and dreads the consequences of it at the same time.

The financing of the first oil shock increased international indebtedness. The effect of the level of interest rates on the level of indebtedness is clear: it influences the size of the existing debt by generating new debt without moving goods and services. At the rate of 7 per cent the debt, even remaining unchanged, doubles on a compound basis within ten years, at the rate of 10 per cent in seven years, at the rate of 20 per cent in four years.

There is little doubt that the years to come will continue to entail a growing nationalization of foreign trade. In the future the risk in international trade will be a political risk in the terminology of the credit insurers: a transfer risk and hopefully only that. The catastrophe would be unavoidable would sovereign risks have to be regarded as potential risks of total loss comparable to the insolvency risk of a private buyer, a problem which has now come into the forefront of discussions with the new administration in power in the USA. This transfer risk will develop regardless of the economic order according to which a national economy is organized.

The philosophy of the credit insurers has been that political risks can only be insured by governments, because political risks can be diversified to only a limited extent: with the political risks between the number of sovereign states as a maximum.

The current export credit insurance systems of the world are badly equipped to deal with the challenge the future presents us with. They originated at a time when there was practically no political risk associated with international trade. The insurance of political risks has been added later. But the political risk has become and will be, however, the major risk in international trade.

When one analyzes the situation as it will face us the following observation has to be made.

The risk in financing international trade is twofold: there is the risk which evolves between the trading partners. It is the risk of orderly execution of contractual arrangements connected with the delivery and the financing of goods and services. The risk can be ascertained, there can be a cash-flow analysis and there is a way to measure the pay-back period.

But there is also the transfer risk which is one of a different nature arising between different parties. The transfer risk exists, however careful the contractual parties analyze the risk originating from the execution of their contractual arrangements. It is latent all the time. It will be dealt with by the credit insurers when the execution of contracts is discontinued because of the lack of foreign exchange reserves of the debtor country. Then there will be negotiations between the governments to reschedule.

In the first phase of recycling it was successfully undertaken by the private banking sector. The role of international financing institutions or governments per se was marginal.

At present and in the future the private banking sector will be confronted with the same task at greater risk because the level of indebtedness has increased and the present level of interest rates makes this debt grow autonomously at a very accelerated pace without the benefit of increasing the flows of goods and investments connected normally with the growth of debt laying the foundation for its redemption.

IV

While there are highly developed export credit insurance systems throughout the world, there is no comparable system to deal with the risks connected with the transfer of financial assets from the surplus regions. On the contrary, there are conflicting interests. The export financing and insurance organizations try to limit their involvement to as short maturities as possible thereby producing a crowding-out effect on the short-term maturities for the private banking sector which has to recycle financial assets into the higher risk area or not recycle at all.[2]

V

The future, however, requires us to look for as *decentralized* solutions as possible; to make use of the *existing talent* as much as possible because there is a lack of experience and not an over-abundance of it.

After World War II, as late as in the early 1960s, export financing assumed a further role which is still growing: export credits were used as investment credits in project financing. The tool was the *buyer credit* formula together with credit insurance not any more offered to exporters but by *banks lending to importers*. From an institutional point of view, the administration of the credits as well as of the insurance, is handled in the majority of cases by *commercial banks* and the already *existing credit insurance organizations* which operated in the field of insuring supplier credits. This is also the reason why today buyer credits are still treated – wrongly as I believe – as a mere substitute for supplier credits which in the majority of cases they are not.

This approach in itself could involve the possibility of engaging governments in the insurance of transfer risks the existence of which is one of the major obstacles for the future recycling process. This is in itself an advantage. It needs to be developed. The association of governments in the risk sharing process by itself does not necessarily guarantee a beneficial development.

But there is no question that the export financing agencies in the industrialized world would be able to be first class borrowers with diversified and interest earning assets which allow the allocation of funds with comparatively little risk to the lender. It seems that in this field cooperation between these agencies and the commercial banks could be developed in that these agencies substitute for the ultimate borrowers which do not qualify any more for direct lending by commercial forms.[3]

The involvement of sovereign governments in most of the industrialized countries necessitates the intervention of parliaments and their commitment cannot be achieved by telling them that they should assume and vote for additional risks on the vague promise that this commitment will provide jobs if and when their industries are competitive enough to win orders in international competition. This might be a regrettable fact but nonetheless it is a fact. This is why it is so difficult to win assistance for international financing organizations because they all insist on international bidding and there is no assurance that the benefits and the burdens are matched.

As a first step toward the solution of the transformation problem we are confronted with the role of the export financing organizations as international borrowers; this role should be strengthened as a deliberate step of policy. A number of export financing organizations borrow already in the international markets. But they do so in the majority of cases because the funds required are not available in their domestic markets. They would prefer to borrow domestically.

Their involvement in international markets could bring about another advantage. It could lead to the gradual shift in the use of exchange risk guarantees from the export and export financing contracts to their financing operations; the advantage being that the exchange risk connected with borrowing operations of these agencies can be diversified because the borrowing institutions can create their own managed unit of account. Exchange risk guarantees on lending operations do not allow the diversification of risks. But this is only a first step in the process. *A second and important one would be that the export financing institutions and the private banking sector closely cooperate in the financing of development projects.* Do they not so far? Not to the extent needed. It should be made a strategy that long-term financing of development projects should be shared in such a way that the private sector assumes the short-term maturities and the specialized institutions the long-term risk with government intervention.

VI

Current account surpluses in one region of the world economy mean deficits in one or more other regions of the world economy. In some future time these deficits and surpluses will have to be adjusted in real terms. Should the surplus regions be prepared to invest their financial surpluses directly on the long term and predominantly in the form of investments into the deficit regions this process of real adjustment could take place at a slower pace, time could be won to achieve the additional growth in the deficit regions necessary to permit the adjustment.

Presently, however, and in the near future these financial surpluses are not and will not be made available sufficiently in the form of direct investments, nor are and will credits be extended directly to the structural deficit regions, nor made available on a long-term basis. As a consequence the international financial markets are and will be liquid, despite the current shift of many OPEC countries from the lending to the borrowing side.

In order that demand for investment is met the risks of transformation have to be borne by intermediaries or, if this is not the case, the recycling of financial surpluses becomes continuously more difficult. Of course, ex post, a recycling problem cannot exist. But it is in the highest interest of the world economy that this recycling takes place on acceptable terms for the holders of financial assets because the other alternative would be to curtail production of oil in order to avoid the monetization of oil reserves.

The international financial markets in the 1980s will therefore increasingly become borrowers' markets. Evidently the recycling of financial surpluses which is regarded as essential for the future well-being of the world economy shall only be possible if there are enough borrowers who are

(i) prepared to borrow in a foreign currency and
(ii) the viability of which conforms to the expectations of the prospective lenders.

These two preconditions, however, limit the number of possible borrowers substantially.

Should the current account surpluses and deficits increase, this must lead to a further and progressive nationalization of the credit risk quite apart from the nature in which individual national economies are organized. A credit risk with reference to the contractual parties which is different from the credit risk of a country presupposes the existence of a market economy.[4]

Can it be assumed, therefore, that the 1980s will offer good prospects for borrowers of exceptional qualifications? Possibly the answer is yes if judged from the point of view of liquidity only. It is probable that the over-abundance of liquidity will continue to exert pressure on the margins which have been compressed already below sound banking standards.

However, even borrowers who are prepared to borrow and regard them-selves as qualified borrowers shall be confronted with the problem that the volumes for single transactions which are acceptable internationally today are too small in order to allow the recycling in sufficient quantity even if the credit standing of the borrower is no problem.

The answer is no if the question is regarded from the point of view of the quality of the funds, if judged from the point of view of the risk of the variation of interest rates and the exchange risk (if the latter is regarded as being different from the interest variation risk for the purpose of argument).

But even if the horror visions do not come true new policies to tackle the challenges of the future are required. It has been argued that difficulties could arise because there are no qualified borrowers for the type of financial surpluses which are offered and that the capacity to transform these financial assets through the private banking community has already reached its limits.

If one regards the borrowers according to their qualifications in the international financial markets it can be seen that banks are among the borrowers in increasing numbers. There are three types of banks:

(a) the important international and regional development banks such as the World Bank, the Interamerican Development Bank or the European Investment Bank;
(b) export financing institutions;
(c) other banks.

The increasing importance of the first of these groups conforms with the expectations. Relatively new, however, is the role of the export financing institutions.

VII

Without any doubt the current account imbalances can only be readjusted if further growth of world trade is maintained as in the past. In order to achieve this goal, the financing of exports will have central importance. It is true that even today 43 per cent of world trade is transacted between industrial nations. However, it is this concentration which will have to be changed if imbalances are to be adjusted.

The demand for investment goods will come from the deficit regions. It will only be satisfied if long-term credits for their purchases can be offered. If, however, the private banking sector has reached the limits of its transformation capacity other institutions have to step in to fill the gap. One way would be the creation of new large development organizations. The other, more promising way would be to expand the institutional export financing facilities which have to be turned purposely into a form of international investment financing. There are indications that a development in this direction is already on the way.

Export financing institutions finance mainly capital exports from their countries. Inasmuch as exporting countries entertain current account surpluses they can mobilize their own financial resources for that purpose. Inasmuch as they have, however, current account deficits they are only able to finance capital exports by capital imports; this is the case for instance in Austria. In this way those countries assume through their export finance agencies a role in the transformation process, a role which is supported by the weight of their entire economy because their financial assets are guaranteed through government export insurance.

Whether these export financing institutions use the insurance cover provided by their countries as a means to facilitate the recycling of financial surpluses only or use the insurance cover to substitute risks with regard to the ultimate borrower depends on the quality of the financial assets in which export institutions have invested and which in turn is dependent on the measure to which the relevant risks are diversified. The extent to which the first aim of only facilitating the recycling is achieved can be measured by the extent to which the financial assets accrued are marketable. Risk substitution does not take place if the share of marketable financial assets of these export financing institutions does not surpass the amount for which they have borrowed internationally.

Which are the advantages of a further and increased role of export financing institutions?

First: they are borrowers who offer financial assets for refinancing which in any case are better diversified than in the case of direct lending to their ultimate borrowers. New borrowers are introduced indirectly to the financial markets who cannot appear as borrowers themselves. The rate of diversification increases. Even if a further nationalization of risks in international trade occurs, past experience shows that project financing is preferable to balance of payments financing.

Secondly: through the intervention of the governments on the side of the borrowing export credit institutions, the borrowing capacity of countries can be used which otherwise is not available or only to a limited extent.

Thirdly: the export capacity of the ultimate borrowing countries could be increased by linking their exports to imports and by developing new ways of distribution of their commodities which in turn will help to adjust the deficits.

Fourthly: this type of financing has not to be restricted to institutions of industrial countries; on the contrary, it should not be restricted to these countries. It could serve as a model for the developing nations and assist to develop their exporting capacities. In this case, a new type of borrower from developing countries could be created which is supported by the guaranty potential of the relevant countries but which is, however, a different borrower from its own government. It should be noted for example that the exports of manufactured goods from newly industrialized countries are directed at a rate of 80 per cent to the OECD region and therefore are a highly diversified potential of financial assets directed towards potential borrowers and borrowing countries.

The task of export financing institutions is to finance financial assets. They finance not single transactions but cash flows. Their demand for funds is more flexible, the funds at relatively short maturities which are available can be more easily digested because they are able also to diversify according to the maturities they receive.

VIII

The absolute level of interest rates defined as the total of the effective interest rates and the consequences of exchange variations, however, constitutes a severe problem for the export financing institutions because the terms at which they offer credits bear direct consequences on the competition for the sale of goods and services in the various import markets.

During the last three decades the average inflation rate has increased and with it the level of interest rates. This development started from the United

States, the largest single economy in the world. In the period 1950-59 the US average inflation rate was at 2.3 per cent, the average short-term interest level at 2 per cent and the long-term interest level at 3.3 per cent. The relevant percentages for the period of 1960-69 were 2.5 per cent, 4 per cent and 5 per cent respectively, and for 1970-79, 7.2 per cent, 6.3 per cent and 8.2 per cent. In the remaining period it escalated to 10.5 per cent, 14.1 per cent and 13.5 per cent.

The inflation differentials between the various economies have not only influenced the level of interest rates as such but also the exchange rates.

Since the beginning of the 1970s the world economy has lacked a corset which curtails excessive movements of exchange rates. It is not very important to ask whether the system before 1970 could have sustained the tribulations of the 1970s or in which way it would have had to be amended to be a success. It was abandoned.

The consequence of the development for today and tomorrow is, in any case, that a much larger portion in the effective cost of borrowing is related to the differences in exchange rates than the actual rate of interest than ever before. Only the latter is, however, the cost element which is determined at the time the contract is entered into.[5]

It can hardly be assumed that these problems will be reduced in the near future. This can only take place, firstly, when the rates of inflation decline generally and, secondly, the inflation differentials between the various economies become less extravagant.

For the time being one has to assume that the level of interest rates in the United States will remain high. The positive rate of interest has reoccurred and grown to excessive proportions. But interest rates did not adjust to a normal real rate of interest. Other countries with an inflation differential to the United States will not be in a position to adapt their interest level to the inflation differential without large capital movements taking place. The prospective dollar borrowers are therefore in a doubly dangerous position to borrow at high interest rates in a currency which becomes stronger. As far as export financing institutions are concerned, these prospects will result in a fierce battle between the institutions from hard currency areas and those from weaker currency areas.

If the export institutions should assume a more important role in the recycling of financial surpluses, then international agreements on minimum interest rates and maximum lending periods – as currently negotiated within the framework of the OECD – are *unreasonable* and *counterproductive*.

It should be mentioned, however, that the exchange risk can also be minimized by diversification and in this respect export financing institutions enjoy advantages because they can undertake this diversification much more easily than their borrowers.

IX

The role of the commercial banks in facilitating international trade consisted in the period after World War II in

(i) providing the services necessary to effect and secure payment for goods and services which were internationally exchanged; and
(ii) bridging deferred payment.

The latter aspect became of increasing importance as the extension of credit for the purchase of goods and services between contractual parties residing in different countries became a tool of financing international investment.

The objective of commercial banks with the exception of those organized as "universal" banks (Germany, Switzerland and Austria) at least in theory is to provide short-term finance since their main resources are made available on short term.[6]

To allow the commercial banks to provide financial assistance with regard to this new dimension of services required which coincided with most governments' general economic policies to promote exports (be it for balance of payments reasons, employment objectives or development assistance) governments in all industrial countries created mechanisms to provide to commercial banks

(i) liquidity through various forms of refinancing which invariably involve in the end ear-marked assistance by central banks;
(ii) protection for credit risks through special agencies thus nationalizing the credit risk in international operations.

This development resulted in practice in that operations of commercial banks in the context of export financing became to an increasing degree investment (or merchant) bank activities. The creation of enormous financial assets which were not transformed into flows of goods and services means that financial flows are divided from real flows of goods and services.

X

As indicated above the commercial banks performed an extremely efficient job in recycling financial assets. However, as this recycling was separated from the real flow of goods and services the banks did not enjoy the risk protection which is connected with exports. They assumed the credit risk themselves.

It has been pointed out that international credit risks became increasingly nationalized: this means limited potential to diversify. The rule that short-term credits are only short-term or repaid by a contractual party other than the borrower applies also, or even more so, internationally. In the absence of a lender of last resort – the IMF performs this role only to a limited extent in view of the volumes involved – the recycling process is followed increasingly by a rescheduling process.

This would be less unpleasant and tragical would one continue to keep applicable that which was the basis of the success story of international trade development during the "glorieuses trente" and the not less glorious ten of the 1970s: the assumption that a sovereign credit risk cannot result in losses in principle. There might be a refinancing risk, which might entail losses in interest; there might be a liquidity problem; but not a loss risk. Credits to sovereign borrowers are not to be written off.

This assumption may have been put into question recently. Hopefully, this anxiety will not become reality. The idea that countries could be declared insolvent as a means of foreign policy could set a dangerous, a lethal precedent which could destroy the world economy without need of another hot world war.

It would put into question the possibility of recycling financial assets which is a pre-condition for the further continuity of an increase in the flow of goods and services. It would lead to a discontinuation of the monetization of natural resources. It would set off a domino effect which could very easily destroy the very foundations of the international banking community.

NOTES

1. One of the sources for optimism is no doubt the development of world trade and the world economy as a whole since World War II. It was a period of unprecedented prosperity in the absence of the hitherto legendary cyclical sequences of booms and depressions. World trade grew by leaps and bounds as never before in world history. The world economy has become more integrated. This is true both with regard to the so-called socialist countries and the developing world. This integration has also its disadvantage – namely the evolving of a parallelism

in worldwide economic development – but the advantages are greater if only the world leadership, their electorate or the human basis to which they owe their power – as the case may be – recognized the very fact of a growing interdependence which leaves less room for an autonomous national economic policy.

Contrary to the widely propagated belief the so-called less developed or developing countries fully participated in the general prosperity and in the growth of world trade. And this is true in the same way for the group of centrally planned economies.

2. One of the proposals to deal with these effects is the strengthening of international lending institutions and the creation of a new International Development Fund. Though this approach has some merits theoretically, one may have reservations as regards the creation of new institutions. The creation of institutions rarely, if ever, solves a problem. An institution may provide the framework within which people are working. Banking is, however, the job of enterprising people and not of however highly trained bureaucrats. New bureaucracies have their own problems. The situation is to some extent comparable to the social limits of the economies of scale in the field of production.

The same is true in many international organizations. However well balanced the staff of such organizations may be, the representatives of the recipient countries are not anymore in touch with the actual needs and problems of their countries of origin because they have been uprooted and live in a different environment.

3. A first class example is provided by the case of Poland. Of the total foreign debt of Poland to the OECD countries of some $ 28 billion, 35-40 per cent has been made available with the assistance of export insurance or export financing agencies, the rest through the commercial banks. In the case of rescheduling, this division between creditors has proven to be quite a severe obstacle to arrive at solutions – alone because of the mere number of participants from the private banking sector.

4. Of the 150 economies in the world only some 34 can be regarded as market economies. It is simple to imagine that a further limitation of the numbers of suitable borrowers must be the consequence because of the overwhelming importance of the transfer risk which is a political risk. The very foundation of the art of banking, which lies in the diversification of risks, therefore becomes increasingly fragile.

5. To give an example, take the cost of borrowing which has been contracted in 1970 at a rate of 7 per cent in US dollars and converted into schillings and repaid in dollars in 1980 at par. If the total interest cost is computed at a compound interest rate of 7 per cent, the value of the total transaction at the end of the transaction is 196.7 per cent of the original amount. When the changes in the exchange rates between schillings and dollars are included, the equivalent value is only 120.5 per cent. The effective cost of the financing lies in this case 501 basic points below the effective interest rate.

For an importer who accepts schillings as his contractual currency, whose foreign exchange income, however, accrues in US dollars, the calculation is exactly the contrary. The effective total cost of the borrowing is almost twice as high as the effective interest cost.

6. The question which type of lending is short-term has always been a topic of dispute. Probably, short-term lending really means the creation of self-liquidating assets which are repaid by other parties than the original borrower; when financial resources of the borrower are used to repay, repayment can only originate from earnings of the borrower which means that regardless of the juridical form of the lending operation, economically the lending operation has become in principle an investment credit, the repayment of which is dependent on the future earnings position of the borrower.

ASPECTS OF GROWING INTERNATIONAL INDEBTEDNESS

Chapter XIII

LIMITS TO INTERNATIONAL INDEBTEDNESS

by *Armin Gutowski* and *Manfred Holthus*

I. DEBT SERVICE – A PROBLEM OF COMPETING CLAIMS ON RESOURCES

The 1970s will be remembered as a period of drastically expanding interna
tional capital movements in the course of which a fundamental change in
the financing of the current account deficits of developing countries took
place. Grants, grant-like flows and direct investments, which in the
mid-1960s accounted for well over half of the net flow of financial resources
to developing countries, had fallen to one third of the net flow in 1979. Furthermore, within the increasing debt-creating flows the share of bilateral official sources had decreased in favour of loans from private creditors. Financial institutions, in particular, have become the main source of deficit
financing.

The shift in borrowing to private sources in combination with a general
hardening of terms caused a fall in average maturities and grace periods and
an increase in interest rates on which developing countries now borrow. The
growing external debt on harder terms and some acute debt servicing difficulties have given rise to concern over the debt servicing capacity and
future borrowing ability of developing countries.

Debt servicing raises once more the problem of reconciling competing
claims on available resources, as simple macroeconomic accounting illustrates. From equation

$$(1) \quad Y = C + I + X - M$$

which means that gross domestic production (Y) and imports (M) are used
for consumption (C), investment (I) and exports (X), and equation

$$(2) \quad Y' = Y - r D = C + S$$

238

which shows that the income generated by domestic production is to be reduced by interest payments at rate (r) on foreign debt (D)[1] before gross national income (Y ') could either be spent on consumption (C) or be saved (S), we derive equation

(3) $S = I + X - M - r D.$

Thus, debt servicing competes for the available resources with other possible uses such as consumption and investment. A country's capability of raising funds for interest (and amortization)[2] is therefore greatly dependent on economic policy, which is called upon to resolve these competing claims in favour of debt service. This is the price for using foreign capital.

For the debtors, the resolution of competing claims in favour of external debt servicing is the easier to achieve the more the country is able to employ the additional capital effectively. If the growth of real income resulting from the use of capital inflow is high enough to allow for a rise in per capita income, and hence in consumption and investment, after the deduction of debt servicing, indebtedness will be felt as less of a burden than if debt servicing results in a check on the standard of living. The developing country thus has to examine whether it is possible to achieve a rate of growth of its gross national product which is higher than that to be gained without employing external savings. The difference is the gain from external borrowing.

The creditors' main interest is to know whether the debtor country is able or willing to service its debt. The ability to employ the external capital effectively is just one aspect of this. Even if foreign savings are invested, and do result in additional production and income high enough to make the servicing of the credit possible a debt servicing crisis may occur because of rising aspirations of the population which the government is not able to frustrate. On the other hand, even if foreign capital is channelled into consumption or into investments which do not result in sufficient additional income to service the debt, a debt servicing crisis need not develop if the debtor is willing and able to service the debt out of his remaining income.

Most of the following discussion will deal with the debtors' point of view. Seen from this standpoint, the capacity of any one particular country to incur foreign debt depends, as it does in private enterprises, on whether or not it has at its disposal investment opportunities profitable enough to meet the costs resulting from the debt. Subsequently the question arises as to what will have to be done to maintain the ability to borrow and to service the debt as a precondition for improving economic growth.

II. VARIOUS APPROACHES TO ESTIMATING
DEBT SERVICING ABILITY

The cost of foreign capital is determined by the international interest rate (r). Very often, it is contractually fixed; in the case of private loans with fluctuating rates interest obligations have to be estimated. More difficult to assess is the benefit of external borrowing.

One approach quite often proposed is the case-by-case examination of the investment projects using cost-benefit techniques. Unfortunately, in most of the developing countries the data necessary to quantify all direct, indirect and, especially all possible external effects, are not available. From the theoretical point of view, it is even less satisfactory that it is impossible to determine which project is financed by which amount of imported capital.

As long as there are foreign exchange earnings from other sources not controlled by foreign creditors, a country will always be able to propose a project for financing which it expects to meet the creditors' requirements and which it would have financed at any rate, that means even without the credit. Since monetary capital is fungible, as soon as the credit is disbursed, the authorities will be able to implement projects which the creditors would not have financed, because of insufficient expected returns from their point of view. Thus, the inflow of capital may not result in the financing of additional profitable investments.[3]

There are plausible grounds for believing that capital imports can lead to a reduction of national saving and that investments either do not rise at all or only slightly.[4] If, for example, savings stem largely from the government or are determined by its policy, the availability of foreign resources can lead to a decrease of the (government's) propensity to save, especially if its main concern is a target growth rate and the target investment is incidental to this. To the degree to which external savings substitute for national savings the economy will have to bear additional costs in terms of foreign exchange to pay interest; an additional return will arise only to the extent to which foreign capital is transformed into investments producing a higher return than the investment of domestic savings would have done.

There are equally plausible grounds for believing that capital imports lead to an increase in national savings. If, for instance, the profitability of investment depends to a large degree on the availability of foreign exchange for the import of capital goods, additional borrowing abroad might mobilize additional savings from the increased income. In such a case there will be additional returns which surpass the additional interest costs, provided that there are sufficient profitable investment opportunities.

240

The effects of capital imports on national savings and investments vary considerably from country to country. They certainly also depend on the form in which the transfer of capital takes place – as development aid, as commercial credit or as direct investment. It is impossible to add up all these macroeconomic effects in a case-by-case examination of projects.

As debt service difficulties often culminate in a liquidity crisis with regard to the balance of payments, another approach to estimating debt servicing capacity, is to look for indicators which compare the debt service obligations with foreign exchange earnings.

One of these indicators is the debt service ratio, i.e. amortization and interest in per cent of earnings from exports of goods and services, which for most countries is published by the World Bank in the World Development Report. A high debt service ratio is supposed to indicate that the country concerned might soon get into balance of payments difficulties especially when for some reason or other all of a sudden export earnings decline or certain import requirements rise.

But the ratio does not say anything as to whether or to which extent a decline in export earnings or a rise in certain import outlays could be balanced out by other changes in the balance of payments without too great a damage to the economy. It is quite possible that some countries with a high debt service ratio are more flexible in this respect than others with a low ratio. A critical value for the ratio which indicates future debt servicing problems in the case of short-run unfavourable developments cannot be determined.

Liquidity crises arise in the short run because economic development, despite all attempts at controlling it, takes place in a discontinuous fashion whereas continuous debt servicing is required. Exports fluctuate with the prospects of foreign markets, import needs depend on changing conditions of domestic supply. Inflation without equivalent exchange rate adjustments lead to higher imports. Changing expectations as to the prospects for investment at home and abroad influence capital flows. Serious problems arise, if the maturities of debts accumulate in periods when unfavourable conditions prevail.

The possibilities for cutting back imports in the short run are often limited. The industrialization process leads to increasing imports of oil and other raw materials, of spare parts and capital goods. A limitation of imports could cause a reduction of growth and employment and only make the problem worse. Furthermore, in many countries food production lags behind the demand of the rapidly increasing population and the urban population can sometimes only be supplied by means of food imports. Only imports puffed-up by inflation can be reduced by an economic policy aimed at stability, but the minimum volume of unavoidable imports remains high.

Fluctuation of foreign exchange receipts and expenditures can be compensated by a variation of the holdings of foreign exchange reserves to the extent that such reserves exist.

Liquidity crises can thus be caused by a combination of[5]

– fluctuating variables, such as exports, capital imports and imports caused by inflation,
– compensating variables, such as foreign exchange reserves and reduceable imports,
– inflexible variables, such as unavoidable minimum imports, amortization and interest.

The debt service ratio includes only three of the eight above-named variables, that is export earnings, amortization and interest. This is another important reason why the ratio is not of much help in forecasting debt service difficulties even in the short run.

The limited evidential value of the debt service ratio and of other single indicators has led, since the beginning of the 1970s, to a third approach, i.e. the development of indicator systems based on empirical studies. They are conceived of as early warning systems and are supposed – by defining critical values for the selected basket of indicators – to allow the recognition of crises of indebtedness early enough to forestall the beginning of a crisis by appropriate action. The studies of Frank and Cline (1971), Dhonte (1975), Feder and Just (1977) and Peterson (1977) aim in this direction. The methodological effort varies greatly but all of these studies are based on the same approach[6]: they attempt to find indicators which in the past showed significant differences between countries with debt problems and those without.

In the HWWA-Institute one of these systems – Petersen's – was brought up to date, i.e. for the period 1976 to 1979, for 36 countries. The system is designed to identify critical constellations of indicators which have been associated in the past with multilateral rescheduling of debts. For the period 1976 to 1979, 53 critical cases in 26 countries were identified, among them some of the large debtor countries. Only 5 of the 26 countries in fact rescheduled debts in this period. Thus, the system frequently identifies crises which do not lead to multilateral debt consolidation. That is hardly surprising, however. First of all, the hypothesis of a stable functional relationship between the value of certain sectoral or overall economic variables and the beginning of a crisis of indebtedness, which is necessary for the application of the system, must be rejected.[7] Secondly, the definition of crisis of indebtedness is a very narrow one. As already pointed out, crises do not only express themselves in the need for a multilateral rescheduling of debts but can also manifest themselves, for example, in not allowing vital imports to be effected, so that serious losses in terms of growth are suffered. The aim of borrowing funds abroad – the speeding up of growth – is thus counter-checked without affecting the creditors.

Thus, there is still need for a reasonably reliable method of assessing the capability of a country to incur foreign debt. This has to be based on a theory which shows in macroeconomic terms the main relationships between the process of growth and the ways it can be financed without dramatic interruptions under different sets of typical circumstances.

III. A CONCEPT OF ECONOMIC GROWTH WITH FOREIGN DEBT

The line of reasoning in sections I and II makes it plain, that the capacity of any one country to incur debt has to be studied in the context of the formation and utilization of total available capital. The rearrangement of equation (3) into

$$(4) \quad I = S + r D + M - X$$

shows that the investments must be financed out of national savings plus net capital inflow. But irrespective of what type of savings – external or internal – is transformed into capital goods, production and income resulting from the utilization of these investments must at least equal the cost of that capital. As the additional output (ΔY), all other factors of production being constant, is determined by the productivity (i) of the new capital stock ($\Delta K = I$), it is economically justified for the country concerned to realize out of all conceivable investment opportunities only those, which meet the condition

$$(5) \quad \frac{\Delta Y}{I} = i \geqq r.$$

Financial resources can be transformed into real capital goods either by using domestic physical resources or by importing capital goods from abroad. Some of the investment opportunities under consideration will not meet the above condition (5) if it is impossible to import foreign capital goods; in other cases it will be more profitable to use domestic resources for the formation of the necessary capital stock. Hence, production and utilization of domestic capital goods depends on the profitability of these in comparison to those which have to be imported.

This may be illustrated by a simple case[8]: a developing country is examining whether it is worthwhile to raise a loan for further investments, since national savings are completely exhausted. The choice is to implement either an investment which would entail domestic resources (K_d), for example the use of the labour force to construct a road, or an investment which would require the importing of foreign resources (K_f), for instance capital goods for equipping a textile factory, both of which would be profitable enough to reach the interest rate prevailing on the international capital market. Should the first project induce a bigger increase in gross domestic product than the second, the country concerned would make use of indigenous manpower to build the road which would, ceteris paribus, make it necessary to use the loan to import food and other consumer goods to feed and serve the domestic resources utilized. If the construction of the textile factory proved to be the more profitable project as measured in additional domestic product, then emphasis would be placed on the utilization of foreign resources, i.e. the import of textile machinery. In the first case the productivity of the additional capital stock K_d, i.e. the road, will exceed that of K_f, i.e. the textile factory, and vice-versa; in both cases, however, the investment will be financed by foreign savings.

Over a given period of time more and more of the conceivable investment opportunities which are sufficiently profitable will be realized, utilizing partly foreign and partly domestic physical resources. The marginal productivities of the respective capital stocks K_d and K_f will decline. The limit to absorb financial resources, regardless of whether these stem from national or foreign savings, is reached when the productivity of the last financial unit spent for the formation of capital stock utilizing domestic physical resources is not only equal to the productivity of the last financial unit spent for the formation of capital stock utilizing foreign physical resources but also to the interest rate prevailing on the international capital market. The capital stock at the moment has acquired its optimal level as well as its optimal composition. Thus, condition (5) turns to condition

$$(6) \quad \frac{dY}{dK_d} = \frac{dY}{dK_f} = \frac{dY}{dK} = i = r$$

The above condition is valid for all countries irrespective of the stage of development of the economy of the country concerned. The capacity to absorb *foreign* capital in this context is a residual magnitude: i.e. that part of sufficiently profitable ($i \geq r$) investment opportunities which cannot be financed optimally out of national savings. What, however, does the term "optimally" mean in this context?

Usually in a developing country the ability to save is limited. If it is less than the target volume of investments this phenomenon is referred to in the literature[9] as the savings gap. However, as little as a poor country may be able to save, if there are no investment opportunities available which at least pay for the external interest, there is also no savings gap. Hence, a savings gap can only be established by comparing the national profitability of investment opportunities with the international capital market interest rate. A savings gap in this sense is one dimension of the term "cannot be financed optimally".[10]

Even if sufficient national savings can be generated for the target volume of investment, a part of the foreign component of investments has to be financed by foreign capital in order to make investment profitable (i $\geq$ r) because inflexibility in the structure of their economies as well as an unfavourable endowment with natural resources prevent many developing countries from increasing exports or substituting imports in order to acquire the necessary foreign exchange. This more or less short-run rigidity in the substitutability of domestic and foreign physical resources is referred to in the literature as the foreign exchange gap. Incurring foreign debts to finance this gap is justified as long as "it can be convincingly claimed that it would at present be more profitable to run up debts than to finance import requirements by means of additional exports or substitution of imports and that domestic product minus interest payable would still be greater with foreign indebtedness than without".[11] Even if it might be technically possible to replace foreign physical resources by domestic physical resources, economically the result would be a decline of the national profitability of the investment opportunities. Thus, the foreign exchange gap in the above sense is the second dimension of the term "cannot be financed optimally".

If the two gaps are defined as above, the closing of either gap by borrowing foreign financial resources is justified. The marginal productivity of the capital stock, and hence the ability to incur debts is at its peak, if in the course of further investments the optimal combination of domestic and foreign physical resources determined by the productivities of the respective resources is maintained. As soon as the marginal productivity, however, has declined to the international market interest rate, any further attempt to increase the capital stock utilizing foreign financial resources would no longer be economical. As saving continues, the interest rate on national savings tend to fall below the international level. Nationals of the country concerned will try to invest in foreign currency, i.e. to export capital, causing a devaluation of the country's currency.

In reality, of course, the marginal productivities of the respective capital stocks are not a given constant. They will grow in the course of technological progress. The technological progress of foreign physical resources can be taken as given. It is incorporated in the capital goods and related services imported. The capacity of a country to absorb domestic and foreign financial resources, however, can repeatedly be enhanced beyond the level determined by the technological progress of foreign physical resources if the country succeeds in improving the quality of domestic physical resources by technological and organizational progress in such a way that the productivity of the capital stock formed by domestic physical resources (K_d) is increasing. In the course of this process additional investment opportunities become profitable so that external indebtedness, interest payments and national income can grow further.[12]

The capability of a country to improve the quality and hence the productivity of domestic resources continuously is of significance in the context of another problem of external indebtedness. The funds for interest payments (and amortization) have not only to be earned; they must also be transferred. This can, however, only be done if productive utilization of the imported financial resources results in a corresponding increase in exports or decrease in imports. But it is not necessarily the production of export goods or of import substitution goods which is the most profitable in terms of additional national product. Producing additional capital stock by utilizing domestic physical resources may be more profitable.

Again, the above mentioned examples can be used to illustrate this. In the case of an investment in a textile factory production of cloth may be higher than that which the domestic population can afford to buy. The residual material can be exported and the foreign exchange earnings from these exports can be used to pay up interest. It may happen as well that the texiles which had to be imported before the investment may now be produced in the new factory. Foreign exchange proceeds which formerly had been used for imports of textiles can now be made available for interest payments. It may also occur, however, that as a result of the investment the domestic production of textiles becomes more efficient. The labour thus saved can be utilized for the formation of additional capital stock (K_d), for instance for improving the infrastructure.

In the case of an investment in road construction, the resources made available by a more efficient transport system could be employed, for example, in the production of textiles, which could be exported or which could make textile imports superfluous. But the physical resources saved can also be used to expand the capital stock (K_d), e.g. by building loading facilities in the harbour at the end of the new road.

Which of the three possibilities – more exports, less imports or additional capital stock from domestic physical resources – is best depends on which represents the highest rate of return on the investment. If additional capital stock (K_d) turns out to have the highest return, the balance of trade is not affected. In this case, the interest owed in foreign currency can only be paid if a creditor abroad is willing to grant an additional loan, equivalent to the value of that additional capital stock, which, of course, has to induce an additional product the proceeds of which must be sufficient to cover the interest payable on the additional loan. This does not mean, that the problem of interest payment has been solved for ever. In the next payment period, interest payments will be greater due to the additional loan. The question is, how long it will take the country to be able to produce exportable goods profitably so that interest can be paid out of export earnings.

Particularly in an early stage of development and indebtedness, it is easy to imagine that investments utilizing domestic physical resources, for instance to improve the infrastructure, will be highly productive. The country concerned will use the borrowed financial resources for imports of consumer goods rather than for imports of foreign capital goods, in order to make domestic physical resources available which are to be used for the augmentation of its capital stock (K_d). Let us suppose that it is most profitable to reinvest the interest payable in the same manner.

In the course of the investment process it will become more and more probable that a shift in the optimal composition of the growing capital stock will take place in favour of that part of the capital stock which is created by foreign physical resources. Importing consumer goods in order to set free domestic resources will become less advisable. Foreign capital goods will be imported instead, as K_f must increase at a higher rate than K_d in order to maintain the optimal composition of the capital stock.

Let us assume that this process, including the reinvestment of interest, lasts until, at diminishing marginal productivity of both partial capital stocks, K_d and K_f, reach a level of marginal productivity equal to the interest rate prevailing on the international capital market. To increase the capital stock further is no longer profitable. However, the obligation to pay interest still remains. As the reinvestment of due interest by utilizing domestic physical resources will no longer pay for the additional costs, the country concerned will run into structural difficulties if additional goods suitable for exporting or substituting imports are not available. Thus, sooner or later the necessity will arise to produce goods which are competitive and can profitably be sold in the world market or substituted for goods which previously had to be imported. The point in time at which this becomes necessary can be postponed if the country succeeds in improving the quality and productivity of domestic resources, so that the share of the capital stock from domestic resources in the total capital stock can grow without its productivity falling short of the interest rate on the international capital market. The more it succeeds in doing so, the better the chances that it will become able to produce goods which are competitive in the world market, the proceeds from the sales of which can be used for interest payments on, and finally repayment of, foreign debt.

Such a strategy, carried to excess, can be more risky than a strategy of using foreign capital for the production of goods which, though perhaps less sophisticated, can either be exported or substituted for imports at an earlier stage. In the latter case, the indebtedness is not growing that fast and even if the marginal productivity of the total capital stock in an optimal composition should decrease to the international capital market interest rate, the accumulated indebtedness does not pose any problems since the interest can continually be transferred. In this case too, however, further growth and indebtedness is possible only if the quality of domestic resources can be improved.

Thus, the capacity of a country to absorb national and foreign savings productively is determined by the quality and the utilization of domestic non-financial resources. This has to be considered in any attempt to estimate the limits of a country's capacity to incur external debt.

IV. POSSIBLE EMPIRICAL RESEARCH

Any strategy of development that relies on inflows of additional financial resources from abroad has to consider that three criteria must be fulfilled if foreign debt is to make a lasting contribution to development.[13]

First of all there is the *efficiency criterion*, which relates the benefits of the inflowing resources to the cost of the debt. The efficiency is highly dependent upon the quality of the utilized domestic non-financial resources as well as the imported capital goods. As explained above, it is in particular the improvement of the utilized domestic resources which allows the capacity of a country to absorb financial resources productively to be continually increased.

The second is the *transfer criterion*, which must be fulfilled, when the country has exhausted the possibility to hold the marginal productivity above the external interest and must pay the interest on foreign debt by producing for export or import substitution. At this time at the latest the country must have established industries that are able to compete on foreign markets to earn the necessary foreign exchange, if its currency is not to depreciate.

The third criterion, which could be called the *transformation criterion*, is met, if the financial resources borrowed abroad are channelled into productive investments, i.e. if they are not consumed. As argued above, the inflow of foreign funds will not necessarily increase the sum total of investible funds to the same extent. Foreign capital may substitute for domestic savings. The extent to which this is the case has to be estimated.

An empirical analysis of a country's capacity to incur debt must examine these three criteria. The calculation of the marginal productivity of capital, the relationship between additional net domestic product and net investment, offers a first indicator for the efficiency criterion. A high value for the marginal productivity of capital taken on its own, however, does not necessarily mean that there are no objections to foreign indebtedness. Almost every country would probably – if cyclical fluctuations are ignored – show a level of productivity of capital lying above the interest rate on the international capital market.

The increase of net domestic product is, however, not necessarily, or not only, the result of the utilization of additional capital but can also be due to other factors, for example to an increase and qualitative improvement in the factor labour, to the extension of the infrastructure, to the composition of the capital stock as regards domestically and foreign-produced capital goods, to the importing of technical progress, to domestic progress in technology, organization and factor allocation, to the type of economic policy, etc. The efficiency criterion is fulfilled only if it is certain that the additional utilization of capital would lead to a sufficiently high increase in production the other factors remaining constant, or if the additional utilization of capital would lead to an increase in the contribution to productivity of the remaining factors.

The individual determining factors' contribution to productivity could, in the ideal case, be determined using production functions. However, with the available statistical data and the available econometric methods it is an illusion to believe that usable production functions can be derived which are appropriate for estimating the capacity to incur debt. Many of the decisive factors – in particular technical progress in its various forms – cannot be measured directly.

In addition there are time-lags between determinants and production results and the influence of the individual determining factors changes within the period under observation. Furthermore, the production function only shows the relationship between output quantity and input quantity. But what matters for the efficiency criterion is the relationship in terms of value, i.e. not only quantities but also prices. The input and output prices are, however, influenced not only by domestic but also by foreign determinants; the average output price also depends on the industrial structure of the economy and the average price of capital depends on the composition of the capital stock.

The attempt in HWWA to obtain information about the capacity to incur debt and, in particular, the occurrence of debt crises using simple macroeconomic production functions did not produce any satisfactory results. We are therefore attempting to develop indicators for those influencing factors which are taken into account only inadequately, or not at all, in the production function and to test their informational value by means of a time series analysis for individual countries and cross-sectional comparisons using several countries.

In our theoretical analysis the most important determinant was the capability of a country to improve its own productive resources. This factor is characterized in several ways: by indicators as to the quality of labour (proportion of skilled workers, level of education) and the infrastructure (for example, investment and value added in transportation) and by the determination of technical progress by means of residuals in the production functions. An important indicator for the quality of domestic resources is the existence of a productive domestic capital goods industry. If the proportion of domestically produced capital goods in the total capital stock increases without a decline in growth, then this is a sign of the improvement of domestic resources. The country can then continue to increase its indebtedness and is not forced to transfer its interest payments in the form of additional exports or by reducing imports. If, on the other hand, there is a reduction of growth, the country will have to pay more attention to the fulfilment of the transfer criterion. An analysis of the structure of the economy must be made so as to show whether the country is on its way to producing goods which could bring in the necessary foreign exchange without the state having continually to subsidize the relevant branches of industry and without unfavourable prices having to be accepted. The development of the structure of the economy according to both quantities and prices as well as the country's development strategy must, therefore, also be included in the catalogue of indicators for the capacity to incur debt. As additional indicators the share of foreign trade in domestic product and the diversification of tradeable goods industries in particular in the manufacturing sector can be used.

The third criterion can, in principle, be examined using savings functions in which domestic savings do not only depend on the level of national income but also on the amount of foreign credit. To the extent that foreign credits are partially used for consumption, there is, correspondingly, no increase in net domestic product and the marginal productivity of capital is thus reduced.[14] Here too, however, simple econometric estimating methods are inadequate since they do not take account of the direction of causality between domestic savings and foreign indebtedness. For if the reduction in domestic savings is autonomous and the fall in domestic savings is compensated for by the borrowing of foreign capital, then it is incorrect to speak of the use of foreign credits for consumption since the renunciation of foreign credit would in that case have meant a renunciation of the financing of investment. Furthermore, econometric savings functions do not adequately take into account that domestic savings are determined to a far greater degree than in the industrialized countries not so much by private households as by the state budget. The examination of the third criterion must take the behaviour of the state into account.

Economic policy, which is reflected, for example, in the state budget, is important not only for the assessment of the third criterion, but also in respect to the efficiency and transfer criteria. The figures for revenue and expenditure show whether the country is conducting a growth policy directed at the support of profitable investments, and what type of development strategy it is following. In the final analysis it is the type and quality of its economic policy which is decisive for a country's capacity to incur debt.

NOTES

1. For the sake of simplicity it is assumed that there are no factor payments other than interest payments.

2. During the course of this paper revolving borrowing for amortization purposes is assumed to be always possible. This does not imply, however, that revolving does not entail problems of its own.

3. Cf. H.W. Singer, "External Aid: For Plans or Projects?", in: *Economic Journal*, vol. 75 (1965), p. 531 ff. and A. Gutowski, "Projektgebundene, nicht projektgebundene Kapitalhilfe oder Programmfinanzierung", in: R. Meimberg (ed.), *Voraussetzungen einer globalen Entwicklungspolitik und Beiträge zur Kosten- und Nutzenanalyse*, Schriften des Vereins für Sozialpolitik NF Bd. 59, Berlin 1971, p. 197 ff.

4. For the following cf. M. Holthus, "Verschuldung und Verschuldungsfähigkeit von Entwicklungsländern", in: *Hamburger Jahrbuch für Wirtschafts- und Gesellschaftspolitik*, 26. Jahr (1981), p. 250 ff. and the literature quoted.

5. Cf. D. Avramovic, et al., *Economic Growth and External Debt*, Baltimore 1964, p. 13 ff.

6. Cf. P.D. Dhonte, "Describing External Debt Situations: A Roll-over-approach", in: *IMF-Papers*, vol. XXII, no. 1 (1975); C.R. Frank, W.R. Cline, "Measurement of Debt Servic-

ing Capacity: An Application of Discriminant Analysis", in: *Journal of International Economics*, no. 1 (1971); G. Feder, R.E. Just, "A Study of Debt Servicing Capacity Applying Logical Analysis", in: *Journal of Development Economics*, no. 4 (1977); and H.J. Petersen, "Debt Crisis of Developing Countries: A Pragmatic Approach to an Early Warning System", in: *Konjunkturpolitik*, Jg. 23 (1977), II. 2.

7. Cf. R. Erbe, S. Schattner, "Indicator System for the Assessment of External Debt Situation of Developing Countries", in: *Intereconomics*, no. 6 (1980), p. 287.

8. Cf. A. Gutowski, *Foreign Indebtedness and Economic Growth: Is There a Limit to Foreign Financing?* Paper presented to the Conference of the International Economic Association on Financing Problems of Developing Countries, Buenos Aires, October 26-30, 1981, p. 2.

9. Cf. for example H.B. Chenery, A.M. Strout, "Foreign Assistance and Economic Development", in: *The American Economic Review*, vol. 56 (1966), no. 4.

10. Such a savings gap corresponds to a savings surplus in other countries in which the marginal rate of return on domestic investment falls below the prevailing external long-term interest rate before all domestic savings are utilized.

11. Cf. A. Gutowski, *op. cit.*, p. 6. A similar interpretation of the two gaps methodology has been given by W.J. Stevens, *Capital Absorptive Capacity in Developing Countries*, Leiden 1971, p. 43 ff.

12. Cf. A. Gutowski, *op. cit.*

13. Cf. M. Holthus, "Desenvolvimento Economico com Endividamento Externo: Riscos e Chances", in: *Divida Externa e Estrategia Brasiliera de Desenvolvimento*, Rio de Janeiro 1981.

14. Cf. R. Erbe, "Foreign Indebtedness and Economic Growth: The Philippines", in: *Intereconomics*, no. 3 (1982), p. 125.

Chapter XIV

LIMITS TO INTERNATIONAL INDEBTEDNESS*

by *Alfred Kuehn*

INTRODUCTION

1. Recent cases of countries experiencing a substantial worsening of their balance of payments position and problems in servicing their foreign debt have led to renewed worries about the strength of the international financial system and to raising the question of the limit to international indebtedness. Put in a general way, this latter question, of course, makes little sense. Rising indebtedness – both domestically and on the international plane – normally goes hand in hand with economic growth. It is the means by which money capital is transformed from savings into productive investments. Furthermore, the greater the division of labour in the world economy, the greater will be financial markets and the more diversified financial intermediation will become. Far from being detrimental to healthy economic development, expanding international indebtedness is a precondition of efficient transfer of resources and of the growth of world trade. Thus, in a global sense there can be no finite limits to international indebtedness.

2. However, just as an individual debtor may become insolvent through putting borrowed funds to uneconomic use or by experiencing a shortfall of revenues, an individual debtor country, or groups of countries, can run into debt servicing problems for the same reasons. In the last ten years, the developing countries as a group have rapidly expanded their foreign indebtedness and several of them have experienced debt service problems which in some cases could only be solved by rescheduling maturities of debt falling due. The question is thus legitimate to ask whether in the present world economic context of low growth, high inflation and high cost of imported energy, the developing countries are not particularly vulnerable to external shocks like the deterioration of terms of trade, or high international rates of interest.

* The present paper reflects the opinions of the author and does not purport to represent those of the institute (OECD) of which he is an official.

3. The subject has been treated in several recent studies published by international organisations.[1] This note tries, briefly, to set out the facts and summarise the major issues arising from current and projected developments.

I. THE FOREIGN DEBT OF DEVELOPING COUNTRIES

4. According to the report by the OECD,[2] the total medium- and long-term debt of developing countries has risen from US$ 87 billion in 1971 to US$ 524 billion at the end of 1981; this represents an annual average increase of 20 per cent. However, if inflation is taken into account the increase in real terms works out somewhere around 10 per cent and, in the last few years, the real rate of growth of the debt of developing countries has, in fact, fallen to around 5 per cent, approximately in line with the growth of their collective GNP (Table 1).

Table 1. *Total debt disbursed at year end and total annual debt service of developing countries by terms of lending*

	1971		1981 estimate		Average annual increase (per cent)
	US$ bill.	per cent of total	US$ bill.	per cent of total	
Debt					
1. Bilateral and multilateral ODA	32.4	37.4	118.0	22.5	13.8
2. Other multilateral lending	6.8	7.9	38.0	7.3	18.8
3. Total export credits	30.8	35.5	148.0	28.2	17.0
4. Other lending at market terms	16.6	19.2	220.0	42.0	29.5
of which: bank loans	9.4	10.9	172.0	32.8	33.7
Total debt	86.6	100.0	524.0	100.0	19.7
Debt service					
1. Bilateral and multilateral ODA	1.8	16.5	5.9	5.3	12.6
2. Other multilateral lending	0.6	5.5	5.0	4.5	23.6
3. Total export credits	5.8	53.2	41.9	37.5	21.9
4. Other lending at market terms	2.7	24.8	58.9	52.7	36.1
of which: bank loans	n.a.	n.a.	51.0	45.7	—
Total debt service	10.9	100.0	111.7	100.0	26.2
of which: interest	3.3	30.3	46.5	41.6	
amortisation	7.6	69.7	65.2	58.4	

Source: OECD.

5. Eleven newly industrialising countries accounted for more than 40 per cent of the increase in the nominal debt of developing countries, another 24 per cent was due to increased borrowing by middle-income countries. In addition, thirteen OPEC countries took up 18 per cent of the total increase of external debt; the low income countries accounted for the rest, 16 per cent. As a result, the share of the low income countries in the total foreign debt has fallen from 21 per cent in 1971 to 17 per cent in 1981, whilst the share of the industrialising countries has risen from one-third to two-fifths (Table 2).

Table 2. *Debt disbursed and annual debt service by income groups (US $ billion)*

	1971	1975	1979	1981 estimate	Increase 1971/81 Total	Per cent
Debt						
1. Low income countries	18	35	69	89	71	16.2
2. Middle income countries	25	46	95	131	106	24.3
3. Newly industrialising countries (11)	30	66	160	210	180	41.2
Total non-OPEC	73	147	324	430	357	81.7
4. OPEC (13)	14	32	73	94	80	18.3
Total	87	179	397	524	437	100.0
Debt service						
1. Low income countries	1.1	3.0	5.2	7.8	6.7	6.6
2. Middle income countries	3.5	6.4	14.7	20.2	16.7	16.6
3. Newly industrialising countries (11)	4.8	11.6	36.1	54.7	49.9	49.5
Total non-OPEC	9.4	21.0	56.0	82.7	73.3	72.7
4. OPEC (13)	1.5	5.2	17.6	29.0	27.5	27.3
Total	10.9	26.2	73.6	111.7	100.8	100.0

Source: OECD.

6. Both the composition of the foreign debt of developing countries by source of lending and by groups of developing countries as debtor have changed considerably over the last decade. Table 1 also shows that the share (but not its total value which has approximately quadrupled) of official development aid on concessional terms (ODA) has fallen from 37 per cent of the debt of developing countries in 1971 to 23 per cent in 1981, whilst the share of commercial lending at market terms has risen rather significantly from a relatively low 19 per cent to 42 per cent in the same period. Floating interest rate bank loans accounted for as much as one-third of the total. The

share of offical and officially guaranteed export credits has declined some-what from 36 per cent to 28 per cent, but not as much as ODA.

7. The first observation one needs to make in interpreting these figures is that the expansion of the foreign debt of developing countries during the last ten years can hardly be considered as excessive, in particular as, in the more recent period, growth of the foreign debt in real terms has not exceeded the growth of GDP of these countries. Whilst it is true that borrowing for con-sumptive purposes would lead a country sooner or later into debt service problems, it makes economic sense to borrow funds during periods of in-creased tightness of foreign exchange in order to finance on-going invest-ments and, in particular, programmes of economic adjustment. It takes time for production processes to be restructured, for factors of production to be reallocated, and meanwhile real income is likely to decline. Without foreign loans a developing country may have to cut real expenditure far more drasti-cally in order to deal with a rising current account deficit of the balance of payments than would otherwise be the case. Thus, it was correct, generally speaking, to step up borrowing abroad in times of balance of payments strain, such as was caused by the two oil-price shocks of 1974 and 1979/80.

8. The debt data also spell out that in the last decade – though the process started during the 1960s – the generally more dynamic, faster-growing mid-dle income countries have outgrown their needs for concessional external fi-nancing and have financed their savings gap through increased commercial borrowing, in particular Euro-loans. Several of these countries also bor-rowed abroad to some extent to increase holdings of foreign exchange re-serves in order to improve creditworthiness. At present, three-quarters of the external debt of developing middle income and industrialising countries is of commercial origin. On the other hand, concessional development aid has been concentrated increasingly on the poorer countries, whose vulner able balance of payments position does not warrant extensive commercial borrowing.

9. The question as to the limits of external indebtedness thus boils down principally to an analysis of a limited number of middle-income and indus-trialising developing countries, of which several have become relatively heavy borrowers on commercial terms. Some twenty countries could be con-sidered as falling into this category; among these, by far the largest bor-rowers are Brazil and Mexico which together owe debt totalling US$ 100 bil-lion (Table 3). Countries with a disbursed foreign debt in the range of US$ 15-20 billion are: Korea, Spain, Algeria, Indonesia, India, Yugoslavia and Turkey. These are followed by Argentina, Venezuela and Egypt, with debt exceeding US$ 10 billion. This is rather a mixed bag of countries in respect

Table 3. *The 20 developing countries with the largest debt-service payments* [1] *(US $ billion)*

Country (ranked by average debt service in 1979/1980)	Debt service paid				Disbursed debt year-end			Total reserves year-end	
	1978	1979	1980 prelim.	1981 estim.	1978	1979	1980 prelim.	1978	1980
1. Brazil	8.1	10.8	13.4	16.0	44.2	50.6	56.6	11.9	5.9
2. Mexico[3]	7.0	11.0	9.0	12.2	30.5	34.5	42.4	1.9	2.9
3. Venezuela[2]	1.6	2.8	5.1	6.8	9.7	11.6	13.2	6.6	7.1
4. Algeria[2]	2.0	3.3	4.2	4.6	14.7	17.4	17.8	2.2	4.0
5. Spain	3.0	3.2	4.1	4.9	13.1	15.0	18.2	10.8	12.5
6. Saudi Arabia[2]	1.8	2.9	(3.5)	(4.0)	2.3	3.1	4.0	19.4	23.6
7. Korea	2.0	2.9	3.3	4.0	12.5	15.5	20.5	2.8	2.9
8. Yugoslavia	1.8	2.5	2.9	3.5	11.3	13.3	15.0	2.5	1.5
9. Argentina	2.2	1.8	2.8	3.6	7.8	11.3	14.0	5.2	6.9
10. Indonesia[2]	1.6	2.3	2.3	2.7	14.5	15.6	17.0	2.6	5.5
11. Chile	1.5	1.6	1.9	2.5	5.3	7.1	8.8	1.2	3.2
12. Iran[2]	2.4	1.9	(1.4)	(6.5)	10.6	(9.9)	(9.5)	12.1	10.0
13. Peru[3]	0.8	1.1	1.9	2.1	6.0	6.8	6.9	0.4	2.0
14. Egypt[3]	1.4	1.2	1.7	2.0	10.3	12.0	12.7	0.6	1.2
15. Philippines	1.3	1.3	1.5	2.0	6.2	7.2	9.5	1.8	2.9
16. Greece	0.9	1.2	1.6	2.0	4.8	5.6	6.5	1.2	1.3
17. Taiwan	0.9	0.9	1.3	1.6	3.5	3.9	4.9	1.5	2.4
18. India	1.1	1.1	1.1	1.3	15.9	16.6	16.7	6.8	7.3
19. Morocco	0.6	0.9	1.2	1.6	5.4	6.6	7.5	0.7	0.4
20. Thailand	0.8	1.0	1.1	1.4	2.6	3.7	5.6	2.1	1.7
Total 20 countries	42.8	55.7	65.3	85.3	231.2	267.4	307.3	94.3	105.2
% of grand total LDCs	76	76	72	76	69	67	67	62	51

1. Next-ranking countries include Turkey (whose original debt-service obligations of over US$ 2 billion in 1980 were substantially reduced by debt relief), Israel (excluding military debt), Ecuador, Libya and Portugal.
2. OPEC member.   3. Net oil exporter.
Source: OECD.

of size of per capita income, and economic activity and prospects. Egypt and India are low-income countries with a small private debt, several countries (including Egypt) are net oil exporters and hence are not affected adversely by rising oil prices, and eight others are newly industrialising countries. Nevertheless, five of these major debtor countries – Chile, Indonesia, India, Peru and Turkey – have had some of their foreign debt rescheduled during the 1970s, as they were unable to meet a rising foreign debt burden.

10. It is also a fact that, altogether, some fifteen developing countries have had to ask once or several times for a rollover of their official debt since the beginning of 1974, considerably more than in the preceding five to six years. Moreover, in analysing these cases, the IMF reports that usually a specific pattern of developments leading up to acute debt servicing problems could be noticed: economic policy in these debtor countries was mainly inward-oriented, giving little encouragement to exports; the exchange rate tended to be overvalued, and there was high pressure of domestic demand, in particular of consumption.

11. However, these were exceptional cases; it must be underlined that most middle-income developing countries, and in particular the newly-industrialising countries, have followed sound economic policies during the difficult 1970s, increasing productive investment, expanding exports and providing in turn a growing market for imports of goods and services as well as capital from the industrial North, thus helping to recycle oil revenues of OPEC countries.

12. Two principal factors may, however, change this picture in the near future. First, oil demand has fallen considerably through the effect of energy conservation and world recession. There are grounds for believing that oil prices will remain relatively weak for some time which will affect export revenues and overall demand of net oil exporters. Secondly, recovery of economic activity in industrial countries may take longer than initially expected. Hence, developing countries, in particular large debtors, net oil exporters, as well as primary producing countries, will probably find their balance of payments affected to some degree and it will depend on the domestic economic policies of these countries whether the difficulties will be temporary or might lead to more serious developments, possibly affecting debt servicing capacity.

13. Concern is sometimes expressed that the current high level of international interest rates may create debt servicing problems for developing countries. There can be no doubt that a country borrowing in the Euro-market will find that its interest burden has risen as a result of the rise in the cost of floating rate debt. But most countries receive a mix of foreign credits, in-

Table 4. Current interest cost to developing countries by type of credits outstanding [1] (percentages)

Categories of outstanding debt	1972	1973	1974	1975	1976	1977	1978	1979	1980 (prel.)	1981 (est.)
A. Fixed-interest debt	4.2	4.5	4.6	4.8	4.8	5.0	5.2	5.5	5.7	6.2
1. DAC – ODA	2.5	2.5	2.4	2.4	2.4	2.2	2.3	2.2	1.9	1.8
2. DAC – Official export credits	n.a.	6.0	6.0	6.3	6.3	6.0	6.2	6.3	6.8	7.3
3. DAC – Private export credits	n.a.	6.6	6.8	7.5	7.6	7.9	8.1	8.3	8.6	8.9
4. International organisations	5.2	5.5	5.5	5.4	5.5	5.6	6.2	6.2	6.6	7.3
5. Bonds	4.9	5.5	5.2	5.5	5.0	5.6	7.0	7.3	8.3	9.0
6. Other private debt	n.a.	(8.5)	(9.0)	8.6	8.5	8.4	8.6	9.2	9.8	10.5
7. Non-DAC total bilateral	(2.6)	(2.7)	(2.8)	3.0	3.0	3.0	3.3	4.0	4.5	5.0
B. Floating-interest debt [2]	7.9	9.0	10.0	11.0	8.5	7.8	9.0	12.0	15.3	18.0
C. Total debt	4.6	5.4	6.1	6.6	6.6	6.6	7.5	7.7	8.8	10.2

1. Annual interest payments and other charges as a percentage of debt outstanding at the beginning of the year, adjusted for exchange rate variations.
2. Weighted average annual cost to debtors (including spreads and fees), based on the average LIBOR during the period July 1st to June 30th, assuming 6-months average revolving basis.

Source: OECD.

cluding a large share of generally cheaper official or officially-guaranteed export credits and, for all developing countries taken together, the average interest cost stands at around 10 per cent, compared to 5 per cent in 1972 (Table 4).

14. For the low income countries the rise in nominal interest cost was modest (from 3 per cent in the period 1974/78 to 4 per cent in 1981). In fact, real interest rates have remained significantly negative. For the middle income countries the nominal interest cost on their debt grew from 5.1 per cent to 8.6 per cent, which is still a negative rate in real terms. Only for the newly industrialising countries has interest cost gone up to a relatively high 13.3 per cent. What is more, for quite a number of developing countries high short-term and floating rate interest rates have had a net positive influence on the balance of payments. This is because countries have contracted most of their debt at fixed rates of interest, whilst their foreign exchange assets are invested at floating rates. Table 5 shows that in 1981 developing countries had liabilities on floating interest rates totalling US$ 209 billion which were offset by assets of US$ 139 billion; low income countries as a group, in fact, held more floating interest rate assets than liabilities. The major exceptions among developing countries are Brazil and Mexico, whose floating interest rate foreign liabilities are covered by similar foreign assets to only 21 per cent. Hence, if there is a problem in respect of the interest burden, it affects at present only a very small number of countries.

II. DEBT-BURDEN INDICATORS

15. In discussions of developing countries' debt burden, reference is frequently made to a variety of external debt indicators, such as the relation between debt or debt service to national product, or exports of goods and services. The IMF report[3] points out that, while being a useful tool for preliminary analysis, debt indicators must be used with caution, as otherwise misleading inferences may be drawn. First, the change in a particular debt ratio over time may be more significant than its absolute level; second, in cross-country comparison, two countries with a similar debt service ratio may have entirely different underlying economic structures and hence prospects. These are but a few of the reasons that invite caution in using such mechanical devices in analysing a country's debt position and it must be underlined that the calculation of debt ratios cannot take the place of serious and comprehensive assessment of a developing country's economic situation and policy when trying to ascertain country risk.

Table 5. *Estimated total[1] external assets and liabilities of non-OPEC, non-OECD developing countries at year-end, 1979-1981 ($ billion)*

	Liabilities			Assets			Balance		
	1979	1980	1981	1979	1980	1981	1979	1980	1981
I. *Medium and long term*	269	309	354	9	10	13	−260	−299	−341
A. Fixed interest[2]	180	206	235	8	9	11	−172	−197	−224
B. Floating interest[3]	89	103	119	1	1	2	−88	−102	−117
II. *Short-term*[4]	60	75	90	115	126	137	55	51	47
of which: foreign exchange reserves[5]	−	−	−	(69)	(70)	(70)	−	−	−
III. *Total*	329	384	444	124	136	150	−205	−248	−294
A. Fixed interest	180	206	235	8	9	11	−172	−197	−224
B. Floating interest	149	178	209	116	127	139	−33	−51	−70
of which: Brazil/Mexico	60½	71	87	15½	15½	18	−45	−51	−69
LICs	9½	11	13½	14	15	15	4½	4	1½

1. Excluding direct foreign investment and IMF transactions.
2. The bulk of which is *not* denominated in US dollars.
3. The bulk of which is denominated in US dollars.
4. Liabilities include arrears, assets exclude flight capital deposited in foreign banks. All short-term transactions are assumed to be on floating interest, although a part of trade credits (for both imports and exports) and of arrears are below market rates.
5. All foreign exchange reserves are assumed here to be invested in short-term instruments.

Source: OECD.

16. Taking an aggregate view, debt service of non-oil developing countries, which was about 1.5 per cent of GNP in 1971, rose to about 3 per cent at the end of the 1970s, and interest payments as a proportion of exports have risen from 3 per cent to 5 per cent. Amortisation payments have increased from 7 per cent to 9 per cent of exports, but since, under normal conditions, amortisation may be expected to be rolled over, this item might, in fact, be disregarded. The increase of the interest payments ratio of non-oil developing countries — whether measured as a percentage of GNP or of exports — represents a noticeable, but not alarming increase of the debt burden in real terms.

17. Table 6 shows debt service ratios measured against exports for 40 of the largest debtors, or countries with high debt service ratios. The first observation one can make is that these ratios vary widely, between a low 3-5 per cent (Nigeria, Malaysia, Senegal, Taiwan, Venezuela) to a high 55-68 per cent (Brazil, Mexico). Secondly, for quite a number of these countries, the debt service ratios have had a marked tendency to increase over the last three to four years. Thirdly, if a ratio of 20 per cent is taken as an arbitrary threshold where "prudent" limits might appear to be exceeded for the typical developing country, it should be noted that there were only nine such cases in 1971/72, but twenty-three in 1981. These last two observations are related and the recent, quasi-general increase in debt service ratios should provoke further thought, first and foremost on the part of borrowing countries in respect of the right economic policy orientations, lest debt service should become too onerous a charge on their foreign exchange earning capacity, as well as on the part of aid donors and, where relevant, of commercial banks who, evidently, do not wish to see a developing country default.

III. LIMITS TO COMMERCIAL BANK LENDING

18. Lending to developing countries represents, overall, only about 3 per cent of commercial banks' assets, though in individual cases the ratio is likely to be higher. The ratio of lending to oil importers to banks' capital, nevertheless, has been rising and represented some 60 per cent in 1978. To what extent increased exposure will cause banks to slow their lending to developing countries depends on many factors apart from a perception of increasing risk. In the past, many individual banks found lending to developing countries profitable, not least in the short-term Euro-loan market where high spreads and front-end fees could be earned. The slow-down in world trade and the recent substantial fall in oil prices has affected individual developing

Table 6. *Debt service ratios: debt-service payments as per cent of total exports**

Country	Average 1971/72	1975	1976	1977	1978	1979	1980 prelim.	1981 estim.
Algeria	9	17	20	21	29	31	30	36
Argentina	26	30	30	20	28	18	25	27
Bangladesh	—	14	17	13	13	10	11	12
Bolivia	16	19	20	23	50	31	34	33
Brazil	51	37	43	47	55	60	57	58
Chile	20	34	32	31	45	32	34	45
Colombia	15	13	11	11	13	14	15	12
Congo	10	16	20	21	27	28	26	25
Dominican Rep.	7	9	10	10	11	21	24	25
Ecuador	12	7	9	10	16	34	21	22
Egypt	31	22	19	24	22	19	20	20
Gabon	9	9	11	16	25	26	21	22
Greece	12	15	15	15	13	14	16	18
India	22	14	12	11	11	10	9	10
Indonesia	10	10	11	13	15	15	11	12
Ivory Coast	10	9	9	11	17	23	36	39
Jamaica	8	8	12	15	17	17	21	24
Korea	19	12	10	10	11	15	14	16
Malaysia	4	5	6	7	9	5	4	5
Mexico	34	37	50	63	59	68	41	60
Morocco	10	7	10	13	22	26	28	35
Nicaragua	12	14	14	15	15	26	13	25
Nigeria	3	3	4	4	6	4	4	4
Pakistan	19	18	17	17	14	12	11	10
Peru	23	28	27	32	32	26	36	42
Philippines	9	12	16	13	23	20	18	24
Portugal	6	6	8	9	8	10	13	15
Senegal	5	7	7	8	17	21	27	28
Spain	12	7	7	9	13	10	11	13
Sri Lanka	12	19	19	16	9	7	7	8
Sudan	13	37	24	17	17	35	39	44
Taiwan	5	5	5	5	6	5	6	6
Thailand	11	9	8	13	15	15	14	17
Tunisia	16	10	10	13	14	14	14	15
Turkey	12	10	12	12	16	18	14	17
Uruguay	28	24	21	30	47	12	12	13
Venezuela	6	5	5	11	15	17	26	37
Yugoslavia	20	16	15	17	15	18	16	20
Zaire	8	19	15	15	15	17	24	24
Zambia	13	15	14	21	26	21	21	24

* Exports of goods and services and net private transfers (including reported workers' remittances).
Note: The Table includes mainly the largest debtors and countries with high debt service ratios. It excludes countries for which consistent data over the decade were not available.
Source: OECD.

countries differently and will, no doubt, influence both availability of international funds to commercial banks, as well as lending policies. However, as the World Bank points out in its report,[4] it seems highly probable that borrowers and lenders will adapt to changing conditions without precipitating a general crisis of confidence. While some economies might find it harder to service their debt, others by contrast may find it easier. Different countries are involved with different banks and the degree of their involvement also varies. Banks that feel they are over-exposed internationally can generally be replaced by others. This is what has been happening during the last decade when international lending by European and Japanese banks accelerated whilst American banks were slowing down the growth of overseas lending. More recently, there are indications that OPEC-Arab banks have increased their participation in international lending, in particular to oil-importing developing countries. Hence, whilst lending to developing countries will no doubt continue to grow, its composition and speed will very much depend on prevailing circumstances. No doubt also, in isolated cases, developing countries (and the banks involved with them) may not escape the consequences associated with debt servicing difficulties. Defaults by debtor countries are usually preceded by a fairly long period in which indicators of economic performance emit adequate warning signals, and a prudent borrower would seek appropriate remedies at an early stage, thus attempting to avoid the worst.

19. Lending to developing countries has become a specialised business requiring a great deal of experience and close contact to borrowers. Banks engaged in international lending can, no doubt, contribute to maintaining orderly conditions in this market by careful assessment of country risk, by increasing co-operation among themselves and by becoming more inventive in dealing with the foreign financing needs of particular clients.

NOTES

1. *External Indebtedness of Developing Countries*, IMF, Washington, DC, May 1981; *World Development Report 1981*, The World Bank, Washington, DC, August 1981; *External Debt of Developing Countries*, OECD, Paris, October 1981.

2. *External Debt of Developing Countries*, Paris, 1981: The OECD regularly collects and publishes external debt statistics for some 150 developing countries. The statistics relate to amounts disbursed and cover, in principle, all types of debt, with the exception of debt with an original maturity of less than one year, military debt, debt to the IMF and debt in local currency.

3. *External Indebtedness of Developing Countries*, IMF, Washington, 1981, p. 12.

4. *World Development Report 1981*, The World Bank, Washington, August 1981, pp. 60-61.

Chapter XV

PROSPECTS FOR THE EXTERNAL POSITION OF NON-OIL DEVELOPING COUNTRIES*

by *Jacques R. Artus*

I. INTRODUCTION

External factors have been extremely unfavorable to non-oil developing countries over the past ten years. In particular, two rounds of oil price increases and the stagflation problem in industrial countries have worsened the terms of trade of non-oil developing countries and reduced the growth of their exports. As a result, many non-oil developing countries have found their margins for policy mistakes greatly reduced. Many have found the resolve to adopt comprehensive adjustment programs, but many have not. In recent years, the sharp increase in interest rates in world financial markets and the strength of the US dollar – the currency of denomination of the bulk of the foreign debt of non-oil developing countries – have increased the cost of delaying adjustment and have resulted in severe financing constraints for countries that have delayed adjustment.

The present paper addresses itself to these problems. It briefly reviews the evolution of the external position of non-oil developing countries over the past ten years in section II. Then, it considers the prospects for the external position of non-oil developing countries over the short term (1982-83) and the medium term (1984-86) in section III. It is impossible in the context of the present paper to consider separately a large number of countries. To strike a medium ground between an analysis that is too general to be meaningful and an analysis that is too detailed to be presented in a few pages, the paper distinguishes four subgroups of non-oil developing countries. The subgroup of net oil exporters includes countries that export more oil than they import, but are not major oil exporters. The other three subgroups, referred to together as the net oil importers, are the major exporters of manu-

---

* This paper draws in part on World Economic Outlook reports prepared by the staff of the IMF. Nevertheless, the views expressed in this paper represent the opinions of the author and should not be interpreted as official Fund views.

factures, the low-income countries, and the "other" net oil importers.[1]
The composition of the subgroups is given in the Appendix.[2]

II. HISTORICAL DEVELOPMENTS

On the whole, the external position of non-oil developing countries weakened more sharply after the second round of oil price increases in 1979-80
than after the first round in 1973. Before assessing the prospects for the external position of non-oil developing countries, it is important to understand
the reasons for these developments

1. *The Period 1972-78*

The data in Tables 1 and 2 indicate that the external position of the non-oil
developing countries was only moderately weaker by 1978 than in 1972, the
last year before the first round of oil price increases and the other major disturbances of the 1970s.[3] After adjustment for the growth of exports of
goods and services from 1972 to 1978, the current account deficit was significantly larger in 1978 than in 1972 for the low income countries and the
"other" net oil importers, but it was about the same for the other two subgroups. More important the debt service ratio was about the same by 1978
as in 1972 for the net oil exporters, the low income countries, and the
"other" net oil importers; it was lower by 1978 than in 1972 for the major
exporters of manufactures.[4] The ratio of external reserves to imports of
goods and services was significantly lower by 1978 than in 1972 for the four
subgroups, but the change in the international monetary system toward
greater exchange rate flexibility was in part responsible for this development.

Three factors were responsible for this relatively favorable outturn. First,
many non-oil developing countries benefited from the boom in practically
all commodity prices in 1973, and from the boom in the prices of coffee, tea,
and cocoa, in 1976-77. These developments helped to offset the negative effects that the 1973 oil price increases and the 1974-75 recession in the industrial world had on their terms of trade. By 1978, when more normal levels
of economic activity had been restored in the industrial world and the boom
in the prices of tropical beverages had abated, the terms of trade of the major
exporters of manufactures, low income countries and "other" net oil importers were only moderately lower than in 1972 (see Table 3). Not surprisingly, the terms of trade of the net oil exporters were much higher.

Table 1. *External debt position of non-oil developing countries*
(in per cent)

	1972	1978	1981
Net oil exporters			
Gross reserves ratio[1]	26.7	22.2	19.5
Debt ratio[2]	130.8	157.4	114.7
Debt service ratio[3]	25.3	29.3	32.4
Interest payments ratio	6.9	9.5	11.7
Amortization ratio	18.4	19.8	20.7
Major exporters of manufactures			
Gross reserves ratio[1]	40.2	27.7	13.7
Debt ratio[2]	96.0	87.4	77.9
Debt service ratio[3]	17.7	15.6	18.6
Interest payments ratio	5.8	5.2	7.9
Amortization ratio	11.9	10.4	10.7
Low income countries [4]			
Gross reserves ratio[1]	23.7	16.3	11.7
Debt ratio[2]	144.7	220.2	251.7
Debt service ratio[3]	10.1	11.5	26.8
Interest payments ratio	3.2	4.7	8.7
Amortization ratio	6.9	6.8	19.1[5]
Other net oil importers			
Gross reserves ratio[1]	30.2	26.6	20.4
Debt ratio[2]	89.6	95.5	106.6
Debt service ratio[3]	12.3	13.7	20.2
Interest payments ratio	3.7	4.8	8.7
Amortization ratio	8.7	8.8	11.5

1. Total external reserves (with gold valued at SDR 35 per ounce) at end of year in per cent of imports of goods and services during the year indicated.

2. Total of medium-term and long-term debt, with and without public guarantee, at end of year in per cent of exports of goods and services during the year indicated.

3. Payments as percentage of exports of goods and services.

4. India and the People's Republic of China have been excluded because their balance of payments and external debt developments would dominate too much the developments for other countries in the subgroup. Both countries have a relatively small external debt.

5. The amortization ratio was abnormally high in 1981 because of debt rescheduling in a number of countries.

Table 2. *Payments balances on current account* [1]

	1972	1978	1979	1980	1981
(In billions of US dollars)					
Industrial countries	16.2	30.1	− 10.3	− 44.7	− 3.9
Oil exporting countries	3.0	2.9	69.8	115.0	70.8
Non-oil developing countries[2]	− 10.6	− 38.9	− 58.8	− 85.6	− 102.0
Net oil exporters	− 2.3	− 7.9	− 8.5	− 11.0	− 20.6
Net oil importers[2]	− 8.3	− 31.0	− 50.3	− 74.6	− 81.5
Major exporters of manufactures	− 2.4	− 9.9	− 21.5	− 32.4	− 36.0
Low income countries[2]	− 2.8	− 7.8	− 9.6	− 11.8	− 10.9
Other net oil importers	− 2.4	− 13.2	− 17.4	− 25.8	− 30.2
Total[3]	8.6	− 5.8	0.7	− 15.3	− 35.1
(In per cent of exports of goods and services)					
Industrial countries	4.1	2.6	0.7	2.6	− 0.2
Oil exporting countries	11.5	1.8	29.1	35.2	20.0
Non-oil developing countries[2]	− 12.1	− 15.0	− 17.7	− 20.4	− 22.7
Net oil exporters	− 21.3	− 20.2	− 15.5	− 14.8	− 25.7
Net oil importers	− 10.8	− 14.1	− 18.1	− 21.6	− 22.0
Major exporters of manufactures	− 6.8	− 8.0	− 13.7	− 16.3	− 16.6
Low income countries[2]	− 45.2	− 55.7	− 57.8	− 61.5	− 59.6
Other net oil importers	− 11.1	− 21.2	− 22.3	− 26.9	− 30.3
Total[3]	1.7	− 0.3	0.1	− 0.5	− 1.4

1. Excluding official transfers.

2. The figures for India and the People's Republic of China are excluded from the estimates for low income countries, but are included in the totals for net oil importers and for non-oil developing countries.

3. Reflects errors, omissions, and asymmetries in reported balance of payments statistics, plus balances of listed groups with other countries (mainly, the USSR and other non-member countries in Eastern Europe).

Second, many of the developing countries classified as net oil importers were able to reduce significantly the growth of their imports without much reduction in their economic growth. For the major exporters of manufactures, the rate of growth of the volume of imports was only ½ percentage point more than the rate of growth of real GDP during the period 1973-78, instead of about 4½ percentage points more during the period 1968-72. A similar reduction in the ratio of import growth to GDP growth was observed for the low income countries. The reduction was less impressive for the "other" net oil importers, but, in part, this was because the ratio of import growth to GDP growth of this subgroup was already low during the period 1968-72. Methods of adjustment differed widely among countries. Many countries, including most major exporters of manufactures, adopted broad

Table 3. *Foreign trade developments (changes in per cent)*

	Average change		
	1968-72	1973-78	1979-81
Net oil exporters			
Export volume	5.3	4.0	7.0
Import volume	3.7	7.7	13.2
Terms of trade	− 1.3	4.0	5.9
Real GDP	7.0	6.2	6.3
Import volume/real GDP	− 3.1	1.5	6.5
Major exporters of manufactures			
Export volume	11.8	8.7	6.4
Import volume	12.9	6.6	6.4
Terms of trade	0.6	− 1.1	− 1.7
Real GDP	8.1	6.0	3.5
Import volume/real GDP	4.4	0.6	2.8
Low income countries [1]			
Export volume	5.6	0.9	1.8
Import volume	4.8	2.0	− 3.2
Terms of trade	− 1.4	− 1.1	− 8.2
Real GDP	3.4	3.7	2.9
Import volume/real GDP	1.4	− 1.6	− 6.0
Other net oil importers			
Export volume	6.7	2.0	4.6
Import volume	5.2	3.3	1.9
Terms of trade	− 0.9	− 0.2	− 6.4
Real GDP	5.5	4.9	3.3
Import volume/real GDP	− 0.3	− 1.5	− 1.4

1. India and the People's Republic of China are excluded (see footnote 4, Table 1).

adjustment programs including a depreciation of their exchange rates and supportive demand management policies. Many other countries relied mainly on import quotas and other trade restrictions. On the whole, countries that relied on broad adjustment programs experienced relatively good export performance, while countries that relied on import quotas did not. However, this observation is subject to many exceptions due to differences in the composition of exports and the geographical location of countries.

Third, non-oil developing countries benefited from low interest rates in a period of high inflation (see Chart 1). Many countries, in particular in the subgroups of low income countries and "other" net oil importers, had large debts granted by foreign official institutions at fixed nominal interest rates.

Chart 1. *Nominal interest rates (in per cent)*

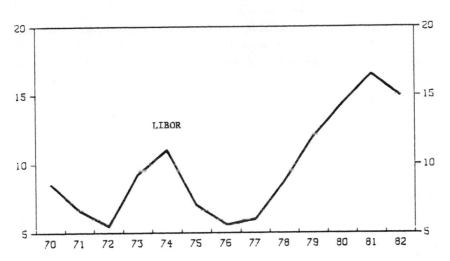

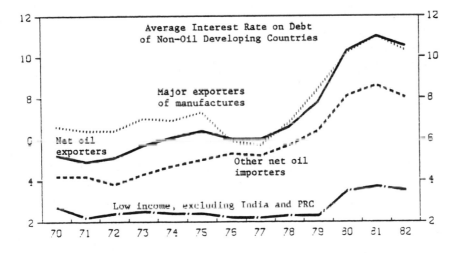

The real burden of this debt was practically wiped out as a result of world inflation. Even with respect to newly acquired debt, the cost of borrowing remained low. For most of the low income countries and the "other" net oil importers, the bulk of financing was still provided at low concessionary rates. For the major exporters of manufactures, the bulk of financing was provided by banks at market rates, but these rates remained significantly below inflation rates. *Ex post* real interest rates on debts denominated in US dollars in the world financial markets averaged only about ½ per cent in real terms during 1973-78, when interest rates are deflated by the rate of increase of the US GDP deflator.

Not only did non-oil developing countries benefit from low interest rates during 1973-78, but, given that most of their debts were denominated in US dollars, they also benefited from the large depreciation of the US dollar that took place during that period. As a result, the real interest rates faced by non-oil developing countries, measured by deflating the average nominal interest rates on their foreign debts by the rates of increase of their export prices, were very low. The low income countries as a group paid an average nominal interest rate of 2½ per cent on their external debt during this period, while their export prices, measured in the depreciating US dollar, rose at an average annual rate of 14 per cent. With such a real interest rate of − 11½ per cent, it is not surprising that their debt position did not deteriorate. The same is true for the other subgroups. The real interest rate for the "other" net oil importers taken as a group was also − 11½ per cent. Even for the major exporters of manufactures, the real interest rate was, on average, about − 7½ per cent.

2. *The Period 1979-81*

Developments during and after the second round of oil price increases were much more unfavorable to non-oil developing countries, and their external position weakened significantly. The weakening was particularly marked for the low income countries and the "other" net oil importers, which together comprise nearly four fifths of the non-oil developing countries. The debt service ratio of the low-income countries increased from about 10 to 11 per cent in 1972 and 1978 to 27 per cent in 1981.[5] The debt service ratio of the "other" net oil importers increased from about 12 to 15 per cent in 1972 and 1978 to 20 per cent in 1981. In addition, both subgroups experienced a sharp increase in their debts to the Fund, which are not taken into account in these debt service ratios. By 1981, both subgroups had low foreign exchange reserves. They also had large current account deficits; the deficit of the low income countries amounted to 60 per cent of their exports of goods and services versus 45 per cent in 1972, while the deficit of the ''other'' net oil importers amounted to 30 per cent of their exports of goods and services versus 11 per cent in 1972.

While less marked, the weakening of the external positions of the major exporters of manufactures and the net oil exporters was significant. The increase in the debt service ratio of the major exporters of manufactures from 1978 to 1981 amounted to only 3 percentage points, and by 1981, this ratio was only marginally higher than in 1972. But this is to some extent misleading because most major exporters of manufactures made large short-term borrowings during 1980-81 that are not taken into account in the debt service ratios considered here. In addition, this subgroup had low foreign exchange reserves by 1981, and its current account deficit was twice as large in 1981 as in 1978 or 1972. While the debt service ratio of the net oil exporters did not increase from 1978 to 1981 thanks to the second round of oil price increases, even this subgroup had a large current account deficit by 1981.

In part, the weakening in the external positions of non-oil developing countries was caused by the low or negative rates of economic growth experienced by most industrial countries in 1980-81. The stagnation in industrial countries reduced the growth of the volume of exports of the non-oil developing countries. It also depressed the prices of many raw materials exported by non-oil developing countries. This effect, combined with the effects of rising prices for oil and falling prices for products such as coffee, tea, and cocoa, led to a marked decline in the terms of trade of most non-oil developing countries. From 1978 to 1981, the terms of trade of the major exporters of manufactures, the low income countries, and the ''other'' net oil importers declined at an average annual rate of 1½ per cent, 8 per cent, and 6½ per cent, respectively. Only the net oil exporters experienced a rise in their terms of trade during this period.

The large increase in interest rates in world financial markets was a further factor behind the weakening in the external position of non-oil developing countries. In about one and a half years, from mid-1978 to end-1979, the three-month London interbank offer rate (LIBOR) increased from 7½ per cent to 15 per cent, and it has fluctuated around this level since then. In addition, the US dollar appreciated sharply during this period, making it even more costly for non-oil developing countries to service the large portion of their foreign debt that is denominated in US dollars. As if this was not enough, official loans at concessionary interest rates did not increase proportionately to the increase in current account deficits so that non-oil developing countries, in particular in the subgroup of ''other'' net oil importers, had to increase the proportion of their financing obtained from the private credit markets at prevailing market-related interest rates.

As a result of these developments, the real interest rates faced by non-oil developing countries increased drastically. If we compare 1981 with the period 1973-78, the average real interest rate increased from − 7½ per cent to 7 per cent for major exporters of manufactures, from − 11½ per cent to 8½ per cent for low income countries, and from − 11½ per cent to 9½ per cent for "other" net oil importers. The subgroup of net oil exporters was the only one that did not experience an increase in real interest rates during 1979-81 thanks to the large increase in oil prices.

Adjustment policies followed by many non-oil developing countries, while unable to offset fully these unfavorable external factors, had significant effects. In particular, the real growth of imports of the three subgroups of net oil importers was cut back a good deal more sharply than their domestic output. By far the greatest curtailment occurred in the low income countries, whose imports in volume rose by 6 percentage points less than their average rate of growth of real GDP during 1979-81. Average import volume growth was 3 percentage points more than average real GDP growth in major exporters of manufactures, but 1½ percentage points less in "other" net oil importers. In addition, some adjustment was evident on the export side. The major exporters of manufactures were able to maintain a high rate of growth of exports despite sluggish growth in the rest of the world. The low income countries and the "other" net oil importers were unable to expand their exports rapidly because their exports are concentrated on primary products, for which world demand has in general been increasing only slowly. But even these countries were relatively successful in sustaining export growth, in part through the expansion of their trade with each other.

Nevertheless, it must be recognized that many non-oil developing countries have so far failed to adopt sufficiently comprehensive adjustment programs. Too often the tendency is to rely on import restrictions, while maintaining excessive fiscal deficits that are monetized because of narrow domestic markets for public securities. Rigid exchange rate and interest rate policies backed up by domestic price controls compound the problem by reducing production incentives. Such a lack of effective adjustment can only lead to severe financial difficulties when real interest rates are high, and this is exactly what has happened to many countries over the past two or three years.

This inadequate amount of adjustment or, more precisely, the inefficient manner in which the adjustment has been sought, is in part responsible for the recent poor growth performance of many non-oil developing countries.

The average rate of growth in real GDP of non-oil developing countries dropped to 2½ per cent in 1981 – only about half the rate prevailing in the previous two years and still farther below the rates of 1977 and 1978.[6] However, it must be recognized that in many low income countries the adjustment is extremely difficult because of the lack of diversification in production and exports, and because of the limited availability of resources for investment. The decline in the real level of foreign aid to these countries in recent years has made the adjustment even more difficult. The growth performance, as well as the external position, of the African region (excluding South Africa) is of particular concern in this context. Real GDP in African countries, on average, grew by only 1½ per cent in 1981, after an average growth of only 3 per cent in 1978-80. In combination with a population growth rate on the order of 2½ per cent per annum, this record implies that real per capita income has stagnated during the whole period 1978-81. In a number of the sub-Saharan countries, indeed, per capita output declined. In 1981, the current account deficit of the region reached $ 13¼ billion, amounting to about one third of the level of its exports of goods and services.

III. PROSPECTS FOR 1982 – 86

Looking ahead, it is difficult to be optimistic for 1982-83, but one can envisage a significant improvement in the external position of non-oil developing countries in 1984-86 if they strengthen their adjustment efforts and if industrial countries make significant progress in solving their stagflation problem. Of course, these are two big "ifs".

1. Prospects for 1982-83

The current account position of non-oil developing countries is likely to improve only moderately in 1982-83. On the favorable side, the moderate growth in the industrial countries that is now expected to begin in the second half of 1982 and in 1983 should lead to an increase in their import demands and in world trade generally. In particular, renewed buoyancy of final demand in industrial countries should lead to a pickup in inventory accumulation after a prolonged period of reduction of stocks or extreme caution in stock-building, reflecting in part the high costs of financing investment in inventories. The resumption of growth in industrial countries also points toward some improvement in the terms of trade of non-oil developing countries by 1983. In addition, the current softness of the world oil market offers a prospect of stabilized oil import bills to non-oil developing countries.

On the unfavorable side, three factors are likely to limit the improvement in the current account position of non-oil developing countries. First, interest rates remain extremely high in world financial markets. Even if they moderate in forthcoming months, the amount of external interest payments of the non-oil developing countries will increase substantially in 1982 because of the rise in outstanding debt and lagged effects of the high interest rates prevailing in 1981 and in the first part of 1982. Second, as discussed above, many non-oil developing countries have so far failed to adopt comprehensive adjustment programs. Third, even in countries with comprehensive adjustment programs, imports may remain high in 1982-83 because such programs often require the importation of capital goods and other inputs in their initial phases.

On the whole, the aggregate deficit of the non-oil developing countries could stay close to its 1981 level of about $ 100 billion in 1982 and 1983. The deficit of the subgroups of net oil exporters and low income countries could increase slightly, while the deficit of the major exporters of manufactures and the "other" net oil importers could decrease slightly. But, more important, the deficit of the four subgroups as a percentage of their exports of goods and services, could decline significantly, even though they would remain much above their 1972 levels.

These projected current account deficits would imply further, albeit small, increases in the debt service ratios of the four subgroups of non-oil developing countries in 1982 and 1983. The factors behind these increases remain the same as during 1979-81, namely, large current account deficits, high interest rates, and the strength of the US dollar. In particular, in 1982, the real interest rates paid by non-oil developing countries could remain at their high 1981 levels, given that the LIBOR rate was still around 15 per cent in March 1982, while the average of export prices of non-oil developing countries is likely to increase by only 4 to 5 per cent in terms of US dollars from 1981 to 1982. In addition, some movement away from the recent pronounced degree of reliance on short-term financing and back toward a higher proportion of longer-term funds in the financing pattern of non-oil developing countries might be anticipated, along with a lower annual rate of reduction in the real value of their international reserve holdings. These latter factors would lead to a more rapid increase in debt service ratios, but, of course, they would not imply a weakening of external positions.

A large number of countries, in particular in the subgroups of low income countries and "other" net oil importers, are likely to continue to experience serious strains on their external financial positions in 1982 and 1983. African countries (excluding South Africa) will remain a particular source of concern. Present projections for the African region envisage a weak recovery in the rate of growth of real GDP in 1982. But even this weak recovery would imply a continuation of the aggregate current account deficit of the region at its extremely high 1981 level. The prospect is that the debt service ratio of this region will continue to rise sharply, and that an increasing number of countries in the region are likely to encounter serious difficulties in obtaining financing for the projected current account deficits, and hence in financing an adequate flow of imports.

2. Prospects for 1984-86

Looking beyond 1983, the degree of uncertainty is such that one can only discuss "scenarios". The Fund staff has developed a number of these scenarios to assess the medium-term implications of alternative policy stances in industrial countries and other factors on the industrial world itself and on the performance of non-oil developing countries. In this context, projections of trade, growth, and financing flows for the four analytic subgroups of non-oil developing countries are developed for 1984-86 under the assumptions pertaining to the alternative policy stances of industrial countries. I will review here two of these scenarios.

Scenario A – the "central" scenario – is based on the assumption that industrial countries affected by inflation persist with policies of monetary restraint aimed at reducing this inflation by restricting the growth of nominal demand. Monetary restraint is presumed to be reinforced by compatible and supportive fiscal policies and by a certain effort to deal effectively with structural rigidities in labor and goods markets. Adherence to such a balanced policy course might be expected to create an economic environment that would encourage the increased saving and investment necessary for structural adaptations of the industrial economies and for a return to non-inflationary growth. It is assumed that persistence with such a policy course would enable industrial countries to increase their average rate of growth to slightly more than 3 per cent per annum over the 1984-86 period, and at the same time gradually reduce the average rate of inflation, measured in terms of GNP deflators, from its projected 1983 level of about 7 per cent to 5-5½ per cent by 1986.

Scenario B, which is more pessimistic, indicates what might happen if national authorities in the industrial countries should fail to implement coherent policy strategies to deal with the problems of inflation and structural adjustment. Such failure could arise from a relaxation of monetary restraint in the face of rising unemployment, or from an inability to develop fiscal policies and policies affecting the supply side that are consistent with restrictive monetary policies. Experience over the past decade provides strong evidence that the probable outcome of a shift to more stimulative monetary policies at this time would be higher growth in the short term followed by an acceleration of inflation and, ultimately, by a sharp economic recession. Alternatively, failure of national governments to bring fiscal policy in line with restrictive monetary policy would be likely to result in continued high (nominal and real) rates of interest in a "crowding out" of the private investment so essential to sustained economic recovery. In either case, the medium-term outcome would be characterized by lower growth and higher inflation than in Scenario A. On balance, under Scenario B, economic growth would average about 2 per cent over the 1984-86 period, with an average rate of inflation that would rise to around 8½ per cent. Progress has been made during 1981 and early 1982 in the direction of Scenario A, but the possibility that Scenario B will prevail cannot be ruled out.

A number of assumptions need to be made to develop the projections for non-oil developing countries. With respect to policies, a crucial assumption is that countries that are confronted with serious external imbalances will implement comprehensive programs of adjustment. Most such programs will have to include fiscal reform leading to a reduction in excessively high rates of growth of the monetary aggregates; adoption of a realistic exchange rate, combined with a change in domestic prices so that they reflect world market prices; an attenuation of government controls and regulations, including more realistic pricing policies by official marketing agencies, and interest rates that are allowed to reflect real rates of return. In the case of Scenario B, the adjustment programs that have been assumed are necessarily more severe than those required under A.

Several other important assumptions are common to the two scenarios. These are: (i) Real interest rates in international financial markets are gradually reduced, bringing the LIBOR rate to about 2 per cent in real terms by 1986. (ii) Oil prices are assumed to stay constant in real terms at their 1983 projected levels. (iii) The trade restrictiveness of the industrial countries toward the exports of the non-oil developing countries is assumed to remain about the same as it is now. And (iv): Official development assistance is projected to be maintained in real terms from 1983 through 1986.

The above assumptions provide the framework within which the consequences of the alternative paths for industrial country growth and inflation are analyzed. Clearly, the implications for the various groups of countries would be altered if these assumptions do not hold over the medium term. For example, an increase in the degree of trade restrictiveness in industrial countries could have a markedly adverse impact on the outcome for the non-oil developing countries. The outcome would also be worse if oil importing countries do not maintain their energy conservation and development programs and, for this or other reasons, real oil prices increase again. On the other hand, if energy conservation and development programs are successfully implemented, there could be a further decline in the real price of oil that would improve the outcome for oil importing countries. The results of the scenarios should therefore be viewed with a certain degree of caution, given their sensitivity to the common assumptions set forth above, in addition to the great uncertainty always involved in medium-term projections of foreign trade flows.

The main results of Scenario A for the subgroups of non-oil developing countries generally include an acceleration through 1986 of the gradual tendency for improvement that is expected for 1982-83. The improvement is particularly marked for the net oil exporters and the major exporters of manufactures. The subgroup of net oil exporters experiences a decline in its current account deficit as a proportion of exports of goods and services from 1983 to 1986, back to the level observed in 1972. Its debt service ratio also starts to decline, but by 1986 it still remains significantly higher than in 1977.[7] A significant part of this improvement is due to the projected decline in the current account deficit in Mexico and in its rate of foreign borrowing. The current account deficit of the major exporters of manufactures also declines when measured as a percentage of exports of goods and services, while its debt service ratio falls somewhat below its 1972 level by 1986.

The other two groups of non-oil developing countries show steady, but less marked, improvement from 1983 to 1986. The subgroup of low income countries shows a gradual decline in its current account deficit measured as a percentage of exports of goods and services. Its debt service ratio also declines, but by 1986 it remains twice as high as in 1972. Similarly, the current account deficit measured as a proportion of the exports of goods and services and the debt service of the subgroup of "other" net oil importers decline, but by 1986 the debt service ratio remains 50 per cent higher than in 1972.

The results for Scenario B are considerably worse for all four subgroups of non-oil developing countries. This deterioration arises from sluggish world demand, higher inflation, and 4 per cent higher nominal interest rates than those assumed in Scenario A. In each of the subgroups, the debt service ratio fails to decline, or continues to rise, from 1983 to 1986.

The projections for non-oil developing countries under Scenario A and B clearly raise a number of issues concerning the feasibility of the financing and the appropriateness of the assumed rates of economic growth. The projections from Scenario A should not pose serious financing problems for the subgroups of net oil exporters and the major exporters of manufactures as a whole. However, the rate of external borrowing for some of these countries is likely to be constrained because of the rapid buildup of external debt in recent years. While, in the aggregate, a similar assessment applies to the low income countries and the "other" net oil importers, a considerable number of countries within these two subgroups will continue to face severe financing constraints. Many of the countries with the most severe constraints are in Africa. These constraints are reflected in the considerable amount of adjustment with respect to export volumes, import volumes, and economic growth assumed in the projections to 1986, as discussed below.

The staff's assessment that the financing of the current account deficits for 1986 as estimated in Scenario A is feasible, is based on considerations related to both private capital markets and official capital flows. Scenario A assumes an environment of lower inflation, declining interest rates, and improved industrial country growth. Under these conditions, the capacity of the international financial markets to intermediate between surplus groups – whether oil exporting or industrial countries – and deficit developing country groups would be enhanced through a strengthening of bank capital positions, ensuring a flow of financing similar to that of recent years. The average annual increase in the total long-term private debt of non-oil developing countries was 26 per cent from 1975 to 1978 and 18 per cent from 1978 to 1981, and Scenario A would imply a continuation of this slowdown. Based on the experience of recent years, the increase in international bank claims on non-oil developing countries implicit in the deficits projected under Scenario A, together with expected domestic credit demands in the major financial market countries, need not unduly strain the capital positions of the banking system.

The behavior of interest rates is a particularly important factor in this assessment. An improved world economic environment combined with lower, less volatile interest rates would increase bond market activity, freeing bank lending capacity and improving the ability of banks to raise new capital. Strengthened capital positions would ease banks' internal country-limit constraints and thus enable them to sustain their financing flows to countries with relatively large existing debt that are pursuing economic policies the markets regard as appropriate. An interruption of the anti-inflationary policies of the industrial countries, with its adverse effects on nominal interest rates, could only serve to weaken the underlying capacity of the international capital markets. In these circumstances, which are characterized by Scenario B, the possibility of an adequate response by the market to the financing needs of the developing countries would become problematic.

Whether individual countries can maintain market access, even under Scenario A, on a scale commensurate with their estimated current account needs will depend crucially on their policies and prospects. The current account projections under Scenario A were based in large part on individual country assessments. Thus, the potential aggregate deficit and the deficits of the analytic subgroups were constrained by an evaluation of the adjustment and financing prospects of a wide range of countries. Ultimately, it is because these countries are assumed to follow appropriate adjustment policies that the deficits are deemed "financeable". Adjustment programs in the three subgroups of net oil importers will be accompanied, in many cases, by a continuation of the lower rates of economic growth that have prevailed since the mid-1970s.

For the low income countries and, to a lesser extent, for the "other" net oil importers, an important part of the financing is assumed to take the form of long-term capital from official sources, as well as funds from reserve-related credit facilities, including mainly loans from the Fund. The assumption that such flows will be forthcoming reflects the view that countries in these two subgroups will follow comprehensive programs of adjustment, and that industrial and oil exporting countries, directly or through international organizations, will continue to play an important role in supporting such adjustment programs.

It must be stressed that the two scenarios considered here differ greatly as to their implications for global economic prospects for the second half of the 1980s. Insofar as the industrial countries are concerned, the basis for a return to noninflationary growth during the latter part of the decade, with a marked decline in unemployment, would have been developed under Scenario A, whereas the prospects for that period under Scenario B would be for continued high unemployment as national authorities struggled with embedded inflationary expectations. The implications for the non-oil developing countries are evident in the projections for 1986. Under Scenario A, these countries would have made significant progress in reducing the debt burden sustained in the late 1970s and early 1980s, and would be in a position to expand their exports in the latter 1980s as world growth prospects improved. With Scenario B, however, not only would there be no improvement in the debt burden, but poorer economic performance of the non-oil developing countries would impair their ability to borrow. Under these conditions, it is difficult to see how their debt burden could be sustained without further reduction of their growth rates.

NOTES

1. This "other" subgroup consists of countries that, in general, export mainly primary commodities (other than oil or gold).

2. In the context of the present paper, India and the People's Republic of China are excluded from the low income subgroup, but included in the totals for net oil importers. The reason is that their balance of payments and external debt developments tend to be different from those of other low income countries; and, given the economic size of the two countries, they would dominate developments in this subgroup.

3. In terms of debt service ratios, or current account deficits in per cent of exports of goods and services, the external positions of non-oil developing countries was also only moderately weaker in 1976 or 1977 than in 1972.

4. The debt service ratios considered in this paper take into account medium-term and long-term debts, with and without public guarantee.

5. As noted in footnote 5 to Table 1, the amortization ratio of the low income countries was abnormally high in 1981 because of debt rescheduling in a number of countries. But, even after adjustment for this factor, the debt service ratio of the low-income countries is still more than twice as large in 1981 as in 1972 or 1978.

6. In 1981, the average growth for the group of non-oil developing countries was markedly reduced by a sharp decline in the growth rates of Argentina and South Africa. But, even if the median growth rate is considered instead of the average growth rate, the decline in economic growth is still large. The median growth rate is 3 per cent in 1981, versus 4.3 in 1979-80 and 5.3 in 1977-78.

7. Debt service ratios are quite sensitive to variations in estimates of rates of amortization. Such estimates are not very reliable since they depend on the term structure of external debt, which cannot be projected with any degree of reliability.

APPENDIX
COUNTRY CLASSIFICATION OF NON-OIL DEVELOPING COUNTRIES

Major exporters of manufactures

Greece	South Africa	Israel	Korea
Portugal	Argentina	Hong Kong	Singapore
Yugoslavia	Brazil		

Net oil exporters

Bolivia	Peru	Syrian Arab Rep.	Malaysia
Ecuador	Trinidad & Tobago	Egypt	Congo, People's Rep.
Mexico	Bahrain	Tunisia	Gabon

Low income countries

Haiti	India	Ethiopia	Niger
Afghanistan	China, People's Rep.	Gambia, The	Rwanda
Bangladesh	Viet Nam	Guinea-Bissau	Senegal
Burma	Burundi	Guinea	Sierra Leone
Kampuchea	Cape Verde	Kenya	Somalia
Sri Lanka	C. African Rep.	Lesotho	Sudan
Lao, P.D. Rep.	Chad	Madagascar	Tanzania
Maldives	Comoros	Malawi	Togo
Nepal	Zaire	Mali	Uganda
Pakistan	Benin	Mauritania	Upper Volta

Other net oil importers

Malta	Uruguay	Jordan	Mauritius
Turkey	Bahamas	Lebanon	Morocco
Chile	Barbados	Yemen, P.D. Rep.	Sao Tome & Principe
Colombia	Dominica	Philippines	Seychelles
Costa Rica	Grenada	Thailand	Senegal
Dominican Rep.	Guyana	Djibouti	Swaziland
El Salvador	Jamaica	Botswana	Zambia
Guatemala	Netherlands Antilles	Cameroon	Fiji
Honduras	St. Lucia	Equatorial Guinea	Papua New Guinea
Nicaragua	St. Vincent	Ghana	Samoa, Western
Panama	Suriname	Ivory Coast	Romania
Paraguay	Cyprus	Liberia	

Chapter XVI

MANAGING INTERNATIONAL INDEBTEDNESS

by *H. Robert Heller*

During the decade of the 1970s, international lending and borrowing activity expanded at an extremely rapid rate and involved an ever wider group of countries and institutions both on the borrowing and the lending side. This paper deals with some of the special portfolio management challenges that arise out of this foreign exposure. The focus is on exposure management from the viewpoint of the lender. Particular attention is paid to the international debt management problems faced by commercial banks that are active in the international lending business.

There are several characteristics that distinguish international lending activity from domestic lending. These include the involvement of foreign exchange transactions; the special problems posed by different economic, political, and legal regulatory environments; the unique factors associated with sovereign risk; and all the portfolio management considerations arising from these differences.

In this paper we will focus first on monitoring and controlling international exposures from a fairly narrowly perceived accounting perspective. Second we will analyze the special risk evaluation problems that have to be faced in international lending. Third, rate of return considerations will be introduced. Finally, the various aspects affecting international portfolio management will be brought together.

1. MONITORING INTERNATIONAL INDEBTEDNESS

The mere task of monitoring international indebtedness poses a formidable challenge. The Euro-currency markets grew from $110 billion in 1970 to $1.5 trillion in 1980[1] for an average annual growth rate of 30 per cent. The outstanding long-term debt of the developing countries increased from $78 billion in 1971 to $426 billion in 1980.[2]

At the same time banks expanded rapidly overseas through branches, subsidiaries, agencies and a host of other vehicles. In each country, special legal, tax and reporting requirements had to be accommodated, while fulfilling the regular domestic reporting requirements as well. Especially in the United States with its patchwork quilt of regulatory agencies this poses formidable challenges. The internationally active US banks operating under a national charter typically have to deal with three key regulatory and examining agencies: the Federal Reserve, The Comptroller of the Currency, and the FDIC. To accommodate all the reporting demands imposed by the various agencies while providing for adequate management reporting is no mean task. This is particularly true in a time of rapid expansion when branches and subsidiaries are being added at a fast rate.

The problems faced by the various national regulatory agencies are no less formidable. Frequently, market developments advance very rapidly, rendering old and tried reporting forms obsolete. The task of gathering internationally comparable and comprehensive data is particularly difficult. On a macro-level it mirrors the problems faced by individual lending institutions on a micro-level.

a. *Monitoring Individual Bank Exposures.* Every international bank – or other lending institution – needs a system to monitor its international commitments and outstandings. While we discuss some of the portfolio management techniques in section 4, it is clear that certain rudimentary accounting information regarding tenor and borrower must be maintained at all times. Exhibit 1 shows a sample reporting matrix that differentiates between short- (up to one year), medium- (one to three years), and long-term (over three years) exposures. It also allows for a distinction between borrowing sectors: government, other banks, and commercial borrowers. This basic matrix has to be prepared for each country for both commitments and for actual outstandings.

Determining the ultimate source of repayment and thereby the country where any particular loan should be booked is not always an easy task. A loan by the UK subsidiary of a US bank to a Liberian shipping company that hauls Saudi Arabian oil under charter to a German oil company that is a subsidiary of a Dutch corporation may pose certain challenges to the accountant trying to determine where to domicile the loan.

A further problem is posed by the necessity to distinguish between loans denominated in the lender's home currency, the borrower's currency, or a third-country currency.

Loans denominated in the lender's own currency are the classical international vehicle. This instrument is particularly important for US banks as

Exhibit 1. *Country exposure control matrix*

Sector Tenor	Government	Banks	Commercial	Total
Short (to 1 year)				
Medium (1–3 year)				
Long (over 3 year)				
Total				

dollar loans constitute the largest share of all international loans. At the end of 1980, domestic US banks had $173 billion in dollar denominated assets outstanding to foreign borrowers, but only $4.2 billion in similar foreign currency denominated foreign assets. In addition, offshore branches had some $142 billion in external assets, including negligible amounts in the domestic currency of the offshore locality. Undisclosed amounts of foreign currency loans were outstanding at other foreign branches of US banks.

Among the other countries one can readily distinguish between various patterns. There are countries, such as Germany and Switzerland, where the local currency is also the predominant currency in international lending. In other countries foreign currency lending predominates (see Exhibit 2). In the latter group some countries have a preponderance of US dollar lending – such as Belgium, France, Italy, the UK, Canada, and Japan. In still other countries, such as Austria and Luxembourg, foreign lending is dominated by the currencies of large neighbor countries.

Exhibit 2. *External bank assets*
(December 1980 in billions of dollars equivalent)

Country	Currency		
	Domestic	US dollar	Other foreign
Austria	4.8	7.2	7.8
Belgium	3.3	33.4	18.9
Luxembourg	1.3	33.6	53.7
Denmark	0.2	2.1	1.5
France	24.4	87.7	31.1
Germany	51.8	14.2	7.3
Ireland	0.1	0.5	1.4
Italy	1.0	23.3	6.4
Netherlands	11.3	28.0	22.9
Sweden	1.2	4.3	2.1
Switzerland	29.5	21.6	8.5
UK	22.7	262.8	70.9
Canada	0.6	31.8	3.0
Japan	17.0	44.0	4.7
US	172.7	4.2	135.5

Source: BIS, *Annual Report*, 1981, p. 114-5.

It is clearly necessary to distinguish carefully between these three types of international exposure. While any exposue in a non-domestic currency creates special problems for the borrower, the same is true from the viewpoint of the lender. The continuing debate about the appropriate accounting treatment of foreign currency exposures (FASB 8 versus FASB 52) highlights the problem involved. It may be argued that as far as country risk is concerned, an exposure in any currency foreign to the borrower is subject to similar potential debt service difficulties and that these exposures may therefore be lumped together. But from the viewpoint of the lender any foreign currency exposure creates its own management problems and it is therefore appropriate to develop the country exposure matrix for the three relevant currency categories: domestic to the borrower, domestic to the lender, and third currency.

A different set of monitoring problems arises for the international bank through the assumption of non-funded foreign credit risks, such as letters of credit, the provision of back-up lines of credit, leases, and foreign exchange contracts. These items do not enter the traditional balance sheet of the bank and may therefore escape the attention that they deserve. While they tend to be contingent liabilities, they nevertheless expose the bank to risks not unlike traditional credit risks. Because these non-credit financial services yield often significant returns to the institution without encumbering the balance sheet, they frequently seem to be particularly attractive to an institution that tries to improve the traditional financial ratios. It is all the more important that appropriate monitoring and control systems are in place so as to keep the exposure to these special kinds of risk within acceptable limits.

In a decentralized institution the problem of monitoring and controlling foreign exposures become particularly complex. Often, the various foreign subsidiaries operate like domestic financial institutions in the various countries and it is a difficult task to integrate their own exposure control systems with those of the parent company. The difficulties encountered with the switch-over to consolidated balance sheet reporting for the German banks offers a very instructive example.

Modern computer systems offer the advantage of great speed and accuracy, but the programming difficulties that have to be overcome are challenging indeed. These problems are particularly great when previously disparate systems have to be integrated.

Computer based systems are indispensable to accurate monitoring and control of international exposures – especially in a highly decentralized organization. A modern and comprehensive exposure monitoring system enables management to exercise appropriate control and to manage the institution's exposure effectively.

b. *National and International Bank Exposure Monitoring.* [3] The Federal Financial Institutions Examination Council, which is composed of the Board of Governors of the Federal Reserve System, the FDIC, the Federal Home Loan Bank Board, the National Credit Union Administration, and the Comptroller of the Currency, now publishes comprehensive data on international lending by US banks. The bank exposure data are broken down as to sector and maturity and distinguish externally guaranteed loans where applicable. Similar data are available for most European countries, Canada, and Japan. These data are compiled by the Bank for International Settlements and published in their *Annual Report* as well as in periodic press releases. In total, the monitoring of international bank exposures versus other countries is quite comprehensive and timely on both a national and an international level for those countries reporting to the BIS.

Data on international bond issues are good, thanks to the monitoring systems developed by the OECD and the World Bank.

Unfortunately, the same cannot be said for other non-bank lending. Official agencies do provide data on bilateral and multilateral lending to developing countries, but these reports typically do not include short-term trade credits granted by official agencies. Also, there is virtually no coverage of short-term trade credits granted by suppliers and of portfolio investments by other private parties. This situation is particularly troublesome because in times of balance of payments difficulties countries may well rely increasingly upon supplier's credits to finance needed imports. The data actually reported through banking and official channels may therefore give a very different picture from the actual situation.

The data monitoring activities of the lenders are usefully supplemented by direct monitoring of the indebtedness of borrowers. The World Bank regularly monitors the external indebtedness of its developing member countries. The coverage of the system is comprehensive for public debt with a maturity of more than one year. In addition, an increasing number of countries also provide data on the foreign indebtedness of their private sector. Unfortunately, few short-term data are available. Also, there is little coverage of the industrialized countries, so that global monitoring and reporting efforts are frustrated. Thus, the curious situation exists that the data sources for the developing countries are often better than those for the industrialized countries. It should also be pointed out that the data for Socialist countries are either non-existent or highly incomplete.

It is unfortunate that the *creditor* reporting systems maintained by the BIS, OECD, and World Bank (Capital Markets System) do not complement the *debtor* reporting system of the World Bank. Unfortunately, it is impossible to arrive at a truly comprehensive picture. In particular, data on short-term debt to non-bank lenders are not readily available from any source. Thus, the BIS comes to the conclusion that "there are no countries for which a fully comprehensive statement of the external debt situation is available, or can be derived, from these data".[4]

Nevertheless, it is possible to ascertain quite a bit of information on the external indebtedness of the various countries, so that analysts, bankers, and officials can arrive at well reasoned conclusions. While the system is not perfect, it is quite comprehensive. Vast strides in improving the debt statistics have been made in the last half dozen years and a continuing cooperative effort of the international organization should result in a filling-in of the remaining gaps.

2. EVALUATING COUNTRY RISK

Country risk assessment is an integral part of any international portfolio management process. It is important to recognize that any country risk evaluation system has to be tailored to the specific needs of the institution it is designed to serve. This is a fundamental requirement if the country assessment procedure is to be an integral part of the portfolio decision-making process by management. There is no one country risk evaluation system that is the "best" in the sense that it optimally fulfills the requirements of all organizations. Instead, the nature of the institution will shape the country evaluation system.

Several factors are certain to influence the country evaluation system in important ways: the type of business the corporation is engaged in; the organizational structure of the corporation and the availability of special information sources; the ultimate use that is made of the output of the system; and the capability of the support staff. It may be useful to elaborate briefly upon these factors.

a. *Type of Business.* The type of foreign business that the corporation is engaged in is clearly of importance. A financial institution will face different risks in its international operations compared to a multinational oil company or a retail store chain considering a foreign acquisition. Among financial institutions, the requirements will be different for a bank that focuses on trade financing or the occasional participation in a syndicated Euro-loan and a bank that has a physical presence abroad and does a large volume of business there. For an institution that engages in a broad spectrum of international lending activity it is unlikely that all relevant information can be compressed into just one single number as an overall country risk indicator.

b. *Organizational Structure.* A decentralized organization will need a country evaluation system different from a highly centralized operation. A decentralized organization's ability to rely upon first-hand information gathered by its foreign staff represents a unique source of strength that should be fully utilized. For that purpose as wide a variety of staff as possible should be involved in the country evaluation process so as to bring their expertise to bear upon the issue. But because such a wide spectrum of officers is involved, ease of understanding and the ability to communicate effectively also becomes highly important.

At the same time, care must be taken to preserve a global perspective while maintaining both equity among competing regions for resource allocation and identification of attractive risk/reward opportunities. Hence, standardization of procedures and common, understandable rules become important. Emphasis also has to be placed on the development of a system that produces globally consistent results. But at the same time, the system must retain flexibility to take account of unique factors that might be present in a specific country.

c. *Purpose.* Another consideration that is of great significance in designing a country evaluation system is the specific purpose for which the system will be utilized. For instance, if the country evaluations are to be used to establish lending limits or loan loss provisions, a quantitatively oriented country risk rating system will be required. In contrast, if the sole purpose of the country evaluation system is to provide background material for the bank's senior loan committee, a set of country reports might serve that purpose as well.

d. *Staff Capability.* It would be an expensive proposition to build up an entire staff of country experts for the sole purpose of running a country risk evaluation system. There are clear economics of scale to be achieved as similar information is also required for general economic forecasting, foreign exchange forecasting, the formulation of detailed business and marketing plans, customer service, and the like.

e. *Country Risk Evaluation.* At this juncture it may be useful to focus on a specific country risk evaluation system that can be utilized in managing international portfolios. Bank of America's country risk program utilizes a three-pronged evaluation system. It is composed of: (1) a set of leading economic indicators pertaining to a country's debt service capacity; (2) a judgmental economic indicator; and (3) a judgmental political indicator. Here we will focus on the quantified debt service capacity index because it is best suited for quantitative analysis.

The debt service capacity indicators are akin to leading economic indicators and focus on a country's ability to avoid arrears, reschedulings, and actual default on its foreign debt.

In the estimation procedure the economic characteristics of over 80 countries for, say, 1974 were correlated with the debt service record of the country during the following years to derive the debt service capacity indicators. By applying the formula derived to current data, the country's debt service capacity for the ensuing years can then be assessed.

There are three indicators: one focusing on the coming year, one on the next three years, and one on the following five year period (see Exhibit 3). It was found that a country's ability to service its external debt in a timely fashion is related in a statistically significant fashion to three broad groups of variables: (a) a country's external liquidity situation, (b) the fiscal and monetary policies pursued, and (c) its economic structure. The analysis shows that external liquidity factors are particularly relevant in an assess-

Exhibit 3. *Debt service index use as leading indicator*

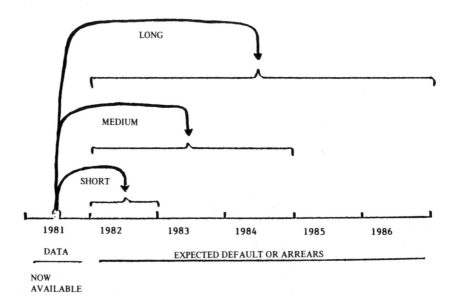

ment of a country's debt service capacity over the short term (next year), while governmental policies have a strong influence on medium-term debt service capacity (1-3 years), and structural factors tend to dominate in the long run (1-5 years). These relationships are illustrated in Exhibit 4.

Exhibit 4. *Debt service capacity*

Indicators	Short to 1 year	(Basic) medium 1-3 year	Long 1-5 year
External liquidity	X		
Government policy		X	
Economic structure			X

Exhibit 5 shows a sample printout for a country that is characterized by a good external liquidity situation as evidenced by a short-term index that ranges between 95 and 100. The basic debt service capacity index as shown by the solid line deteriorated between 1974 and 1979, but shows some improvement in 1980. However, the long-term index shows a substantial decline over the time period shown, indicating that there is about a fifty-fifty chance that some debt service problems such as arrears or reschedulings might occur in the next five years unless steps are taken to improve the basic economic structure of the economy. Together the three indicators offer a rather comprehensive picture of the debt service capacity of a country as far as it can be ascertained in hard economic data.

One of the advantages of an objective debt service capacity indicator of the type described here is that it offers a basis for comparing the debt service

Exhibit 5. *Sample country debt service capacity index*

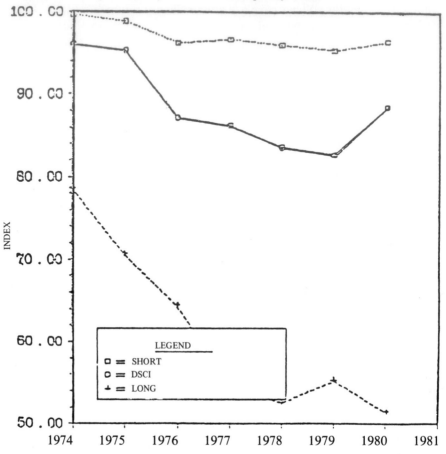

capacity of different countries. It is possible to aggregate the index for various countries to arrive at an average debt service capacity index for a region or the entire world. Exhibit 6 shows the average debt service capacity index for the world. Over 80 countries are covered, although the coverage varies slightly from year to year due to unavailability of information. It should be noted that each country is accorded the same weight in these calculations.

For the world as a whole, the indicators show a slight downward trend over the 1973-81 period, which saw the two major oil shocks, a global recession, and unprecedented inflation. The *short-term index*, which focuses on the liquidity situation, shows considerable deterioration from 1974 to 1976 as the first oil crisis impinges upon the world economy. There is some re-

Exhibit 6. *World average DSCI*

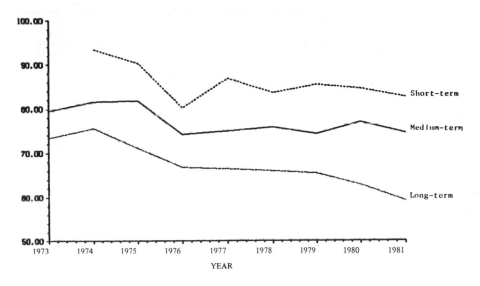

Exhibit 7. *Debt service capacity index, short term*

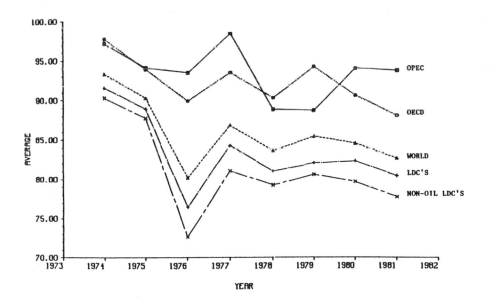

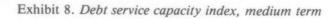

Exhibit 8. *Debt service capacity index, medium term*

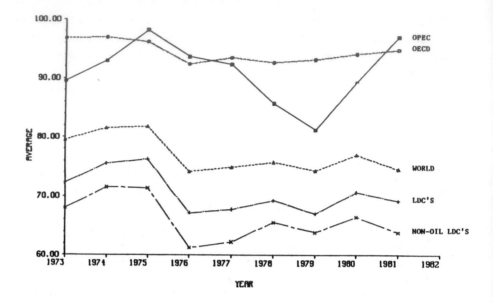

Exhibit 9. *Debt service capacity index, long term*

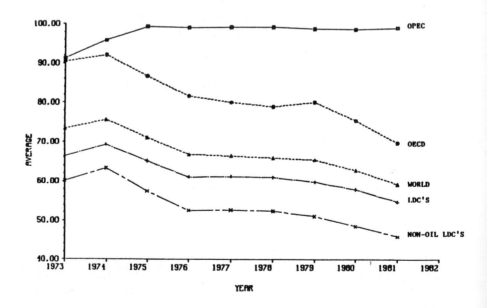

covery in 1977 and after that the index is virtually stable – indicating that world liquidity has not suffered materially. The *medium-term index* also does not change very much, moving from 80 out of a possible 100 in 1973 to 75 in 1981. Overall, this may be indicative of the fact that governments have implemented reasonable policies during the period. In contrast, the *long-term index* moves from a high of 76 in 1974 to 60 in 1981 reflecting the continuing structural deterioration of the world economy over the period.

Exhibits 7, 8 and 9 show a disaggregated picture for the three time horizons. The deterioration of the short-term index (Exhibit 7) in 1976 for the developing countries and the subsequent rapid recovery are remarkable, but they cannot mask the secular downward trend from a score of 90 in 1974 to 77 in 1981 for the non-oil developing countries. Also, the situation in the OECD countries deteriorates from 98 to 88 over the same period. The OPEC countries show rather large fluctuations, with no discernible overall pattern. But by 1980-81, OPEC had pulled ahead of the industrialized countries as far as their liquidity situation is concerned.

The medium-term index (Exhibit 8) shows greater stability, but also here the OPEC countries show large fluctuations. In 1975 their medium-term debt service capacity reached a peak, deteriorated until 1979, only to improve again after the second oil shock. The OECD countries continued to show good results throughout the period, and even the non-oil LDCs exhibited remarkable stability – albeit at a rather low level.

Exhibit 9 shows the long-term debt service capacity index. There was a uniform secular deterioration in economic structure as it affects debt service capacity – with the exception of the OPEC countries.

While these results are rather sanguine, they are not overly comforting. They indicate that there has indeed been a deterioration in the debt service capacity during the 1970s, but that this deterioration has been rather slow and gradual. In those cases where a significant disturbance occurred – such as in the liquidity situation in 1976, it was not allowed to deteriorate further.

f. *Reschedulings*. Arrears and reschedulings did, of course, occur with increasing frequency during the last three years (1979-81). It is interesting to compare the indicators of those countries that actually got into difficulties with the indicators for countries that did not. This is done in Exhibits 10 to 12.

The one common message that is conveyed by these figures is that there is a marked difference in the indicators for those countries that did encounter arrears or reschedulings and those that did not. The debt service capacity indicators for all the countries that did *not* reschedule or accumulate arrears

296

Exhibit 10. *Annual average debt service capacity index, short term*

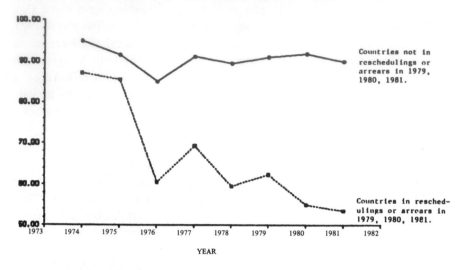

YEAR

Exhibit 11. *Annual average debt service capacity index, medium term*

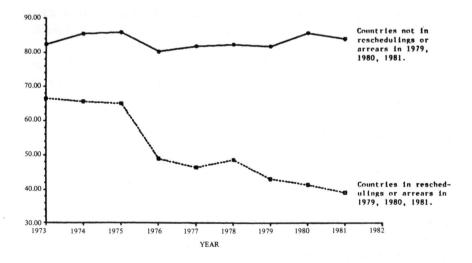

YEAR

Exhibit 12. *Annual average debt service capacity index, long term*

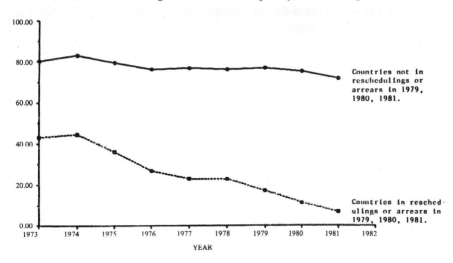

stayed remarkably stable during the decade. In contrast, the indicators for those countries that got into actual difficulties late in the period show already a significant deterioration early in the period. This may be taken as evidence for the generally good predictive qualities of the indicators.

However, certain non-quantifiable economic and political factors cannot readily be captured in these objective indices. Separate economic and political judgmental indicators that focus on the non-quantifiable factors are therefore developed as part of Bank of America's country assessment system as well. It may be worthwhile to briefly describe these judgmental indicators.

g. *The Judgmental Economic Indicator* ranges from *A* (highest rating) through *F* (lowest rating) and is based on a questionnaire filled out initially by the bank's country or regional managers. The questionnaire focuses on those factors that are thought to influence a country's debt service capacity but are not adequately covered in the debt service index. The structure of the questionnaire is flexible so as to permit analysis of all relevant and possibly unique environmental factors while preserving a consistent framework that is common to all countries.

The questionnaire focuses attention on certain areas considered important for the purpose of assessing a country's debt service capacity. Specifically, the questionnaire calls for an evaluation of the effectiveness of monetary policy, the government's fiscal policy – including the sources and uses of funds – as well as the means of financing the government deficit. An evaluation of regulatory policies in the financial sector is also undertaken. An appraisal of the government's attitude towards domestic and foreign investment follows. The government's economic development program is appraised, and the quality of its management is commented upon. The appraisal of the essentially domestic factors covered so far closes with an analysis of the country's economic structure, focusing on the availability of natural resources, the country's labor force, its infrastructure, and the composition of total output.

Turning to mainly external factors, the country's export and import diversification patterns are studied. Next, the country's access to international sources of credit is evaluated and the exchange rate policy is described and analyzed. Certain special regional considerations, such as membership in trade pacts, are then commented upon, and available sources of concessionary finance are identified. The economic questionnaire closes with an open-ended question pertaining to any other important considerations not covered elsewhere and a level of confidence indicator.

After the individual country managers have filled out these questionnaires, the responses are collected and collated at divisional headquarters (London, Tokyo, Caracas, or Los Angeles) and ratings are assigned to each country on a preliminary basis. These rating suggestions are then forwarded to Bank of America's San Francisco World Headquarters where they are consolidated and checked for global consistency. The worldwide ratings are then reviewed and approved by senior management of the bank in its chief financial policy council.

h. *The Political Judgmental Rating* focuses on the political factors affecting a country's ability or willingness to service its foreign debts. It focuses on three general areas of concern: governmental control, the potential for social unrest, and external factors. The section on government control begins with an evaluation of the government's effectiveness in formulating a coherent policy regarding important social and political problems. The institutions designed to provide for a resolution of political and social conflict are assessed next. Other factors considered in this section pertain to the orderly succession of government and institutional structures designed to bring competing influences to bear upon government policy. The section evaluating the potential for social unrest as it might influence the country's debt service ability follows. The political questionnaire closes with a set of questions regarding external factors including potential security threats, the country's special relations with the United States, and an assessment of relevant regional alliances in which the country might participate. Again, an indication of the level of confidence in the assessment is included.

The procedure in arriving at political judgment ratings is the same as that for the economic judgmental ratings.

It is important to note that the entire process moves from on-site knowledgeable officers up to senior management review and approval. The one major addition that occurs as the process moves up the organizational hierarchy is the addition of a global perspective. Ultimately the entire process is designed to be a tool of risk and portfolio management.

3. RETURN CONSIDERATIONS

The rate of return is an important parameter in a bank's lending decision. Most banks have explicitly stated rate-of-return objectives that must be met before they will consider lending to a specific customer.

The international lending market is very efficient and closely approximates the stylized economic model of perfect competition: there are many participants in this market and there is reasonably free entry from the even larger number of banks that are currently only involved in domestic business but might consider participating in the international market if this should be attractive. Furthermore, all banks deal in a highly homogeneous product: credit. Consequently, no individual bank has any leverage over the price of credit. Instead it is determined by the interplay of aggregate supply and demand and reflects the market's assessment of the perceived risk associated with the loan.

However, each bank does have control over how much it wishes to lend to a specific customer at the going interest rate.

These relationships become particularly apparent in international syndicated credits, where each bank participating in the syndicate is free to choose the amount that it wishes to participate with. That is, each bank is a pure quantity-adjuster, thereby determining its portfolio.

Clearly, there are other features of a particular loan that influence its attractiveness for a particular bank. Among these are commitment fees, management fees, participation fees, agent fees, the tenor of the loan, and a wide range of other stipulations that may materially affect the attractiveness of a loan.

4. MANAGING THE INTERNATIONAL PORTFOLIO

The management of the international portfolio of a large commercial bank
is by necessity a complex task. In a bank operating on a global scale many
of the decisions regarding individual assets and liabilities are taken by a relatively large number of individual officers and committees. Delegation of
authority for many of the relevant decisions is not only an accepted management principle, but also a necessity because no individual officer or single
committee would be able to cope with the volume of decisions to be made.
Especially in international banking the separation of the various country officers from headquarters in both a space and time dimension makes it mandatory to rely extensively on delegation of decision-making authority.

Of course, the bank's total asset and liability portfolio is the net result of
the individual decisions taken. The greater the degree of decentralization,
the greater will therefore also be the need for a central framework for portfolio management. This is essential to ensure that the sum total of the individual decisions taken will add up to a total bank-wide portfolio that is optimal and consistent with the bank's objectives.

The portfolio management process brings all relevant elements, such as
risk, return, and diversification together and considers them in one interde-
pendent decision making process.

a. *Country Limits.* The key tool in managing an international portfolio is
the establishment of country limits that represent the maximum exposure
that the bank is willing to take. In a decentralized organization these limits
are then delegated to the respective regional or country officers who are responsible for adhering to them.

There is an important distinction between the bank's *commitments* to
grant loans and the actual *outstandings*. The difference is due to the fact that
not every credit line is always fully utilized. The country limit governs the
maximum amount of outstandings that the bank is willing to have in a specific country.[5] But just as airlines allow a certain amount of overbooking to
fill a plane reasonably close to capacity, so do banks typically permit commitments to exceed the actual country limit. Key to the successful adherence
to a country limit is that the limit on commitments be gradually reduced as
the actual outstandings approach the country limit. Ideally, as actual outstandings reach the country limit from "below", the limit on commitments
just reaches the country limit from "above" (see also Exhibit 13).

One additional variable has to be tracked: actual commitments (the
dashed line in Exhibit 13). Actual commitments will be lower than the com-

Exhibit 13. *Commitments and outstandings: actual and limits*

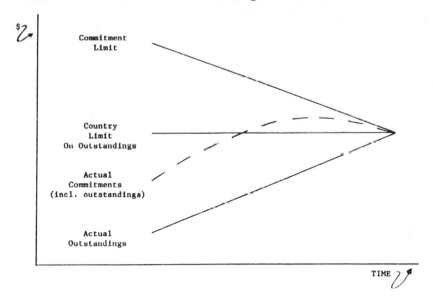

mitment limit, but higher than outstandings because they include the latter. But actual commitments may be higher or lower than the country limit on outstandings. If actual commitments are lower than the country limit on outstandings, this is an indication that the bank may aggressively be pursuing additional business in that country.

b. *Portfolio Quality*. We may utilize the debt service capacity indicator to assess the quality of the actual international portfolio held by a bank or group of banks. Of course, other factors in addition to the country's debt service capacity influence a portfolio's quality. Among these factors are the creditworthiness of the individual firm, the type of loan, its tenor, security guarantees, and a wide range of other factors. But if one abstracts for the time being from these considerations, it is possible to weigh the actual outstandings in the various countries by the debt service capacity indicator to arrive at an overall portfolio quality indicator. The results of such an exercise are shown in Exhibits 14 and 15.

  Exhibit 14 utilizes the data on outstanding international loans collected regularly by the Comptroller of the Currency for US banks and the three debt service capacity indicators to arrive at overall portfolio quality assessments. Two observations can be made: (1) as expected, the short-term quali-

Exhibit 14. *Portfolio quality indicators. United States banks: world*

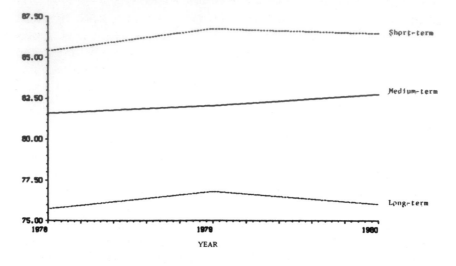

Exhibit 15. *Portfolio quality indicators. Bank for International Settlements: world*

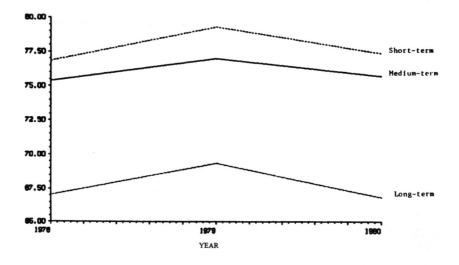

ty (one year time span) of the portfolio is greater than the medium-term quality (three year time span), which in turn is greater than the long-term quality (five year time span). This is only rational as the probability that a country will incur arrears or reschedulings over a longer period will always be greater than it is over a shorter period. (2) For both the medium-term and the long-term portfolio the average quality is much higher than the average debt service capacity index on an unweighted basis (Exhibit 6). This indicates that US banks selectively place their loans in those countries that are more creditworthy than the average country.

Exhibit 15 shows the same information for all the banks reporting to the BIS. Here the results are not quite as favorable. This broader group of banks which comprises Europe, Canada and Japan in addition to the United States has a portfolio that is according to some criteria worse than the quality of the average country around the world. For instance, the short-term DSCI for all countries in the world averaged 82 in 1980, but the score on the exposure-weighted portfolio for the BIS banks was only 77 in the same year. Similar observations pertain if one uses the medium-term DSCI, but not for the long-term DSCI.

Exhibit 16. *Portfolio quality indicators, short term, world*

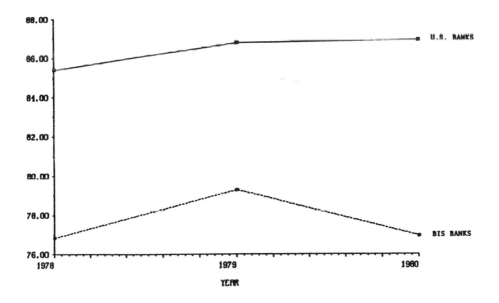

Exhibit 17. *Portfolio quality indicators, medium term, world*

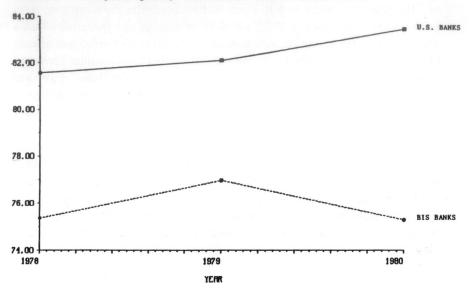

Exhibit 18. *Portfolio quality indicators, long term, world*

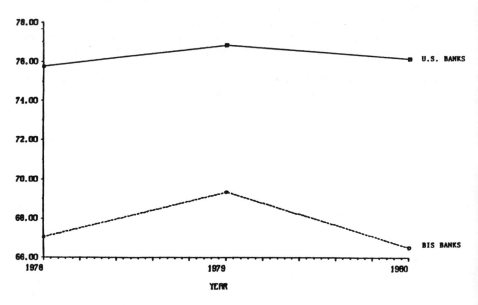

From these observations it also follows that the average portfolio quality of US banks is markedly better than that for the entire group of BIS-reporting banks. Exhibits 16, 17, and 18 illustrate this point graphically. There are two *caveats* to be added to the conclusion. For one, virtually all of the non-US banks have loans outstanding in the United States. US exposures are not included in the analysis, and to the extent that US country risk is lesser than that of the average country around the world, the quality of the portfolio of non-US banks is understated in our analysis. Two, the US banks are included in the universe of the BIS banks and because they have a higher than average portfolio quality, we may conclude on this score that the portfolio quality of the non-US banks is overstated by the BIS sample of banks. To some extent the two factors discussed will offset each other, but the precise extent is not clear. In any case, the conclusion that the US banks' portfolio quality is on average higher than that of the non-US banks reporting through the BIS is unlikely to be affected materially by these considerations.

NOTES

1. Morgan Guaranty, *International Financial Markets.*
2. World Bank, *World Debt Tables*, December 1981, p. xv.
3. Much of this presentation relies upon the comprehensive BIS *Manual on Statistics Compiled by International Organizations on Countries' External Indebtedness*, Basle, 1979.
4. BIS, *ibid.*, p. 106.
5. Loans guaranteed by a third country are domiciled in that country of guarantee and do not appear on the tally of the borrowing country.

Part E

THE STABILITY OF THE INTERNATIONAL FINANCIAL SYSTEM

Chapter XVII

GESTION DES RISQUES ET STABILITÉ
DU SYSTÈME FINANCIER INTERNATIONAL

par *Jeanne-Marie Parly*

Fragilité ou résistance du système financier international? La réponse à cette question est bien entendu contrastée. Les uns tirent argument de la remarquable faculté d'adaptation dont a fait preuve le système bancaire international privé, confronté au problème du recyclage des capitaux ou aux perturbations plus ou moins sensibles qui agitent périodiquement les marchés des changes, pour conforter leur position optimiste. Les autres, considérant la pyramide de dettes et de créances qui caractérise les économies d'endettement contemporaines, sur le plan international comme sur le plan domestique, la voient porteuse d'une crise monétaire généralisée à laquelle l'économie mondiale aurait peu de chances d'échapper.

Le propre des crises est leur caractère imprévisible: comment sinon se produiraient-elles dès lors qu'aucun des acteurs du système ne semble avoir objectivement intérêt à les déclencher sauf à jouer les apprentis-sorciers?

Aussi bien, notre propos ici n'est-il pas de tenter de percer un futur incertain. Il est d'abord de montrer comment les évolutions fondamentales de la structure et des modes de fonctionnement du système financier international ont mis au premier plan des préoccupations les problèmes touchant aux risques d'intermédiation.

Il est ensuite de mettre en évidence les difficultés méthodologiques auxquelles se heurtent les efforts d'appréciation du degré de risque atteint par le système financier international et de repérer les fils conducteurs que propose dans ce domaine la théorie économique.

Il est enfin, et pour conclure, d'avancer quelques éléments de réflexion sur des voies possibles d'évolution du système susceptibles de faire reculer le spectre d'une crise monétaire mondiale.

I. L'EVOLUTION DU SYSTEME FINANCIER INTERNATIONAL ET L'ATTENTION CROISSANTE PORTEE AU PROBLEME DES RISQUES

Ce n'est pas tout à fait un hasard si les problèmes de stabilité sont de nos jours volontiers posés à propos du système *financier* international alors que récemment encore ils concernaient plutôt le système *monétaire* international. Ce glissement conceptuel est en effet significatif d'une évolution profonde des relations monétaires et financières internationales.

Jusqu'au début des années 60 la scène monétaire internationale était dominée par les institutions officielles, Banques Centrales et Fonds Monétaire International qui avaient pour fonction essentielle de gérer le système de taux de change hérité de Bretton-Woods, les flux internationaux de capitaux se trouvant à l'époque limités par l'ampleur du déficit de la balance de base des Etats-Unis.

Le développement progressif d'euromarchés, opérant essentiellement en dollars, mais sur lesquels l'offre de liquidités est de plus en plus autonome par rapport à la situation des paiements extérieurs américains, a permis de répondre à l'accroissement très rapide des besoins de financement qu'entraînait une intégration mondiale de plus en plus poussée des échanges et de la production. Ce mouvement a abouti à l'économie d'endettement international que nous connaissons aujourd'hui et qui repose pour l'essentiel sur l'activité d'intermédiation de très grandes banques commerciales à vocation internationale.

Ce financement par crédit bancaire permet de distinguer l'économie d'endettement international contemporaine des phases de financement international par émissions d'obligations sur les places financières des pays dominants qu'ont connu le XIXème siècle et le début du XXème. Mais les conditions dans lesquelles fonctionne le système financier international contribuent à amplifier les caractères communs aux économies d'endettement[1] et donc à poser le problème des risques dans un contexte spécifique.

Le trait le plus frappant du système de crédit géré par les banques internationales est sa très grande élasticité de réponse à l'accroissement de la demande. En effet, la masse des opérations sur les marchés d'eurodevises augmente plus rapidement que les masses monétaires internes des pays émetteurs des monnaies convertibles, notamment les Etats-Unis. Ceci s'explique essentiellement par le fait que les couples risque-rendement ont été dans les années récentes plus favorables pour les opérations internationales des banques que pour leurs opérations domestiques ce qui les a incitées à délocaliser une fraction croissante de leurs activités de crédit.[2]

Ce processus d'arbitrage explique la communication étroite que l'on constate entre le marché monétaire international et les marchés internes, surtout en ce qui concerne le marché monétaire américain.

Le fait que les euromarchés aient jusqu'à présent largement échappé (pour des raisons d'opportunité plus que d'impossibilités techniques) au contrôle des autorités monétaires centrales ne fait bien sûr que renforcer l'élasticité de l'offre de crédit international.

(Au contraire, l'extension de l'endettement dans les économies domestiques peut se trouver freinée soit par des phénomènes de désintermédiation soit par des interventions contraignantes des autorités monétaires centrales).

A côté de cette modification de situation relative des acteurs sur la scène financière internationale, un autre facteur important d'évolution a bien sûr été, depuis 1971, le remplacement du système de l'étalon dollar or, dominé par les Etats-Unis, par un système de devises-clé inconvertibles. L'hégémonie du dollar s'est trouvée remise en cause du fait que les devises des pays qui connaissaient de forts excédents du commerce extérieur concurrençaient le dollar dans sa fonction de monnaie de réserve. La possibilité d'arbitrage entre plusieurs monnaies fortes a favorisé la spéculation et accru par là l'instabilité sur les marchés des changes.

Cette internationalisation des monnaies se traduit par une grande sensibilité des demandes de monnaie aux différentiels d'intérêt sur les principales devises-clé: la fonction de réserve de la monnaie au plan international gagne de l'importance par rapport à sa fonction de transaction. Cette évolution qui tend à réduire le rôle dominant du dollar lorsque celui-ci n'est pas conforté par des taux d'intérêt élevés aux Etats-Unis est susceptible d'engendrer des déplacements massifs de capitaux en fonction des différentiels d'intérêt et des anticipations de change.

A ces facteurs, que l'on peut qualifier de structurels, d'instabilité du système monétaire international, s'est ajoutée depuis deux ans l'influence de la politique monétaire des Etats-Unis. En effet, les efforts du Système de la Réserve Fédérale pour contenir la croissance des agrégats monétaires, dans un contexte institutionnel dont l'évolution au cours des dix dernières années a abouti à ce que la masse des actifs monétaires et quasi monétaires évolue dans le même sens que les taux d'intérêt, engendrent inévitablement des niveaux élevés et des fluctuations erratiques de ces taux.

Il est intéressant de constater que cette très forte instabilité des taux de change et d'intérêt même si elle est porteuse de difficultés et de tensions, notamment en raison de l'alourdissement des charges qui pèsent sur les débiteurs, ne semble pas avoir dans un premier temps constitué un obstacle à la poursuite du processus d'endettement.

Ceci tient sans doute au fait que la technique des eurocrédits permet très généralement aux intermédiaires financiers de reporter sur les emprunteurs finaux et le risque de change et le risque lié à la variabilité des taux d'intérêt. Le processus d'indexation des taux joint au fait que sur les marchés d'euro-devises les mécanismes de transformation de depôts à court terme en prêts à moyen ou long terme sont extrêmement progressifs et diffus explique que les banques qui ont toujours perçu ces deux risques comme particulièrement lourds aient pu, dans le domaine des financements internationaux, accepter des risques plus élevés au niveau des créances figurant à leur actif.

La conséquence en est, dès lors que les banques financent des opérations pour lesquelles le risque de défaut n'est pas négligeable, que l'évaluation de ce risque joue un rôle essentiel dans la manière dont les banques gèrent leur portefeuille de créances internationales.

La troisième caractéristique notable de l'évolution des relations finan-cières internationales au cours des dix dernières années est la polarisation à laquelle on a assisté des excédents et déficits des balances des paiements. Ce phénomène que la réduction récente des excédents pétroliers contribuera peut-être à remettre en cause, a deux implications importantes du point de vue des risques qui pèsent sur le système financier international. Il a entraîné l'ouverture des PVD à l'intermédiation financière internationale et l'endet-tement massif de certains de ces pays. Il s'est par ailleurs traduit par la con-centration des dépôts sur les euromarchés entre les mains d'un nombre re-streint de créanciers qui ont ainsi acquis un pouvoir potentiel de déstabilisa-tion des marchés de change par des déplacements marginaux de liquidité d'une devise à une autre. Ces déposants ont également acquis la possibilité de mettre en difficulté certaines banques membres du réseau international par des retraits massifs de fonds.

Si l'on considère donc la mutation très profonde qu'a connue le système financier international depuis l'émergence des euromarchés il apparaît que ce système remplit actuellement deux fonctions étroitement imbriquées: sup-port des mouvements monétaires internationaux et notamment des varia-tions de taux de change, il est en même temps le vecteur de flux de finance-ment international d'une ampleur croissante. Faiblement régulé, ce système est soumis à des tensions déstabilisantes tant en raison de la polarisation des excédents et déficits des balances commerciales que sous l'influence des poli-tiques économiques et monétaires des pays dominants.

Ces faits justifient largement l'attention croissante que les banquiers, les observateurs extérieurs des marchés internationaux de capitaux et les autori-tés monétaires centrales attachent à l'évolution des risques sur ces marchés. En témoigne le volume croissant des ressources que les banques consacrent à l'analyse des risques, qu'il s'agisse des procédures longues et détaillées conduisant à la mise en place du financement de projets ou qu'il s'agisse des méthodes de plus en plus sophistiquées permettant d'apprécier le risque-pays. En témoignent également le raffinement et la complexité croissante des systèmes de garanties associés aux financements internationaux. En témoignent enfin les projets récurrents de soumission des euromarchés au contrôle des banques centrales.

Mais cette convergence des préoccupations ne doit pas nous dissimuler la complexité des problèmes méthodologiques que soulève l'étude des risques du système financier international en l'absence d'une théorie suffisamment élaborée de l'intermédiation financière qui soit centrée sur sa fonction essentielle: le traitement de l'information et du risque.

II. QUELQUES DIFFICULTES METHODOLOGIQUE DE L'ANALYSE DES RISQUES D'INTERMEDIATION FINANCIERE INTERNATIONALE

"De notre point de vue un cadre adapté à l'analyse de l'intermédiation financière est encore à construire" écrivaient G.J. Benston et C.W. Smith en 1976.[3] En dépit de la percée théorique extrêmement stimulante que représentent leurs propres travaux sur le sujet, ce jugement nous semble encore largement pertinent aujourd'hui. Pour résumer l'essentiel de leur apport on peut dire que prenant le contre-pied des analyses antérieures qui décrivaient les intermédiaires financiers soit comme produisant de la monnaie sur la base de prêts, soit comme produisant du crédit sur la base de dépôts, ces deux auteurs ont affirmé que le rôle des intermédiaires financiers est de créer des produits financiers spécialisés. Selon eux la raison d'être de ces intermédiaires résiderait dans la réduction des coûts de transaction liés à la recherche d'une allocation intertemporelle optimale du revenu et de la dépense des agents économiques.

L'émergence d'intermédiaires financiers s'explique, en effet, par l'existence d'économies d'échelle dans la collecte et le traitement de l'information puisque l'essentiel de l'activité d'intermédiation financière consiste justement à traiter de l'information portant notamment sur des variables de risque. En effet, les intermédiaires financiers se doivent d'exercer un contrôle suffisant sur la qualité des créances figurant à l'actif de leur bilan pour garantir la liquidité des instruments financiers figurant à leur passif.

En général les intermédiaires financiers produisent plus d'un type de produit financier et disposent donc de plusieurs types de ressources et de diverses utilisations de leurs fonds. Si l'on en croit les enseignements de la théorie microéconomique, les intermédiaires financiers devraient pour maximiser leurs profits tendre vers une situation d'équilibre caractérisée par le fait que le coût marginal d'un Franc supplémentaire soit le même quelle que soit son origine (augmentation de capital, émission d'obligations, accroissement des dépôts . . .) de même que le rendement marginal d'un Franc supplémentaire quelle que soit son affectation (crédits commerciaux, prêts à long terme, créances hypothécaires . . .). Un tel comportement marginaliste débouche sur le principe de non affectation des ressources aux emplois. Mais se trouve alors posé le problème de la séparabilité des décisions portant sur la structure de l'actif de celles concernant la structure du passif. Sur ce point, tout à fait central, les auteurs expriment l'idée que sans aller jusqu'à établir une correspondance rigide de la structure des échéances de part et d'autre du bilan, une certaine couverture des risques est rendue nécessaire par les relations d'interdépendance entre actif et passif.

C'est à partir de là que nous pensons que leur analyse devrait être complétée et approfondie. En effet, tout en conservant l'idée clé suivant laquelle la spécificité des intermédiaires financiers est de traiter de l'information et d'analyser des risques, il nous semble que devrait être davantage explicitée la fonction de gestion des risques que remplissent conjointement et les intermédiaires financiers considérés individuellement et le système financier dans son ensemble.

Une telle démarche devrait notamment conduire à évaluer les risques d'intermédiation et d'en préciser la nature, mais elle se heurte à des difficultés méthodologiques non triviales. De plus elle soulève des problèmes spécifiques dans le domaine de la finance internationale.

Les analyses théoriques de l'intermédiation financière dont nous disposons ne nous fournissent en effet pas un cadre distinguant clairement les trois niveaux successifs mais interdépendants auxquels doit être menée l'analyse du risque et mettant en évidence les effets de structure et de composition qui interviennent entre chacun de ces niveaux. S'il est intuitivement évident pour chacun qu'on ne saurait passer par addition ou agrégation pure et simple des risques d'opérations de crédit particulières au risque de l'actif de l'intermédiaire financier et encore moins au risque global d'intermédiation qu'il supporte, pas plus que le cumul des risques des différents intermédiaires qui le composent ne permettrait d'approcher le risque d'un système financier, force est de convenir que l'analyse théorique ne fournit que des éléments de réponse limités aux questions que nous nous posons sur le risque d'intermédiation et la stabilité des systèmes financiers.

Cet état de fait ne saurait totalement nous surprendre. Ce n'est que récemment en effet que les économistes ont perçu l'écart qui se creusait entre une théorie financière fondée pour l'essentiel sur le fonctionnement de marchés d'actifs quasi-parfaits sur lesquels se rencontreraient les capacités et besoins de financement des agents économiques, et une réalité dans laquelle un système structuré et hiérarchisé d'intermédiaires financiers constitue le principal support des flux de financement.

Au plan des économies nationales une typologie des systèmes financiers se dessine assez clairement. Une situation extrême est celle des États-Unis caractérisé par un ensemble de marchés monétaires et financiers interdépendants et faiblement contrôlés par les autorités centrales; on peut lui opposer les traits particuliers à l'économie d'endettement qu'a largement conservés le système financier français en dépit de la vague de réformes libérales qu'il a connu au tournant des années 70: faible rôle des marchés, persistance de circuits de financement dominés par des intermédiaires puissants, eux-mêmes sous la dépendance des autorités étatiques. Des modèles théoriques décrivant les modalités de fonctionnement de l'un et l'autre de ces deux systèmes ont été élaborés au cours des années récentes.[4]

Les mécanismes de financement international que nous connaissons aujourd'hui sont extrêmement intéressants à analyser de ce point de vue car ils combinent des caractères qui relèvent de la logique de l'économie de marché avec d'autres plus proches de l'économie d'endettement.

Sur les marchés d'euro-obligations se rencontrent bien les capacités et besoins de financement des prêteurs et des emprunteurs mais ces marchés fonctionnent grâce à l'intervention d'intermédiaires financiers spécialisés dans le montage des émissions (tout comme la présence de "dealers" est nécessaire au bon fonctionnement des différents compartiments du marché monétaire américain). Il faut être conscient de ce que l'intervention de ces agents est la manifestation d'inégalités d'accès à l'information et de processus de rationnement des emprunteurs qui ne sont pas totalement cohérents avec la pure théorie du fonctionnement des marchés.

On pourrait être tenté de présenter les marchés d'eurodevises comme les archétypes du marché pour manuel d'économie puisque se retrouvent à leur propos les maîtres-mots d'homogénéité du produit, de transparence, de concurrence . . . Mais cette vision doit être corrigée du fait qu'une part très importante des opérations sur ces marchés se nouent entre intermédiaires financiers. La chaîne des opérations qui permet à un dépôt initial sur ce marché de venir éventuellement financer un emprunt final est souvent longue et riche d'implications: transformation de montants, d'échéances, de devises. Il serait dans ces conditions difficilement admissible d'effacer, au moyen commode d'une consolidation du système bancaire cette chaîne d'intermédiation, cette imbrication de créances et dettes interbancaires car elles sont indispensables à l'accès des agents non financiers au financement sur euro-devises.

En définitive l'essentiel du financement international repose sur l'activité d'un nombre réduit de banques, nouant entre elles des relations complexes sur un réseau de marchés faiblement contrôlés par les autorités centrales. Ce relatif défaut d'intervention s'explique par l'absence d'une autorité moné-taire supranationale et d'une définition claire des responsabilités respectives du FMI et des banques centrales à l'égard du système financier internatio-nal.

L'opposition ''économie de marché'' – ''économie d'endettement'' est importante du point de vue de l'analyse théorique des risques. En effet, l'es-sentiel de la très riche littérature sur la gestion des risques financiers a été éla-boré dans le cadre de la théorie des marchés de capitaux, cependant que les enseignements de la théorie des assurances n'ont que faiblement fécondé la littérature concernant les intermédiaires financiers notamment bancaires.

La théorie de la sélection des portefeuilles fondée sur l'axiomatique des choix dans l'incertain a fourni les bases permettant la construction de mo-dèles théoriques ou appliqués de gestion optimale de portefeuilles d'actifs négociables sur des marchés (actions et obligations). Ces modèles recher-chent une combinaison optimale, pour le gestionnaire du portefeuille, du rendement et du risque, le risque pris en compte dans l'analyse étant celui de variabilité des rendements, gains et pertes en capital compris. Les en-seignements de ces travaux apparaissent particulièrement pertinents pour les intermédiaires financiers dont les ressources sont plutôt issues de souscrip-tions de part que de dépôts et qui gèrent des portefeuilles de titres sur des marchés boursiers (SICAV, Investment Trust . . .).

Les développements récents de cette théorie (largement connus sous le terme de modèles des ''Bêta'') s'appuient sur une distinction tout à fait es-sentielle entre risques diversifiables et risques non diversifiables. En effet, la variabilité du rendement d'un actif peut être imputable d'une part à des causes spécifiques à l'actif considéré, d'autre part à un risque conditionnel au comportement d'ensemble du marché boursier: les coefficients Bêta me-surent donc le degré d'amplification ou de réduction des fluctuations des cours d'une action donnée par rapport à l'évolution de l'indice du marché boursier. Une diversification raisonnable des portefeuilles financiers permet de réduire fortement ou même d'éliminer les risques spécifiques à chacun des actifs qui le composent, de sorte que le risque global du portefeuille ne dé-pend plus par l'intermédiaire d'une moyenne pondérée des coefficients Bêta, que des fluctuations de l'indice des valeurs boursières.

Ce type d'analyse est particulièrement adapté à la gestion de portefeuilles d'actions. Il permet de mettre en évidence les facteurs de risque propres à chaque secteur d'activité ou à chaque entreprise. Pour les obligations, le risque systématique ou non diversifiable lié aux variations du taux d'intérêt induites par la politique monétaire joue évidemment un rôle tout à fait prédominant.

Un certain nombre de modèles de comportement des intermédiaires financiers bancaires a été construit dans la lignée de la théorie de la sélection des portefeuilles.

Jusqu'à la fin des années 60 les modèles de comportement bancaire considéraient que le volume des dépôts – susceptible de connaître des fluctuations aléatoires – constituait pour la banque une contrainte exogène; la gestion des risques se bornait alors à déterminer la part de l'actif détenue sous forme de monnaie centrale et de titres négociables pour assurer à la banque une position de liquidité satisfaisante et à gérer par ailleurs le portefeuille de crédits aux entreprises et aux particuliers sur la base des principes de diversification des risques et de limitation des engagements à l'égard de tout emprunteur particulier.

Le développement des marchés de certificats de dépôts négociables ou du marché des eurodevises a obligé à tenir compte de ce que les banques ont une relative maîtrise de leur passif. Leur marge de jeu dépend des différentiels d'intérêt qu'elles sont prêtes à consentir sur les dépôts mais elle est limitée par la confiance qu'inspire aux déposants l'attitude de la banque à l'égard du risque.

Des modèles récents mettent en évidence la complexité des problèmes de gestion des risques posés aux intermédiaires financiers bancaires du fait des interdépendances des décisions portant sur l'actif et le passif de leur bilan. Dans le modèle de Klein,[5] l'intermédiaire financier est supposé maximiser le taux de rendement anticipé de ses fonds propres sur la base de fonctions de distribution de probabilité du rendement des actifs qu'il détient (encaisse, titres de dette publique, crédits) et des mouvements aléatoires des dépôts. Ce modèle conclut que le rendement moyen de l'actif détermine les taux d'intérêt offerts sur les dépôts à vue et à terme et par là à la fois la taille totale du bilan et la structure du passif. Par contre, la répartition optimale de l'actif entre ses trois composantes y est indépendante du coût des ressources bancaires. Dans cette analyse par conséquent le problème de l'interdépendance des décisions portant sur la structure du passif et sur celle de l'actif est abordé au travers des relations entre taux d'intérêt débiteurs et créditeurs.

D'autres modèles[6] permettent de situer cette question difficile dans un

cadre explicitant les comportements d'arbitrage des intermédiaires bancaires entre le risque et le rendement: sous certaines hypothèses ces comportements impliquent non seulement une diversification de l'actif en fonction
des variances et covariances des rendements des différentes créances qui y
figurent, ainsi que de la variabilité anticipée du montant des dépôts, mais
encore ils sont influencés par la covariance entre mouvements des dépôts et
rentabilité de l'actif.

En dépit de leur très grand intérêt ces modèles ne nous semblent pas se prêter parfaitement à l'étude des risques d'intermédiation dans le domaine des
prêts internationaux. En expliciter les raisons essentielles nous conduira à
suggérer une approche assez différente du problème.

Les premiers décalages que nous pouvons relever entre les hypothèses fondamentales des modèles théoriques et la pratique actuelle du financement international se situent au niveau du traitement des risques de l'actif.

Tout d'abord, la diversification des risques ne s'y heurte à aucun obstacle:
qu'il s'agisse des modèles de gestion de portefeuilles d'actions et d'obligations ou de modèles de comportements bancaires, l'élimination des risques
diversifiables est toujours supposée réalisable au travers d'un choix judi-
cieux de secteurs d'activité ou de types d'emprunteurs. Dans le domaine des
prêts internationaux une telle diversification des risques est bien entendu
souhaitable et peut sembler rendue plus facile par l'ouverture des choix offerts aux intermédiaires financiers. En réalité, les banques doivent tenir
compte des risques-pays et donc du lieu d'implantation des activités produc-
tives et des projets qu'elles financent. Un emprunteur privé parfaitement
solvable peut en effet se trouver empêché de verser les intérêts ou de rembourser le principal de sa dette non point de son fait mais parceque la situation des paiements extérieurs du pays considéré interdit tout réglement en
devises convertibles. Par ailleurs, les emprunts effectués directement par les
Etats ou par des organismes publics bénéficiant de leur garantie représentent
une fraction notable des prêts internationaux.

Dans ces conditions, les banques sont conduites à attacher une importance
toute particulière à la diversification des risques par pays. Or, le nombre des
pays ayant régulièrement accès au financement international est forcément
limité: parmi les pays ayant un besoin net de financement extérieur ne sont
en effet éligibles que ceux dont la situation économique, politique et sociale
paraît suffisamment rassurante aux prêteurs potentiels.

Dans ces conditions la pratique bancaire courante semble être de fixer des
limites d'engagement par pays et de rechercher la meilleure diversification
des risques en termes de catégorie d'emprunteur ou de secteur d'activité à
l'intérieur de ces limites. Rien n'interdit a priori d'imaginer de construire des

modèles à deux niveaux de diversification, mais rationnement et diversification des risques ne procèdent pas de la même logique et ne relèvent pas de mécanismes identiques. Le rationnement se trouve justifié par l'incertitude et l'imperfection de l'information, alors que la diversification (telle qu'elle est analysée dans les modèles) repose sur la notion de risques probabilisables.

Nous situant toujours sur le plan des risques de l'actif, il nous paraît intéressant de souligner que paradoxalement les approches théoriques de l'intermédiation financière sont largement marquées par leur parenté avec les théories de la sélection des portefeuilles sur le terrain même où elles devraient s'en écarter le plus.

En effet, la théorie des choix financiers en univers incertain a été pour l'essentiel élaborée par référence aux actions et obligations, c'est à dire à des titres négociables sur des marchés ouverts à des opérateurs non professionnels. Cette donnée implique pour ces titres un contenu contractuel et juridique relativement simple, sinon frustre. Propriété d'une fraction du capital de l'entreprise donnant droit à un dividende annuel variable, prêt à long terme associé au paiement d'un coupon, dans les deux cas la décision de détenir le titre est fondée sur la capacité globale de l'émetteur à réaliser des profits ou à rembourser ses dettes. Ce qui est offert sur le marché boursier c'est un couple rendement-risque dans lequel le risque est évalué sur la base des performances passées du titre et d'une appréciation globale de la situation de son émetteur. Ce couple risque-rendement est identique quels que soient les détenteurs du titre et la répartition du risque entre les agents économiques se fait au prorata du nombre d'actions ou d'obligations détenu par chacun (sous réserve de distinctions entre diverses catégories d'actions par exemple). Une telle formule ne se prête évidemment pas à un traitement différencié des risques en fonction de leur nature. Dès lors, le comportement des détenteurs de titres se ramène dans la théorie comme dans la pratique à panacher au mieux, en fonction de leur attitude à l'égard du risque, les différents ensembles risque-rendement qui leur sont proposés sur le marché.

Bien que les opérations de crédit bancaire ne relèvent en rien de la logique des marchés boursiers et qu'il soit reconnu, en particulier depuis les travaux de Benston et Smith, que les intermédiaires financiers bénéficient d'avantages comparatifs dans l'analyse et le traitement des risques individuels, les modèles théoriques de gestion des risques d'intermédiation n'ont pas remis en cause les bases du principe de diversification: les banques sont supposées diversifier leur portefeuille de crédits en fonction de l'évaluation du risque global qu'elles attribuent à telle ou telle catégorie d'emprunteur.

Difficilement acceptable pour certaines opérations de crédit domestique, cette position nous paraît intenable dans le domaine du financement international. En effet, les opérations que l'on peut y observer présentent des caractéristiques particulières. Les montants concernés sont le plus souvent très importants, ce qui justifie à la fois le recours à la syndication et l'élaboration de modalités de financement adaptées aux caractères propres à l'opération faisant l'objet du financement. Ce montage s'accompagne d'études préalables et d'une analyse approfondie des différents types de risques susceptibles de peser sur l'emprunteur et les divers organismes participant au financement. La mise en place des financements internationaux implique donc en général la signature de contrats juridiques détaillés et complexes précisant les droits et obligations de chacun en fonction de la nature des risques encourus.

Cette spécificité des financements internationaux apparaît très clairement lorsqu'il y a cofinancement mais aussi dans le domaine, actuellement en expansion, du financement de projets. En effet, dès lors que le prêt repose non sur les garanties de remboursement offertes par la société ou l'Etat emprunteurs mais sur la faisabilité du projet et son cash flow anticipé, la responsabilité essentielle des banques chefs de file de ces opérations est de déterminer et d'évaluer précisément les risques assumés par les prêteurs et ceux qui doivent au contraire être pris en charge par les constructeurs ou fournisseurs, les organismes d'assurance des crédits à l'exportation, le pays d'accueil et la société qui promeut l'opération.

Ce constat nous incite à tirer deux conclusions complémentaires:

– à côté de la pratique traditionnelle consistant pour les banques à évaluer globalement le crédit que l'on peut accorder à tel ou tel emprunteur (dont la forme la plus spécifique au domaine des relations internationales est l'analyse des risques-pays) se développent d'autres techniques permettant aux banquiers de choisir dans la panoplie très ouverte des risques associés aux opérations de financement international (risques politiques, industriels, commerciaux, risques de transformation, de taux de change ou d'intérêt . . .) ceux qui leur paraissent compatibles avec leur savoir faire professionnel et avec la structure de leurs ressources.

– qu'il s'agisse de l'une ou l'autre de ces approches du problème des risques de l'actif, il apparaît que le risque d'intermédiation tout autant que de la structure du portefeuille de créances de chaque intermédiaire financier dépend de l'organisation globale du système économique et financier dans lequel s'insère son activité.

Cette conclusion qui incite à déplacer l'analyse du plan de la structure du bilan des intermédiaires financiers à celui des relations fonctionnelles qui fondent le système financier international, se trouve confirmée par la prise en compte des interrelations dynamiques entre risque de l'actif et risque du passif.

Ceci constitue en effet le deuxième niveau auquel se manifeste un divorce profond entre les approches théoriques, y compris dans leurs formulations les plus récentes ou les plus sophistiquées, et les réalités de la finance internationale. Deux points méritent particulièrement d'être soulignés:

– si dans les modèles de comportements bancaires le montant des dépôts est une variable aléatoire, la distribution de probabilité de cette variable est connue et dépend soit du taux de croissance relatif des activités de la banque par rapport à ses concurrents, soit de la variabilité du rendement de l'actif. En aucun cas ne sont pris en compte les processus dynamique au travers desquels des pertes notables sur certains éléments d'actif provoquent la fuite des dépôts et par là le risque de faillites bancaires et d'une crise financière.

– les déposants dont les comportements sont pris en compte dans les modèles sont, pour l'essentiel, des agents non financiers, ce qui explique peut-être partiellement le faible intérêt porté par ces modèles aux relations dynamiques entre les deux parties du bilan. Dès lors que l'on admet d'une part que les opérations de financement international relèvent davantage d'une analyse en termes d'incertitude que de risque probabilisable et que l'on se souvient d'autre part du rôle essentiel que jouent les prêts interbancaires dans l'intermédiation financière internationale, on est obligé de considérer les choses autrement.

Il existe en effet des liens de concurrence et de solidarité entre banques internationales qui peuvent soit jouer dans le sens d'une plus grande stabilité du système soit au contraire en accentuer la fragilité.

En effet, si la communauté des banquiers estimait trop risquée la stratégie de prêts d'un de ses membres, ce dernier pourrait se trouver confronté à des graves problèmes de liquidité. Des effets de domino secouant l'ensemble du système ne seraient alors pas à exclure. Il semble donc que le retrait de dépôts interbancaires ait une toute autre portée potentielle à l'égard des risques d'illiquidité qui pèsent sur un intermédiaire financier que les retraits de dépôts émanant d'agents non financiers. En effet, tant que la communauté bancaire conserve sa confiance à l'égard de la banque qui subit des pertes de dépôts du fait des déposants primaires, son problème de liquidité se résoud par des ajustements à la marge sur les taux d'intérêt qu'elle doit consentir sur les prêts qu'elle obtient auprès d'autres banques.

A l'inverse, les relations complexes qui se nouent entre banques à vocation internationale tant au travers des prêts interbancaires que de la syndication ont contribué jusqu'à présent à stabiliser le système: c'est ainsi que les banquiers reconnaissent que les liens de solidarité qui les unissent à l'intérieur d'un syndicat contribuent à empêcher chacun d'entre eux d'essayer de récupérer sa mise en provoquant le défaut d'un débiteur en difficultés: les banques se protègent donc collectivement contre ce risque en recherchant au travers des procédures de consolidation de la dette une sortie de la crise évitant la matérialisation de leurs pertes potentielles et par là l'ébranlement du système financier.

L'importance du rôle que joue le réseau serré de relations interbancaires dans la stabilité du système financier international rend de notre point de vue faiblement pertinents les modèles de comportement d'un intermédiaire financier isolé dans la mesure où ses relations avec le reste du système y sont réduites à la prise en compte du coût éventuel du recours à l'escompte auprès de la banque centrale.

Sur ce point encore il nous semble que l'appréciation du risque d'intermédiation lié aux opérations de crédit international dépend étroitement de l'idée que l'on peut avoir de l'attitude qu'adopteraient les banques centrales à l'égard des banques dont elles assurent la supervision et le contrôle des opérations en cas de crise majeure. L'intériorisation par les banques internationales des règles du jeu plus ou moins explicites qu'elles prêtent à la banque centrale dont elles relèvent n'est sûrement pas sans influence sur leur stratégie de prêts internationaux, et donc sur le niveau de risque qu'elles acceptent d'assumer.

Deux considérations complémentaires s'imposent à nous en guise de conclusion. La première concerne l'orientation des recherches dans le domaine financier international. La mondialisation des échanges et de la production implique en effet que tant les problèmes d'équilibre macroéconomique que de financement soient désormais traités à l'échelle de la planète. Il est donc temps que les fabricants de modèles se penchent sur les caractères structurels qui commandent le comportement dynamique du système financier qui a la charge de l'ajustement des capacités et besoins de financement des nations. Trois points principaux devraient retenir l'attention des modélisateurs: les mécanismes de rationnement; les particularités d'un oligopole financier par rapport à un oligopole industriel; l'alternative entre une régulation de ce système par un organisme supra ou international et une régulation décentralisée confiée aux banques centrales des pays émetteurs des monnaies convertibles.

La deuxième considération porte sur ce qui pourrait être fait pour renforcer la stabilité du système financier international. Les développements qui précèdent nous incitent à penser qu'un progrès pourrait être réalisé à ce niveau à partir d'une analyse poussée de la répartition des responsabilités en matière de risques entre les diverses parties prenantes: entreprises multinationales, Etats, organismes multilatéraux de financement, banques privées.

Cette analyse conduirait sans doute à faire apparaître des vides institution-
nels: la mise en place d'organismes multilatéraux d'assurance de certains
types de risques ou une définition plus précise des responsabilités relatives
du FMI et des banques centrales pourraient ainsi contribuer à assurer un avenir plus serein au financement international dans une économie mondiale
fragile.

NOTES

1. Dans une économie d'endettement au sens de Hicks, le système des banques commerciales,
largement refinancé par la banque centrale, joue dans le financement de l'économie un rôle
beaucoup plus important que les marchés financiers. De là découle la généralisation de l'opposition théorique entre économies de marché et économies d'endettement.

2. Cf. J. Métais, *La multinationalisation des banques commerciales américaines*, thèse de
doctorat d'Etat, Université de Paris-Dauphine, 1978.

3. "A Transaction Cost Approach to the Theory of Financial Intermediation", *Journal of
Finance*, 1976.

4. Ils sont présentés notamment dans D. Lacoue-Labarthe, *Economie Monétaire*, Bordas
1980, chapitres 9 et 10.

5. M. Klein, "A Theory of the Banking Firm", *Journal of Money Credit and Banking*, 1970.

6. Cf. D.H. Pyle, "Descriptive Theories of Financial Institutions under Uncertainty", *Journal of Financial and Quantitative Analysis*, déc. 1972.

Chapter XVIII

RISKS TO THE STABILITY
OF THE INTERNATIONAL FINANCIAL SYSTEM:
GLOOM WITHOUT DRAMA

by *Luigi Spaventa*

INTRODUCTION

1. What can economists say on the issue of the risks to the stability of the international financial system? Though well supplied with aggregate data on international lending, country debt and so on, they are unfamiliar with the microeconomic facts of individual banks, which are more relevant for assessing the stability and resilience of the system. Above all, they feel that in these matters conventions are at least as important as economic criteria: conventions being in turn shaped by the actual or presumed attitude of the authorities, they sense a powerful intrusion of political elements amongst the factors determining the course of events. Will a large debtor country ever be pushed to the point where it cannot but default? Or, for that matter, will a large bank engaged in international transactions ever be allowed to default? How one fares between gloom and unguarded complacency very much depends on the (non-economic) answers to these questions.

In view of these limitations I may be forgiven if I do not provide a clear-cut prognosis: "it depends" is after all the economist's motto. Without reviewing past developments in international private lending (well known from a vast body of literature and statistical sources), I shall first examine some symptoms of deterioration in the international financial system which have recently aroused some concern amongst the observers. Should they be treated seriously, as a genuine cause of worry? I shall look at the problem from the point of view of the financial position of international debtors, first in simple theoretical terms and then with reference to current trends. Beyond the pathology of specific cases, which can be explained in terms of specific causes, there have been general factors at work affecting adversely the financial position of all debtor countries alike. Such factors are external to the behaviour of both the lenders and the borrowers: if they persist (as they well may), the outlook for debtor countries is depressing and the cases of debt service difficulties (as well as the number of rescheduling operations) are likely to become more numerous.

Does it necessarily follow that there is an impending danger of a financial crisis? In the final section I shall observe that conventional rules of the game resting on largely justified political assumptions may help the system to pass unscathed, or more precisely to muddle through a very difficult period. I shall however maintain that such muddling through is a costly and relatively inefficient solution. More efficient solutions, though advantageous to the international banking system, lie outside its specific responsibilities: they are however unlikely if the now dominant approach to policy problems continues to prevail.

I

2. Concern at the growth of international bank lending and of the external indebtedness of some countries – mostly LDCs – has often been voiced in the past. Total external debt of 150 developing countries and territories reached $ 489 billion at the end of 1979 and $ 572 billion at the end of 1980. (Some data on the medium- and long-term debt of the non-oil developing countries are reproduced in Table 1). The size and the growth rates of the aggregates have made some fear that the international banking system has proceeded too rapidly and too lightly on a path of increasing risk and that defaults have not only become more probable, but, owing to the extent of inter-bank links, are likely to cause disastrous domino effects.

Such fears and concerns have commonly been dismissed on several grounds.[1] As regards size and growth rates it has been noted, first, that one should not be overly impressed by the "wondrous working of compound interest"[2]; second, that if some inflation accounting is done, real growth rates appear far less impressive; third, that one should consider not the gross, but the net debt position of debtor countries and take into account official reserves, which have increased very consistently in most years of the decade, other deposits with the international banks and unused credit lines. As regards the debtors' position, no drastic and irreversible deterioration in the usual ratios is noticeable over the decade. Finally, as regards the creditors' position, it has been observed, first, that by far the largest share of private credits goes to middle-income and newly-industrialized developing countries, with highly dynamic growth records and prospects; second, that claims on developing countries are but a small share of total assets of the banks involved in international lending activity; third, that the number of such banks has been growing all the time, thus allowing risks to be more diffusedly spread; fourth, that there has been no marked deterioration in the banks' capital/assets ratios.

Table 1. *Long-term external debt of non-oil developing countries*

	1979	1980	1981	Annual growth rates 1973-79	1979-81
Non-oil developing countries					
Total outstanding debt (bn $)	322.8	370.1	425.2	+ 22.1	+ 14.8
Id. to private creditors (bn $)	188.0	214.3	245.3	+ 25.4	+ 14.2
Debt service (bn $)	60.5	75.2	96.4	+ 24.7	+ 26.2
Ratio of external debt to export of goods and services × 100	102.3	93.4	92.7		
Debt service ratio	18.3	18.2	20.1		
Sub-group 1: Major exporters of manufactures					
Total outstanding debt (bn $)	128.6	143.0	162.7	+ 22.1	+ 12.5
Debt service (bn $)	27.4	36.4	44.9	+ 23.0	+ 28.0
Ratio of external debt to exports of goods and services × 100	82.4	73.0	72.5		
Debt service ratio	17.6	18.5	20.0		

Source: IMF, *World Economic Outlook.*

3. Though these arguments appear convincing enough, it may be asked how far they only reflect (and are validated by) the experience of the past and whether they will apply under different circumstances in the future. As a matter of fact, the tranquil and unconcerned view of the situation which prevailed until recently enjoys now less widespread support and is held with far less certainty. In the cautious words of an international agency, "a greater element of doubt and concern has in recent months been evident in the pronouncements of analysts who have traditionally discounted the possibility of a full-fledged debt crisis".

Why have such clouds appeared on the horizon of the international financial scene? There are, first, some specific facts. Foremost, of course, comes the Polish case, on which not many words need to be spent. Poland's total external debt in 1981 has been estimated at some $ 24 billion, of which over 60 per cent due to foreign banks; before rescheduling, the ratios of debt service and of interest payments to exports had reached the extraordinary levels of 1.4 and 0.4. Considering the arrears of 1980-81, the overdue interest payments which have accumulated since and the state and prospects of the Polish current balance, it is difficult to escape the conclusion that, in spite of rescheduling, Poland is in a state of "effective but undeclared default".[3] Poland, however, though the most dramatic case, is not the only socialist country where problems of debt servicing have arisen or may arise. Thus Rumania has accumulated arrears worth $ 1.2-1.8 billion (according to sources) and has notified her wish to defer also the payments due for the current year, while Yugoslavia is also in trouble. Future difficulties for other CMEA countries, thus far considered perfectly sound borrowers, may be caused or compounded by the drying up of new credit, as banks have belatedly come to realize that there is no lender of the last resort for that group of economies.

Even leaving the problem of the socialist countries' debt aside, there was last year a sudden and remarkable increase in the number of rescheduling operations: eight countries engaged in multilateral debt negotiations (the highest number ever, the average for previous years being 2-3 cases), for some $ 800 million. Further, there were four cases of direct renegotiations with commercial banks for more substantial sums.

To complete the list of symptoms justifying some uneasiness, a deterioration of the liquidity situation of the LDCs in general and specifically of some of the largest borrowers from private sources has been noticeable in the past year or so. Official reserves net of gold of non-OPEC LDCs fell in 1981 and overall reserves of oil-importing LDCs fell both in 1980 and in 1981.[4] Deposits with banks of all LDCs decreased and, "for the first time in five years, LDCs' debts to banks maturing during the year exceeded their deposits with banks"; further, for the ten non-OPEC LDCs accounting for the larger share of debts to banks, debts maturing between mid-1981 and mid-1982 exceed deposits and unused credit facilities combined.[5]

4. Some recent developments in international lending may seem *prima facie* to allay the concern caused by such symptoms of deterioration. As is clear from Table 1, the growth rate of non-oil LDCs' medium- and long-term debt fell considerably in the last three years with respect to past trends. More important, the net flow of medium- and long-term funds (loan disbursements minus amortization payments) has remained more or less constant in *absolute* terms in 1979 and 1980, while the net financial transfer (disbursements minus debt service), after peaking in 1978, has since been falling each year.[6] The changes in the past three years or so are even more striking if, instead of medium and long-term debt to all creditors, all debt (including short-term debt) to private banks is considered: in 1981, for the first time, debt service to banks exceeded inflows of new credit by a substantial amount, which was barely compensated by the interest payments received by the LDCs on their deposits.[7]

To those worried by the excessive growth of the debt this may appear good news; and indeed it would be, if such recent developments reflected a structural improvement in the situation of debtor countries and a greater degree of self-sufficiency after the initial stages of growth. This, however, is hardly the case.

The reduction in the growth of the debt and the rapid fall of net inflows in absolute terms has been accompanied by a marked deterioration of the LDCs' current account position: as deficits had to be partly financed at the expense of reserves, there occured a deterioration in the liquidity and net debt situation of such countries and a fall in their financial receipts. Further, maturities have shortened, especially for the larger borrowers, and the share of total debt maturing each year increased, just as the cost of new debt was rising: as a result, the rise in the average cost of total debt must be more than proportional to the rise in the cost of new debt,[8] while shorter maturities may cause some bunching of repayments. Finally, the fall of net transfers is due not only to a slow-down in the growth of gross inflows, but also to a sharp rise in interest and amortization payments: with positive and rising real interest rates, this has implied a growing real burden on debtor countries.

The reduction in the growth of the debt, far from being the welcome symptom of improved conditions of the borrowing countries, appears to be the result of increasing constraints on credit supply and also on credit demand. Concern over the financial position of the traditional borrowers (LDCs and Eastern European countries alike) has made the lenders far more reluctant to extend new credit. On the other hand, the higher cost and the reduced availability of credit have compelled the borrowers to cut their investment plans and to reduce their growth rates (with true recessions in some cases) and this has in turn reduced demand. Thus, the borrowing countries' disequilibria have, if anything, increased: in such conditions, even the choice open to the lenders between providing more or less credit may turn out to be for them a choice between two equally dangerous courses.

5. Are these difficulties only due to transient causes or is it possible that they will persist and become more intractable?

Preliminary to a brief discussion of these matters, a distinction must be drawn, at least in principle, between pathological cases, where the responsibility for actual or potential debt crises can be attributed to specific factors, and more general causes of chronic deterioration, affecting all debtors alike. Of course, the distinction can be sharp only in principle, insofar as general adverse factors make specific cases worse. Still, the Polish case is a glaring example of wrong policies and misallocation of resources on the part of the borrower and of erroneous judgements on the part of the lenders, so that a crisis would have occurred even in more favourable overall conditions.

In what follows I shall only be concerned with the more general factors which affect the financial situation of borrowers as a group.

II

6. The simple analytics of debt capacity can be a useful starting point (but not much more than that) to consider present problems. This is an old issue in the literature and I shall not even attempt to summarize the relevant contributions. I shall only recall that the problem was studied by Domar from the point of view of a lending country wishing to maintain an export surplus and hence a steady rate of *net* capital outflow.[9] Subsequently Hayes set up a simple analytical framework to determine the conditions under which the growth of debt would not exceed that of national product in the borrowing country. More recently Solomon provided a more concise and simplified version of Hayes' model to show that, if one crucial condition holds, the ratio of external debt to gross national product will grow at a decreasing rate, approaching a limiting value.[10]

Net foreign capital inflow must finance the country's gap between investment and savings, equal to the current balance. Both Hayes and Solomon take an exogenously given growth rate, g, and a given capital output ratio k, so that, with a fixed-coefficient Harrod-Domar production function, investment in t is

(1) $I_t = k\ g\ Y_0\ e^{gt}$.

With a simple savings function

(2) $S_t = s\ Y_0\ e^{gt}$.

If i is the interest rate and D_t is the debt accumulated at $t = T$,

(3) $D_T = \int_0^T Y_0\ e^{gt}\ ^T(kg - s)\ e^{i(T - t)}\ dt = \dfrac{kg - s}{g - i}\ Y_0\ (e^{gT} - e^{iT})$

and

(4) $\dfrac{D_T}{Y_T} = \dfrac{kg - s}{g - i}\ [1 - e^{T(i - g)}]$

so that, with g > i,

(5) $\displaystyle\lim_{T\to\infty}\ \dfrac{D_T}{Y_T} = \dfrac{kg - s}{g - i}$

Hayes has a more plausible savings function, with a marginal rate of savings higher than the investment rate, which is in turn higher than the initial average rate of savings: also in this case, given the value of the other parameters, there is a critical value of the rate of interest (which may now be higher than the growth rate) insuring a tendency towards equi-proportionate growth of debt and GNP.

7. This is a very crude model, with rigid and unrealistic assumptions. Still, it brings home some relevant points. First, if all the parameters are given, the existence of a limit to the ratio of external debt to GDP may be a meagre consolation, since, as the ratio approaches that limit, the levels of gross borrowing and debt service may become so high as to cause unmanageable liquidity problems.[11] Second, the size of debt accumulation and the level of its ratio to GDP crucially depend upon the level of the real interest rate: the higher the interest rate, the higher the accumulation of debt and the higher, at any moment of time, the ratio of debt to GDP. The accumulation of debt relative to GDP becomes explosive as the interest rate becomes greater than the growth rate, in the version of the model given above, or greater than a certain critical value in the version with a rising savings ratio. In this latter version, equilibrium with a higher interest rate requires a lower growth rate. In the simpler version, an offsetting rise in the growth rate may raise the ratio of debt to GDP and in any case requires greater net flows of capital each period.

The limitations of the model are obvious: it is a steady-state model, where demand growth must always be in equilibrium with capacity growth, determined at an exogenously fixed rate. Since the savings gap is a constant share of income, if imports are also a constant share, exports must grow at whatever constant rate is assumed for capacity growth: this in turn implies either the same growth rate for world demand or, if the latter is lower, a growing share of the debtor country's exports on world exports. The effects of a fall in world demand would be portrayed by such model in a very round-about way. The fall in exports would increase the savings gap by lowering absolute savings and hence, *ex post*, the savings ratio relative to capacity output (or, if the savings ratio is measured with respect to income, by raising the capital coefficient relative to income).

When dealing with a representative debtor country, however, the very assumption of capacity-determined growth at an exogenously given rate becomes questionable. Income growth in such country must depend on the growth rate of world demand, which affects both the volume of its exports (of primary products as well as of manufactures) and, when there are substantial exports of primary products, its terms of trade. Such dependence can be captured by making savings dependent on income, rather than on a given capacity output, by establishing the usual dependence of income on exports, and by making exports grow at a rate dictated by the growth of world demand. Investment can be taken to comprise an autonomous part, growing at some exogenously given rate, and an endogenous part, related to income.[12]

In this revised model the results of the effects of the level of the real interest rate on debt accumulation and debt service still hold, but the growth rate of world demand now assumes an equally crucial role. The slower is the growth of world demand, the greater the debt and the higher the debt/GDP ratio; further, worse terms of trade cause a higher import propensity which raises the debt/GDP ratio.

8. Nor is this the end of the story, as the level of interest rates and the growth of world demand cannot be considered two separate factors.

In the case of LDCs, private bank lending is concentrated to a group of newly industrialized middle-income countries, where loans from private sources at non-concessional terms represent the larger share of total debt. This is also true for the Eastern European debtors. The cost of such debt is therefore highly dependent on the level of interest rates charged in international markets, which in turn reflects that prevailing in a few large industrialized countries and particularly in the US. Further, the shortening of maturities and the increase in the proportion of floating-interest loans which has occurred in recent years has made the cost of debt far more sensitive to movements of the interest rate. Finally, world demand is affected, through direct effects on the levels of activity in each country and through transmission mechanisms, by medium-term movements of internal and international interest rates.

Adverse movements of interest rates thus cause a deterioration of the financial situation of debtor countries in two ways: directly, as shown above, and by lowering the growth of world demand and hence of their exports. Higher interest rates and lower growth rates of world demand interact to reduce the debt servicing capacity of debtor countries and their overall growth rate; at the same time, they raise the gross capital inflow required to maintain a certain growth rate of autonomous investment.

Simple theoretical analysis thus confirms the penetrating conclusions reached by Avramovic and his associates at the World Bank in the early 1960s.[13] In earlier periods of economic history a considerable share of the total flow consisted of direct investment, the returns of which fluctuated together with the country's export sales. Nowadays the larger part of capital inflows gives rise to contractually fixed debt service obligations and a substantial part serves internal development purposes. Hence, "if world demand for primary products rises only moderately; if possibilities to expand exports of light manufactures are circumscribed by restrictions resulting from concern with domestic employment in the importing countries; and if it takes time to develop competitive exports of heavy industrial goods, it is virtually inevitable that the ratio of debt service to exports will increase quickly and will attain a high level'', with growing rigidities in the balance of payments.[14] For such a system of international lending at hard terms to work successfully, returns on capital must be high with respect to the interest rate; a high rate of investment must allow a sufficiently high growth rate; creditors must be ready to lend continuously, despite high debt service ratios; debtors must pay their bills as they fall due; fluctuations in the debtors' export earnings must be avoided; reasonable solutions to the liquidity problems of some countries, as they may arise, must be found.

9. Real interest rates in the world have been at unprecedentedly high levels for quite some time now. Activity in industrialized countries has been stagnating; the growth of world demand has fallen, and is still falling, and so has the growth of developing countries' exports, while protectionism in the industrialized countries is increasing; in spite of the decline of nominal prices of oil, terms of trade have deteriorated for the developing countries.

This is not the place to discuss the causes of the remarkable rise in real interest rates which has occurred in the past eighteen months or so, and it is a matter of speculation whether and for how long this situation will persist. Old-fashioned theories raise their head and attribute high real interest rates to a world scarcity of savings: we will need some convincing to accept this explanation when investment is so low and unemployment in industrialized countries so high. Over-tight monetary policies coupled with cyclically very large budget deficits offer a more plausible clue, as is also shown by economists who cannot certainly be accused of Keynesian sympathies.[15] One thing can be said with some certainty: neutrality theorems, whereby monetary policies would affect inflation leaving output undisturbed, have been proven wrong. On the other hand simple short-run Keynesian remedies are also out of question, when structural unemployment is emerging also in industrialized countries and the policies pursued have so shaped expectations as to make ineffective or self-contradictory any sudden change in policy stance. It is therefore doubtful whether lower real interest rates will be attained again through lower nominal rates or through a new spell of higher inflation.

10. High levels of interest rates, flagging world demand, worsening terms of trade have already caused great damage to the financial situation of all debtor countries and are a basic cause of the present difficulties. What may happen if this situation persists for some time?

A likely scenario would be in this case one of gloom, though not necessarily of drama. As the debtors' financial conditions deteriorate, owing to high interest rates and low export demand, it is improbable that the flow of capital towards them continues at the same rates as in the past. Not only would lenders be less willing to extend credit, but also borrowers will hesitate to contract loans at high rates and at the increasing spreads attendant upon rising risks on debt service. This, as was noted above, is already happening and the emergence of negative net flows and negative net transfers for the non-oil LDCs and for other countries are the most obvious symptom.

In order to adapt their borrowing requirement to supply constraints or to new supply conditions, borrowers will have to "readjust", as they are increasingly urged to do. "Readjustment" is however an ambiguous term, as its benefits and its costs depend on external conditions, outside the control of the individual country, no less than on internal conditions. In a situation of expanding world economy and in one where only one or few countries engage in readjustment, such benefits are high and such costs are low. The reverse is true if stagnation prevails and if the number of countries compelled to cut their financial requirements is large. In the latter case, collective readjustment would lower further overall demand and would thus contribute less to reducing relative disequilibria and to increasing the debtors' ability to service foreign debt. The recent examples of some South-American countries and in particular of Brazil serve as a good reminder.

Less investment and lower growth rates may impair the debtors' ability to service foreign debt in the long run: present financial difficulties may cause the cancellation of projects with high medium-term rates of return which would increase the country's export capacity in the future. In the shorter run, readjustment and a reduction of growth rates may not be sufficient to avoid debt service problems, as the repayment of past loans falls due, as interest payments rise and as the current balance does not improve *pari passu* with the reduction of internal demand. Debt service ratios may keep rising and the decline of gross inflows may precipitate liquidity crises.

III

11. This is a scenario of gloom but not necessarily of drama. It would become one of drama if the increase in the number of cases of debt service difficulties, delay in repayments, accumulation of arrears gave rise to a proper banking crisis, with domino effects and the rest. How likely is this to happen, if the debtors' conditions persist or develop in the way sketched above?

I said in the introduction to this paper that this is not a question to which there exists a purely economic answer, as conventions and political decisions appear to play a dominant role. It is to a large extent a matter of mutually, though implicitly, accepted convention to decide how to treat a claim on a large debtor who has experienced financial difficulties for a long time and will experience them in the foreseeable future. Such conventions, in turn, are shaped both by the desire to postpone unpleasant truths and by assumptions as to the behaviour of the authorities in the lending country and in the creditor's country.

In the "new concept of international financial morality" debtors are not expected ever to default, unlike in earlier periods of economic history.[16] But the rules of the game also require that creditors cooperate to avoid the debtor's default, both by refraining from actions which would make default unavoidable and by accepting those further commitments which allow everybody concerned to pretend that the debtor is not defaulting. It is not in the creditor's interest to write off an asset as long as pretence can be kept that returns on it are being paid, even though this often implies an indefinite lengthening of that particular asset's maturity, the concessions of periods of grace and even the granting of new credit. This is, after all, what rescheduling operations are about: both parties agreeing that formal default is to be eschewed, the outcome will depend on the bargaining power of the debtor. Such bargaining power may vary directly with the size of the debt, but inversely with the needs for further financing in the future (so that it is very difficult to decide where it stands in the case of Poland); but it is also affected by the political situation in, and the political and strategic relevance of, the country involved (and here again it is difficult to assess the Polish case).

The intrusion of political and discretionary elements in the rules and conventions of the international financial system works also in more relevant, though less obvious ways. One is the tacit assumption that there is a lender of the last resort for some debtors, who is expected to step in to prevent default if debt service difficulties arise. It is thus generally felt that lenders to CMEA countries have acted on the presumption that the USSR would perform such role if needs arise; as it turned out, US government guarantee has proved more effective in the case of some overdue payments from Poland to American banks.

The conventions and practices of the "new financial morality", though helping to prevent a debtor's difficulties from developing into a full-fledged financial crisis, may push maturity transformation to a point of dangerous mismatching between assets and liabilities. Another silent but widespread assumption serves here to placate uneasy feelings: namely that the central banks and the governments of the 1980s will never allow a major financial crisis to develop. In the event monetary authorities would stand ready to supply the necessary liquidity, whatever their current monetary orthodoxy: after all, the shivers caused by the Herstatt case were a good lesson and the international financial system showed on later occasions to have learnt from it.

These assumptions are probably correct to a considerable degree and the conventions and rules of the game which follow from them may certainly help the international financial system to muddle through a period of growing financial difficulties of the debtor countries, if the scenario depicted above comes true.

The question – a largely academic question, given the spirit of the times – is whether such muddling-through is an efficient solution. My answer is that it is not. First, it still leaves very high margins of risk and instability. Second, the set of conventions and practices on which it is based have caused a great deal of inefficient allocation of resources. Private bankers often speak and write on the techniques of risk assessment they employ when deciding to make loans. Still, there is little doubt that a lot of money has been poured into countries which have later become hopeless cases without paying much regard to the viability and prospective returns of the projects or plans which were thus being financed: clearly, the crude assumption that somebody somehow would eventually pay was more important than sophisticated risk assessment. Third, such a solution may serve to keep creditors and debtors afloat: but only just in the case of many debtor countries, which will still have to bear permanent damages to their standard of living, to the development of their export capacity, to their future growth prospects.

Nobody is, or should be, foolish enough to ask international banks to lend more and on more generous terms: it is not their individual task to do so. Nobody is, or should be, foolish enough to deny that conditionality is necessary in general financing, even though one may desire that conditions imposed in individual cases were mutually consistent. It is however legitimate to argue that, at least as long as conditions of impossibly high interest rates and depressed world demand prevail, international agencies should be more active in providing far larger amounts of concessional *and* conditional finance. This would be in the short- and in the long-run interests of the international banking system: it would reduce the risks and dangers of the current situation; it would relieve the banks somewhat from the unsavoury task of providing finance, which has an exceedingly high cost not only for the borrower but, beyond the appearances, also for the lender, if due account is taken of the quality of the assets; it would compel borrowers to adopt the necessary policy changes before a crisis occurs (and not after it has occurred), but it would also save them a great deal of unnecessary sacrifices in terms of growth of income and investment.

Mine was an academic question and I gave an academic answer. Neither belong to the prevailing mode of thought, according to which all that is real in the markets is also rational and does not require correction – a conception not far removed from the belief that whatever happens is an act of God with which man should not interfere, no matter how painful the possible effects.

NOTES

1. See, amongst others, Charles S. Ganoe, "Loans to LDCs: Five Myths", in M.G. Franko, M.J. Seiber (eds.), *Developing Country Debt*, 1979; Robert Solomon, "A Perspective on the Debt of Developing Countries", *Brookings Papers on Economic Activity*, 1977, 1; and "The Debt of Developing Countries: Another Look", *ibid.*, 1981, 2; Jeffrey D. Sachs, "The Current Account and Macroeconomic Adjustment in the 1970s", *Brookings Papers on Economic Activity*, 1981, 2.

2. The expression is by Jacob Viner (who was indeed impressed), quoted by Evsey D. Domar, "The Effect of Foreign Investment on the Balance of Payments", *The American Economic Review*, December 1950, repr. in Evsey D. Domar, *Essays in the Theory of Economic Growth*, 1957.

3. "Communist bloc debt and world banking tensions", *International Currency Review*, March 1982, p. 24.

4. "LDC Liquidity Levels – How Serious is the Decline?", *The Amex Bank Review*, 1982, 2, and F.X. Colaço, *Capital Requirements in Economic Development: The Decade Ahead*, mimeo., October 1981.

5. *Ibid.*

6. "External Indebtedness of Developing Countries", *International Monetary Fund, Occasional Paper*, 3, May 1981.

7. See "LDC Debt Service Burden: A Cash Flow Analysis", *The Amex Bank Review*, 1982, 4.

8. Let P be interest payments, r the cost of the debt, D the debt and α the share of the debt which must be renewed in the period. Then

$$dP = dr\alpha D + (r + dr)\, dD \text{ and } \frac{d}{dt}\left(\frac{P}{D}\right) = \frac{P}{D}\frac{dr}{r}\left(\alpha + \frac{dD}{D}\right):$$

see OECD, *Economic Outlook*, December 1981, p. 159.

9. Evsey D. Domar, *op. cit.* in note 2.

10. J.P. Hayes, "Long-Run Growth and Debt Servicing Problems: Projections of Debt Servicing Burden and the Conditions of Debt Failure", in Dragoslav Avramovic et al., *Economic Growth and External Debt*, 1964; Robert Solomon, "A Perspective . . .", *cit.*, note 1. See also "External Indebtedness . . .", *cit.*, note 6, appendix 3.

11. Hayes, *cit.*, p. 181.

12. Let $I_t = A_0 e^{rt} + bY_t$, the sum of an autonomous and an endogenous part. Let exports equal $m^+ W_0 e^{zt}$, where W is world demand and z its growth rate. Let $k = 1/(s - b + m)$,

where s is the propensity to save and m the propensity to import. Then

$$Y_t = k (A_0 e^{rt} + m^+ W_0 e^{zt}) \text{ and } I_t - S_t = k [mA_0 e^{rt} - (s - b) m^+ W_0 e^{zt}]. \ s > b$$

$$D_T = \int_0^T (I_t - S_t) \, e^{i (T - t)} dt = k \left[\frac{mA_0}{r - i} (e^{rT} - e^{iT}) - \frac{m^+ (s - b)}{z - i} W_0 (e^{zT} - e^{iT}) \right]$$

13. "An Analytical Framework" in Dragoslav Avramovic et al., *Economic Growth . . .*", *cit.*, note 9, volume I.

14. Avramovic et al., *cit.*, pp. 85 ff.

15. See Thomas J. Sargent, Neil Wallace, "Some Unpleasant Monetarist Arithmetic", *Federal Reserve Bank of Minneapolis Quarterly Review*, Fall 1981.

16. Avramovic et al., *cit.*, p. 87.

338

Chapter XIX

EXPERIENCE WITH THE RESCHEDULING OF INTERNATIONAL DEBT

by *Helmut von der Bey*

The wording of the topic itself suggests as the most convenient approach to choose the case of a specific country for demonstration. Much to the regret of international banks there is no great lack of debt reschedulings for sovereign debtors from which to select. The first three years after the Second World War saw relatively few cases: to begin with the settlement of old German debt by the Federal Republic of Germany in the early 1950s. There was a debt rescheduling for Turkey at the end of the 1950s and another, quite substantial one for Indonesia in the second half of the 1960s. It was only from the mid-1970s onwards, when developing countries increasingly felt the consequences of oil price increases coupled with insufficient or slow adjustment to changed economic conditions, that debt reschedulings became more frequent.

For the topic of this paper Turkey appeared to be the most suitable case for several reasons: the rescheduling of Turkish debt was quite comprehensive, it involved very substantial amounts, various kinds of creditors, various forms of debt and – at least a loose – coordination between several groups of lenders for the subsequent efforts to help the country on its way to recovery. Besides it should not be overlooked that, although a country debt rescheduling is always to some extent a public affair, a sovereign borrower is also entitled to some extent to confidentiality from its bankers. In this respect Turkey presents a suitable case as it is virtually concluded and the country is on its way to recovery.

The paper deals with the subject in four parts: the phase leading to the breakdown of transfers, the actual rescheduling operations and the subsequent developments. The fourth part attempts to draw general conclusions.

I. THE CREATION OF A CRITICAL VOLUME OF FOREIGN DEBT AND THE BREAKDOWN OF TRANSFERS (APPROXIMATELY FROM APRIL 1975 UNTIL THE END OF 1977)

Through the 1960s and the early 1970s Turkey had been able to achieve average real growth rates of 6 to 7 per cent annually, noticeably above the average of the OECD countries as a whole. During this period budget deficits and inflation by and large did not exceed acceptable levels. With comparatively moderate foreign borrowing Turkey presented a better balance of payments during the first years of the 1970s than ever before and the currency reserves showed the record figure of US$ 2.4 billion in August 1974. The thrust of the economic development of the country had largely been inward-orientated, domestic demand for investment and consumption and import substitution had priority over the development of export industries. The energy sector showed a noticeable structural dependence on oil imports.

The pace of economic expansion continued almost undiminished also after the oil price increases of 1974. Consumption spending and investment, in particular in the public sector, provided a strong stimulant for demand. Total investment increased from approximately 18 per cent of GDP during the first years of the 1970s to nearly 25 per cent in 1977 while the savings quota remained virtually unchanged at around 16 per cent.

The public sector accounted for approximately half of total fixed investment of which again slightly more than 50 per cent concentrated on the State Economic Enterprises (SEEs). From a small overall surplus at the beginning of the 1970s their losses reached nearly 13 per cent of sales on average for the years 1974-1977. These deficits were largely met by transfers from the central government's budget, the deficit of which in turn grew from about 1.5 per cent of GNP to approximately 4 per cent in 1977. Growing portions of budget deficit were covered by central bank credit: approximately one third during the first three years of the decade and two thirds on average in the following three years. Between 1974 and 1977 money supply increased yearly by rates varying between 24 and 30 per cent, and domestic credit by approximately 40 per cent annually. Growing inflation rates, which by and by left the officially regulated interest levels behind, and a Turkish Lira that was overvalued most of the time were conducive to rather excessive stockpiling.

After several years of surplus the Turkish balance of payments turned into deficit from 1974 onwards. The trade deficit grew from US$ 2.2 billion in 1974 to US$ 3.2 billion in 1976. The unrealistic external value of the Turkish Lira had a negative effect on remittances from Turkish workers abroad, which dropped by one third from 1974 to 1976. Over the same period the current account deficit grew from US$ 720 million to US$ 2.3 billion and the overall deficit from US$ 360 million to US$ 1.8 billion.

In order to sustain economic expansion in spite of the deteriorating balance of payments situation Turkey resorted increasingly to borrowing abroad. In April 1975 and the following months Turkey introduced two schemes which proved in the end rather problematic for both Turkey and its foreign creditors.

A. *The Convertible Turkish Lira Deposit Scheme (CTLD Scheme)* [1]

Under this scheme foreign banks could place term deposits with Turkish commercial banks. They were TL deposits only in name, in fact they consisted of term deposits in foreign exchange with a swap arrangement being concluded at no cost between the Turkish commercial banks and the Turkish central bank. The TL proceeds were used by Turkish commercial banks to finance domestic credits. When the scheme was introduced the Turkish authorities were probably genuinely convinced that the CTLD scheme could be kept going on a revolving basis if there were sufficiently strong incentives for all the parties involved in such operations. As late as spring 1977 Turkish authorities and banks were still unwilling to agree that short- or barely medium-term CTL deposits were an inadequate and more than just potentially dangerous instrument for financing chronic balance of payments deficits.

The initial success of the CTLD scheme was largely due to the aforementioned incentives. Internal bank credits were tight and considered expensive. Import licenses, needed also for industrial requirements, were more and more difficult to obtain. As a consequence foreign banks were continuously urged by customers to place CTL deposits with Turkish banks in order to arrange TL credits for their Turkish subsidiaries or buyers, especially if the latter could, in addition, obtain import licenses against the foreign exchange flowing in. In fact much more than half of all CTLDs which were established were made on behalf and in the interest of customers and tied to the granting of TL credits to designated borrowers in Turkey. A considerable portion of these were made by banks at the risk and at times also with funds of their customers ("fiduciary deposits"). In view of the comparatively low cost of the refinancing arranged on behalf of the borrower these TL credits were given at rates well below the normal Turkish interest level.

Turkish commercial banks also prevailed strongly on their foreign correspondent banks to reciprocate for business received from Turkey by placing untied CTLDs with them, preferably in DM or Sfrs. on which the Turkish banks could obtain gross interest margins of 10 to 12 per cent p.a. while the currency risk was borne by the central bank. Most CTLDs were for maturities between 12 and 24 months but a minor portion (for an estimated aggregate of US$ 150 million) had maturities beyond the end of 1980.

B. *Imports under the "Cash Against Goods" and "Cash Against Documents" Schemes* [1]

Under these schemes Turkish buyers could import goods and have them cleared through customs without immediate transfer of the purchase price. Upon import clearance they had to have the TL equivalent deposited with the central bank and to apply for transfer. Foreign suppliers who undertook to ship goods to Turkey on this basis incurred an unsecured export credit risk. Some could and did take out government export credit insurance for such risks. Others agreed to ship goods only after having received the whole purchase price, or part thereof, from the Turkish buyer, usually from unoffical foreign exchange sources. Many foreign exporters, however, were prepared to supply goods without any such safeguards to their own Turkish subsidiaries in order to maintain production, or to long-standing Turkish importers in order to maintain market positions.

At this point a few general remarks may be in place. In several respects the Turkish method of financing part of the external deficit differed considerably from the approach usually taken by borrower countries. In addition to capital aid and suppliers' credits most countries try to raise medium-term loans from organized international markets, mainly through syndicated Euro-loans. With few exceptions these are widely publicized and thus the international banking community is able to follow by and large all major country borrowings. The CTLD scheme, however, operated almost exclusively on a bilateral relationship, one foreign bank lending to one Turkish commercial bank without any publicity. Neither the Turkish central bank nor the Turkish commercial banks used to report any figures about CTLD operations concluded or the accumulated volume. Only banks with closer business relationships with Turkey, visiting there frequently, had the possibility to follow developments by obtaining verbal statements from central bank officials or from their Turkish correspondent banks. Quite a few foreign banks may not have learned until late or too late about the full extent of this form of borrowing abroad. Furthermore, most borrower countries try to finance their own payments deficits by raising medium-term loans abroad, leaving the roll-over risk to the lending banks, which fund themselves by raising short-term money on the international markets. Turkey, however, borrowed mainly short- or barely medium-term for rather long-term needs and thus incurred the roll-over risk herself, assuming that the combination of the internal circumstances described above and sufficiently attractive interest spreads offered to foreign banks would permit maturities to be continuously rolled-over as they came up. While it was already difficult for foreign banks to keep aware of the growing Turkish short-term debt under the CTLD scheme it was nearly impossible to monitor the accumulating short-term suppliers' credits under the cash against goods and cash against documents scheme.

In spite of the inflow of foreign exchange under the CTLD scheme and the factual postponement of foreign exchange outflows on the import side, the reserve position of the central bank continued to decline until in the course of 1976 the total outstanding CTL deposits exceeded gross foreign exchange reserves. Besides, the conversion of short-term borrowings abroad into Turkish Lira had in the course of 1975 and 1976 contributed to a great extent to the rapid growth of money supply in Turkey. Aware of the increasingly unfavourable developments, some banks started to grow more and more reluctant in the course of 1976 to enter into new CTLD operations; other banks, however, were still actively engaged in this kind of operation and enabled Turkey to continue borrowing short-term.

In October 1976 the Turkish central bank urgently requested several of its closest correspondent banks abroad to supply substantial emergency assistance. The then central bank Governor explained verbally that this was in line with the views of the IMF which had urged the central bank to raise a considerable volume of credits from foreign banks immediately without the internal inflationary side effects of CTL deposits. Well aware of the increased Turkish transfer risk twelve banks responded favourably as this request for assistance came from the monetary authority of Turkey itself and was not related to any particular commercial interest. These short-term lendings to the Turkish central bank were later on termed "bankers' credits".

Foreign suppliers were the first to notice transfer delays under the cash against goods scheme towards the end of 1976. With the last sources for short-term foreign borrowing drying up the situation deteriorated rapidly in the first months of 1977, leading to substantial payment arrears to foreign suppliers. Banks were not directly affected until about April or May 1977 when the first defaults on CTL deposits became known. In autumn transfers to suppliers and to banks had nearly, though not completely, come to a standstill. For lack of funds or insufficient replenishment of overdrawn accounts of the central bank its foreign correspondent banks were no longer in a position to honour reimbursement claims from third banks for payment under Turkish import letters of credit.

In contrast to the breakdown of official transfers a parallel grey foreign exchange market had developed in Turkey, the annual volume of which was estimated by non-official sources to have an order of magnitude of around US$ 2 billion. Import entitlements due to Turkish exporters under an export incentive scheme were sold domestically at a premium of up to one hundred per cent to importers who were not able to obtain import licenses or supplies under the cash against goods scheme.

II. THE DEBT RESCHEDULING (1978-1979)

During the last months of 1977 the Turkish Ministry of Finance and the central bank were still confident that a formal debt rescheduling could be avoided if only foreign banks were prepared to arrange a substantial medium-term loan for Turkey. Although at the time still without any organized coordination among themselves, the banks which had been approached explained almost uniformly that the situation had already deteriorated so much that neither individual assistance, as in October 1976, nor a large syndicated loan could be an adequate solution to the Turkish transfer problems even if such financial assistance were feasible. Only if Turkey went in for a comprehensive rescheduling of all major areas of foreign debt and could obtain a stand-by facility from the Fund – less for the financial impact involved than for the visible approval of the IMF for new economic, fiscal and financial policies to be adopted – could it expect a medium-term loan from the international market.

Around the same time first contacts took place between individual banks and officials of the Turkey Consortium at the OECD in Paris and of the International Monetary Fund. A delegation of the Fund went for initial negotiations to Ankara. The first meeting between fifteen leading creditor banks took place in mid-December 1977 in Frankfurt and confirmed the previously rather individual views of the banks that the aforementioned link between a stand-by agreement and a comprehensive debt rescheduling should not be abandoned. Banks keeping in loose telephone contact thereafter learned from further talks with the IMF that, although the Fund could not enter into any formal coordination with the banks in view of its position, it appreciated the banks' insisting on such a link and was prepared to exchange views and information within appropriate limits.

The OECD was likewise interested in obtaining information about what went on between the international banks and Turkey. They were considering whether the transfer problems of Turkey should be handled by the Turkey Consortium in the form of a debt rescheduling in order to avoid an outright moratorium, which would have put the ultimate financial stigma on Turkey and made it even more difficult for the country to regain some confidence abroad.

On their own initiative a few banks in mid-February 1978 submitted to the Turkish Ministry a memorandum on how the necessary external financial arrangements could be organized. In response to the paper the Ministry of Finance invited several banks to a meeting in Ankara in mid-April 1978. These were three banks from the United States and one each from the United Kingdom, Switzerland, and the Federal Republic of Germany. These banks plus another German bank which joined in shortly thereafter, formed what was later called the Working Group or the Club Banks.

The essential outlines of the debt rescheduling with banks and an accompanying new money loan were already established at this meeting:

- All bankers' credits and all CTLDs overdue or falling due by the end of 1980 were to be rescheduled (except CTLDs held by Turkish nationals abroad as the central bank was quite confident that most of them would not demand retransfer). In view of their comparatively minor volume, CTLDs maturing after 1980 were excluded from the rescheduling and to be repaid on due dates.
- Although banks were aware that a period of 10 years was more in line with Turkish requirements, the lifetime of the rescheduling agreements was proposed to be 7 years as this was closer to the terms then prevailing on the Euro-loan market and, more important, the OECD had just before agreed to the same period for rescheduling government-to-government debts. A grace period of 3 years, slightly longer than under the OECD arrangement, was envisaged with the intention of enabling the Turkish central bank to resume payments on trade arrears with foreign suppliers in the meantime.
- A participation of 85 per cent was considered to be the necessary minimum quota for the CTLD rescheduling (which, as it turned out later, involved approximately 260 banks with nearly 2,700 individual claims representing 99.5 per cent of the amount for which it was intended and proposed).
- The interest rate was to be 1 ¾ per cent per annum over the 6-month London Interbank Offered Rate (except for individual CTLDs which were to continue on a fixed-interest basis).

- Repayment in 48 monthly instalments in order to avoid too heavy debt service burdens on any individual payment dates.
- The Working Group considered feasible a new medium-term loan (later called the New Money Loan) for financing the import of goods which were vital for the recovery of the Turkish economy, conditional upon a stand-by agreement being concluded with the IMF, the rescheduling of government-to-government debt being continued on no less favourable terms, an orderly payment of instalments for settling trade arrears with foreign suppliers, unpaid reimbursement claims from third banks being settled within a reasonable period, excessively overdrawn current accounts of the central bank with foreign correspondent banks being brought back into agreed credit lines and overdue interest on CTLDs being brought up to date. While the Turkish authorities aimed at a higher amount for the New Money Loan, the banks believed anything beyond US$ 500 million to be unrealistic. (The banks considered the New Money Loan necessary and justified in order to help protect the Turkish economy, if possible, from a near collapse, which in turn would have rendered the rescheduling exercise useless. At the time the New Money Loan was conceived, the Turkish Government – and the banks – had no reason to expect the substantial financial assistance from OECD countries which followed the Guadeloupe summit at the end of 1978.)
- Terms and conditions for the New Money Loan were to be the same as for the rescheduling agreements.
- The proceeds of the New Money Loan were to be disbursed in four equal instalments, each one tied to a stand-by tranche being disbursed by the IMF (this precaution turned out to be not entirely unfounded later on).
- All agreements were to be guaranteed by the Republic of Turkey.
- Repayments due during the next years under a few outstanding syndicated medium-term loans, mostly bearing a government guarantee or being co-financings with the International Finance Corporation, were not to be rescheduled not only because of possible consequences of cross-default clauses in the agreement, but largely because the government still wanted to protect its own creditworthiness by not defaulting on any of its own obligations, even though the central bank was already in default on the bankers' credits.

The aforementioned elements of the financial package could, naturally, only be discussed in principle at this meeting in Ankara. It may be observed here that a debt rescheduling of this complexity and dimension was largely unknown territory not only for the Turkish side but also for the Club Banks.

Between the Turkish representatives and the Club Banks the various types of debt and the different categories of creditor to be dealt with could be quite precisely ascertained, less so, however, the details of the outstanding debts. Matters were complicated by the fact that the central bank itself was the contractual debtor only to the bankers' credits, the precise details of which were on hand, while the CTL deposits were liabilities of a number of Turkish commercial banks. Here the central bank did have the maturity profile and the breakdown by currencies on record, also amounts overdue, but not the number or geographical distribution of creditor banks and even less so details about applicable interest rates, interest falling due or overdue or whether the CTL deposits were made by the creditor banks for their own account or for account of customers as fiduciary deposits. It also remained to be established in the later course to what extent foreign correspondent banks of the central bank were ready to continue overdraft facilities and which portion of central bank debt in current account over and above such lines needed to be settled. The amount of unpaid reimbursement claims of third banks against the central bank under Turkish import letters of credit could only be estimated to be around US$ 300 million, the number and the names of creditors being unknown. No estimate was possible on how much of this represented actual claims of third banks for payments effected and how much was to be considered suppliers' claims in arrears. While the identification of liabilities to foreign banks was already quite complex the suppliers' debt in arrears was even more complicated. The total outstanding could only be estimated to be around US$ 2 billion.

During the weeks following the meeting in Ankara, the Club Banks prepared a detailed proposal along the aforementioned lines, including a commitment for participating in the New Money Loan with US$ 25 million each, provided a total amount of at least US$ 400 million could be achieved; if not, the commitments would be reduced accordingly. On the basis of their proposal they were formally mandated by the central bank to act as a Working Group. Its role was to structure the procedural and operational details of the rescheduling operation and the New Money Loan and to prepare the draft agreements. In view of possible legal implications, however, the Club Banks felt unable to act as classical syndicate managers inviting third banks to join the rescheduling operation and especially, to participate in the New Money Loan. The Working Group would structure the operation in detail, but the Turkish central bank was to approach the approximately 260 other banks itself. For assistance in the extensive communications with so many banks, in the follow-up efforts with those unwilling to participate, the lengthy reconciliation of every detail of CTLD claims between foreign banks and the Turkish records and also in the preparation of an information memorandum and the invitation letters to the banks, the central bank was to engage the professional assistance of one or several experienced merchant banks.

In addition to the major elements mentioned above several further intricate issues had to be discussed. As the CTL deposits formally constituted TL liabilities of Turkish commercial banks and as the central bank was not permitted by its by-laws to guarantee liabilities of private institutions, the following legal form was chosen for the CTLD rescheduling. The Turkish central bank would purchase the CTLD claims on the Turkish commercial banks from the foreign banks against central bank obligations in US dollars, DM or Sfrs. CTLDs which had originally been established in other currencies were to be converted to one of the three settlement currencies. A system was to be agreed upon between the Working Group, the central bank and the Turkish commercial banks on how to avoid an abrupt loss of liquidity for the latter owing to the disappearance of the existing CTLDs and to enable them to continue fulfilling their TL loan commitments with designated Turkish borrowers. This system was also desirable in order to induce non-bank fiduciary holders of CTLDs to join the rescheduling as these could probably best be motivated by ensuring the continued supply of TL credits to their Turkish subsidiaries. A suitable and capable entity outside of Turkey had to be found to handle the extremely complex interest and debt service payments to approximately 260-270 individual creditors with monthly payments in three different currencies. Again, in view of possible legal implications, none of the Club Banks was prepared to undertake this in the classical role of an agent bank. Finally, one of them agreed to assume the technical tasks involved merely as a servicing institution. (To describe the complex technical settlement procedures for imports under the New Money Loan or provisions in case of payment default would definitely overtax the reader's patience.)

Shortly before the first meeting with the banks in Ankara, Turkey had reached an understanding with the OECD countries about the rescheduling of approximately US$ 1.4 billion of principal and interest payments overdue or falling due shortly under previous capital aid and of foreign export claims covered by national export credit insurance agencies. The terms obtained were repayment over seven years including one or two years of grace, depending on the original payment conditions. These terms set a precedent also for the negotiation with the banks. Although the Working Group felt that seven years were probably not in line with the future Turkish capacity for debt servicing and that a rescheduling term of ten years would be more adequate, it saw little chance of obtaining the approval of more than 250 other banks if softer terms than those conceded by governments were proposed for the settlement of Turkish liabilities to banks.

In May 1978, when the bank rescheduling was still far from being finalized, the Turkish government concluded the stand-by agreement for SDR 300 million, available over two years, with the International Monetary Fund. The government committed itself to a series of measures aimed mainly at restoring the balance of payments equilibrium and reducing the inflation rate while at the same time maintaining a satisfactory growth rate of the economy and trying to reduce unemployment. Several corrective measures had already been taken by the Turkish government towards the end of 1977: prices and fees of State Economic Enterprises (SEEs) had been increased by between 50 and 100 per cent and the Turkish Lira had been devalued by 9.1 per cent. Anticipating the expectations of the Fund the Turkish Lira was again devalued by 23 per cent in March 1978.[3]

The major measures to be undertaken by the Turkish government consisted of incentives to exports, limitations to expenditure and investment by SEEs, limits to central bank lending to the public sector, restrictions on commercial bank lending, an increase of interest rates on deposits and bank loans, limits on new foreign borrowing by the public sector (except by the central bank) and a tax reform package. Besides, the government committed itself to prevent any further increase of arrears on foreign debt.

As result of these measures the current account deficit of the balance of payments was expected to decrease from approximately 7 per cent of GNP in 1977 to about 4 per cent in 1978 and to bring the inflation rate down from 35 per cent in 1977 to around 20 per cent by the beginning of 1979.

Towards year-end, however, it turned out that Turkey was not quite able to meet all the envisaged targets. The current account deficit of the balance of payments was actually slashed in half from 1977 to 1978 but payment obligations with OECD countries, also under the rescheduling arrangements of spring 1978, could not be met entirely and arrears increased further. Also central bank lending to the public sector remained well above the envisaged levels and the inflation rate turned out much higher than expected, largely due to the widening gap between domestic demand and production which was more and more severely hampered by import constraints. The tax reform package did not pass through Parliament. (Actually, a tax reform could only be enacted in the later course of 1980 after government had been taken over by the armed forces.)

Turkey and the Fund being in disagreement with respect to Turkey's compliance with the letter of intent or the necessity of new measures to be taken in Turkey, the dialogue beween the Fund and Ankara virtually ceased owing to the sensitive political situation in Turkey. In view of the link between the bank agreements and the stand-by agreement with the IMF the Turkish authorities considered even the continuation of negotiations with the banks to be politically too delicate. Therefore the work of the Club Banks also suffered an interruption of several months. The summit meeting at Guadeloupe over the year-end of 1978 laid the basis for the coordination of economic assistance to Turkey by the Western world. Only after Herr Walter Leisler-Kiep, acting as an intermediary on behalf of the West German government and the other OECD countries, was able to bring the Turkish government and the Fund on to speaking terms again in spring 1979 could negotiations with the banks be resumed. Shortly after that OECD countries agreed with Turkey on the rescheduling of another US$ 800 million of principal and interest payments due under previous capital aid and export-insured trade arrears. This was followed in May by a pledge of OECD countries for US$ 906 million special assistance to Turkey, US$ 661 million thereof being programme aid and US$ 245 million project aid.[4]

In July 1979 the first stand-by agreement between Turkey and the IMF was cancelled and replaced by a new one for SDR 250 million, available over one year. The major aims and the measures of the economic, monetary and fiscal package agreed upon between Turkey and the Fund were essentially the same as in 1978 but more stringent.

In the meantime the work on the bank rescheduling and the New Money Loan had been continued and agreements were signed as follows:

July 1979:   US$ 407 million letter of credit facility by thirty-eight banks for financing vital imports for Turkey.
US$ 429 million rescheduling of previous bankers' credits to the Turkish Central Bank.
August 1979: rescheduling of approximately US$ 2.2 billion CTL deposits.

Rescheduling terms were identical for the three parts: repayment in 48 consecutive monthly instalments after three years of grace and monthly payment of interest at current market rates or individually negotiated fixed rates. Disbursement under the letter of credit facility was to take place in various drawings linked to disbursements under the IMF stand-by facility. This was to ensure that banks did not have to disburse the loan even if the new economic package for Turkey should break down. As agreed, the Turkish central bank had, prior to the signing of the agreements, brought its overdrawn current accounts into line and settled all overdue interest on CTL deposits and bankers' credits.

At this stage two areas of Turkish foreign debt still remained to be settled: the unpaid reimbursement claims of third banks of approximately US$ 300 million and the very wide and diverse field of trade arrears with foreign suppliers who were not covered by national export credit insurance agencies. Guided by the concept that the rescheduling exercise could only fulfill its objectives if all major areas of Turkish foreign debt were settled, the banks had originally insisted that the Turkish government should present and possibly even start implementing a repayment programme for the non-guaranteed trade arrears before the bank agreements became effective. In order not to delay the conclusion of the bank agreements and especially the disbursements under the New Money Loan any further the banks had, however, to relax this condition when it turned out that the immense organizational efforts could not be undertaken in time. Even the settlement of the comparatively modest US$ 300 million reimbursement claims of third parties proved to be so difficult that the agreements have only recently been concluded.

The economic crisis of the country culminated towards the end of 1979/beginning of 1980. The inflation rate had climbed to around 50 per cent. Industry operated far below installed capacity because of a shortage of imported components, which also affected negatively export performance, and because of frequent power cuts. Transport suffered from lack of diesel oil. Black markets in foreign exchange and in price-controlled domestically manufactured goods flourished. Hoarding of essential commodities was a current phenomenon. To make things worse the winter of 1979/80 turned out to be extremely severe. The comprehensive debt relief itself brought no immediate material alleviation. Only part of the new financial assistance was disbursed quickly. As the future of the country still looked rather bleak short-term commercial credit for Turkey had virtually dried up. Banks and suppliers were most reluctant to enter into new exposures and national export credit insurance agencies, except one, had ceased covering exports to Turkey in view of the ongoing default situation. What probably saved the country from final collapse was that it was always self-sufficient in food and even during the most difficult period in a position to produce an exportable agricultural surplus.

III. THE RECOVERY (FROM JANUARY 1980)

In the last weeks of 1979 the government of Bulent Ecevit and the Peoples' Republican Party was succeeded by Suleiman Demirel and the Justice Party. By then the economic situation of the country was so desperate that the new government felt politically able to apply a full dose of economic, monetary and fiscal reform measures. End of January 1980 Türgut Özal, then Under-Secretary of State and Head of the State Planning Organization, presented a reform package which surpassed even the expectations of the IMF: devaluation of the Turkish Lira by 33 per cent, almost complete abolition of price controls, prices of SEEs were raised drastically, in some cases by several hundred per cent, further export incentives were introduced and administrative procedures for exchange controls on exports eased. With a few exceptions State Economic Enterprises were denied access to subsidies from the government's budget for financing deficits. The public investment programme was streamlined. Regulations on procedures for the authorization of direct foreign investment were considerably liberalized. Exchange rates for the Turkish Lira were to be continuously adjusted in order to avoid any significant over- or undervaluation of the currency. The two essential aims of the programme package were to restrict domestic demand in favour of export performance and – in the longer run – to turn towards a more and more market-oriented economy.

The practical results became visible quite soon. The inflation rate exceeded 120 per cent in March 1980 but started to decline noticeably thereafter. In May the price increase over the previous month was down to around 3 per cent. (Since 1981 the year-on-year inflation rate has been fluctuating around 35 per cent.) Previously widespread hoarding and black markets for foreign exchange and goods virtually collapsed. Domestically manufactured durables like passenger cars, refrigerators, television sets, and electrical household appliances, which previously had been sold with long delivery terms or above official prices, were soon immediately available or even sold at a discount or on deferred payment terms. Domestic investment and consumption were further discouraged when towards mid-year 1980 bank interest rates were liberalized and rose to a level which offered depositors a real return for the first time in years.

The economic reforms were the basis on which the IMF granted an Extended Stand-by Facility of US$ 1.6 billion, available over three years. In April the OECD had again pledged special assistance of US$ 1.16 billion. This was followed in July by further debt relief from the OECD countries: 90 per cent of maturities under previous capital aid and interest due between mid-1980 and mid-1983 were to be rescheduled for ten years, the remaining 10 per cent for five years. Payments due until mid-1981 and some arrears under previous reschedulings were likewise to be rescheduled over eight years. The aggregate debt relief of these agreements amounted to US$ 3 billion.

Together with its economic reform package the Turkish government announced at the end of January 1980 a programme for the repayment of trade arrears. Compared with the conditions of the bank agreements the terms for the trade creditors appeared to be very unfavourable and provoked widespread criticism, not only outside of Turkey. So far Turkey had carefully avoided the term "moratorium" even being mentioned and had concluded all reschedulings by negotiated agreements. In line with this policy, the trade arrears were also to be settled by way of a general offer of repayment terms and their individual acceptance by trade creditors. The proposal, however, did not stipulate a debtor. Turkish commercial banks were expected to pay interest, and later on the instalments on principal from their own foreign exchange positions (if they could); they would obtain the Turkish Lira-equivalents from the central bank where they had been deposited before or at the time of import. This might have been formally acceptable as the contractual debtors of the trade arrears were still the Turkish importers or, where letters of credit had been opened, Turkish commercial banks, but was hardly acceptable for trade creditors from the practical point of view. Furthermore, regardless of the contract currency of the trade transactions, all claims were to be converted into US dollars at cross rates as at end of January 1980. This would have exposed many trade creditors to undue currency risks. The interest rate offered was far below the US dollar market rate. Trade creditors were given the option to demand repayment over ten years including four years of grace in escalating instalments in foreign exchange or to request payment in twelve two-monthly instalments in Turkish Lira at the quite unfavourable exchange rate prevailing the day before the 33 per cent devaluation of January 1980 and thus excluding them also from any subsequent devaluation of the Lira. Non-convertible Turkish Lira proceeds under this option could be used for direct investment in Turkey[5] and several other purposes of lesser importance and for granting 20-year credits at virtually no interest to the original Turkish importers.

The possibility to grant loans to the original importers had a special purpose. The Turkish authorities, probably quite rightly, assumed that an unknown portion of the trade arrears, estimated to total approximately US$ 1.8 to 2 billion, had actually been prepaid wholly or partly from unofficial foreign exchange funds of the importers but nevertheless also been submitted for official payment and transfer. There was no effective way to identify these cases out of perhaps a hundred thousand individual import transactions. To induce exporters – and in particular the Turkish importers who had deposited the Turkish Lira equivalents and part of subsequent devaluation differentials with the central bank – to forgo voluntarily repayment in foreign exchange, importers had to get their Turkish Lira back from the central bank without having to admit formally to previous unofficial payments. Another disadvantage of the Turkish Lira option, besides the very unfavourable exchange rate, was the necessity for foreign trade creditors to make the decision in one way or the other between the foreign exchange and the Turkish Lira option at the moment of presenting their claim for settlement. Furthermore, TL proceeds were not allowed to be transferred by original holders to third parties who might have use for TL funds. This involved a disadvantage for Turkey too: in view of the then still quite uncertain economic future of the country foreign companies could hardly be expected to take major investment decisions at the time and most trade creditors would, to be on the safe side, therefore prefer the foreign exchange option (except in cases of unofficial prepayments).

Heavy criticism from many trade organizations and official bodies abroad and the conviction that the repayment proposal for trade arrears really left some room for improvement led to the presentation of a revised debt settlement proposal for trade arrears at the end of May 1980. Although the central bank was not formally made the legal debtor, the registration of trade arrears and the debt servicing were centralized with the central bank. Besides the US Dollar, DM and Sfrs. were also accepted as settlement currencies. Interest rates offered remained, however, unsatisfactory compared with market levels. For trade claims in US Dollars 7 per cent per annum, for DM 4 per cent per annum and for Sfrs. 3 per cent per annum were offered as fixed rates throughout the 10-year repayment period.

Most improvements were made on the TL option. Trade creditors could register first for payment in foreign exchange and within one year change to payment in Turkish Lira (the period was subsequently extended into 1981). The transfer of TL proceeds to third parties who had use for them for purposes allowed under the settlement scheme was permitted. (The original hesitation against this possibility came largely from – not entirely unjustified – fears of the Turkish authorities that this might lead to disorderly speculative trading of rescheduled trade claims.) Several foreign banks were authorized by the Turkish central bank to act as intermediaries between sellers and buyers of rescheduled trade arrears. The exchange rates to be applied for conversion of foreign exchange claims into Turkish Lira were substantially improved for the most important purposes allowed under the scheme and tied to the current rates, although not for all purposes permitted.

The logistic task of registering and counter-checking about one hundred thousand individual trade arrears was immense. It spread over many months. Banks, chambers of commerce and business associations all over the Western world were busy advising and assisting exporters on how to submit their claims for registration. In the end, of the estimated amount of US$ 1.8 billion, only arrears of approximately US$ 1.2 billion were registered, out of which some US$ 400 million for payment in Turkish Lira and only two thirds for repayment in foreign exchange. Very soon thereafter a kind of market developed for trade arrears convertible into Turkish Lira. In view of the extremely tight and very expensive domestic market for bank loans quite a number of foreign companies felt the need to improve the working capital of their Turkish subsidiaries and saw the advantage of obtaining Turkish Lira for capital increases at a fraction of their normal cost. Initially transactions were done at discounts on the face value of trade claims of around 75 to 78 per cent. By now prices between 40 and 50 per cent of face value are being paid. A considerable portion of the applications for new foreign capital investments in Turkey filed with or approved by the Turkish authorities in the last year represents capital increases under the TL option of the trade arrears settlement.

While the economic downslide was being arrested the internal political situation kept deteriorating in 1980. Terrorism seemed to grow out of hand. Work days lost in strikes during the first three quarters were more than during the eight preceding years together. On September 12 government was taken over by the armed forces and parliament was dissolved. A few days later the spiritus rector of the economic policy in Turkey, Türgut Özal, was appointed Deputy Prime Minister. The National Security Council endorsed and supported the continuation of his economic concepts. This also opened the way to put into practice the tax reform package which two preceding governments had been unable to put through the parliament.

In the same month of September exports began to pick up. It soon became apparent that relative growth was faster in the export of processed and manufactured goods than in the traditional agricultural exports. In 1981 Turkish exports grew by 53 per cent to approximately US$ 4.5 billion against imports of US$ 8.8 billion. Workers' remittances increased from US$ 2.1 billion in 1980 to US$ 2.5 billion. OECD governments again pledged special assistance to Turkey for nearly US$ 1 billion. These favourable developments permitted the restrictions on imports to be relaxed to some extent and remaining bottlenecks in oil supplies to be removed. With domestic demand still kept in check and industry, on average, not yet working on full capacity, import requirements have probably not yet regained their full dimensions. Even so, Turkey already achieved a real growth rate of 4.4 per cent in 1981.

A revision of the bank agreements of 1979 is presently about to be concluded. In 1981 the Turkish Government requested the banks to consider an extension of repayment terms under the rescheduling and the New Money Loan agreements. Creditors agreed to extend the grace period from three to five years and the repayment period from four to five years. For each of the two additional years of grace this means a net debt relief to the country of approximately US$ 700 million, which coincides partly with the period during which the OECD special assistance is likely to run out. The extension of the repayment terms of the bank agreements was not only to bring the debt service burden more into line with Turkish repayment capabilities but also to contribute to public economic assistance for Turkey.

Based on the economic performance to date the Turkish authorities – and not only they – are confident that by 1984/85 the country will be able to earn the foreign exchange to pay for its entire imports and even a portion or all of the current interest service. In 1983 the special financial assistance to Turkey is likely to be terminated and the stand-by facility of the IMF should by then be fully drawn. Trade from government sources and from supranational institutions should thereafter consist only of project loans. It therefore becomes vital for Turkey that by 1984/85 the – probably still substantial – additional borrowing requirements can be met at commercial conditions on the international financial market and by medium term suppliers' credits under national export credit insurance schemes. Notwithstanding the very remarkable success achieved up to now by the new economic policies the Turkish authorities are fully aware that it will still take years of effort to stabilize the Turkish economy further. One of the most difficult problems for the second half of this decade will probably be the rising unemployment which is now over 16 per cent. Viewed from today it appears as yet unlikely that average real growth rates high enough to allow a noticeable reduction of unemployment can be achieved without again incurring external deficits of a size which the balance of payments cannot support.

IV. GENERAL CONSIDERATIONS

In the three first sections the paper attempts to outline the parallel developments in the Turkish economy and the rescheduling and new financial assistance. But for a few remarks, the domestic and the – no less important – international political background has been omitted although political aspects had a substantial impact both on the economic deterioration and the subsequent path to recovery.

The following remarks are not exhaustive, in part subjective, and probably disputable. Some of them are not, or not equally, applicable to every case of country debt rescheduling. Operations of this nature for countries like Bolivia, Sudan, Peru, Zaire, Madagascar, Indonesia, Costa Rica, to name but some, besides those which are presently on many people's minds have only a limited range of similarities and are highly individual in other respects.

The following remarks try to generalize the more important aspects:

- Of the three main groups of factors, political, economic, and operational, the political aspects are probably the most important, controversial and – at least seen from a banker's point of view – the most irritating. To a great extent political factors are at the root of economic developments which lead to reschedulings, when political conditions make it difficult or impossible to carry out economic adjustment policies which are painful or unpopular. Likewise, while a rescheduling is under way or has been concluded, domestic – or even international – political considerations may stand in the way of thorough economic reforms and halfheartedly implemented measures may jeopardize the effects of the rescheduling. In the case of Turkey two attempts to arrest the economic deterioration did not bring the desired results.
- Unfortunately, this applies at times also to a country's – or its government's – attitude towards turning to the International Monetary Fund in time. Reluctance to do so may have different reasons: the fear that this may be considered an official distress signal, public opinion critical of supposed foreign or international interference with sovereign affairs, or just the conditionality of the Fund. At times continued lending by international banks, especially when on inadequate terms, may even contribute to some extent to enabling a country to postpone a call on the Fund, and add to the dimensions of the subsequent problems.
- If a government in the end approaches the IMF and negotiates a stand-by agreement it may – rightly or wrongly – feel that corrective economic measures overtax the political and/or social elasticity of the country.
- Another question may be whether the external political situation is favourable or unfavourable to temporary special financial assistance from foreign public sources.
- The possible economic scenarios surrounding a debt rescheduling can be so varied that there is little use in dwelling on this subject. Therefore only a few remarks: the main objective of a debt rescheduling should be a phasing-out of maturities to such an extent that the debt servicing on the rescheduled debt does not afterwards unduly restrict the capability of the

country to raise and service the new foreign debt necessary to cover reasonable future balance of payments deficits and capital needs.

– This objective can, however, be in conflict with the terms which commercial – and even public – creditors may be prepared to concede. In 1968/69 Indonesia obtained for the rescheduling of its foreign debt, mostly with public creditors, repayment terms of thirty years including fifteen years of grace with the additional option of having the interest for the first eight years capitalized. Such conditions would be hardly conceivable today for government creditors, not to speak of commercial creditors. In any large rescheduling involving different types of creditor it is quite difficult to strike the right balance between the conditions which public and commercial creditors are willing or able to concede and the extent to which adjustment policies can bring about economic improvements and the time that will take – and finally the size and terms of additional assistance necessary to help the country over the adjustment period. Such assessments are made additionally difficult by wide fluctuations of exchange rates and interest levels on the international markets or unforeseen shifts in the terms of trade.

– The operational side naturally requires first of all a comprehensive review of the composition of a country's foreign debt by maturity structure, currencies, different kinds of debt and different types of creditor. This already determines to a large extent how to organize a debt rescheduling. In order to avoid unnecessary additional damage to its creditworthiness a debtor country will try to negotiate a debt rescheduling rather than unilaterally declare a moratorium. As individual or collective negotiations with hundreds of creditors of the same category would be impossible, the work group approach, with or without separate advisors to the debtor government, has meanwhile proved quite suitable. The normal preference would be to combine major creditor positions with a suitable geographical coverage when composing the work group, as member banks would have to check back frequently with other creditor banks in their area to make sure that terms under negotiation remain within the acceptable in order to achieve in the end a participation quota which comes as close as possible to 100 per cent. This obliges parties to agree on a reasonable balance between the needs and wishes of the debtor country and preferences of the creditors. While the number of bank creditors should always remain within manageable limits there is hardly a way for thousands of trade creditors with very different types of claim for exports of goods, services, royalties, dividends, short-term or long-term, against private firms or public entities or banks to effectively organize themselves worldwide.

Only a few of them may be in a position to enter into direct negotiations with the central bank or the government of a debtor country. In substance most of them have hardly any choice but to accept the rescheduling terms offered by the debtor country if they do not want to see their claims left in a very unclear legal and financial situation. Obviously the strongest position is that of government creditors (leaving aside the World Bank which never accepts a formal rescheduling); they are much fewer in number, can coordinate their views and policies directly without even the intermediation of a working group; and the debtor countries may be looking to them for new financial assistance during the recovery period.

– The position of the International Monetary Fund is a unique one. Formally it is not a creditor; it does not conclude loan agreements. Given its undisputed experience, and with no political or commercial interests of its own, it may not be the easiest, but is certainly the most neutral partner when it comes to the evaluation of the debtor countries' economic reform programme. Even when the size of its own financial contribution may not give the Fund a great weight of its own in one or another case, its role is compounded when creditor governments and bank creditors make their agreement to the proposed rescheduling conditional upon the conclusion of a stand-by agreement with the IMF. The conclusion of a stand-by agreement, especially when the disbursement period is not a very short one, is in turn one of the most convincing arguments vis-à-vis banks when, alongside with the actual rescheduling, new credit facilities for the debtor country are required for starting the recovery programme, at which point many commercial creditors start asking themselves whether this would not mean throwing good money after bad.

– The principle of equal treatment can become a very thorny issue. It is certainly a very fair principle, for an outright moratorium. It may, however, not be very practical in the case of a comprehensive rescheduling operation which involves several different classes of creditor with many different kinds of claim. It would not be surprising if trade creditors, for instance, held the view that their claims, at least if they had not sold on deferred payment terms, should be treated more favourably than claims from public creditors under capital aid or claims from banks who professionally lend money and incur credit risks. Banks in turn may argue that rescheduling conditions must not exceed the limits of what is acceptable in the market; otherwise too many creditor banks might refuse and try to recover their money by any form of legal action open to them, which in turn would disrupt the already difficult payment situation of a debtor country even more.

— The cooperation and coordination between the IMF, governments, banks and trade creditors practised in the case of the rescheduling of the Turkish debt was probably as close as it could possibly be, which does not mean that it was very close. The Fund has to take care of its neutrality and impartiality, also of its privileged access to economic data of a country, which may not normally be available to commercial parties. While it can and does cooperate closely with governments it can probably not go beyond a rather loose exchange of views and information with banks; it can hardly agree to joint negotiations with representatives of banks. But even this modest level of contact should be sufficient to avoid the Fund and banks being at cross-purposes. The same applies by and large to the relationship between a group of governments and banks, even if some governments may have closer dialogues with banks in their respective countries than others. In turn, banks are usually to some extent aware of the problems which their customers may have with the debtor country.

Growing country exposure in the balance sheets of banks, mounting international debt of many non-oil exporting developing countries and the growing number of country debt reschedulings during more recent years have made supranational financial institutions and national banking supervisory authorities increasingly aware of the problems involved in international lending by banks and their very substantial role in the recycling process. Wider and more accurate and detailed financial information about growth and structure of country indebtedness and official regulations and guidelines may be helpful and sound but they cannot relieve banks of their responsibility to make their own assessment of country risks and their own judgement on how much individual country risk they can afford.

NOTES

1. The scheme was not entirely new, it had already once been operative at the beginning of the 1970s but was abolished after a short while.

2. The names of the schemes were adopted from the corresponding Turkish concepts; the wording is misleading.

3. In view of the very sensitive political situation between the government, the opposition, the news media and the public, the Turkish government adopted the procedure of anticipating the Fund's expectations and introducing unpopular measures on its own as an almost regular feature of its relationship with the Fund.

4. Further financial assistance granted to Turkey in mid-1979 consisted of a US$ 150 million programme loan and a US$ 300 million project loan from the World Bank and US$ 150 million project aid by the European Investment Bank.

5. In practical terms: after the necessary investment approvals had been obtained, TL proceeds could be used to pay up capital in new Turkish subsidiaries or capital increases in existing ones for meeting local expenditure or fixed investments or to improve the financial structure of the subsidiaries.

Subsidiaries were naturally not entitled to use the capital increases for importing foreign equipment. Direct capital investments made under this option, however, were immediately entitled to transfer of the corresponding dividends and to the retransfer of capital after several years.

Chapter XX

THE STABILITY OF THE INTERNATIONAL FINANCIAL SYSTEM: CAN WE COPE WITH THE RISK?

by *Tom de Vries*

The outline suggested by our secretary general, Prof.Dr. H.W.J. Bosman, provides a convenient way to approach the subject assigned to me, and I intend to follow its main lines. In doing so, I shall concentrate on policy issues and bring in analysis only insofar as it is relevant to those issues.

I. THE LACK OF INTERNATIONAL SUPERVISION AND CONTROL AND ITS EFFECTS

National banking systems are subject to supervision and control by the monetary authorities so as to ensure the public good of stability. The reason is twofold: first, commercial banks are private institutions, yet they provide a major part of the money supply, and secondly, commercial banking is inherently a fair weather activity. The liquid reserves of a bank are only a minuscule proportion of its liquid liabilities and its capital is only a small portion of the total credit it has extended. If the fair weather turns foul the liquid reserves of the bank are quickly exhausted, it must sell assets in distress, which therefore fall in value, and thus its solvency is threatened. In order to guard against these dangers within the national context, the monetary authorities supervise the banking system so as to minimize unwarranted risks and in return stand ready to provide the banking system with needed liquidity in time of stress.

This apparatus is absent when it comes to international credit. For lack of an international authority, there is no adequate supervision of the international activities of the major banks. Insofar as they are carried out by branches and subsidiaries located abroad transactions take place largely outside the purview of the national monetary authorities. The inevitable concomitant is that there is no lender of last resort. While it is true that the efforts of some central banks have resulted in a beginning of supervision over the elusive transactions with the cooperative framework of the Bank for International Settlements in Basle, the very cooperative nature of these efforts, and therefore the need for general agreement, have put severe limits on their progress. Central banks often reflect, at least to a degree, the interests of the domestic banking system that they supervise. It is therefore not surprising that some central banks, notably the Bank of England in contact with a banking community making large profits on its international credit business, were for a long time opposed to measures of supervision that might restrict that lending. Other central banks in a different position, e.g. the Netherlands Bank, had an easier time insisting on the dangers inherent in the uncontrolled expansion of international credit and pleaded for both prudential and macroeconomic surveillance and control.[1] As noted, these differences of opinion and of financial interest have slowed progress.

The sudden increase on two separate occasions of the price of energy and the enormous surpluses accumulated as a consequence by a few major oil producers, with small populations and therefore unable and unwilling to suddenly spend their vastly increased income, has been an important immediate cause for the expansion of international bank lending to an annual rate of some 25 per cent. The large surpluses of a few oil producers were necessarily matched by large deficits in other countries. The stronger industrial countries were able to reduce their deficits rather quickly and thus push them on to the less developed countries. Hence, a need for "recycling" from the oil surplus countries to the developing countries arose. In the beginning, rather than cautioning prudence, the monetary authorities were pleased to see the commercial banking system take on this role of recycling. In fact, they positively encouraged it.

In this way an old well-known and often recurring dangerous situation arose for the banking community. The banks were flooded with sizable deposits from the oil producing surplus countries. Faced with an abundance of loanable funds banks have always found it difficult to maintain their former prudential standards. An early example of this phenomenon is provided by the Medici Bank, and the following account of it deserves our attention:

"As deposits poured in, it became increasingly difficult to find suitable investments . . . Rather than refuse deposits, the Medici succumbed to the temptation of seeking an outlet for surplus cash in making dangerous loans to princes. This policy proved to be their undoing as it had caused the ruin of the Peruzzi in the fourteenth century and later brought the Fuggers to the brink of bankruptcy. It seems that there was a general weakness . . . to drift from private banking into government finance. Nearly always the results were catastrophic".[2]

Since 1973 the commercial banks have not acted differently. Faced with surplus deposits the bankers almost started to "sell" loans to foreign governments. Anthony Sampson reports overhearing a contact man telling a group of American bankers at one of the Annual Meetings of IMF and World Bank: "I have good news for you. I think they will be able to take your money".[3] Although journalistic exaggeration may be at play here, the basic tendency is confirmed by the action of successive Treasurers-General of the Netherlands, who upon arriving at the Annual Meetings have invariably found it necessary to tell their secretaries that they absolutely refused to see any banker, in order to drive home the point that the Netherlands had no intention to take up international bank loans. It is also confirmed by the experience of many Executive Directors of the International Monetary Fund when the Fund was considering borrowing from private institutions. They were besieged by bankers anxious not to miss out on the possibility of lending money to the Fund.

In short, the banking system has for years accepted the deposits offered to it and has tried to find outlets for them only afterwards. For a long time this was a riskless procedure because any money for which no borrower could be found quickly could be placed with other banks in the inter-bank market, thus spurring on other banks to look for potential debtors. It is small wonder that in this process the solidity of the debtor as well as prudence suffered. The result has been twofold. On the one hand, a large number of countries have become saddled with a heavy debt burden, part of which has been contracted not to increase productive capacity and thus the capability to service the international debt, but to pay for oil. The second result has been to reinforce international inflationary tendencies.

This brings us to a curious paradox in the attitude of policy makers and analysts alike. In an age of monetarism domestic monetary expansion is closely watched and much emphasis – in my view too exclusive an emphasis – is placed on strict control. But if a bank grants a credit, not to the friendly neighborhood drugstore but instead to some foreign government or entity, it is no longer called monetary expansion but becomes part of "international capital movements", and while monetary expansion is "bad", somehow international capital movements are "good". This is, of course, an untenable position and so are the policy attitudes that have followed from it.

After experiencing for more than a decade the increasingly destructive impact that serious and continuous inflation has on the productivity and the possibilities for sustainable growth of market economies, the industrial nations are now embarked with grim determination on a policy to break the addiction of their economies to the inflationary drug. This is not an easy or a quick process and it involves severe withdrawal symptoms. The less developed countries as well as domestic business in the industrial countries have no choice but to undergo the cure. But it is far from certain that all of them will be able to withstand the difficult process of withdrawal without suffering a nervous breakdown. The question then becomes what to do to alleviate such a breakdown. While the answer is not immediately obvious, it *is* clear from the start that the solution cannot lie in administering a new dose of addictive inflationary liquidity.

Thus the initial consequences of the absence of effective international supervision and control, together with the needs and opportunities created by the enormous "oil surpluses and deficits" of the 1970s have been a rapid acceleration in industrial bank lending. Three factors have come together of late to produce some reversal of this tendency. The deposits offered to the banking system by the main oil producers and lent to the developing countries constituted a drain on the domestic circulation in the major industrial countries where these banks are headquartered. This process could go on only as long as the "headquarter" countries pursued an easy monetary policy. With the shift to strict monetary policies in the major industrial countries the leeway for this "international" monetary expansion has been reduced. At the same time, and not unrelated, the surpluses of the oil producers are diminishing rapidly. Lastly, the political risks involved in international bank lending are becoming more apparent. The result has been less easy access by deficit countries to bank credit.

II. AN INTERNATIONAL LENDER OF LAST RESORT?

An apparently easy way out, at least for imprudent banks and their debtors, would be for the central banks of the major industrial countries to act as lenders of last resort if the international credits turn sour. While the going was easy and large profits were to be made there was much opposition from both banks and debtors against the involvement of the monetary authorities with international lending. In the words of a report published by the Group of Thirty: "Bankers and their customers in developing countries have expressed concern that unnecessarily 'fussy' regulations could hamper the smooth operation of the recycling process".[4] But there is less objection from either banks or debtors against the central banks bailing them out if the going gets rough and difficulties accumulate. The central banks are unlikely to oblige and they would be unwise to do so.

The role of the central bank as a lender of last resort is intimately connected with its role as supervisor of the domestic banking system and with its macroeconomic task of maintaining the stability of the currency through policies designed to ensure an appropriate rate of money growth. Central banks have rightly accepted the role of lender of last resort as an integral part of those functions but they have always, equally rightly, refused an obligation to act as a lender of last resort without supervisory authority. They would, of course, be put in an untenable position if they were made responsible for preventing a breakdown in activities over which they could exercise no control. Since much international lending has taken place outside the control of the central banks, they have refused to give any clear guarantee that they will act as lender of last resort should any difficulties arise from it.

It is hard to see how they could act differently. If the central banks did give such a guarantee, the result would simply be a temporary new acceleration of the international money creating machine. At the same time, the central banks are, of course, aware that a serious breakdown in the international financial system would have serious consequences for the domestic banking system which it is their task to avoid. Faced with this dilemma they have expressed themselves in very cautious terms:

"3. In view of the present volume of international bank lending and of its prospective future role, the Governors are agreed on the importance of maintaining the soundness and stability of the international banking system".

"5. Recognizing that individual banks, or the international banking system as a whole, could in future be exposed to greater risks than in the past, the Governors reaffirm the cardinal importance which they attach to the maintenance of sound banking standards – particularly with regard to capital adequacy, liquidity, and concentration of risks. To this end they place high priority on bringing into full effect the initiatives already taken by the Committee on Banking Regulations and Supervisory Practices with regard to the supervision of banks' international business on a consolidated basis, improved assessment of country risk exposure, and the development of more comprehensive and consistent data for monitoring the extent of banks' maturity transformation".[5]

The central bank governors have thus put their main emphasis on sound banking standards. There is no mention anywhere of central bank credits to stabilize the international banking system. If mishaps were to occur as a result of past independent actions by commercial banks, they will be on their own and will be the first to bear the brunt. But it is of course the task of the central banks to see that such an unhoped for development would not degenerate into a cumulative deflationary downturn.

The central banks must therefore walk a tight-rope: the commercial banks must be fully aware of their responsibility to avoid a financial crisis and of the consequences for their profits should one occur. Yet the central banks must prevent any mishap from bringing down the entire banking system. Given the limited supervisory powers of central banks in the international domain, it is difficult to see any neat solution. We are faced with the consequences of economic interdependence analyzed already 15 years ago.[6] The jurisdiction of the central banks extends over a much smaller geographical area than the domain of the large commercial banks and this renders effective action by the monetary authorities extremely difficult, both in the upswing and in the downswing.

The position of the International Monetary Fund is similar and simpler at the same time. The IMF has no responsibility at all for the activities of the commercial banks either in the international or in the domestic sphere. The Fund has however warned its member countries when they were accumulating international indebtedness at an unsustainable rate, and the Fund has adopted a policy of granting credit to its members only on the basis of a program that would lead to a sustainable balance of payments position – one that could be maintained without excessive international borrowing. Thus on a "micro-level", that is to say in its relations with *individual* countries, the Fund has tried to strengthen the external debt position of its members. But in the absence of a wider authority it has had to leave the macroeconomic aspects unaddressed.

In any situation of stress the responsibility of the Fund would not be towards the commercial banks but to member countries that might get into difficult situations because of it. Thus, if it became necessary to see to it that some mishap would not spread to the financial system as a whole, it would be the task of the Fund to assist individual debtor countries, whereas the position of individual commercial banks would be closer to the field of competence of the central banks. This separation of responsibilities has been underlined by a hardening over the past year of the Fund's policy against "bailing out banks". The Fund is insisting with an increasing emphasis in a number of cases that the banks maintain their exposure in member countries with which the Fund is about to conclude a credit arrangement, and it has refused in a number of cases to finally approve such an arrangement unless and until such parallel sources of financing were assured.

III. POSSIBILITIES AND LIMITATIONS OF A LENDER OF LAST RESORT

Thus our provisional conclusion is that it is neither possible nor desirable to take any formalized action at this time that would ensure that there would be a lender of last resort. But there are institutions that have responsibilities to prevent any difficulty from magnifying itself: the central banks to shield their national monetary system against the consequences of mishaps in international credit and the IMF to help its member countries overcome the consequences of a break-down in international lending. It may be useful to speculate on what this may mean for future developments.

It was pointed out above that central monetary institutions have always resisted an obligation to extend financial assistance for activities beyond their control. But the reverse relationship is also at work. If monetary authorities are in the end drawn into a crisis after all, they have always insisted on increased powers of supervision.[7] The increasing tensions manifesting themselves at present in international financial relations may thus *over the long run* lead to increased supervision of the international financial system and hence to increased responsibilities of central monetary authorities to shield the system against liquidity crises through lending of last resort.

It is, however, necessary to be clear about what a lender of last resort can and cannot do. Kindleberger in his history of financial crises presents himself at the outset as a supporter of the existence of a lender of last resort.[8] Yet he concludes that as overexpansion mounts, "it must be slowed down without precipitating a panic. After a crash has occurred, it is important to wait long enough for the insolvent firms to fail, but not so long as to let the crisis spread to solvent firms needing liquidity",[9] and his final conclusion is modest: "At most there remains a presumption, but perhaps not a strong one, that halting a cumulative deflation helps shorten the depression that follows".[10]

A lender of last resort can provide liquidity but not solvency, although the question as to who is still solvent also depends on whether a panic is stopped or not. Thus there is no safe haven for the imprudent creditor or debtor. They will have to face the consequences of any past mistakes. Lenders of last resort can prevent the damage from spreading to the sounder creditors and debtors but they will insist that in doing so their powers of supervision be extended. There is, moreover, a clear division of responsibility between the Fund having to look after debtor member countries and national central banks with their responsibility for commercial banks headquartered in their country.

42

IV. PRUDENTIAL CONTROLS AND SELF-HELP BY COMMERCIAL BANKS

If there are clear limitations on a number of approaches by monetary authorities towards strengthening international bank lending under present institutional arrangements, the authorities can make an important contribution by enhancing the prudential control over those of the international activities of the banks that fall or can by consolidated reporting be brought under their national supervisory jurisdiction. This is precisely what a number of central banks have done. Under present circumstances such a policy could be further reinforced by requiring the commercial banks to write off certain parts of their international credits about which questions have arisen. Of course, details of implementation would not have to be made public. But the rules would require commercial banks to increase their equity reserves against certain of their international credits.

If such a policy were adopted, it would of course in time become known which national monetary authority did require their commercial banks as well as their overseas branches and subsidiaries to submit to such strict rules, and which monetary authorities did not. In times of tension such as the present one, there might be a tendency for a two-tier interbank market to develop. In one tier commercial banks under strict national rules would deal with one another. But there might develop some hesitancy to deal with some banks that were not subject to strict rules. In this way the stricter regime would be likely to spread, at least if adopted initially for a large enough segment of the banking community. It would thus have to involve the US authorities, who have been in the forefront of moving to stricter supervision of the international activities of their commercial banks.

However, the main contribution must come from the commercial banks themselves as they tighten up their own prudential guidelines and resolve to abide by them more strictly in the future than they have done in the past. Yet the question remains whether the banks are able to fully evaluate country risk including political risk.

The question has also been raised in the outline presented to the authors whether a voluntary safety net of commercial banks could strengthen the system. It is important to recognize that such a scheme would be concerned mainly with transfers of equity from strong banks to banks having suffered important losses. There are indeed historical examples of such transfers in actual conditions of crisis, because the spreading of a crisis would engender a fall in the value of the assets of all banks and would involve all of them in losses that would rise as the crisis would spread. But it would be unreasonable to expect prudent banks to underwrite in advance imprudent banks whose action they could in no way control.

The monetary authorities cannot provide insolvent banks with equity either. When acting as lenders of last resort they can provide liquidity to the banking system – whether or not this is judged desirable but they cannot provide capital. It is therefore essential that the individual commercial banks provide themselves with an additional financial safety margin.

V. ARE PRESENT APPROACHES ADEQUATE OR SUFFICIENT?

I have some difficulty with the last question in the outline presented to the authors. The crime of negligence has already been committed in some cases and there are no approaches or arrangements that can any longer prevent it. If some banks and debtors have become overextended, they will have to face the consequences of past lighthcartedness.

At best, this will take the form of a painful process of reducing the bank's overextension and of a difficult policy of adjustment to a harsh world on the part of the debtor country. At worst, accidents will occur on the road to a more solid situation. As explained above, it is the difficult task of the monetary authorities to see to it that, insofar as necessary, the adjustment process takes place steadily and continuously while avoiding accidents, or at least ensuring that such accidents as are no longer avoidable remain localized and are prevented from endangering the entire financial system.

The present tensions are in part the result of the judgment of the commercial banks that the so-called "sovereign risk" was nil since countries cannot go bankrupt. But the risk is not that the sovereign will go bankrupt, but that he will disappear as a result of revolution or be unable to pay as a result of social strife. These dangers have become more apparent of late.

The problems may be less severe than in the winter of 1975-76 when the Federal Reserve Board staff is reported to have had a problem list that included 12 of the 50 largest bank holding companies in the United States.[11] A major part of international lending is now done by a rather small number of banks and their financial position strengthened from 1976-80. But there are at present risks of a political origin and they seem to be spreading as the banks have suddenly and in a somewhat irrational and herdlike fashion stopped extending credit to all Eastern European countries after the difficulties in Poland. [As this paper is being sent off, the question has suddenly arisen how Argentina's military action and the freezing of its assets in London will affect that country's credit-worthiness and ability to service its debt by new borrowing. Reserve centers have always frozen the assets of countries with which they got into serious political difficulties. But such risks have been discounted too heavily by bankers. It is by no means certain that international bank lending has been fully in tune with today's political realities.]

Thus the situation is far from easy. But I do not want to be misunderstood. I am not implying that a crisis is likely or that there is a 50/50 per cent chance of one. Things may well fall back into their old channels and confidence may revive. But even a 10 per cent or a 5 per cent chance of crisis is too high for comfort. The Group of Thirty noted already a year ago "In short, there are default risks in international lending; in our view, these risks are increasing".[12]

Nor are present stresses limited to international credit activities. More generally, there is at present a tension between indebtedness, both international and domestic, and the possibility of the real economy to bear that debt burden. The extension of bank credit and the excessive inflation of the past fifteen years are of course intimately connected. Now that the authorities in most industrial countries are determined to break the back of inflation, growth and economic activity in the real sector necessarily suffer temporarily. The ability of the real sector to service its debt is therefore diminished at the same time that the anti-inflationary policy at last results in positive real interest rates. This puts a second burden on the real sector for it is no longer relieved of part of its indebtedness by the decline in the value of money. The resulting tensions and uncertainties lead to a further rise in real interest rates, increasing the difficulties of servicing the debt.

In the mid-1970s financial stress originated within the banking sector as some banks incurred big losses by speculating in the exchange markets. This time, any difficulties are more likely to originate with the debtors rather than with the banks, and may occur with either foreign or domestic loans. Significant losses through domestic bankruptcies might well be the bigger danger. In the United States, for instance, a "Chrysler bail-out" is unlikely to be repeated if some other major firm were to get into difficulties.

The authorities are now applying stricter policies in answer to the more difficult situation. Bank supervision in a number of important countries such as the United States, Germany and Switzerland has been considerably reinforced, and international cooperation, difficult as it is, is progressing. The International Monetary Fund has become stricter in its credit policies since the spring of 1981. The change in policy came about at the request of the main industrial countries, and because the commercial banks stopped considering a country's credit arrangement with the Fund as a "seal of good housekeeping'' as long as the Fund pursued the lax standards prevalent at that time.

In their turn the banks have also become more prudent in their lending. Instead of adjusting the credit volume to the funds available, they now make more careful judgments about what credits they do or do not wish to extend and adjust their financing activities accordingly. This tendency must be further encouraged. There is no better way to induce the banks to persist in such an attitude than to implement balanced rules requiring them to keep equity reserves that are realistic in the light of a sober evaluation of the credit risks that they have assumed.

NOTES

1. The position of the Netherlands Bank is clearly set out by one of its Directors, Dr. H.J. Muller, in its *Quarterly Bulletin*, September 1979, pp. 36-44.

2. Raymond de Roover, *The Medici Bank*, New York University Press, 1948, p. 66. (Also published in London: Oxford University Press).

3. Anthony Sampson, *The Money Lenders*, New York: The Viking Press, 1982, p. 12.

4. *Balance-of-Payments Problems of Developing Countries*, A report by a Study Group, Group of Thirty, 1981, p. 12.

5. Communiqué of central bank Governors issued by the BIS on April 14, 1980. Its background is discussed by Dr. J.A.H. de Beaufort Wijnholds in the *Quarterly Bulletin* of the Netherlands Bank, June 1980, pp. 38-48.

6. Richard N. Cooper, *The Economies of Interdependence*, New York: McGraw-Hill, 1968, pp. 91-94, and *passim*.

7. The gradual extension of "conditionality" by the IMF is but another example of this tendency.

8. Charles P. Kindleberger, *Manias, Panics, and Crashes*, A History of Financial Crises, New York: Basic Books, 1978, p. 4.

9. *Ibid.*, p. 180.

10. *Ibid.*, p. 215.

11. *Ibid.*, p. 175.

12. *Op. cit.*, p. 11.

Chapter XXI

SAFEGUARDING THE INTERNATIONAL BANKING SYSTEM:
PRESENT ARRANGEMENTS
AND A FRAMEWORK FOR REFORM

by *Richard Dale*

The stability of the international banking system clearly depends on a number of factors which are beyond the immediate control of national supervisory authorities. In particular the global economic environment, the volatility of both interest rates and exchange rates, the willingness and ability of debtor countries to undertake balance of payments adjustment and the availability of non-bank sources of credit, all have a direct bearing on the riskiness of international lending. The present paper, however, focuses more narrowly on the role of prudential regulation and the scope for increased international co-operation in this area. The discussion is divided into three parts: a comparative overview of national regulatory arrangements; a critical appraisal of the present approach to international co-ordination; and alternative proposals for improving the supervisory system.

I. A COMPARATIVE OVERVIEW OF PRUDENTIAL BANK REGULATION*

National authorities use a variety of approaches and controls to foster bank safety and soundness and to maintain confidence in the banking system as a whole. The techniques employed may be broadly categorised into (1) preventive regulation designed to limit the risks incurred by banks; (2) schemes which offer protection to depositors in the event of bank failure; (3) support provided by national monetary authorities to banks experiencing liquidity difficulties (the lender of last resort function).

---

* This discussion, which is based on a study undertaken by the author for the Group of Thirty, is confined largely to leading industrial countries other than Japan.

(1) *Preventive Regulation*

Among measures aimed at controlling the levels of risk incurred by banks are those concerned with market entry, capital and liquidity adequacy, functional diversification, foreign currency exposure and concentration of loans (including country risk exposure). National practices in each of these areas, as well as the method and scope of bank examinations, are considered below.

(a) *Entry Controls*

National banking laws generally require the formal authorisation of all banks. Typically, the conditions specified include a reputable management and some minimum amount of subscribed capital, although the capital requirement may or may not apply to branches of foreign banks, may or may not be formalised and where formalised can range from the equivalent of US$ 1 million (Switzerland) to nearly US$ 10 million (UK).

In addition, several countries apply an economic need criterion and in such cases market entry may be restricted or (as in Italy) suspended altogether with a view to avoiding excessive and destabilising competition. Foreign-owned banking operations may be formally limited to subsidiaries (as in Canada) on the grounds that locally incorporated entities can be more effectively regulated by the host authority, or largely confined to branches (as in Singapore) on the grounds that a branch enjoys the full support of the group to which it belongs.

(b) *Capital Adequacy*

Minimum capital requirements apart, banks are generally required to maintain an appropriate relationship between capital on the one hand and total assets, risk assets or liabilities on the other. The definition of capital for this purpose varies: for instance, subordinated debt may be excluded (as in West Germany), included up to a limit of between 10 per cent (Switzerland) and 50 per cent (Netherlands) of total capital or included without formal limit (France). Some countries (Italy, Canada) do not formally regulate capital adequacy, some (including the US) make an essentially judgemental assessment while most European countries apply solvency ratios of varying complexity which incorporate different weightings for different categories of risk asset. In this last case, the weightings applied to similar categories of asset may vary: for instance, whereas Switzerland applies a premium weighting to all foreign assets, the Netherlands accords a preferential zero weighting to loans to foreign governments. In addition, one country (Belgium) applies a solvency ratio which discriminates in favour of larger banks on the grounds that risk is a function of bank size. Because of the variety of methods used in capital adequacy assessment it is not possible to make direct comparisons between requirements in different countries.

Finally, capital adequacy may or may not be assessed on a worldwide consolidated basis and branches of foreign banks may or may not be separately assessed. However, the general trend is towards consolidation as indicated by recent moves in this direction by Switzerland and Germany. Even so, the treatment for consolidation purposes of non-wholly owned subsidiaries and minority interests may vary.

(c) *Liquidity*

As with capital adequacy, approaches to the measurement and control of liquidity vary considerably. Some countries (including the US and Canada) choose not to lay down formal prudential liquidity requirements while others (notably the Netherlands, Germany and Switzerland) apply a number of ratios designed to limit the extent of maturity mismatching in banks' balance sheets. In a few cases (for instance France and Italy) banks which accept short-term deposits are regulated separately from those engaging in longer-term banking business and limits may be placed on their term lending. Where regulation is formalised, distinctions may or may not be drawn on the assets side between primary, secondary and other classes of liquidity, on the liabilities side between interest-sensitive money market funds and retail deposits, and on both sides of the balance sheet between local and foreign currency items (France, for instance, requires separate calculations for local and foreign currency liquidity). Although most national schemes seek to classify liabilities both by maturity and volatility with a view to determining the extent to which funds may prudently be used as a basis for maturity transformation, direct comparisons of permissible transformation are not possible because of the variety of assessment methods and other institutional differences.

In general, liquidity regulation does not take account of undue deposit concentrations, although the Netherlands impose extra liquidity requirements on "large item" liabilities. Some countries (notably the US) assess liquidity on a worldwide consolidated basis, others (such as France) confine their assessment to banks' domestic offices, while branches of foreign banks may or may not be included in the assessment process.

(d) *Functional Diversification*

Typically, banks are restricted as to the kinds of business they can engage in with a view to limiting the risks they may incur. However, these restrictions are imposed in a number of different ways. Some countries (notably the US, Canada and France) prohibit the mixing of banking and non-banking business within the bank entity itself, while permitting participation in at least some kinds of non-banking activity through bank holding companies, subsidiaries and/or minority interests. Other countries (such as the Netherlands) permit the bank entity itself to engage directly in non-banking business but limit the scope for investment in non-bank companies. A third approach (also illustrated by France) permits a wider range of activities to be undertaken by a special category of separately regulated universal banks. Finally, some countries (such as the UK, Switzerland and Germany) impose few restrictions on the kinds of business banks may engage in, whether directly or through affiliates. In the case of international operations, restrictions may be relaxed so as to enable foreign branches of domestic banks to compete more equally in their country of residence with local banks.

(e) *Foreign Currency Exposure*

Whereas all countries monitor banks' foreign currency exposure and seek to ensure adequate internal control procedures, there are a number of approaches to regulating risks in this area. Some countries (including the US, Canada and France) prefer to avoid general limits or norms, others (such as the Netherlands and Switzerland) apply incremental capital requirements to uncovered positions, while a third group imposes guidelines or formal limits on aggregate (and in some cases individual) foreign currency positions. Where limits are indicated, they are generally stated as a percentage of bank capital and, in the case of aggregate exposure, vary from 15 per cent (UK) to 30 per cent (Germany). The monitoring and control of foreign currency exposure may (as in the US) embrace foreign branches and subsidiaries of domestic banks, but in some other cases foreign subsidiaries are excluded, while the treatment of local branches of foreign banks also varies.

(f) *Loan Concentrations and Country Risk*

Countries frequently impose formal or informal limits on loans to a single borrower. Stated as a percentage of the lending bank's capital, the limits vary between 100 per cent (Italy) and 10 per cent (US), subject to varying definitions of capital for this purpose. In general these lending ceilings are not directly applicable to country risk exposure involving several borrowing entities from the same country, although in the US case the 10 per cent limit may so apply where there is a common source of repayment.

Most countries do, however, attempt to measure and monitor their banks' country risk exposure. Sometimes (as in the US) this is done on the basis of worldwide consolidated data, embracing cross-border and non-local currency loans to foreign borrowers adjusted for third party guarantees. In other cases (for instance Italy, France and Germany) exposure data is not fully consolidated while risk transfers via third party guarantees are generally ignored. Several countries (notably Germany, Switzerland and Belgium) require banks to report their methods of country risk evaluation, while the US and UK categorise countries into three risk classes in order to assess the extent of banks' exposure to potential defaults (in the US the country designation provides a basis for "listing" loans). Such exceptions apart, regulators do not generally seek to form an independent judgement as to individual countries' financial prospects. Nor do regulators impose an absolute limit on total country risk exposure, although Switzerland applies a special premium capital requirement to banks' foreign assets.

(g) *Bank Examinations*

The role of bank inspections in the regulatory process varies considerably from country to country. At one end of the spectrum is the US where regular on-site examinations lie at the heart of the supervisory system and where examiners are required to provide a composite rating of each bank on a standardised basis. At the other end of the spectrum is the UK which eschews bank inspections in favour of a surveillance system based on interviews with management backed by extensive reported data. Routine on-site bank examinations, where they occur, may be conducted by the supervisory authorities' own inspectorate (as in the US, Canada, Italy and France), special auditors appointed and paid for by the authorities (Belgium), auditors licensed by the authorities and subject to special statutory duties (Switzerland) or general auditors (Germany). Examinations may take place annually (as in Canada), every 3-4 years (Italy) or at intervals varying between 1 to 2 and 10 years depending on the size and standing of the institution concerned (France). Several countries confine on-site examinations to banks' head offices while few (a major exception being the US) conduct routine inspections of banks' foreign establishments.

(2) *Deposit Insurance*

Most countries either have or are in the process of introducing deposit protection schemes. Such schemes may be official (as in the US, Canada and UK) but frequently they are organised by the banking industry itself with the encouragement of the authorities (as in France, Germany and the Netherlands). Countries which do not have any formal deposit protection arrangements include Italy and Luxembourg. Typically, the protection offered is territorial in scope, thereby embracing branches and subsidiaries of foreign banks and excluding deposits with foreign offices of domestic banks. However, there are exceptions: the German scheme covers foreign branches of German banks and the Belgian scheme excludes local branches of foreign banks. Foreign currency deposits may or may not be protected, there are variations in the eligibility of both deposits (for instance certificates of deposit) and depositors (most but not all schemes exclude interbank deposits) and the size limits imposed on protected deposits vary from the equivalent of under US$ 20,000 (Canada, UK) to US$ 100,000 (US). In addition the UK and Swiss schemes (as proposed) require that the depositor bear a certain proportion of any loss. Some schemes provide for a deposit protection fund while others are unfunded but in either case banks are typically subject to a flat-rate contribution based on the total of their deposits (France being an exception in providing for a scale of graduated contributions which discriminates in favour of larger banks).

(3) *Lender of Last Resort/Emergency Measures*

Generally, national monetary authorities are prepared to provide financial assistance to commercial banks experiencing temporary liquidity difficulties, although in some centres (for instance Luxembourg and Hong Kong) there is no indigenous central bank to perform this function. A distinction can usually be drawn between routine use of the official discount window, where the conditions of access are often formalised, and emergency support operations undertaken on a discretionary basis. In general, emergency assistance is provided directly by the central bank but in some countries (Belgium and Germany) it is channelled through a special fund jointly established by the authorities and the commercial banks. Frequently, such assistance can be offered only to solvent institutions and on a secured basis but some authorities (including the Bank of England) have broader powers of intervention where insolvency is threatened. In other cases (as in the US and Canada) the deposit insurance agency has lender of last resort powers which, at least in respect of potentially insolvent institutions, may exceed those of the central bank. Finally, whereas emergency assistance is typically extended directly to troubled banks at a penal interest rate, this is not necessarily the case: for instance, the Bank of Italy's practice is to lend at below market rates to institutions prepared to acquire/assist the problem bank (a technique also employed by the US deposit insurance agency).

As a matter of policy, the precise scope of the lender of last resort function in the emergency assistance sense is not publicly stated. However, national authorities generally look to foreign parent institutions for the support of their local subsidiaries and for this purpose some countries (notably the UK and Canada) require non-legally binding undertakings or "letters of comfort" from the parent acknowledging responsibility to support its subsidiary beyond the limits of strict legal liability. On the other hand, in the US subsidiaries as well as branches of foreign banks have a formalised right of access to the central bank's discount window, at least for the purpose of routine liquidity assistance.

Among other emergency measures that may be available are the regulation of interest rates to ease pressures on financial markets (as provided for in France and the Netherlands), assisted mergers, the appointent of caretaker managers to troubled banks and special liquidation proceedings. In this last case, local branches of foreign banks may, in the event of the parent institution's failure, be subject to separate liquidation proceedings in which case (as under New York State and Dutch law) branch creditors sometimes enjoy a preferential claim to branch assets.

II. INTERNATIONAL CO-ORDINATION OF REGULATORY PRACTICES

The disparities in national regulatory arrangements outlined above may undermine the stability of the international banking system in various ways. This is most obviously the case where there are regulatory gaps, as in the supervision of foreign currency liquidity, the inspection of banks' foreign establishments and the monitoring of country and foreign exchange risks incurred by foreign subsidiaries. But the uneven severity with which certain types of regulations are applied may give rise to similar problems and distortions. In either case, banks may gravitate to the least regulated financial centres,[1] seek to substitute unregulated for regulated risks,[2] book or even transfer high risk loans to offices located in permissive jurisdictions[3] and more generally take advantage of the fact that even in tightly controlled regimes such as the US, foreign offices of domestic banks are authorised to engage in a wider range of activities than would be permitted domestically.[4] In addition, banks headquartered in permissive centres may enjoy competitive advantages, such as higher financial leverage, thereby enabling them both to operate on narrower spreads and to increase their market share at the expense of more tightly constrained institutions. Moreover, closely regulated banks are, through the interlocking mechanism of the inter-bank market, exposed at one remove to the risks incurred by less regulated banks, suggesting that within the global banking system now emerging bank safety is indivisible.

Disparities in national preventive regulation are compounded by serious inconsistencies in the protection afforded by deposit insurance schemes and lender of last resort arrangements. So far as the former are concerned it has been noted above that some countries have no formal deposit protection, that the geographic and currency coverage of existing schemes varies and that limitations as to the ownership, type and size of deposit subject to protection differ from country to country. Nor is there any common understanding as to the proper role and purpose of deposit protection. For instance, in the US the Federal Deposit Insurance Corporation has, through its policy of assisted mergers for failing institutions, moved de facto towards a policy of 100 per cent insurance coverage for all depositors with a view to sustaining confidence and stabilising the domestic financial system.[5] By contrast, the proposed UK and Swiss deposit insurance schemes are designed merely to provide a limited form of consumer protection which, as it involves the depositor in some proportion of any loss, cannot be expected to prevent bank failures via precautionary deposit withdrawals.[6] In the event of a general crisis of confidence these differences between national deposit protection arrangements could prove highly damaging since depositors would presumably be induced to shift their funds to those banks and financial centres promising the greatest protection. As matters now stand, this could entail large-scale deposit withdrawals from the Euro-currency market as well as from certain domestic financial markets, and a corresponding influx of funds into perceived safe haven countries such as the US (see p. 385 below).

Lender of last resort arrangements also vary considerably from country to country. As indicated above, some financial centres lack such a facility, certain central banks are statutorily limited to providing assistance to solvent banks on a secured basis while in other cases the relevant authorities may exercise a broad discretion to support even insolvent institutions. More importantly there appears to be no common understanding as to the appropriate allocation of national responsibilities in this area. The Basle communique of September 1974 merely assured the financial community that "means are available" for the provision of temporary liquidity to the Euro-markets and "will be used if and when necessary".[7] However, it is clear that whereas central banks generally accept responsibility for providing liquidity support to the foreign branches of banks headquartered within their jurisdiction (as illustrated by the support provided by the US Federal Reserve to Franklin National's London branch)[8] no such understanding exists in relation to foreign subsidiaries and consortium banks. For instance, it has been widely reported that differences exist between the US and UK authorities as to who is responsible for supporting the subsidiaries of US banks in London,[9] while similar differences appear to exist between the West German and Luxembourg authorities over support for the Luxembourg subsidiaries of West German banks.[10] Moreover, since Luxembourg hosts a large number of bank subsidiaries from West Germany and elsewhere, and has neither an indigenous lender of last resort facility nor deposit protection scheme, banks within its jurisdiction may be regarded as particularly vulnerable to precautionary deposit withdrawals in the event of a general crisis of confidence.*

Finally, effective exercise of the lender of last resort function may be impeded by differences in national laws relating to liquidation. As noted above, some countries require separate liquidation proceedings for local branches of foreign banks while conferring on branch depositors a preferential claim to branch assets. In such cases a foreign central bank may have difficulty in obtaining collateral from the branch concerned. It may then be forced to curtail its liquidity assistance, as illustrated by the US Federal Reserve's (eventually successful) attempts to prevent a sudden collapse of Franklin National Bank by collateralising the assets of its London branch.[11]

The establishment in 1975 of the BIS Committee on Banking Regulations and Supervisory Practices (The "Cooke Committee") represents the response of national supervisory authorities to the dangers posed by uneven regulatory practices. The Committee, whose members are drawn from the Group of Ten Countries plus Switzerland, seeks not to harmonise prudential regulations but rather to mesh disparate national regulatory regimes with a view to ensuring that all banks are supervised according to certain broad principles.[12] Accordingly the Committee's initiatives have focused in particular on the allocation of national supervisory responsibilities, for which purpose the Basle "Concordat"[13] of 1975 establishes general guidelines, as well as the monitoring of banks' international business on a consolidated basis.[14]

The Basle approach to international co-ordination of regulatory practices suffers from a number of drawbacks. To begin with, the scope and effectiveness of the Cooke Committee's initiatives have been severely limited by the need to rely on voluntary compliance with informal and broadly drawn guidelines. The difficulties involved can be illustrated by considering the five

---

* Events surrounding the failure of Banco Ambrosiano's Luxembourg subsidiary have since tended to confirm these observations.

main recommendations of the Basle Concordat which have been described as "a cornerstone of international supervisory co-operation":[15]

1. The supervision of foreign banking establishments is the joint responsibility of parent and host authorities. This principle is linked to the Concordat's further recommendation that supervision should be adequate as judged by both host and parent authorities. However, since national supervisory standards vary, some countries have been more reluctant than others to share or delegate supervisory responsibilities. The US approach, for instance, appears to be based on the view that "bank supervision in foreign countries, at least from an examination standpoint, is generally non-existent or far inferior to that in the US".[16] Accordingly, the US authorities have declined to rely on foreign supervisors' surveillance of US banks' international operations[17] while imposing extensive reporting requirements on the US offices of foreign banks relating to their parent institutions' structure and condition.[18]

2. No foreign banking establishment should escape supervision. This principle requires further elaboration since a bank may be supervised for some purposes but not others. Regulatory practice suggests that certain foreign banking establishments continue to escape supervision in the areas of liquidity management and foreign exchange risk while by no means all are subject to on-site inspections.

3. The supervision of liquidity should be the primary responsibility of the host authorities. A crucial ambiguity is, however, introduced here by the qualification that for foreign currency liquidity (embracing the entire Euro-currency market) "local practices and regulations may be less important and not all host authorities accept the same degree of responsibility". Even within its limited field of application, the liquidity principle is not always followed. For instance the Bank of England has not up to now imposed liquidity guidelines on UK branches of foreign banks, an omission which it concedes, "is not wholly consistent with the views expressed by the Basle Committee of Banking Supervisors in 1975".[19]

4. The supervision of solvency is essentially a matter for the parent authority in the case of foreign branches and primarily the responsibility of the host authority in the case of foreign subsidiaries. This allocation of responsibilities is not easily reconciled with the Cooke Committee's advocacy of solvency supervision on a consolidated basis, but is nevertheless one of the more widely accepted principles. Even so, Canada has declined to accept the principle of delegated parental responsibility in relation to branches of foreign banks and has therefore limited all foreign banking in Canada to the subsidiary form.[20]

5. Practical co-operation should be promoted by the exchange of information between host and parent authorities and by the authorisation of bank inspections by or on behalf of parent authorities. Some progress has been made here in the form of statutory provisions for information exchange and bilateral inspection agreements but bank secrecy laws in some countries continue to present problems[21] while recent European legislation aimed at protecting commercial information has introduced new difficulties (for instance, as a result of such legislation the US authorities are no longer able to carry out inspections of US banks' French establishments).

From the above it may reasonably be concluded that the principle of voluntary co-operation which underlies the Cooke Committee's activities has failed to deliver a fully operational agreement on the allocation of regulatory responsibilities. In addition the Basle Concordat suffers from two major omissions. Firstly, the regulatory practices of non G-10 countries fall outside its purview, although attempts are being made to bridge this gap through discussions with a recently constituted group of supervisors from offshore centres, for which Hong Kong is currently co-ordinator. Given the uncertain progress in implementing the Concordat among G-10 countries it would, however, be unrealistic to expect anything but painfully slow progress in securing the effective participation of others.

The second key omission relates to the lender of last resort function, a subject which has evidently been reserved to the Bank Governors themselves rather than to the Cooke Committee. All that need be said here is that it is difficult to envisage a generally acceptable allocation of regulatory responsibilities which does not take account of the responsibility for emergency support, since there is an understandable reluctance on the part of central banks to extend financial assistance to institutions whose activities are beyond their control and a corresponding reluctance to yield supervisory control over institutions for which they remain financially responsible.

The foregoing comments should be interpreted not as criticism of the Cooke Committee but of its very restricted mandate. Nor need it be supposed that the Committee is superfluous, since the relationships that it has forged between national supervisory authorities could prove to be particularly valuable during crises conditions in the absence of formal guidelines and procedures. What does emerge, however, is the need to address the question of international supervisory co-operation on a more fundamental level.

III. PROPOSALS FOR REFORM

It has been suggested that because the Euro-currency market is part of a closed system, funds can always be recycled back to banks experiencing deposit withdrawals and that prudential regulation of banking in this area is therefore superfluous.[22] Such a view is, however, difficult to accept if only for the reason that automatic recycling, in whatever form, to banks suffering liquidity problems must be expected to undermine market discipline and thereby give rise to the familiar moral hazard problems that underlie the modern theory of bank regulation.[23]

More typically, the Euro-currency market has attracted the critical attention of those who believe that supervision of international banking is seriously deficient, particularly in today's disturbed financial conditions. Among the many proposals for reform, which have tended to focus on emergency arrangements rather than preventive regulation, the following are prominent:

An International Deposit Insurance Corporation (IDIC)

Professor Grubel has proposed[24] that an IDIC should be established to insure deposits placed with the foreign offices of multinational banks since such deposits, at least when denominated in non-local currencies, are generally unprotected by national insurance schemes. Apart from questions of funding and membership, the major difficulty with such a scheme is that participating countries would be required to protect deposits in banks subject to widely differing regulatory standards. Professor Grubel suggests that this problem might be overcome by authorising the IDIC to impose uniform regulatory standards on the foreign banking establishments concerned and also by setting variable insurance premia related to risk class. However, since the risks incurred by parent banks and their foreign offshoots are not at present severable (see below) this must be regarded as an incomplete solution to the problem.[25]

An International Lender of Last Resort

There have been a number of proposals for a supra-national lender of last resort backed by the major central banks. However, precisely the same difficulties arise here as with the IDIC proposal. Above all, no central bank can be expected to underwrite the activities of banks outside its own regulatory purview, given the present wide variations in regulatory practice.

Private International Safety Net

Dr. Guth, a chief executive of Deutsche Bank, has floated the idea of a private safety net jointly organised by international banks and designed to provide prompt liquidity assistance on a reciprocal basis.[26] However, Dr. Guth has evidently had second thoughts about the practicality of such a proposal on the grounds that a broad-based scheme would necessarily involve considerable risks for the creditor banks who could not be assured of the solvency of the institutions to which they are lending, while a narrowly based scheme would have undesirable consequences for those seen to be excluded from the magic circle.[27] Here again, it may be supposed that commercial banks, like central banks, would be unwilling to enter into open-ended commitments vis-à-vis institutions subject to widely differing regulatory standards.

An Inter-Bank Commitment Network

Professors Dean and Giddy have suggested[28] that central banks should encourage the establishment of a network of formal, guaranteed credit commitments between commercial banks by charging an annual fee for acting as lender of last resort. The fee, which would be based on the amount of each bank's uninsured deposits less the amount of any guaranteed commitments obtained from other banks, would be set high enough to induce banks to switch to inter-bank commitments to back up the bulk of their inter-bank liabilities. However, this ingenious proposal presents a number of difficulties. If the unconditional commitments are for any length of time, the committed bank risks being embroiled in insolvency problems as a result of a deterioration in the potential borrower's condition during the period of the commitment. While if the commitments are rolled over at frequent intervals, the protection afforded may be correspondingly limited. In any event, the scheme would presumably only work if all major countries participated, since commitment fees, by adding materially to the cost of financial intermediation, would impose a competitive penalty on the banks concerned. Furthermore, an international agreement along these lines presupposes agreement also on lender of last resort responsibilities.

A common characteristic of these and other proposals for reform is that they attempt to isolate one aspect of the regulatory problem without giving due consideration to the broader policy dilemma posed by the presence of multinational banking networks, straddling numerous regulatory jurisdictions. Accordingly, before examining what improvements might be made to better safeguard the multinational banking system it is necessary to identify the contradictions implicit in the present fragmented regulatory structure.

The most flagrant contradiction lies in the fact that "soft" financial centres (i.e. those adopting permissive regulatory standards) are able to free ride at the expense of "hard" centres. More specifically, a financial centre which seeks to attract banking business by offering a permissive regulatory environment does not bear any prudential cost in the form of a risk premium payable on locally placed deposits. The additional risks attaching to banking business transacted within the centre are not separately "priced" for the simple reason that any difficulties encountered by foreign banks established there are, either by law, convention or commercial necessity, transferred to the respective parent institutions in their countries of origin. Put another way, because parent banks are generally obliged to absorb the financial strains experienced by their foreign subsidiaries and branches, deposits placed with a loosely regulated foreign banking establishment can be no more risky in a *credit* sense[29] than deposits placed with its more tightly regulated parent bank. The net result is that financial centres at best have little incentive to control the risks incurred by foreign banks to whom they are host, and at worst may be induced to attract banking business by engaging in what has been described by a former Chairman of the US Federal Reserve Board as "competition in laxity".[30]

The obvious dangers in this situation are aggravated by the likelihood, during periods of financial stress, of large and destabilising movements of funds both between financial centres and between banking groups. This latent instability is explained by a number of related factors. Firstly, whereas in normal conditions depositors with offshore banks look primarily to the parent institution for security, in times of crisis they can be expected to look beyond the parent bank to the protection afforded by national authorities.[31] Secondly, the principle of parental responsibility that applies to commercial banks is not necessarily followed by central banks in their lender of last resort capacity (that is to say, foreign subsidiaries cannot automatically look to their parent banks' central bank for emergency assistance) and is typically rejected in favour of the territorial principle by national deposit insurance schemes. Finally, official support facilities of both kinds may be available in the national authorities' local currency only. Under these circumstances depositors may reasonably perceive that their funds will, in extremis, be better protected if placed as local currency deposits in the domestic banks of a hard financial centre than they would be if held as Eurocurrency deposits with foreign banking establishments in a soft financial centre. The likely result is an exodus of funds not merely from soft centres themselves but from banking groups headquartered in such jurisdictions.[32]

It should be noted that three regulatory principles combine to bring about this state of affairs. Firstly, there is the principle of national autonomy in regulatory matters which permits wide variations in national regulatory practice. Secondly, there is the neutrality principle which requires that all banks resident in a particular country should be subject to regulatory parity under that country's laws. Thirdly, there is the principle of parental responsibility which asserts that parent institutions are financially responsible for their foreign establishments.

In order to correct the self-destructive tendencies implicit in the present regulatory structure it is necessary to reverse at least one of the above principles. Conceptually the simplest but in practical terms the most far-reaching reform would be to harmonise national regulatory arrangements through a binding international agreement. Central bankers have consistently rejected such an idea although Governor Wallich, of the US Federal Reserve Board, has recently spoken of the need for greater co-ordination of national laws in the following terms:

"Growing integration across national boundaries makes it important for us to attain a better insight into banking laws and practices elsewhere. These laws and practices, which increasingly affect the condition and competitiveness of the banks we supervise, differ enormously across nations. Probably most of us believe that there are good reasons for doing things the way we do. We are not proposing to change each other's ways. But there is a need to individually adapt our national laws and practices into an international framework so that they will accommodate and support each other instead of creating gaps or even conflicts that could pose a threat to the worldwide system".[33]

Clearly, one of the major problems of harmonisation would be to secure the participation of all countries having financial centre status, although this might be achieved if participating countries refused (a) to host banks headquartered in non-participating countries and (b) to permit their own banks to establish offices in such jurisdictions. Financial centres which declined to co-operate might then find themselves left out in the cold – or at the very least relegated to fringe banking status.

An alternative approach would be to reverse the neutrality (or national) principle which currently governs regulatory practice in favour of the so-called equity principle.[34] This would mean that all foreign branches/subsidiaries of a single group would be subject to the same regulatory regime as the parent bank in its country of origin. Under the equity principle soft centres could no longer free ride on hard centres since the foreign banks they host would be permitted to engage in activities no riskier than those of their parent institutions.

On the other hand, such a regime would present numerous practical problems, among which would be the possibly adverse competitive implications of banks conducting business on unequal terms within the same jurisdiction and the likelihood that many countries would not wish to host banks subject to external regulation.

The third approach to reform is to abolish the principle of parental responsibility by preventing risk transfers from foreign banking establishments to their parent institutions. As matters now stand parental responsibility rests on legal, conventional and commercial constraints: banks are legally committed to their foreign branches[35] while commitment to their foreign subsidiaries is secured through letters of comfort extracted by host authorities,[36] persuasive pressure from home authorities,[37] and commercial self-interest arising from the fact that the credit standing of a bank would be seriously damaged by the demise of a subsidiary.[38] The legal and conventional commitments could, presumably, be severed by confining foreign operations to the subsidiary form and limiting financial dealings between parent banks and their foreign subsidiaries. More problematical is the commercial interdependence of banks within a single group, although this difficulty might be mitigated by, for instance, prohibiting foreign subsidiaries from trading under their parent bank's name. In any event further consideration might be given to ways of fragmenting risks within the multinational banking network.[39] If such fragmentation were achieved, soft financial centres would have to bear the burden of risks incurred within their jurisdiction, a consideration which would presumably be reflected in a risk premium on locally placed deposits. Regulatory diversity would therefore no longer give rise to free rider problems.

Any one of the above three approaches to reform would provide an incentive, now altogether lacking, for soft financial centres to put their house in order. Alternatively, those centres which failed to respond to the new arrangements would experience a loss of banking business based on the perception among depositors that their funds would, even during periods of financial stability, be safer elsewhere. Furthermore, initiatives of the kind proposed would help to reduce the risk of a sudden movement of funds from soft to hard centres during times of crisis. Under harmonised rules there would be no basis for such a movement: the equity principle would, by facilitating the extension of parent authority support arrangements to all foreign banking establishments, remove the incentive for shifts between centres (though not necessarily between different banking groups); and the risk severance approach would contribute to the same objective by obliging depositors to focus on local jurisdiction risks while encouraging offshore centres to strengthen their own financial support schemes.

IV. SUMMARY AND CONCLUSIONS

The comparative survey of prudential bank regulation undertaken in the first section of this paper reveals a wide variety of regulatory practices and standards even among the major industrial countries. The second section identifies some of the dangers arising from uneven regulation and underlines the uncertain progress of international co-operation in this area. The final section considers some recent proposals for reform before addressing the broader policy issues raised by the co-existence of diverse national regulatory jurisdictions and multinational banking networks knowing no jurisdictional boundaries. The major conclusion to be drawn from this discussion is that more far-reaching initiatives than those so far undertaken or even proposed are necessary to remove the internal contradictions implicit in the present regulatory free-for-all.

NOTES

1. See, for instance, the Bundesbank's comments on the impact of uneven solvency requirements in "Bank Supervision on the Basis of Consolidated Figures", *Monthly Report of the Deutsche Bundesbank*, August 1981, pp. 25-27.

2. The tendency for banks pursuing high risk strategies to speculate in the foreign exchange markets, where official supervision is particularly difficult, is well documented. For a notorious example see Joan Spero, *The Failure of the Franklin National Bank*, Columbia University Press, 1980, pp. 63-67.

3. An example of this practice is cited by Michael Pakshong, former Managing Director of the Monetary Authority of Singapore, in "Supervision of a Regional Financial Centre", *International Conference of Banking Supervisors*, London, July 5-6, 1979, *Record of Proceedings*, p. 20.

4. "FINE: Financial Institutions and the Nation's Economy", a compendium of papers prepared for the FINE Study, Book I, *Evidence Submitted by the Board of Governors of the Federal Reserve System*, 94th Congress, 2nd Session, 1976, p. 499.

5. For an explanation of the FDIC approach see *Statement on FDIC Procedures in Handling Failed or Failing Banks*, presented by Irvin Sprague to Commerce, Consumer and Monetary Affairs Subcommittee, Committee on Government Operations, House of Representatives, July 16, 1981.

6. Since the transaction cost of switching deposits from one bank to another may be considered close to zero, the prospect of *any* loss will presumably be enough to induce depositors to withdraw their funds.

7. Cited in Spero, p. 155.

8. Andrew Brimmer, *International Finance and the Management of Bank Failures: Herstatt versus Franklin National*, paper prepared for presentation before a joint session of the American Economic Association and the American Finance Association, September 15, 1976, p. 49-50.

9. See, for instance "Fed offers new Approach to Eurocurrency Market" *New York Times*, September 3, 1974; Spero, pp. 156-68; Jack Guttentag and Richard Herring, "The Lender of Last Resort Function in an International Context", *Working Paper no. 9-82, Rodney L. White Centre for Financial Research*, p. 28-32.

10. A Bundesbank director has commented as follows on the question of liquidity assistance to Luxembourg subsidiaries of West German banks: "The central bank that is responsible for the parent bank cannot be under any obligation to provide foreign subsidiaries with liquidity so long as this central bank has no means of exerting any influence on the foreign subsidiaries, for instance by fixing reserve requirements". Panel contribution by S. Burger, *International Conference of Banking Supervisors*, London, 1979, pp. 31-32.

11. Spero, pp. 148-9.

12. The Cooke Committee's approach to international financial co-operation is described by its Chairman, Peter Cooke, in *Developments in Co-operation Among Banking Supervisory Authorities*, a paper presented to the Conference on the Internationalisation of the Capital Markets, New York City, May 19-21, 1981.

13. *Report to the Governors on the Supervision of Banks' Foreign Establishments*, Committee on Banking Regulations and Supervisory Practices, Basle, 26 September 1975. This report was approved by the Governors in December 1975 and released to the public in March 1981. See also H.J. Muller, "The Concordat: A Model for International Co-operation", *De Neder-landsche Bank N.V. Quarterly Statistics*, 1979, vol. 2, pp. 84-91.

14. See *Consideration of Banks' Balance Sheets: Aggregation of Risk-Bearing Assets as a Method of Supervising Bank Solvency*, Committee on Banking Regulations and Supervisory Practices, Basle, October 1978.

15. Peter Cooke, "Developments in Co-operation Among Banking Supervisory Authorities", p. 8.

16. Compendium of papers prepared for the FINE Study, Evidence Submitted by Comptroller of the Currency, p. 385.

17. Compendium of papers prepared for the FINE Study, Evidence Submitted by Board of Governors of the Federal Reserve System, p. 546.

18. These requirements are embodied in the Federal Reserve's reporting form FRY-7 which was first proposed in October 1979 and finally introduced in modified form in February 1981, following strong protests from foreign banks and supervisory authorities. Several national authorities have argued that FRY-7 is in conflict both with the national principle of regulation and also with the Basle Concordat. See, for instance, Comments Regarding Docket No. R-0256 (Proposed Form FRY-7) and Docket No. R-0257 (Proposed FRY-8F): Bank of England, 11 January 1980; Deutsche Bundesbank, 11 March 1980; EEC Commission, 16 June 1980; et al.

19. "The Measurement of Liquidity", *Bank of England, Discussion Paper*, March 1980, p. 13.

20. The Canadian Inspector General of Banks has expressed the Canadian authorities' approach as follows: "I should also note that in one way we have not been prepared to follow completely the precepts of the Concordat. The Canadian Bank Act requires, and will continue to require, the Inspector General of Banks to protect the creditors, and also the shareholders of banks operating under it. It was my predecessor's view, with which I have concurred, that we could not pass that responsibility for the creditors back to the foreign parent or another supervisory authority. Our proposals therefore provide for the entry of foreign banks only in the subsidiary form. It is obviously our view that a well run and supervised subsidiary can survive the bankruptcy of the parent bank". Panel Contribution by William Kennett, International Conference of Banking Supervisors, London, 1979, pp. 70-71.

21. See *Banking Secrecy and International Co-operation in Banking Supervision*, Committee on Banking Regulations and Supervisory Practices, Basle, August 1981.

22. "... if a large depositor withdraws funds from a bank, the bank can borrow readily in the inter-bank market, for the [Euro-currency] market is a closed system. Withdrawals from a particular bank come back into the market or can be brought back into the market one way or another – provided, of course, that the key central banks and in particular the Federal Reserve do not withdraw funds from the system altogether. That feature marks a big difference from national banking where there is the possibility that the public will withdraw deposits in favour of holding currency . . . so the usual modes of government intervention – deposit insurance, reserve requirements and close surveillance over portfolios of banks – would not seem applicable to the Eurocurrency market, whatever their merits may be today in national banking systems". Summary remarks by Richard N. Cooper in Gary Hufbauer (ed.), *The International Framework for Money and Banking in the 1980's*, Georgetown University Law Center, 1981, p. 9.

23. The issue of moral hazard is, for instance, discussed by several authors in Franklin Edwards (ed.), *Issues in Financial Regulation*, New York, McGraw-Hill, 1977.

24. Herbert Grubel, "A Proposal for the Establishment of an International Deposit Insurance Corporation", *Princeton Essays in International Finance*, No. 133, July 1979.

25. A foreign branch may, for instance, be brought down by the activities of the parent institution in its country of origin. Given such interdependence, an acute free-rider problem would arise from the co-existence of (a) national regulatory regimes embracing parent banks and (b) a separate international regulatory regime covering foreign establishments.

26. "Guth Underlines Microeconomic Risks for Private Banks in Recycling Funds", *International Herald Tribune*, June 16, 1980.

27. See Dr. Wilfried Guth, *Trends in International Banking*, Speech given at the 34th International Banking Summer School on August 31, 1981, in Timmendorfer Strand, Federal Republic of Germany, pp. 12-13.

28. James Dean and Ian Giddy, "Averting International Banking Crises", *Monograph Series in Economics and Finance*, Salomon Brothers Center, New York University, 1981.

29. Foreign currency deposits placed in offshore banking centres may, however, be subject to "country risk" in that the host authorities could conceivably apply exchange controls preventing the transfer of such funds to other centres. See Robert Z. Aliber, *Exchange Risk and Corporate International Finance*, John Wiley and Sons, 1978, pp. 86-88.

30. Arthur F. Burns, *Reflections of an Economic Policy Maker*, American Enterprise Institute, 1978, p. 365.

31. This proposition is supported by the behaviour of Euro-bank deposit rates during periods of uncertainty such as 1974: See Guttentag and Herring, *The Lender of Last Resort Function in an International Context*, p. 24. It is also consistent with the argument advanced by Guttentag and Herring that financial markets tend to ignore low-probability events: see *Financial Disorder and the Eurocurrency Markets*, Mimeograph, University of Pennsylvania, March 1981.

32. During the 1974 Euro-market crisis funds moved both between banking groups and from the Euro-markets into the United States. The latter move was partly compensated by the recycling of funds from American parent banks to their foreign branches but there is, of course, no saying that in such a situation individual parent banks will necessarily gain what their foreign branches lose. See Brimmer, *International Finance and the Management of Bank Failures*, pp. 52-54.

33. Remarks by Governor Wallich at the International Conference of Banking Supervisors, Washington, DC, September 24, 1981, p. 2.

34. The equity principle has been advocated by a former Director of Financial Institutions in the EEC Commission. See H.R. Hutton, "The Regulation of Foreign Banks – A European Viewpoint", *Columbia Journal of World Business*, Winter 1975, p. 113.

35. For a full analysis of this relationship under US law see Patrick Heininger, "Liability of US Banks for Deposits Placed in their Foreign Branches", *Law and Policy in International Business*, vol. II, 1979.

36. The legal status of letters of comfort is examined in Jacques Terray, "La Lettre de Confort", *Banque*, no. 393, March 1980.

37. Official pressure was, for instance, brought to bear on United California Bank of Los Angeles to support its majority owned Basle affiliate when the latter incurred large commodity trading losses in 1970. See Francis Lees, *International Banking and Finance*, John Wiley and Sons, 1974, pp. 42-43.

38. See, for instance, views of the Board of Governors of the Federal Reserve presented in Compendium of papers prepared for the FINE Study, Book I, p. 499 and comments by Rt. Hon. Gordon Richardson, Governor of the Bank of England, International Conference of Banking Supervisors, London, 1979, pp. 8-9.

39. For an analogous proposal to fragment risk within the US domestic banking system by "building a wall" between bank holding companies and their bank subsidiaries, see Fischer Black, Merton Miller and Richard Posner, "An Approach to the Regulation of Bank Holding Companies", *Journal of Business*, 1978, vol. 51, no. 3, pp. 400-402.

REPORTS ON THE COLLOQUIUM

Chapter XXII

STABILIZING A FRAGILE INTERNATIONAL FINANCIAL SYSTEM

by *Alexander K. Swoboda*

Webster's Dictionary defines the adjective fragile as "easily broken or destroyed; frail; delicate". The papers presented at this Colloquium reveal divergent views as to how fragile the world economy and the international financial system actually are. Yet a feeling of unease, not to say deep worry, prevails. It may be appropriate, in presenting some general remarks on the over-all theme of this meeting, to focus on three broad questions. First, in what sense and why do we increasingly perceive the world economy and financial system to be fragile? Second, what are the features of international lending that are most troublesome in this context? Third, what policies are appropriate to insure a greater stability of the international financial system?

In attempting fragmentary answers to these questions, I shall draw freely on the papers presented at this conference. I will, however, refrain from trying to summarize their findings leaving that difficult task to Dr. Diwok. I will thus only occasionally refer specifically to the views of authors of papers even when theirs and mine overlap or clash. In keeping with my assignment, this will leave me free to propose a selective, personal, and occasionally provocative menu of issues for discussion.

I. HOW FRAGILE A WORLD ECONOMY?

In many ways, the performance of the world economy over the past few years is evidence of a great deal of resilience rather than of fragility, at least by longer historical standards. Growth rates in both the industrialized and developing world have been low in the late 1970s only as compared to those of the "golden" 1960s. They have been fairly high in comparison to pre-World War II experience. The world economy has weathered two oil shocks, the demise of Bretton Woods, accelerating inflation, high real interest rates, financial market turbulence, and growing political uncertainty without plunging into depression. Inflation, at last, seems to be decreasing significantly in a number of major industrialized countries.

Yet, even on the broad macroeconomic front, the world economy appears to be more fragile at the threshold of the 1980s than it was at the outset of the 1960s. That fragility derives partly from longer-term developments, partly from more recent ones. Some indicators of macroeconomic performance are presented in Table 1. Comparing the 1960-1970 with the 1970-1979 periods, three characteristics stand out: first, a general worsening in terms of growth rates, except for the low-income countries; second, the contrast between the relatively sharp drop in industrialized countries' growth and the relatively mild drop in that of middle-income oil importers; third, the general acceleration of inflation in the 1970s. Part B of Table 1 focuses on selected industrial countries for the more recent 1978-1981 period. The further deterioration of growth in 1980-1981 appears clearly together with the stubbornness of inflation. The concomitant increase in unemployment is equally worrisome. The average weighted rate of unemployment of seven larger industrial countries was 3 per cent for the period 1963-1972, according to IMF estimates.[1] By 1975 it had risen to 5.6 per cent, fell back to 5 per cent in 1979, and rose again to 6.6 per cent in 1981. Current account disequilibria have also been rising dramatically in the 1970s as indicated in Table 2 which is reproduced from the World Bank's *World Development Report 1981*. Finally, as Table 3 indicates, nominal interest rates have been rising steadily throughout the period, realized real rates of interest increasing sharply in the past few years.

In brief, there is a marked deterioration in the world economy's macroeconomic performance in the 1970s as compared with the 1960s. The worsening of macroeconomic performance is, however, not necessarily synonymous with increased fragility. The sequels of over fifteen years of rising inflation, of increasing payments disequilibria and, more recently, of high real interest rates and volatility of financial market variables do, however, leave the world economy more susceptible to further exogenous shocks. Combined with a deterioration of national and international financial relationships (to which I return below), they may also lay the ground for endogenous instability and crises in the international financial system.[2]

In this context, the recent abrupt increase in volatility of financial market variables is particularly striking and worrisome. Table 4 documents this increase in variability. It lists the standard deviation of monthly changes in three groups of variables (asset prices, monetary, and real variables) for five countries, over 1966,2-1981,9 and four subperiods. Similar patterns arise for all countries, though individual variations remain. Most striking is the

Table 1. *Indicators of macroeconomic performance*

A. *Growth and inflation rates: 1960-1979*

	Average annual growth rate of GDP (weighted)		Average annual inflation rate (median)	
	1960-1970	1970-1979	1960-1970	1970-1979
Low-income countries	4.5	4.7	3.0	10.8
Middle-income oil exporters	6.5	5.5	3.0	14.0
Middle-income oil importers	5.9	5.5	3.0	12.2
Industrial market economies	5.1	3.2	4.3	9.4

Source: World Bank, *World Development Report*, 1981.

B. *Growth and inflation rates: selected industrial countries, 1978-1981*

	Growth rate of GNP				Inflation rate (CPI)					
	1978	1979	1980	1981[1]	1978	1979	1980	1981[2]	58-72	73-78
US	4.8	3.2	−.16	0.7	7.5	11.3	13.5	10.9	2.7	8.0
UK	3.3	1.4	−1.4	−2.4	8.3	13.4	18.0	11.2	4.1	16.1
Germany	3.6	4.3	1.8	0.2	2.8	4.1	5.5	6.1	2.8	4.8
Italy	2.7	4.9	4.0	−0.3	12.1	14.7	21.2	17.5	3.7	16.4
France	3.7	3.5	1.6	0.3	9.1	10.7	13.3	13.6	4.4	10.7
Japan	5.1	5.6	4.2	4.2	3.8	3.6	8.0	4.2	5.3	11.3
Switz.	0.4	2.8	3.9	0.7	0.8	3.6	4.1	7.2	3.4	4.0

1. Provisional estimates.
2. 1981.III/1980.III.

Source: IMF, *International Financial Statistics*

Table 2. *Current account balances, 1970-1990 (billions of 1978 dollars)*

Country group	1970	1975	1978	1980	High 1985	High 1990	Low 1985	Low 1990
Oil importers	−18.5	−49.8	−25.5	−52.7	−49	−60	−41	−43
Low-income	−3.5	−7.0	−5.1	−8.6	−12	−15	−8	−9
Middle-income	−15.0	−42.8	−20.4	−44.1	−37	−45	−33	−34
Oil exporters	−4.7	−3.2	−17.6	4.1	−5	−14	−7	−12
All developing countries	−23.2	−53.1	−43.1	−48.6	−54	−74	−48	−55
Capital-surplus oil exporters[a]	6.0	39.7	18.8	85.1	(57)	(35)	(55)	(16)
Industrial market economies[a]	25.9	28.4	29.9	−24.5	(12)	(55)	(8)	(55)
Nonmarket industrial economies and China	3.4	−9.0	−0.2	−0.1	−3	−4	−2	−3
Statistical discrepancy	−12.3	−6.0	−5.4	−11.9	−12	−12	−13	−13

Note: Excludes official transfers.

a. These projections are subject to particular uncertainty.

Source: Reproduced from World Bank, *World Development Report 1981*, August 1981, p. 19.

Table 3. *Nominal and realized real rate of interest: 1966-1981*

	1966	1967	1968	1969	1970	1971	1972	1973	1974	1975	1976	1977	1978	1979	1980	1981
London Euro-dollar rate	6.1	5.5	6.4	9.8	8.5	6.6	5.5	9.2	11.0	7.0	5.6	6.0	8.7	12.0	14.4	16.5
US rate of inflation (CPI)	3.1	2.6	4.2	5.4	5.9	4.3	3.3	6.3	10.9	9.2	5.8	6.5	7.5	11.3	13.5	11.0
Realized real rate	3.0	2.9	2.2	4.4	2.6	2.3	2.2	2.9	0.1	−2.2	−.2	−.5	1.2	0.7	0.9	5.5

Source: IMF, *International Financial Statistics.*

increase in volatility of prices of financial assets in the most recent periods (79,9-81,9 and to a lesser extent 74,1-81,9). This is not only true of exchange rates since 1971 or 1973, but also, more recently and strikingly of both short and long-term interest rates. The surprise in these figures is that no strong systematic increase in the variability of stock prices, consumer prices, industrial production, or money seems to have taken place over the same period. This leaves the variability of exchange and interest rates in search of an explanation. Expectations, commodity price shocks, expected policy instability, and inappropriate policy procedures are the most frequently adduced rationalizations.

The volatility of economic variables, of asset prices in particular, contributes to fragility of the world economy in several ways. The information content of price signals diminishes and the response of production to expansionary incentives may well be reduced significantly. Real resources are diverted from the production of goods and services to that of financial hedges. Long-term investment becomes more risky and its volume may decrease. And important changes in the financial system are induced: floating-rate loans and a substantial shortening of maturity structure, to mention but two. As debt has been growing rapidly in the previous expansionary and inflationary period, the possibility of fairly wide debt defaults arises, especially in view of rising (or high) real interest rates, pessimistic expectations as to the prospects for vigorous real growth, and the ensuing re-financing difficulties of borrowers.

The process I have just described is, however, typical of every recession that follows on a previous boom. It is also typical of every stabilization crisis or, more modestly, stop phase of the stop-go cycle. The present concern with the possibility of a serious financial crisis, followed by a collapse of the real economy, goes beyond the usual gloom associated with every recessionary or stabilization phase for a number of reasons. Among these, the persistence and acceleration of inflation over a twenty-year period has served to imbed serious distortions in the financial system and has left a number of institutions and firms particularly exposed to restrictive monetary policies. The effectiveness of stabilization policies themselves has deteriorated as a result of persistent inflation that has made it difficult to lower inflationary expectations, not entirely irrationally in view of the loss of credibility past performance has inflicted on policy pronouncements. In addition, uncertainty as to the course of economic policy and economic prospects is compounded by the new and extraordinary financial market turbulence referred to above. Finally, the impressive growth of international lending and of international financial markets over the past fifteen years is per-

Table 4. Standard deviations of monthly changes [1]

	Exchange rate (dom./$)	Forward exchange rate	Short-term interest rate	Long-term interest rate	Stock prices	Prices (CPI)	Industrial production	Money (M1)
1. USA[2]								
1966,2-81,9	—	—	.883	.276	.037	.0034	.0097	.030
1966,2-71,1	—	—	.387	.166	.035	.0020	.0073	.027
1971,1-73,1	—	—	.393	.209	.028	.0016	.0056	.031
1974,1-79,7	—	—	.484	.165	.040	.0030	.012	.034
1979,9-81,9	—	—	2.158	.593	.042	.0028	.012	.021
2. UK[3]								
1966,2-81,9	.021	.026	.602	.431	.059	.008	.016	.022
1966,2-71,1	.020	.019	.272	.173	.040	.005	.010	n.a.
1971,1-73,1	.014	.019	.430	.289	.043	.004	.024	.021
1974,1-79,7	.023	.030	.772	.604	.077	.009	.018	.020
1979,9-81,9	.028	.033	.657	.455	.041	.008	.010	.028
3. Germany								
1966,2-81,9	.023	.078	n.a.	.239	.034	.003	.018	.028
1966,2-71,1	.012	.007	n.a.	.182	.037	.003	.022	.024
1971,1-73,1	.009	.010	n.a.	.197	.038	.003	.017	.032
1974,1-79,7	.032	.031	n.a.	.226	.029	.003	.014	.030
1979,9-81,9	.031	.037	n.a.	.363	.025	.003	.016	.032

4. Japan[4]

1966,2-81,9	.021	.032	.451	.251	.035	.009	.014	.041
1966,2-71,1	0	n.a.	.259	.007	.034	.007	.011	.043
1971,1-73,1	.013	.009	.226	.069	.039	.007	.013	.043
1974,1-79,7	.024	.030	.468	.221	.030	.010	.013	.040
1979,9-81,9	.034	.037	.723	.475	.022	.007	.020	.045

5. Switzerland

1966,2-81,9	.025	.031	n.a.	.159	.042	.005	n.a.	.021
1966,2-71,1	0	.003	n.a.	.110	.045	.004	n.a.	.021
1971,1-73,1	.014	.015	n.a.	.129	.040	.004	n.a.	.018
1974,1-79,7	.028	.037	n.a.	.163	.042	.005	n.a.	.021
1979,9-81,9	.034	.043	n.a.	.218	.030	.004	n.a.	.027

1. Except for interest rates, standard deviations of logarithmic approximation to percentage changes.
2. For the US, money variability was calculated on the basis of the M_1 series for 1966,2-1979,3 on the basis of the comparable M1A series for 1979,9-81,9.
3. For the UK, the M_1 series begins in 71,11.
4. For Japan, the forward rate series begins in 1971,9; the long-term interest rate series in 1968,2.

Source: IMF, *International Financial Statistics.*

ceived as having proceeded to a stage where it now constitutes a major source of potential instability of the international monetary and financial system. It is to this last issue that I now turn.

II. INTERNATIONAL LENDING AND FINANCIAL FRAGILITY

Four features of the evolution of international lending over the past one or two decades are often cited as potential sources of instability in the international financial system. The first is the sheer size of rates of growth of international lending which have outstripped those of most other financial stock or flow variables. Second, the past ten years have seen an increasing dominance of bank over bond financing in international capital flows. Third, private capital flows, especially through the intermediary of banks, have come to play an ever increasing role in financing payments disequilibria, of developing as well as industrial countries. Fourth, there appears to have been an increasing concentration of bank exposure to a few large borrowers. I document these four features briefly below before evaluating their contribution (as well as that of a number of additional factors) to the perceived fragility of the international financial system.

Table 5 illustrates the extraordinary growth rates that have characterized international bank lending and international financial market expansion since 1966. The growth rates of these aggregates clearly outstrip not only those of similar domestic aggregates but also those of worldwide aggregates as calculated by the IMF, be it world reserves, world money, world inflation, or the aggregate value of exports.[3] The only exceptions occur in the 1973-80 period where world reserves with gold valued at market prices grew at an annual rate of 19.9 per cent and the value of exports for the world grew at an annual rate of 25.2 per cent. The increase in the value of oil exports of course contributes significantly to this last figure. The fact that the growth of international lending is high both for the 1966-73 and 1973-80 sub-periods is noteworthy. It shows that the expansion of international bank lending predates the oil-price increase, though the initial high growth is partly attributable to the relatively low initial 1966 asset base. The failure of the growth to slow abruptly after 1973 is equally noteworthy.

There are, however, significant changes in the composition of total international lending over the period.[4] Thus, the second half of the 1970s was marked by a decline of international bond financing relative to international bank loans as a source of capital. Table 6 provides some relevant data for the period 1974-1980 (earlier data is hard to obtain on a comparable basis).

Table 5. *Indicators of international banking and lending growth*

	(1) Euro-currency assets Total	(2) Euro-currency claims on non-banks	(3) Euro-currency market Net size	(4) Deposit banks foreign assets	(5) Deposit banks foreign liabilities	(6) Net new international bank lending	(7) Net new international bank lending to non-oil LDCs
Billions of US dollars							
1966	20.3	2.8	17.4	51.8	61.3	n.a.	n.a.
1973	187.6	38.7	132.0	354.5	384.7	71	10
1980	751.2	193.5	575.0	1711.3	1777.8	165.0	41*
Average annual rates of growth (%)							
1966-1980	29.4	35.4	28.4	28.4	27.2	n.a.	n.a.
1966-1973	37.4	45.6	33.6	31.6	30.0	n.a.	n.a.
1973-1980	21.9	25.8	23.4	25.2	24.4	27.0	26.5**

* 1979   ** 1973-79

Sources: Columns (1) – (3), *BIS Annual Reports;* Columns (4) – (5), IMF, *International Financial Statistics;* Columns (6) – (7), BIS and IMF, *International Capital Markets,* Occasional Paper, September 1980. Columns (4) and (5) refer to IMF "world" aggregates (all countries). Reproduced from A.K. Swoboda, *International Banking: Current Issues in Perspective, op. cit.,* p. 5.

Table 6. *International bank and bond financing, 1974-1980* [1,2]
(billions of US dollars)

	1974	1975	1976	1977	1978	1979	1980
Net new international bank lending	50	40	70	75	110	130	145
Net new international bond lending	11	20	30	31	30	29	29
Total new bank and bond financing	61	60	100	105	140	159	174
Percent of bond financing	18%	34%	30%	29%	21%	18%	17%

1. This table is adapted from IMF, *International Capital Markets*, Occasional Paper 1 (September 1980), Table 13, p. 29. Data for 1980 are taken from BIS, *Fifty-First Annual Report* (1981).

2. Total new bank and bond financing contains a minor amount of double counting.

Source: Reproduced from A.K. Swoboda, *International Banking: Current Issues in Perspective, op. cit.*, p. 9.

The "arithmetic" reason for the decline in bond financing is readily apparent: after a rapid initial expansion in new bond lending, the latter stabilized at its (high) 1976 level while new bank lending kept expanding rapidly.

Third, the increasing role of banks of industrial countries in financing balance-of-payments deficits (particularly those of developing countries and subsidiarily Eastern bloc countries) in the 1970s has received much attention recently. Coupled with an increased perception of country risk and an apparent decline in profit margins on lending, this development has been the source of much concern, though it has also been welcomed as a major contribution in solving the recycling problem attendant on increases in oil prices after 1973. The flows involved are illustrated in Table 7 which is reproduced from the World Bank's *World Development Report*. The figures for the middle-income developing countries reveal clearly the large increase in their current account deficit after 1973 and 1979, the relative decline of official development assistance (ODA) in financing these deficits, and the large absolute increase in financing through commercial loans since 1970. Table 8 documents the impact on the outstanding stock of debt of all non-oil developing countries which increased from $ 97.3 billion in 1973 to $370.1 billion in 1980 or at an average annual rate of 21 per cent. The debt to private creditors increased by 23.7 per cent. As a result, the share of claims of private creditors grew from 49.6 per cent to 57.9 per cent of the developing countries' debt. Financial institutions, which accounted for 71.4

Table 7. *Oil-importing developing countries' current account deficit and finance sources, 1970-80*
(billions of 1978 dollars)

	Low-income					Middle-income				
	1970	1973	1975	1978	1980	1970	1973	1975	1978	1980
Current account deficit[a]	3.6	4.9	7.0	5.1	9.1	14.9	6.7	42.8	20.4	48.9
Financed by:										
Net capital flows										
ODA	3.4	4.1	6.6	5.1	5.7	3.3	5.3	5.3	6.5	7.9
Private direct investment	0.3	0.2	0.4	0.2	0.2	3.4	5.1	3.8	4.6	4.5
Commercial loans	0.5	0.6	0.8	0.9	0.7	8.9	13.7	21.0	29.4	27.1
Changes in reserves and short-term borrowing[b]	−0.5	−1.1	−0.7	−1.1	2.4	−0.8	−11.7	12.7	−20.1	9.5
Memorandum item:										
Current account deficit as percentage of GNP	1.9	2.4	3.9	2.6	4.5	2.6	1.0	5.5	2.3	5.0

a. Excludes net official transfers (grants), which are included in capital flows.
b. A minus sign (−) indicates an increase in reserves.

Source: Reproduced from World Bank, *World Development Report* for 1981.

Table 8. *Non-oil developing countries: long-term external debt, 1973-81* [1,2]

	1973	1974	1975	1976	1977	1978	1979	1980	1981
	In billions of US dollars								
Total outstanding debt of non-oil developing countries	97.3	120.6	147.1	176.5	216.7	272.7	322.8	370.1	425.2
By type of creditor									
Official creditors	49.1	59.3	69.3	81.2	97.8	117.8	134.8	155.8	180.0
Governments	36.9	44.2	50.4	58.5	68.9	81.6	92.1	106.0	121.4
International institutions	12.2	15.2	18.8	22.7	28.9	36.2	42.8	49.8	58.6
Private creditors	48.3	61.2	77.9	94.4	118.9	154.9	188.0	214.3	245.3
Unguaranteed debt	21.4	26.0	32.0	37.5	43.1	51.4	60.7	68.2	79.0
Guaranteed debt	27.1	35.4	46.1	57.2	75.8	103.5	127.3	146.1	166.3
To financial institutions	13.1	21.7	29.8	39.2	54.3	73.9	96.1	112.8	127.9
Other private creditors	13.8	13.5	16.1	18.0	21.5	29.6	31.2	33.3	38.4
	In percent								
Total outstanding debt of non-oil developing countries	100.0	100.0	100.0	100.0	100.0	100.0	100.0	100.0	100.0
To official creditors	50.4	49.2	47.1	46.4	45.1	43.2	41.8	42.1	42.3
Governments	32.9	36.6	34.3	33.5	31.8	29.9	28.5	28.7	28.5
International institutions	12.5	12.6	12.7	12.9	13.3	13.3	13.2	13.4	13.7
To private creditors	49.6	50.8	52.9	53.8	54.9	56.8	58.2	57.9	57.8
Financial institutions	35.5	39.6	42.0	43.7	45.0	46.0	48.6	48.9	48.7
Other private creditors	14.2	11.3	10.9	10.0	9.7	10.8	9.6	9.0	9.1

1. Excludes data for the People's Republic of China prior to 1977.
2. Figures from 1981 are Fund projections.

Sources: Extracted and reproduced from IMF, *World Economic Outlook*, Occasional Paper 4 (June 1981), Tables 27, p. 132 and 29, p. 134; World Bank, Debtor Reporting System; and Fund staff estimates and projections.

per cent of private claims on developing countries in 1973, account for 84.5 per cent of that total by 1980.

This increased role of banks in lending to developing countries (particularly middle-income ones) and to Eastern bloc countries has partly led to the fourth feature mentioned at the beginning of this section, the concentration of bank exposure to a few large borrowers, largely governments or government agencies and enterprises. The list is well known: Brazil, Mexico, Argentina, Algeria, Egypt, Indonesia, India, Turkey, Yugoslavia, Korea, and Poland figure prominently.

These developments are part and parcel of the internationalization of banking and capital markets that has taken place since the return to convertibility in 1958. The international capital market has truly become a worldwide one, with banks playing a dominant role. At the same time, bank financing has supplanted bond financing as a major source of international medium- and long-term capital while the short-run Euro-currency markets fulfil the function of main money market for the banking system of several of the smaller industrialized countries. The geographical distribution of the foreign assets and lending of banks has also evolved, with developing countries assuming an important share of international indebtedness, and flows of bank loans playing an increasingly important role in balance-of-payments financing.

With rising and volatile interest rates, diminishing spreads, an increase in perceived country risk and in the actual number of rescheduling negotiations, these developments suggest that the international financial system may have become significantly more fragile than it was ten years ago. The sheer growth of international lending has raised concerns as to the capacity of government to control the growth of both world and national monetary and credit aggregates, an issue to which I return briefly in the next section. The deep involvement of banks in that lending raises the possibility that a foreign monetary or debt crisis will spread to the domestic monetary, banking, and credit system. The role of banks in financing payments disequilibria suggests that necessary adjustment measures may be delayed so long as to lead increasingly to exchange and debt repayment crises. The concentration of lending to a number of developing and Eastern countries is worrisome for a number of reasons. The present macroeconomic environment of low growth, high and variable real interest rates, and shortening maturity structure raises doubts as to the capacity of borrowers to service their debts and finance themselves adequately. The reduction of spreads raises doubts as to the capacity of lenders to set aside sufficient provisions for losses.

Some of these concerns seem exaggerated or misplaced, as I will cursorily argue below and as several of the papers presented at this Colloquium point out. Others are serious enough to warrant at least a brief discussion of possible measures to safeguard the stability of the international financial system.

III. STABILIZING THE INTERNATIONAL FINANCIAL SYSTEM

Among the many policy questions raised by the general theme of, and papers presented at, this Colloquium, I have chosen to comment briefly on four issues that bear on the stabilization of the international financial system. I ask, first, whether the extraordinary growth of international bank lending, especially through Euro-currency markets, calls for co-ordinated or national controls. This is of course one of the main issues discussed by this meeting's first commission. Second, I ask why this extraordinary growth, whether it should be controlled or not, has occurred, a question obviously related to the work of both the first and second commissions. My last questions bear on issues raised by the themes assigned to the third and fourth commissions. I will thus enquire, third, into the proper division of roles between national authorities, the Fund, aid agencies, and the private sector. By way of conclusion, I shall emphasize what appear to me to be a few obvious prerequisites for a sounder international financial system.

1. *Controlling the Growth of International Lending*

The extraordinary growth of Euro-currency markets has been taken to imply that monetary and credit growth are uncontrolled and have become uncontrollable at both a national and international level. As a result, world inflation cannot be curbed and may eventually lead to a credit collapse, national monetary authorities have lost in large part their capacity to influence economic activity, unless controls are imposed on the market.

At a global level, this argument is based either on very high estimates of the so-called Euro-dollar multiplier or on the thesis that the quantity of Euro-currency deposits (and corresponding Euro-currency assets) is entirely demand-determined. Neither economic analysis nor empirical evidence support these views, as I have argued elsewhere and as is brought out in the excellent papers presented at this colloquium, especially that of Barry Johnston.[5] At a national level (and here the Dudler and Llewellyn papers are particularly relevant), exclusive focus on Euro-currency or, for that matter, capital flows as sources of the impotence of domestic monetary policy is counterproductive as it confuses symptoms with causes. This is especially true under fixed or managed exchange rates where, even if there were no Euro-currency transactions, other capital flows and trade in goods and services would rob monetary policy of much of its influence in any event.

This is not to deny that the existence of Euro-currency markets can singularly complicate the task of authorities in monitoring monetary aggregates and in choosing appropriate monetary targets. Nor is it to deny that that unevenness in regulations applying to domestic and international bank transactions creates problems of both stability and competitive equity. Differences in regulations make for disintermediation and instability in global monetary aggregates in response to changes in either asset preferences or in monetary policy. Furthermore, they have serious consequences for the evolution of the competitive position of national banking groups in the international financial market. Some harmonization of national regulations for macroeconomic purposes (especially reserve requirement ratios on *both* domestic and international transactions) is thus highly desirable. This harmonization should, however, be towards a lowering of average reserve requirements (and/or the payment of competitive interest on required reserves) rather than an increase towards the highest common denominator, if further disintermediation is to be avoided and if banks are to play properly their role of channelling saving into productive investment.

2. Determinants of the Growth of Bank Lending

If autonomous growth through a multiplier process is not a convincing explanation of the expansion of the Euro-currency market and of international bank lending, you may well ask what is responsible for that development and for the preponderant role of banks in it. One answer is simply the general expansion of trade and the "multinationalization" of international business activities since the early 1960s. Recycling has, more recently, also played a role but it, itself, needs explaining. The papers by Joël Métais, Tad Rybczynski and Herman Dudler, taken together, provide a convincing and fairly complete set of explanations. This will allow me to concentrate on a few points only.

First, the growth of international financial transactions has taken place within a context of general monetary and credit expansion. The former has proceeded faster than the latter partly as a consequence of the general internationalization of business activities mentioned above, partly as a result of a dramatic decrease of information costs (analogous to the decrease in transport cost in international trade) attendant on the communications revolution. Second, the preponderant role of banks can be explained partly by various informational and risk-diversification advantages but also by rising advantages of shifting from domestic to offshore modes of conducting bank transactions. To the extent that domestic business is subjected to higher reserve requirements than offshore transactions and that required reserves bear low or zero rates of return, there is a cost advantage to transferring activities from regulated to unregulated financial intermediaries. It is worth noting that this cost advantage rises significantly with the nominal rate of interest (the tax rate on the tax base constituted by barren required reserves). The trend increase in nominal interest rates that has occurred over the past two decades in the wake of the simultaneous rise in inflation rates thus constitutes an important determinant of the expansion of international banking activity.

Though these considerations go a long way towards explaining the growth of international lending and the preponderant role of banks, I would argue that another and rather unhealthy factor has been at work for the past ten years or so. My guess is that there has been a widespread perception that banks, or their largest debtors, would not be allowed to fail. As a consequence, depositors have been ready to lend to banks, and investors have been willing to acquire bank stocks, even though they, themselves, would not have been willing to acquire the assets held by banks directly. Banks, in turn, have been willing to acquire assets at rates of return lower than the riskiness of these assets (or of their contribution to the risk of the banks' overall portfolio) would have justified, had the implicit guarantee mentioned above not been available.

One reason for this hypothesis is that international bank lending has kept growing in spite of the increase in perceived country risk, a narrowing of spreads, and diminishing capital-asset or capital-deposit ratios.[6] This raises the question of why, if spreads are inadequate as banks often claim, they have not increased their margins or refused to lend; in addition, why have banks not issued additional capital or refused to engage in unprofitable activities if capital-deposit ratios have become inadequate? On the basis of observed behavior neither the market nor the industry believe that banking is in serious trouble – or, if it is, that it will not be rescued out of trouble.

This perception has several distortive effects. By enabling banks to obtain funds at lower cost than they otherwise could and to invest in assets that are riskier than those their stockholders would choose to hold directly, it confers a distorted advantage to bank over direct finance and biases international bank portfolios towards higher risk (and return). In addition, large lenders and borrowers are advantaged at the expense of smaller ones. For if you may hesitate to let a large entity fail, you may afford to let a small one do so (cf. New York vs. Yonkers or Chrysler vs. Studebaker). An untoward consequence of implicit guarantees to large borrowers and lenders is that it creates incentives for brinkmanship. Banks can raise the probability of a bail-out by concentrating their lending on one large borrower who then cannot be allowed to fail since the banks' stake is too high (or by following one large bank who has a large stake in one country). Similarly, borrowers have an incentive to incur very large liabilities to one or a few banks who cannot be allowed to fail.[7]

The policy issue this argument raises is straightforward. Removing the implicit guarantee to banks requires that there be a perception that banks *can* conceivably fail even if, in fact, important bank failures do not actually occur. I return to the dilemma that implementing such a policy without destabilizing the international financial system as a whole raises, in the next section.

3. *The Proper Division of Supervisory and Functional Roles*

The issue at hand, then, is how to correct existing distortions while ensuring stability of the international financial system and a continuation of its role in transferring funds efficiently from surplus to deficit regions. In this context, there have been proposals for the IMF to supplement (or cooperate with) banks in the recycling process, for banks and/or governments to cooperate in creating various safety net designs, for the creation of some supranational supervisory authority (or at least for close harmonization of supervisory tasks), and for the creation of a lender of last resort at the international level. Like Tom de Vries, David Williams, and Richard Dale, I remain highly skeptical of such proposals. What appears both more practical and more desirable is to ensure a clear and appropriate division of tasks among these bodies.

The problem is reminiscent of the assignment problem in international macroeconomics: there are a number of targets which need to be matched with an equal number of instruments in efficient and stabilizing manner. The targets here are a speed of international adjustment compatible with non-inflationary growth of the world economy, an efficient long-run transfer of resources from surplus to deficit areas and from rich to poor, and a sound international banking and financial system.

The IMF seems to be in the best position to contribute to an adequate adjustment mechanism by restricting its dealings to member governments and monetary authorities and the judicious exercise of conditionality. Doing this in a non-inflationary fashion requires monetary restraint on the part of major countries in a world in which international reserves play a diminished role with exchange-rate flexibility, and where they are neither centrally created nor related to an outside asset such as gold but are, instead, in large portion composed of major national currencies. Such monetary restraint should also help insure that banks will refrain from inappropriate short-term lending for balance-of-payments purposes. The transfer of longer-term resources from surplus to deficit regions can safely be left to private markets, including banks, in response to economic incentives, as long as the latter are not distorted for political or other reasons. The transfer of resources from rich to poor on concessional terms should be the explicit purview of governments and aid agencies.

Insuring the soundness of the international financial and banking system while avoiding a confidence crisis is perhaps the most difficult task. In principle, a clear regulatory framework that puts the risk clearly where it belongs, namely with the banks, would by itself provide sufficient incentives for soundness in international lending. The problem, however, is triple. First, conflicts of jurisdiction and responsibility among supervisory authorities need to be solved, perhaps along the lines suggested by Richard Dale. Second, banks have often engaged in imprudent loans at the implicit or explicit urging of political authorities (as Helmut von der Bey and Helmut Haschek have suggested). The cost of these will probably have to be borne by the taxpayer but the practice needs to be discontinued. This is not to suggest that concessional aid or even bail-outs should not occur (there are often excellent reasons for them), but that they should be explicitly recognized for what they are and undertaken on that basis. Third, higher penalties for mismanagement could be imposed and here I would very much second Tom de Vries' suggestion that early write-off provisions be reinforced. But can this be done without threatening the stability of the international financial system?

This is where a lender of last resort may be useful. However, it is illusory to think that such a lender can be found at an international level. Nor is such an international lender of last resort necessarily needed. National lenders of last resort may, and in any event will have to, suffice. For this to be the case, jurisdictional problems will have to be solved, national central banks whose financial intermediaries have large foreign exchange liability positions will have to keep adequate foreign exchange reserves, and penalties for having to borrow at the lender of last resort will have to be sufficiently high not to encourage imprudent behavior on the part of the private sector.

4. *Prerequisites for a Sounder International Financial System*

The lesson I would draw from recent economic history and from this Colloquium is that there are four prerequisites to a sounder international financial
system, a less distorted system that avoids drifting from one episode of crisis
management to the next. These prerequisites are perhaps obvious but are
worth listing as they are less trivial than they appear at first.

At the most obvious level, stability of the international financial system
is inextricably bound with general economic (and political) stability, that of
the real economy in particular. More stable macroeconomic policies are thus
the first order of the day. Second, where risk has been artificially (and temporarily) removed from the banks, it should be put back, however gently at
first. This implies, third, that politics should be removed from banking and
private international lending and put where it belongs, in foreign policy and
in foreign economic policy.

Finally, it is essential to reverse the trend towards rising protectionism, be
it commercial or financial. This is essential if debtors are to generate the foreign exchange needed to refinance, service and pay their debt. Vienna is an
appropriate city to remind oneself of the role that mounting protectionism
against Austrian trade played in precipitating the Credit-Anstalt debacle.

NOTES

1. See IMF, *World Economic Outlook*, June 1981, p. 114.

2. For a perceptive – and skeptical – analysis of the financial instability hypothesis in the con-
temporary context, see Warren D. McClam, *Financial Fragility and Instability: Monetary
Authorities as Borrowers and Lenders of Last Resort* (mimeo).

3. See A.K. Swoboda, *International Banking: Current Issues in Perspective*, paper presented
at the Ente Einaudi Conference on "International Banking: Its Market and Institutional Structure", Perugia, September 1981, pp. 7-8.

4. The remainder of this paragraph, the next paragraph, and accompanying tables are lifted
from *ibid.*, pp. 7, 9, 10-12.

5. See, for instance, A.K. Swoboda, "Credit Creation in the Euromarket: Alternative
Theories and Implications for Control", *Occasional Paper No. 2, Group of Thirty* (New York,
1980). See also the papers by David Llewellyn and Herman Dudler.

6. The decrease in spreads is partly misleading as it is compensated by various front-end fees.
Furthermore, floating-rate loans have taken part of the interest-risk out of bank financing. But
part only since the counterpart is an increase in default-risk in a period of rising real interest
rates and since loan rates are adjusted only at discrete intervals.

7. For further analysis of the implicit guarantee hypothesis, see A.K. Swoboda, *International
Banking: Current Issues in Perspective, op. cit.*, pp. 27-31.

Chapter XXIII

GENERAL REPORT

by *Fritz Diwok*

As my predecessors have stressed, it is no easy task to choose the most important points from discussions held in several commissions only the day before and to present "results" of a Colloquium to which so many SUERF members and guests have contributed.

The following account of the results is to be understood as a complementary statement to the more detailed analysis of Professor Alexander Swoboda, stressing the practical and policy sides of the matter. It includes points made in the speeches of the opening day together with the discussions which centered around the content of papers and last but not least, points from conversations inside and outside the "court room". It seemed wise to restrict and structure the report into five main theses:

I. AWARENESS AND AVOIDANCE OF RISKS IN FOREIGN LENDING

The seriousness of the situation was made clear at the outset. Peter Cooke pointed to the necessity to take domino-theories and "withdrawal symptoms" seriously. Stephan Koren stated that the Polish crisis had brought about a shock on both sides. Risks which are the result of the long recession, transfer risks, sovereign risks, commercial risks and currency risks seem to pile up in front of the banking community and it is possible that there are types of risks which can be avoided neither by prudent management nor by a global distribution of the loan portfolio.

One situation in which prudent management would not be of great help is the case of the so-called *"general risk"* in the form of a "crash" of the international financial system, a situation in which particular sovereign and commercial risks could – to a certain degree – become irrelevant because of a breakdown of the channels for international capital flows. The general risk would affect both financial intermediaries and individuals (e.g. bond holders and bank customers) and could be triggered off by the failure of too many ultimate borrowers to service their debts. Starting with difficulties and insolvencies of many countries and a marked deterioration of their debt servicing ratio, one could imagine that such a general breakdown is no longer beyond all possibility. Loan losses alone will not be regarded as a reliable indicator – one Scandinavian participant remarked: "Our losses have been low, because we have not been permitted to take them" – especially as regards the evaluation of the sovereign risks of neighbouring countries.

A sudden change in the application of banking rules and usages could present a second form of such a general risk; here one has to be aware of the possibility of a politically motivated application of the default clause which, in conjunction with the instrument of cross default, could lead to the same consequences as the often quoted "big crash".

The situation presents itself in a somewhat tragic way, as the necessity to avoid the perceived big risks could, under certain circumstances, lead to exactly the type of difficulties that many fear. A greater frequency and volume of reschedulings which cannot be executed according to schedule could lead to large scale international insolvencies. An element in this direction could be found in the expectation that international loans will be less readily available in the years to come than the total demand for them (David Llewellyn).

It should be noted at this point that the papers presented and the discussions held were devoted primarily to technical questions such as motivations for and economic causes of the growth of international loans, the role of banks in the international markets and important aspects of growing indebtedness of third world and other debtor countries.

The intensive study and keen application of all methods of risk avoidance, distribution of risks, insurance against risks including the ultimate placing of risks on the shoulders of taxpayers, shareholders (of banks) and other groups do, of course, signal that it is currently à la mode to declare oneself as a risk-avoider. It seems that all parties concerned presently suffer from the discord between the wish to avoid as many risks as possible on the one hand and the need to cope with realities on the other. This situation often results in criticism of "over-lending" and "over-recycling" – there were heated discussions about the nature of the recycling process; whether it was a necessity or a folly; a reality or fiction – by those institutions which bear the brunt of non-performing loans.

It has to be stressed, however, that, so far, the international side of banking business has proved to be altogether less risky than business at home. The higher degree of caution connected with the bigger volume of lending outside one's own borders seems to reflect at least a greater psychological vulnerability.

II. FURTHER GROWTH OF INTERNATIONAL FINANCIAL MARKETS IN THE CONTEXT OF THE TRIANGLE: LIQUIDITY – ADJUSTMENT – CONFIDENCE

Disregarding, for a moment, the comments under point I, namely the "general risk" and the "big crash", we had to deal with the question of how the Euro-markets would continue to grow. The reasons for such further growth: high interest rates, multiplier effects, special productivity of the Euro-markets and the need for further international loans by a vast number of lenders were discussed. As far as I could perceive nobody has really predicted a stand-still in the Euro-markets: "In the long run sterilization is no practicable strategy" (Claude Chouraqui). But in our *couloir* discussions many of us felt that the international part of banking business would grow more in conformity with the domestic business than during recent years and that the slowdown would be influenced much more by outside factors such as declining balance of payments surpluses of OPEC countries rather than policy decisions.

A new "parallelism" between domestic and foreign lending seems probable, as the number of banks that are pressing themselves into the international side of the market for the first time ("new entries") is on the decline whilst those already in the market are observing more conservative relationships between banking at home and banking abroad. A new "parallelism" is also likely as some parts of the international assets have to be regarded as frozen, if not as bad debts. Nationwide banking in the United States could also contribute to such a shift from international loans into domestic assets.

On the other hand, we were strongly reminded that Euro-markets could not be blamed for their efficiency and that a wide framework seems to be in the making, in which central banks of major countries would be in the position to identify common and important criteria for international lending (Hermann Dudler). Such a framework would include the Paris Club and the BIS, and might lead to standard procedures or mechanisms for the rescheduling process at large as well as ad hoc. The opinion seemed to prevail that past procedures for rescheduling might not be sufficient for the needs of the coming years.

Intensified efforts in international lending very often meant "to buy time" and to postpone real adjustment. In this sense international markets have been accused of undermining confidence and adding to the financial burden and difficulties of some countries. Central banks have been worried that the swift growth of international credit markets has led to an erosion of their domestic money and loan targets, thus increasing the potential conflict between monetary policy at home and lending abroad.

As far as the triangle of liquidity, adjustment and confidence is concerned, more and more liquidity has meant slow adjustment and some erosion of confidence. Over and over again during the SUERF Colloquium in Vienna "the will to repay" and the creation of a "safety net" have been in the centre of the discussions, including measures of central bank policy to which I will revert later on.

As far as return of confidence is concerned, it seemed obvious that much will depend on the way in which rescheduling arrangements will be dealt with.

The further proliferation of the number and the volume of rescheduling arrangements came under scrutiny. Suggestions regarding confidence-inspiring measures such as Barry Johnston's proposal to foster empirical analysis (more than theoretical considerations) formed an important part of the discussions. It was recognized that limits of indebtedness were "dynamic" (Hans Eckhart Scharrer).

III. SOME ANSWERS FROM THE BANKS

One of the two speakers from the commercial banks made it clear on the opening day that it would be necessary to "devote more time and better people to the assessment and management of sovereign risks" (Guido Schmidt-Chiari). Others stressed the necessity to intensify co-financing with the World Bank and to put more emphasis on profits.

The desire for stronger co-operation between all types of financial intermediaries, namely commercial banks, export credit institutions, central banks, the BIS, the World Bank, the IMF, the regional development banks and other international organizations like the OECD, was clearly expressed (Helmut Haschek). Robert Heller reminded the participants that computer-based systems of sovereign risk analysis were indispensable for the control of international obligations.

Another point was capital adequacy with regard to the risks in international lending. There were proposals to harmonize the debt-equity ratios of international banks, or, at least, to strive for more similar structures on the assets side – difficult enough in view of the wide variation of tax systems. Other participants stressed the necessity for higher bank profits to defend existing capital ratios and to avoid further deterioration of the debt-equity ratio.

One proposal by David Williams was directed to openly declare swap lines between the big banks. It was also stressed that higher rates of return could be brought about not only by better interest rate margins but also by flat rate fees, facility fees, front end fees, etc.

Banks were confronted not only with risks on the assets side but also with the question of funding risks. The possibility that inter-bank funds might not be available caused concern and had to be seen in the context of the relations with individual lenders of last resort (see point IV).

Interestingly enough, it was not thought that new institutions for monitoring the Euro-markets would be a good idea (Stuart Wilson). Rainer Gut, in pointing to experiences of German, Japanese and Swiss banks, considered that questions of surveying banks in the Euro-market would have to be resolved on a national level.

As far as a wider (geographical and business) distribution of loans by the banks is concerned it was pointed out that banks had gone far through their participation in syndicated loans and that a "total atomization" of international credits could be an instrument to destroy national "centres of gravity" in international lending.

IV. MONETARY AND FISCAL POLICY

In spite of the freedom of important off-shore markets, international loans are given under a system of rules (and sometimes regulations) which have been established by a large number of central banks. Thus individual acts of monetary authorities play their part and will continue to do so.

If we regard central banks, including the BIS and the IMF, as the "second line of defence" and if we think of these institutions as a "fire brigade", as we do, it should be mentioned that there are great uncertainties about putting in this brigade. This naturally presented a topic for discussion at the Colloquium. We have only limited knowledge about the strength and the resolution with which this "second line" of defence would come to the front, if needed. On the one hand it is, of course, necessary, that central banks should be able to keep their secrets and leave participants in the market unclear about what they are going to do in the case of emergency. In public all central banks stress that their support cannot be taken for granted in the supply of liquidity. On the other hand there is a great lack of knowledge about basic attitudes concerning support and the nature of the Basle Concordat.

Some participants felt that powder for the second line of defence should be kept dry in all circumstances and that central banks should not come out too early with swaps or other forms of almost direct lending. To a certain extent these considerations were in contrast to the quest for closer co-operation between commercial and central banks.

As far as monetary policy of industrial countries was concerned, there were no problems in the sense that the banks did not have a clear understanding of the intentions of their respective monetary authorities. Nevertheless, central banks had their views on the adjustment process in the real world (at home and abroad) but did not specify their view about such basic questions as growth, unemployment or other matters of basic economic policy, the welfare aspects of lending.

The question of the policy-mix between fiscal and monetary policy was an important topic of discussion since it had become clear that abrupt changes in international lending could prove counter-productive to the need for consolidation. Too much of the burden of the adjustment process is often placed on monetary policy with fiscal and budgetary policies rather weak or at least not consistent enough to add to the credibility of adjustment policies in the real world. Rising deficits in the public sector were seen to be in very close context with the topic of the Colloquium, namely balance of payments financing and financing of national budget deficits through international lending.

As far as co-operation between the public sector and the banks was concerned, Frans Engering put the question: which forms of risk sharing ought to be aspired to? In other words, to what degree would the burden of non performing international loans be ultimately borne and divided up among shareholders and staff of banks, the taxpayer and the bank customer? These aids included all forms of interest rate subsidies, concessional loans, the costs of rescue operations and write offs.

It was only natural that the question of high interest rate policies and their consequences was raised in all of the commissions. It was stressed that developing countries, especially those depending heavily on the exports of a few raw materials would inevitably get into trouble when confronted with interest rates of 15 per cent or more and declining raw material prices. Robert Piloy raised the question whether we would not soon be compelled to ease the interest rate burden for some of these raw material exporting countries. Hardly anyone will be surprised that in a European study group like SUERF the question "why does the whole world have to pay such high interest rates as a consequence of a one-sided monetary policy in the United States?" was raised.

The predominant line of thought was that success with initiatives to lower interest rates would help to diminish some risks in international lending and increase the feasibility of more international loans later on.

V. STRENGTHENING THE SYSTEM

Jeanne-Marie Parly had drawn our attention to the fact that there is a considerable amount of confusion about the "international financial system". Constant changes with regard to the inclusion or exclusion of certain debtors and creditors, especially governments and monetary authorities, are now part of the picture. We were also reminded that – apart from the confusion about financial intermediaries – a considerable number of weaknesses in the financial structures do exist and that banks are not always free to determine the direction of their foreign lending (Rainer Gut). A strengthening of the international financial system could only be expected if progress was made on three different levels:

a) regarding the relations between debtors and creditors,
b) increasing the share of those responsible for public finance especially in debtor countries and
c) making more clear the auxiliary and supervisory functions of the monetary authorities including their "insurance function" of lender of last resort in order to ease pressures on financial markets.

In spite of all the talk about the importance of central banks and the necessity for closer co-operation between different institutions it was felt that the responsibility for their international lending remains with the participants in the market. "Finally banks will ultimately have to supervise themselves and to rescue themselves".

Looking back at the discussions, it can be said that they contained an element of frank, and to a certain extent, blunt exchange of opinion. One participant in the final discussion did not hesitate to state that there would be significant re-ratings on the international capital and credit markets and that there were signs which had to be taken as an urgent warning.

So: we see the clouds, but we don't know whether it means rain, hail or just a lack of sunshine.

FINANCIAL AND MONETARY POLICY STUDIES
Other volumes in the series*:

1. Multinational Enterprises – Financial and Monetary Aspects.
   Editors: J.S.G. Wilson and C.F. Scheffer, with 16 contributors.
   1974. ISBN 90-286-0124-4
   (SUERF Colloquium Nottingham University, England, April 1969)

2. Floating Exchange Rates – The Lessons of Recent Experience.
   Editors: H. Fournier and J.E. Wadsworth, with 14 contributors.
   1976. ISBN 90-286-0565-7
   (SUERF Colloquium Venice, October 1974)

3. The Development of Financial Institutions in Europe, 1956-76.
   Editors: J.E. Wadsworth, J.S.G. Wilson and H. Fournier, with 26 contributors.
   1977. ISBN 90-286-0337-9
   (SUERF Colloquium Brussels, April 1976)

4. New Approaches in Monetary Policy.
   Editors: J.E. Wadsworth and F. Léonard de Juvigny, with 29 contributors.
   1979. ISBN 90-286-0848-6
   (SUERF Colloquium Wiesbaden, September 1977)

5. Europe and the Dollar in the World-wide Disequilibrium.
   Editor: J.R. Sargent, with 17 contributors.
   1981. ISBN 90-286-0700-5
   (SUERF Colloquium Basle, Switzerland, May 1979)

6. Bank Management in a Changing Domestic and International Environment: The Challenges of the Eighties.
   Editors: D.E. Fair and F. Léonard de Juvigny, with 25 contributors.
   1982. ISBN 90-247-2606-9
   (SUERF Colloquium Helsingør, Denmark, October 1980)

* The first five volumes of this series were published by Sijthoff & Noordhoff International
Publishers, Alphen aan den Rijn.